A THIRST FOR LIFE

WITH THE ACCENT ON CRICKET

Henry Blofeld

Hodder & Stoughton

Copyright © 2000 Henry Blofeld

First published in Great Britain in 2000
by Hodder and Stoughton
a division of Hodder Headline

The right of Henry Blofeld to be identified as the Author of
the Work has been asserted by him in accordance with the
Copyright, Designs and Patents Act 1988.

10 9 8 7 6 5 4 3 2 1

All rights reserved. No part of this publication may be
reproduced, stored in a retrieval system, or transmitted,
in any form or by any means without the prior written
permission of the publisher, nor be otherwise circulated
in any form of binding or cover other than that in which
it is published and without a similar condition being
imposed on the subsequent purchaser.

A CIP catalogue record for this title is available
from the British Library

ISBN 0 340 77049 X

Typeset by Rowland Phototypesetting Ltd.,
Bury St Edmunds, Suffolk
Printed and bound in Great Britain by
Clays Ltd, St Ives plc

Hodder and Stoughton Ltd
A division of Hodder Headline
338 Euston Road
London NW1 3BH

A THIRST FOR LIFE

For Bitten, Rumple and the dogs, but for whom
I might have made the deadline

CONTENTS

1	Hoveton	1
2	Through the Grace Gates in a Rolls	14
3	On not missing the bus	35
4	First assignments	51
5	Package to India	66
6	Arabs in the West Indies	80
7	*TMS* debut	99
8	Bouncers, sledgers and the passing streaker	109
9	In the assistant chauffeur's seat	127
10	From the Saadabad Palace to Bombay	141
11	Enter the Demon King	152
12	Packer triumphant	169
13	The bespectacled Henry Blofly	187
14	Rest day	204
15	West Indian antics	216
16	The Botham phenomenon	229
17	Transported in Pakistan	246
18	Gower to Gatting	263
19	One crisis to the next	279
20	BSkyB	298
21	Passage to India	319
22	Grasping the English nettle	326
23	Storm clouds and Indian bookies	353
24	Retired hurt	371
25	Drawing stumps	388
	Index	403

ACKNOWLEDGEMENTS

I WOULD FIRST LIKE TO THANK my mother and father, sadly *in absentia*, for making the whole thing possible. Then a big vote of thanks to all those hirsute characters of long ago who picked up staves or sticks and invented Creag or whatever the primitive game of cricket was originally called. Johnny Woodcock must receive a special mention for he must take no small part of the blame for unleashing me on the unsuspecting world of cricket journalism. As far as the airwaves are concerned my thanks must go to Messrs Arlott, Johnston, Alston, Swanton and the others who set fire to an early passion for cricket commentary. This book would also never have been written without the draconian enthusiasm of Roddy Bloomfield, my editor, who learned to spell at Harrow and puts it to good effect at Hodders. He is an old friend who, in order to make me keep my eye on the ball, adopted an attitude which would have made Attila the Hun raise an eyebrow. My thanks to Simon Heffer who ploughed through the manuscript a couple of times, put his finger on several spots, gave me great encouragement, as well as spreading the word abroad. His enjoyment of serious claret did no harm either. David and Ursie Lloyd Owen were a great help over the splendid lunches we had at Swainsthorpe when they did their utmost to keep me on the straight and narrow. My wife, Bitten, was a tower of strength from first to last. Thank goodness the Swedes don't play cricket otherwise we might never have come up for air. Thanks also go to my daughter, Suki, to whom I fear I have not done justice in these pages and whose support and enthusiasm was as terrific as her cooking which would always have kept Escoffier on his toes. Finally, a colossal thank you to the Almighty for lending a hand during those grim days first in the King Edward VII Hospital in Windsor and later on in the Harley Street Clinic.

PHOTOGRAPHIC ACKNOWLEDGEMENTS

The author and publisher would like to thank the following for permission to reproduce photographs:

A THIRST FOR LIFE

Allsport, *Daily Mirror*, Patrick Eagar, Hulton Getty, *East Anglian Times*, Lay & Wheeler.

All other photographs are from private collections.

CHAPTER

1

HOVETON

September 1939 was not one of England's greatest months. The war had begun in the first week and as Hitler's ambitions grew frighteningly closer, the job of battening down the hatches began. On 23 September petrol rationing was introduced and that morning my mother, who must cleverly have filled her tank the day before, set off across north Norfolk from the Home Farm in Hoveton St John to a cattle sale. Ingate, my father's farm bailiff, was her only companion, apart from the bulge which announced that she was about to produce her third child. In his time, Ingate had overseen the birth of countless calves and foals and my mother, who was warmingly down to earth about these things, had told my father that morning she had no doubt Ingate would be able to cope if number three decided to put in its first appearance behind a passing haystack. My mother, who had drawn the short straw at the font when she was christened Grizel, will have been wholly unconcerned and will have thought only about the shorthorns she was going to see in the saleyard. I daresay Ingate will have been feeling rather more anxious.

Ingate was Suffolk by birth with an upright, almost military, bearing. When I remember him, after the war, he had a white, elderly, sergeants' mess moustache, a slightly clipped way of speaking in a voice distinctly tinged with Suffolk which instantly marked him down as a foreigner. He wore a flat brown cap and always seemed to me to be a pillar of rectitude. As a small boy, I was almost as anxious not to be caught letting the side down by

Ingate as I was by my father who, at six foot six with a moustache and an eyeglass, did not encourage insubordination. The thought of my mother driving through the byways of Norfolk that day, keeping up a constant flow of conversation and, in her own direct manner, asking Ingate his opinions of one thing after another before adding her own pithy comments, is extremely jolly. I am sure Ingate will have wanted to persuade her to leave the sale at the earliest possible moment and start the journey home. My mother would have said something like, 'Not yet. I want to see how much that handsome beast over there fetches.' She will have gone when she was ready.

Ingate need not have worried. I was on my best behaviour. After a successful day at the sale, the drive home in my mother's small but stately Austin Seven passed off peacefully enough. After dinner that night my parents went for a good walk down to the river at Hill Piece, to try and move things along. It worked, because soon after they got back to the Home Farm, it all began to happen. I was born shortly before midnight under the watchful eye of Dr Bennett, monthly nurse and all the trimmings, but not my father who will have been reading a book in the drawing room with a whisky and soda at hand, apprehensively awaiting my first scream. When Anthea and John, my sister and brother, were born all the Siamese cats, which my mother bred and showed, were in attendance at my mother's decree. By the time I was born, she had moved on to cows, rabbits and bantams, and fortunately did not feel the need to call on them as birthroom companions.

Anthea was ten years older than me and John seven and there was no doubt that I was a mistake. Soon after I was first married, my mother, ever anxious to push along the business of procreation, gave me one of her inimitable talking-tos. 'You see, darling, I bred at the shake of a pair of pants, which was just as well.' Be that as it may, one of the sad aspects of big age gaps is that one's elder siblings seem so enormous when you are young, and they cannot reasonably be expected to do much more than tolerate you. The three of us have always got along all right, although Anthea still tends to talk to me as if I was a scruffy fourteen-year-old, while John, a High Court judge to his boot straps, regards me as being too high a risk factor for comfort. Alas, we see too little of each other, for he is a pragmatist more than a romantic.

The first time I appear to have made any sort of impact was, sadly, in rather a negative sense. At an early stage my family were too easily prepared to sacrifice me to the enemy. During the war there were a great many aerodromes in Norfolk from where bombers were dispatched to make life as uncomfortable as they could for the opposition. The Führer and his minions were therefore hellbent on repaying these aerodromes in kind and so there was much aerial activity in the neighbourhood. As a result, a primitive form of air-raid shelter was built in the middle of the farm buildings at the Home Farm to which everyone rushed when the air-raid warning siren went off. It was not underground but had, I suppose, smelled vaguely of rats and dust and was rather good news when I played games like hide-and-seek with my friends. I am not sure it would have made the enemy scratch their heads for very long. One day the siren went off soon after lunch and everyone fled to the shelter and were busy congratulating each other on the nimbleness of their flight, when someone noticed that I was not among those present. A red-faced search ensued and I was found happily gurgling away in my pram on the lawn and hastily retrieved, but it was some time before I brought myself to forgive them for such gross cowardice.

Hoveton has been whittled away at for years and now the estate can barely muster a thousand acres and that includes the two Broads, Hoveton Great Broad and Hoveton Little Broad and the accompanying marshland and alder carrs. But it was a brilliant place in which to grow up. There were the Broads, with duck and fish, and the marshes where we found bittern, pheasants and even marsh harriers. There were many different varieties of butterfly and most summers my mother would find the chrysalis of a swallowtail which we would carefully take home and hatch in a special glass cage before releasing it. There are still some on the marshes but they are much rarer now. As a child, I was intrigued by the extraordinary colours which nature produced, the green and red on woodpeckers, the green on the wings of a teal, that amazing flashing blue on a kingfisher and a mallard drake in his full plumage, almost as regal in his way as a cock pheasant. Then there were the wild flowers which I was never much good at, although I loved the yellow waterlilies on the two Broads. But there was nothing quite so extraordinary as the colours of those swallowtails.

I was brought up in a shooting family and in my father's day Hoveton was a reasonable pheasant shoot. In those days none of the birds were reared and wild pheasants with an east wind under their tails took some hitting. Norfolk is traditionally thought to be dreadfully flat, and its reputation here was not helped by Noel Coward, but in the east of the county there are gentle undulations which make pheasants sometimes fly rather higher than the height of a room. I found duck-shooting the most exciting. The most convenient way was standing in the front of a wooden rowing boat and being propelled around the Broad by someone standing in the back using a quant. The quant is the Norfolk variation of the punt pole and quanting seems a simple art to the uninitiated until they try for themselves, when the boat either goes round in circles or gently backwards. The other way of shooting duck is flighting them in the early morning or evening, which is much more exciting than being pushed round the edge of a Broad.

We were desperately lucky as children to have this world in which to grow up. But my father never allowed us to take it for granted. He made sure we were taught to respect the country in every way. On the farm, gates that were opened for traffic had to be shut and if they were not, and were left swinging on their hinges, he was furious. Of course litter was never to be left anywhere and safety when learning to shoot was of paramount importance. On one inglorious occasion when he caught me climbing over a fence with my gun still loaded, I was sent straight home. The biggest ticking off I ever got from him was when he discovered I had not cleaned my gun after a day's shooting. If you do not clean the barrels of a shotgun after you have used it, the residue the cartridge leaves behind will eat into the barrels and eventually destroy them. When I was shooting, I was allowed to kill only what I could eat, unless it was vermin, and once a bird had come down, I had to do all I could to find it. I was taught when I was very young how to deal with everything that I shot. I learned how to gut and skin a rabbit and how to pluck and prepare birds for the pot. If I failed in any of these things, my father became rather a frightening figure because he did not have great patience with children.

The names of the fields and the woods at Hoveton have, for me, a wonderful ring to them: Haugh's End, King's Wood, Souter's Close, Poker's Loke, Cooper's Close, Bushes and New Plantation, and how lucky I am to live with them all around me now. When I was young, Hoveton was rich in characters and, being essentially a fruit farm, there were a great many more people employed than there are today. There was Carter the gamekeeper who had fought in the First War and was a small and rather bent man. One of his first jobs in the morning was to press and brush the clothes my father had worn the day before on a small trestle table on the verandah in front of the side door. He had a gruff sense of humour and when I began to play cricket he often came to the small croquet lawn by the tennis court, and bowled to me. He had a three-pace run-up and by then his arm was not as high as it had been in his prime, but he was accurate enough and rather enjoyed showing he could still put the ball on the spot. On Saturdays he used to umpire in the village matches. He was always kind to me but stood no nonsense.

It was Carter who organised the first shot I ever had. I was nine when one morning he got the small single-barrelled four-ten out of the gun cupboard and asked me if I would like to shoot a rabbit. I could hardly believe my luck and we walked across the tennis court at the back of the house and into the wood called the Grove. We walked about twenty yards down the path when Carter stopped, put a cartridge in the gun and, with a half whisper and a half point, showed me a rabbit sitting under a bush to our left. Standing behind me, he helped me hold the gun. I don't think I pushed the stock tightly enough into my shoulder and when I eventually pulled the trigger there was a tremendous jolt, the gun seemed to jump all over the place and, to my dismay, the rabbit lolloped away completely untouched. I haven't got much better since.

As I grew up, I spent more and more time with the gamekeepers, and gave a wide berth to Mrs Porcher who lived in and did the cooking. She was a small woman with a strident voice and I think my mother had quite a job controlling her, although she would never have let on to me. Then there was Maud, the comfortably built parlourmaid, who was quite jolly when she was not being subdued by Mrs Porcher which was most of the time. Maud was related to Johnson the head marshman who lived near the Little Broad Boathouse. It was one of his sons, in the RAF, who brought us back a banana soon after the end of the war. Bananas were an unheard of luxury in those straitened days. By the time it reached us this banana was almost black, but I was given a bit and, although I pretended I liked it at the time, I was quite happy not to have been offered a second helping. I remember it was all made into rather an event and I was happy to be able to bask in the glory of having had a banana which was one up on most of my friends. Johnson quanted my mother around the Big Broad when she fished for pike which she did pretty regularly during the war and with considerable success. We used to eat pike smoked and I think they were also turned into kedgeree. After the war whenever a big pike, above ten or twelve pounds, was pulled out, it was taken up to London and delivered to the Gaudins, Geo and Alex, who ran that splendid restaurant, L'Escargot Bienvenu in Greek Street, Soho where these evil-looking beasts with their horrendous teeth were, by some magical sleight of hand, turned into the most delicious quennelles de brochet.

But the most important person in my life was Nanny. Nanny was magic. Her dark hair was always tied in a bun on the back of her head and she grew a formidable moustache but she was the sweetest person in the world. Her great ally at the Home Farm who often came and had nursery tea with us and whom we adored, was my father's secretary, the effervescent 'See-Saw'. Her name was Miss Easter but as a small child I had been unable to manage that. 'See-Saw' was as close as I could get and it stuck. She was round and cuddly and full of infectious laughter with a loud and cheerful voice. I was devastated when she left to get married. 'See-Saw' worked in the outer office, which is where John's secretary works still. In those days, it was memorable for a door which was particularly noisy when you pushed it open and a notice which hung on the wall at the end of the room which said in large block capitals, 'IT IS WISER TO KEEP YOUR MOUTH SHUT AND LET PEOPLE THINK YOU ARE A FOOL THAN TO OPEN IT AND REMOVE ALL DOUBT.' My father's office was up the step and further through.

I was always slightly frightened of him and I think we were two very different people. I once remember him telling me soon after I became a journalist that he had no problem resisting physical temptations, but that those of an aesthetic nature were another matter. I feared he disapproved of me. A year or two after he had died, I told my mother that I didn't think my father had particularly cared for me. 'Oh, no,' she answered in her usual purposeful voice, 'he was extremely fond of you.' As a boy, I was never wholly at ease with him and I can recall those dreadful days when my school report landed on the dining-room table with all the other letters at breakfast. He did not say anything and never opened it there and then. It was tucked away in the pile he would take with him to his office after breakfast – I was always impressed by the size of the pile but knew it was then only a question of time before I was summoned to account for my sins. My reports never touched the high spots he was hoping for.

Two punt guns which I always considered to be a mark of great distinction, hung on the two large beams over his desk and today look down on what is left of John's hair. I have never fired either but John did so more than once, paddling out into tidal waters on the Wash, lying out of sight in the bottom of the boat and then shooting the duck at the moment they opened their wings to take off and hoping for as many as ten or twelve with one shot. It is a form of shooting that must by now have become extinct.

The door at the far end of my father's office opened into the schoolroom where before I went off to my private school (the Eton term for prep school) I learned the rudiments of reading and writing and adding and subtracting with some friends and cousins who lived nearby. Mrs Hales drove to Hoveton each morning from Sea Palling, on the coast, in what now seems a prehistoric car but it was eminently reliable. She must have been quite good at her job because when I went on to school they didn't immediately award me the dunce's cap but she wouldn't have known what a sense of humour was. She kept us in order but that was not too difficult as any disturbance would bring my father steaming through the door from his office, which was to be avoided at all costs.

Those who knew my father may be surprised that he has come in for a bit of stick in this first chapter. Like my brother John, he was the most charming and courteous of men and those on either side of him at a dinner party will have reckoned they had the best of the draw. One thing at which he was brilliant was reading aloud in the drawing room after tea. I don't think I have ever laughed as much as I did when he read the whole of *Handley Cross* by R.H. Surtees. He was so good at the various accents, not least the Cockney of Mr Jorrocks and the Scottish burr of his obstinate whipper-in, James Pigg. This was also how I was first introduced to P.G. Wodehouse who became a lifelong passion. My father was hugely knowledgeable over a wide range of subjects and, above all, he was an excellent listener. I suppose the external perspective is likely to differ from a family perspective and equally an adult perspective from a child's. I am sure my father never meant to be frightening but this was how he came across to me. I think it was his imposing bearing which alarmed me. He was a stickler for standards which had to be maintained. So too, was my mother and she was also able to make her feelings abundantly clear if she had to, but without ever quite coming across to me as a blood relation of Attila the Hun.

There was one famous occasion when John was a small child. He had gone some way towards perfecting the habit of biting people and my mother had told Nanny that when it happened again in the nursery he should be forcibly ejected into the passage, at which point, my mother, hearing the noise, would rush out of the drawing room and sink her teeth into the wretched child to teach him a lesson. Nanny forgot her instructions and ejected John into the passage for a much more minor infringement that scarcely merited a yellow card, whereupon he was amazed to see the drawing-room door burst open and my mother descend on him in a blur of fury and give him a whacking great bite on the upper arm. This could, of course, be the reason why today the inhabitants of John's dock quiver so violently when the foreman of the jury pronounces the prisoner guilty.

My best friend in the farmyard was Freddie Hunn who was in charge of the barn where all the cattle food for the sizeable herd of pedigree shorthorns was ground and mixed and put into sacks. This gave him a more or less permanently dusty appearance. Freddie who was small, was the most cheerful and engaging of men. His only blemish was that he insisted on supporting Surrey and if you gave him half a chance would bang on about Jack Hobbs. I was a fervent Middlesex supporter and was certain that no one had ever played cricket as well as Denis Compton and Bill Edrich who had the added advantage of having been born only a few miles away near the village of Blofield (no relation). Freddie also worked the farm petrol pump which was a healthy relic from pre-war days when you pumped in half a gallon and then pushed a lever across before pumping in the next half gallon. Amazingly, it is still in something like midseason form. But Freddie's main function, in my eyes at any rate, was as the honorary head groundsman on our cricket ground. His wife, Hilda to everyone but precocious small boys who had to settle for Mrs Hunn, was a large cuddly woman with a loud voice and laugh to match, and an inimitable Norfolk accent. She presided over the cricket teas at village matches with humour, authority, a huge steel teapot and a sharp but jolly rebuke if anyone tried to snaffle a second cream bun. Like Freddie, she was a thoroughly good sort.

The cricket ground was reached by going through the big green gate at the end of the farmyard and walking across a grass field which was part of the old parkland and was known as the Lawn. The ground itself nestled between the Hill Piece Wood which, at the appropriate time of the year, was carpeted with bluebells and King Alfreds, and a clump of stately old oaks just over a hundred yards away. There was in those days a tiny round thatched wooden hut in the middle of Hill Piece Wood and once upon a time the family would walk across from Hoveton and have a picnic there looking down the hill to the River Bure. Those were the days.

The village had once played on a ground in front of Hoveton House where the land is not at all level. This was ploughed up at the start of the war when all available land was used for food production. Towards the end my father had been allocated a contingent of German prisoners of war to work on the farm. When there was nothing else for them to do, he set them to make another cricket ground over by the Hill Piece Wood. I remember them well because at about that time I had been given a German policeman's helmet and I thought it would be a good idea to wear it in front of them. Happily, wiser counsels prevailed and the pitch was laid without incident. When Freddie knocked off for the day he would shake off the dust as best he could and walk across to the ground where he would busy himself until late in the evening. But cricket had not yet embedded itself in my consciousness and that didn't happen until I first went to school at Sunningdale at the age of seven and a half when I had hardly shed my infant's plumage. In the meantime, Mrs Hales and I had put up with each other in a state of more or less constant armed neutrality. At least, she didn't have to bowl to me on the croquet lawn.

The Blofelds first owned Hoveton in the middle of the seventeenth century through shrewdly marrying into the Doughty family who had owned it for two hundred years before that. Hoveton House was built in 1680 and is described by Nikolaus Pevsner as 'one of the most attractive, if not perfect, houses of its time in Norfolk'. When I was a child living at the Home Farm, I found the house somewhat forbidding. Its sole occupant was my father's mother whom I regarded as a stinking old tyrant. She disliked me almost as much. My grandfather, by all accounts a charming man, had died horribly of anthrax which he had picked up from a cow on the estate just after the Great War.

My grandmother was responsible for one of the better family stories. In 1953, when John was twenty-one, there was a party for the tenants and employees of the estate which was held in the big barn at the Home Farm. There were four sizeable trestle tables, three going down the length of the barn and one across at the top. The fatted calf had a bad day of it. The family sat mostly at the top table, although being only thirteen, I was in the lower echelons. My grandmother sat next to my father and during dinner she peered down the full length of the table in front of her. After looking intently for some time at the far end, she turned to my father and asked him who was the woman dressed in blue sitting on the right near the bottom. My father peered down the table and then said in a slightly surprised voice, 'That's Winifred.' Winifred had been my grandmother's cook for many years and she lived in the house.

'I thought it was,' came the measured reply. 'I have never seen her eat before.'

The best thing I can remember about Hoveton, as we knew it, was the dressing-up chest on the landing at the top of the main stairs which came down into the hall at the front of the house. For a small child this was an Aladdin's cave full of the most splendid garments which we, as children, were allowed to use on rare occasions such as Christmas, and only when heavily supervised. The dressing-up chest sparked the one moment of triumph I ever had over my grandmother and, very surprisingly, it did not cost me as dearly as it should have done. My father was extremely good at telling stories in a broad Norfolk accent. The benchmark for Norfolk stories was set by Sidney Grapes who called himself the Boy John in his periodical letters to the *Eastern Daily Press*, written in the Norfolk dialect, and which had the entire county splitting its sides. I had not yet gone to school and so I doubt I was even seven when I heard my father tell a Norfolk story which I can't remember but I do know that the punch line was, 'I don't pay no regard to you.' And I had laughed and laughed. A few days later I went with my mother up to Hoveton to see if we could find something from the famous dressing-up chest for me to wear at a party. I started by trying on some clothes which my mother had told me I really shouldn't and, making a lot of noise, I raced downstairs with them on. At the bottom, I almost bumped into my grandmother who was coming the other way in full sail. She was furious at the noise I was making and not pleased by what I was wearing. She told me to shut up and take the clothes off immediately. I looked her in the eye and out it came in the broadest Norfolk.

'I don't pay no regard to you.'

If anyone had thought she was an extinct volcano, they would have been shocked if they had heard her then. There was a formidable rumble. My mother took me home by the scruff of the neck and sent me straight to my room. My father paid me a visit later on but this time he didn't mark out his long run and I had, to all intents and purposes, got away with it. My mother whose views on anything seldom coincided with those of my paternal grandmother told me many years later that she had found it ungovernably funny. I think she had told my father to go gently with me.

After the dressing-up chest I was mesmerised by the cellar at Hoveton and this, remember, was in the days before I had touched a single drop. There seemed to be something irresistibly romantic about going down into what I considered to be the bowels of the earth and finding bins full of aged bottles of vintage port which were liberally covered with cobwebs and dust. This suggested to me that they had been there for centuries rather than just twenty or so years. I was especially thrilled one day when my father found at the back of a bin of port, a bottle of 1749 rum. My father kept most of his wine in the cellar at Hoveton and when he went to collect some bottles to take to the Home Farm, I never missed the opportunity to go with him. After the 1749 rum, I was sure that Long John Silver himself would soon put in an appearance. What exciting names those bottles of port had, too – Fonseca, Gould Campbell, Taylor and Graham. The last two are very run-of-the-mill but in those far-off days they were only just behind Compton and Edrich. When I played dot cricket between My Side and the Rest, Fonseca went in at number four for My Side for quite a while, although I can't remember why he was eventually dropped. I'm not sure either why Gould Campbell never got a game. Today Hoveton is presided over by John who hares about the country truly and impartially administering justice from Monday to Friday and returns each weekend to flex his muscles on the estate. As for me, I shall take an awful lot of digging out from North Farm, I can promise you, and that digging will have to be done in the family plot in the graveyard of the church of St John's. But we will leave Hoveton for the time being with me wearing my first grey flannel jacket and shorts as I jump into the back of my father's dark green Armstrong Siddeley for the long drive to Sunningdale with my mother sitting in the front beside my father and Nanny waving furiously and a little tearfully from the verandah.

CHAPTER 2

THROUGH THE GRACE GATES IN A ROLLS

I CAN STILL REMEMBER the false parental bonhomie which reverberated through the car as I made that journey for the first time along a road I came to know so well. My mother was pretty convincing and I think probably felt sorry for me, although she made quite sure she never showed it. For some weeks she had done her best to try to prepare me for what lay ahead, even to the extent of calling me Blofeld, which was what I would be called at school. It made me feel rather important. My father hated emotional occasions and longed to get it over with before I started blubbing in the back – he shirked the facts-of-life moment a few years later although my mother stepped nobly into the breach. I didn't let the side down this time, although on a number of future journeys, when I knew exactly what I was going back to, the upper lip was not as stiff as it might have been.

The journey must have taken getting on for four and a half hours. Dual carriageways and bypasses had not really been invented, although when we turned right off the A1 just after Hatfield, there was a quickish stretch leading to Watford and Rickmansworth. We had taken a picnic and pulled off the road somewhere to gulp our hard-boiled eggs and ham sandwiches. By now I was becoming more apprehensive at what lay ahead and my heart was in my mouth as we went over the level crossing in Sunningdale and turned right into Dry Arch Road. Then it was right at the top and left almost at once into the rhododendron-lined school drive.

The reception committee in the drawing room consisted of Mr and Mrs Fox. He looked to me to be older than God with a wrinkle or two more than the Almighty might want to own up to. His strong black hair which went back over his head with a measured sweep, was gleaming with hair oil which I soon discovered was Mr Thomas's best. It had a pungent smell tinged with a slight sweetness I shall never forget. It preceded Mr Fox everywhere he went and stayed on afterwards as a reminder of his visit. He never moved or spoke quickly or impulsively and everything was done with a calculated tread which made him seem mildly sinister. His nickname was Foe. Mrs Fox was bigger and rather a bouncy woman but, as I was not long in discovering, with the sharpest of tongues if need be. We all shook hands and then I met matron and Mr Burrows who did not seem to be in the first flush of youth either, before clinging nervously to my mother who was doing her best to be jolly to parents of other new boys. Having been through the whole process with John, my mother was an old hand at it. This was the summer term and there were only three or four new boys. The great influx always came at the start of the Michaelmas term. Soon, we were taken upstairs and shown the lower dormitory which was to be my initial berth. Then came the dreaded moment when it was time for my parents to go. I kissed them goodbye and watched, mesmerised with disbelief, as they got into the car, circled in front of the school, and drove slowly away through the rhododendrons. I felt spectacularly alone that night.

I soon discovered that I was the youngest boy in the school which was definitely not an asset. The whole process was an extraordinary voyage of discovery. I found that I made friends reasonably easily but there were also certain boys I took against for whatever reason, and once I had done that I was not good at changing my mind. The world in 1947 was a much less child-friendly place than it is today and, even at the age of seven and a half, one was expected to stand on one's own two feet. I muddled through my first term unmemorably but at least I survived. Of course, lots of people remembered John, which was a help as he had won his colours for cricket and was in the team photograph which hung on one of the walls. My stock rose as a result.

It was during this first term at Sunningdale that I was introduced to cricket for the first time as an active participant. The third game was a very humble affair played in a remote outpost. It was a tiny ground with the noisy, clattering electric railway, which ran the full length of the school, at one end and an orchard in a dip at the other. The square boundaries were the wooden fence which marked the end of the school property and some long grass which was eventually cut and turned into hay. Proceedings were presided over by the formidable Miss Paterson who wore rubber-soled shoes that had a slight squeak and who was off-puttingly hearty. She had a strident voice, a bouncing carriage and she formed her Rs in the same way as Harrods, with a loop at the top. This was held against her and it particularly angered a boy called Howard Stepney, although I have no idea why, but he spoke most contemptuously about it and, in fact, seldom spoke about anything else.

Miss Paterson was not a serious forerunner of Rachael Heyhoe-Flint, but she had strong views about fair play. If she caught anyone trying to pull a fast one over her, he was not allowed his innings and had to field long leg at both ends. The bowling in the third game was under-arm and the contestants did not wear pads. Miss Paterson herself was not averse to seizing the ball and doing her best with her under-arm stuff if she felt someone had been in for too long. She took full advantage of an appallingly uneven pitch and by the end of the term would, I am sure, have topped the bowling averages. As well as bowling, she umpired at both ends and perish the boy who doubted any decision. No umpire's word has ever been more final. One of the ruses of playing on the third-form ground was to hit the ball back past the bowler into the orchard. Then everyone ran to try to find it but in reality to pick an apple. Not many achieved their objective because Miss Paterson started screaming at everyone to come back the moment the pursuit began. I don't think we learned very much about cricket under her tutelage but it was all good fun.

By the time I started my third term, I had progressed to the upper dormitory and the tender mercies of the dormitory bully. It was there that I encountered at close quarters a charming little boy called Baring who lived darkly in a bed near to the door. We were sent to bed at six o'clock and it was lights out at seven. A monitor, one of the senior boys, slept in each dormitory to see fair play but the monitor came to bed at eight o'clock and so the forces of evil had a good hour to themselves. I can't remember why I was particularly singled out for third-degree treatment or if I had done something which had made me especially unpopular. It was probably just that I was perceived as a nasty little squirt who was easy meat. Anyway, I was prevailed upon by Baring and his minions, under threat of excommunication and all sorts of physical unpleasantnesses, to take my tortoiseshell hairbrush, dressing gown optional, to the stair well which looked down the two flights of stairs to the passage outside the library.

At a quarter to eight each evening, the rest of the school gathered in the library where they were each given a mug of steaming cocoa and a hunk of bread and butter, which was almost certainly margarine, in the hope that it would keep body and soul together until breakfast. The maid who delivered the cocoa in two huge enamel jugs carried them on a tray from the kitchen to the library and passed directly underneath anyone looking down, as I was, from above. I had been forcibly instructed to drop my hairbrush over the banister at the moment the maid came into vision, so that it would land on the tray and cause mayhem. Quivering considerably, I took a quick aim and let the ruddy thing go. By the grace of God, it narrowly missed everything and fell with a resounding crash onto the dark green lino beside her. Somehow the girl held on, although I expect the jugs wobbled about a bit. I slunk back to bed, half tinpot hero for having done it, half failure for having missed. I lay shivering at the thought of what was to follow, while the dreaded Baring and his colleagues in arms laughed warmly to themselves at the same prospect.

Of course, there was no escaping magisterial retribution because I would be the only member of the dormitory without a hairbrush on the shelf above his bed and my name was anyway written in large letters on a piece of sticking plaster on the back of the brush.

Mr Burrows, as craggy as an Alp, unsmiling, moustached, austere and, unless you played soccer well and supported Newcastle United in general and Jackie Milburn in particular, one to be avoided, had the reputation of being a dab hand with the cane. He lived in two rooms next door to the upper dormitory and presided over discipline in those parts. I think Mr Burrows would have hit it off well with the Ancient Mariner. It was not long now before he burst through the door and the interrogation process began. I had some awkward interviews that night and the next day, awkward because sneaking most certainly wouldn't do. To my astonishment, and Baring and Co.'s sadness, I was not beaten which was just as well because after Mr Burrows had his way sitting down was quite an adventure for several days. Maybe the thought had occurred to him that I had been persuaded against my better judgement. But it was still pretty unpleasant, otherwise I doubt I would have remembered the incident quite so well.

Miss Paterson's influence on the third-form ground must have been strong. In the summer holidays that followed my first term, I was taken by my parents to watch Norfolk play in the Minor Counties Championship on their lovely ground at Lakenham where my father, along with a dozen other members, had his own wigwam-like tent just over the square boundary. I loved every moment of it and there was one particularly exciting occasion when Norfolk played a match against an all-Edrich Eleven captained by the redoubtable W.J. of Middlesex and England. Little did I dream that I would one day play for Norfolk, for some years under W.J.'s captaincy. The cricketers of Norfolk in the late forties and early fifties, although they never won very much, became my heroes. They were captained by Wilfred Thompson, the successor of Mike Falcon who had been in charge of the side from 1911 to 1946. In the thirties, Thompson had been one of the quickest bowlers in England when Norfolk had such a good team they were twice given a game against the touring side. Thompson was now getting on and was not much above medium pace, but he was a giant of a man who contented himself with hitting thrilling straight sixes which usually landed on the bowling green. Thompson himself, the Rought-Roughts (Basil, Desmond and Rodney),

THROUGH THE GRACE GATES IN A ROLLS

Clements, Theobald, Thistleton-Smith and Beresford all made the Greek gods seem like pretty small beer to me.

My love of cricket had reached the point when, in June 1948, my mother and father took me to the third day of the Second Test Match against Australia at Lord's. By now, the game had a more real meaning for me. I had been promoted to the second game at school where I purveyed a form of leg spin and could bat a bit. I had followed the progress of the Australians in detail and had been cutting out each day's scores from the newspapers. I was horrified when England had lost the First Test Match at Trent Bridge, although the blow of this defeat had been softened for me by the brilliant innings of 184 played by Denis Compton. I was given a lift to Lord's by Mr Sheepshanks, who was one of the masters, and I met my father, as planned, outside the Grace Gates in St John's Wood Road. Play had already begun and Australia were being given a good start to their second innings by Barnes and Morris after England's last wicket had put on another 8 first thing. My parents had been there early in order to bag some seats in Q Stand just to the right of the pavilion which is reserved for members' friends. Unless you were a member of MCC, you had to have a Rover ticket which was a most exciting affair in three parts held together by perforation. One part was taken as you came in to the ground, the next bit went when you entered the stand and then you hung on to the third and tiniest bit.

We were near the front of this small stand which has now become the Allen Stand after Gubby Allen, the Eminence Grise of Lord's, the MCC and the game of cricket for so long. My mother had brought along a couple of rugs and also two punnets of strawberries which had been picked only the day before in Four Acres. I was given a scorecard on which I avidly filled in the wickets that fell – sadly, only four Australians were out that day – but I wasn't that sad because it gave me the chance to gawp at Compton and Edrich in the field. The baggy green Australian caps made a deep impression on me. Morris wore his in a splendidly jaunty, left-handed sort of way which suggested he was going to fall over with laughter at any moment. As an opening partnership of 122 would suggest, he did not.

I was allowed one big strawberry soon after I had sat down – my mother dispensed them in miserly fashion – and then another half an hour before the lunch interval and the stalks had to be put carefully into a paper bag. H.M. Bateman might have drawn a cartoon of the spectator who threw his strawberry stalk on the ground at Lord's. Barnes and Morris were still together at lunch and of course when, in the middle of the afternoon, Morris was bowled by Wright who bowled like a demented windmill, I was not looking. By then, we had eaten our picnic lunch, when I was allowed to make more serious inroads on the strawberries, but one punnet was kept back for later.

When Morris was out, I was well aware that Bradman was in next and I strained forward in my seat to see him come out of the pavilion but my view was blocked by the members. Morris was clapped in and then after a moment's break, the applause swelled again. This was the Great Man. I could not see him until he was comfortably out on the ground. I was amazed at how small he was but I delighted in his baggy green cap which seemed to be pulled down over his ears more than the others. He walked quickly, took guard, looked around the field and started scoring runs. When he called Barnes for a single, it was in a loud voice and I liked to think I was able to spot the exciting Australian twang. The moment I enjoyed almost more than any other was when Evans appealed for lbw against Barnes. It was an enormous scream and I couldn't for the life of me understand why the umpire didn't give him out. The one thing I can still remember is that when Bradman received a no-ball or two from Coxon he hit it each time for 4 along the ground to the boundary of Q Stand as it was known then.

The score had reached 296 when Barnes, who had made 141, was out to Yardley who, minutes later, bowled Hassett. I think I was allowed another strawberry to celebrate because I hadn't been allowed to finish them at tea. By now, I was praying I would see Bradman reach his hundred. He was in the eighties and was facing Bedser who had got him in the first innings. Then, to my dismay, when he was 89, he played at a ball outside the off stump from Bedser and it flew to Edrich at first slip who hung on to the catch, by his shoulder as I remember it, and Bradman departed briskly after playing his last Test innings at Lord's. He was clapped all the way back and the members stood to him, which annoyed me as it meant that I was unable to watch him go into the pavilion. I was deeply disappointed. The new batsman had hardly taken guard when we were off. Bradman's dismissal had happily coincided with the time we were meeting up again with Mr Sheepshanks to go back to Sunningdale. It had been the most exceptional day and it made me sure I now knew more of life than my chums.

By then, my father was driving a spectacular Rolls-Royce which was thought to be one of the last half dozen made with the red RR on the front of the car. The letters were changed to black in 1932 after the death of Charles Rolls, one of the firm's founders. It was a huge grey car with a specially built body and a soft roof. I distinctly remember, too, that it had no less than three different horns which seemed to me to be the last word in one-upmanship. At that time my father was the Managing Director of the Country Gentleman's Association and it seemed appropriate that the number of the car should be CG 1000. At school, this was thought to stand for Country Gent one thousand.

The car had a glass partition which wound up behind the front seat and was put in those big cars so that the passengers in the back could talk without being overheard by the chauffeur. On one occasion, John was sitting in the back with this partition wound up and he began to whistle. My father suddenly stopped the car, got out, lifted the bonnet and looked inside, although his knowledge of the internal combustion engine did not fill one with confidence. After a good look, he shut the bonnet, climbed back into the car and set off once more. It was not long before John again started to whistle. The car was brought to a halt and my father had another look at the engine with my mother offering plenty of forceful advice. This time John continued to whistle while my father was outside the car and of course he now knew where the problem came from and all hell was let loose. John's whistling has never been the same again.

My other source of cricket, which was just as important to me, was the village side at home and I followed the progress of

Hoveton and Wroxham just as keenly as Norfolk's, and Compton's progress with Middlesex and England. There were some splendid characters in the side in those days such as Bob Cork, the blacksmith on the estate. Once, at the age of ten or eleven, I was allowed to join in the Friday night fielding practice rather than stand behind and pick up the balls when they had been let through. I was tested by a skier and managed to make the most frightful mess of it and dislocated my thumb in the process. I was in considerable pain and was letting everyone know about it when Bob Cork came up with a wicked grin and gave the thumb a yank. I yelled as the joint went back into place and shuffled off home to be bandaged up.

There was Colonel Ingram-Johnson, Inky to his chums, who was Indian Army to his little toes, with the accompaniment of the inevitable military moustache. He wore an Incogniti cap, batted first wicket down, kept wicket and had rather a curious wife who was as thin as a telegraph pole and smoked about 223 cigarettes a day with a cough to match. There was Fred Roy who later inherited 'Roys of Wroxham, The World's Largest Village Store' which still prospers although it is, in fact, situated over the river bridge in Hoveton, a village which does not have the same alliterative possibilities. He never stopped smiling, opened the batting stoically, bowled the slowest off breaks in the world off a run-up which looked as if he was rehearsing an obscure dance routine, had a delightful chuckle and ended up with a splendid obituary in *The Times*.

Arthur Tink was a man of extremely few words and he didn't give the ball much of a tonk either, although he bowled little seamers at scarcely medium pace and picked up hundreds of wickets. He looked enormously sloggable, as many found to their cost. Although hardly an Adonis, he had managed to lure Mona into matrimony. Mona had long dark hair and was a beauty in a gypsy-like way. Theirs was a communion based on silence for Arthur never smiled and only spoke when he appealed and if Mona had belonged to an order of Trappists, her record would have been unblemished. Then there was Neville Yallop, the captain, dark-haired and thickset, who opened the batting and made himself into an extremely efficient player, topping the batting averages year after year. How he managed to control his rather curious side with such skill I shall never know – they won more than they lost.

In 1949, my leg breaks were deemed to be of a good enough quality to merit elevation to the first game at Sunningdale and on into the first eleven. This gained me a certain respect and put the Barings of this world in their places. I had no more trouble from him after that one unpleasant term. Early on in the following year I hurt my shoulder and couldn't bowl for a few days and, just for fun, one afternoon I put on a pair of wicket-keeping gloves and for ever after they had a hell of a time trying to pull them off me. It was a new world and I loved it. I found I was in the game all the time and with Edward Lane Fox who also got into the first eleven at the age of nine, bowling his extremely accurate left-arm spinners, we had a whale of a time. He turned the ball appreciably and batsman after batsman from opposing schools were drawn inexorably forward and were left floundering down the pitch when the ball spun past their bat. I have no idea how many I stumped off him in three years behind the stumps, but it was quite a few. The pupils of Earlywood, a neighbouring scholastic establishment, were invariably mesmerised by Edward's spinners and I managed to stump five of them in one innings.

Edward was given his colours before me and I was given mine at the last gasp in 1950, when we were being arranged into serried ranks for the team photograph. It was the accepted practice to sleep with your new cap under your pillow that night, presumably so that in the moments before and between sleep you could dive under the bedclothes and try it on. The snag was that I had already been scheduled to spend that night in the Princess Christian Nursing Home in Windsor where I was going to have my tonsils removed the next day. Mrs Fox drove me in her usual no-nonsense way to the nursing home and, with the matron in tow, we went up to my room which I had to share with a stranger, and Mrs Fox unpacked my suitcase. My new dark blue cap was at the top and I can still see the look of surprise on the matron's face when Mrs Fox quickly thrust it under my pillow. With my mind fully concentrated on my forthcoming medical adventures, I don't remember much trying on that night.

By then I was being asked to play in quite a number of boys' matches in the summer holidays and I was for ever being driven across to west Norfolk by my long-suffering mother who had graduated to a pale blue beetle Renault. Some of these journeys were as much as fifty miles each way. They were afternoon affairs and we set off from Hoveton in mid-morning armed with a picnic lunch which we ate on a rug by the side of the road. These games were needle affairs and while we children were competitive enough, we were not a patch on the mothers. If any of them planned to have a boys' match of their own the following year, they would have made football's Premiership managers look like mere selling platers as they raced to sign up each star turn for their own side. There was one ground I adored. Colonel Fitzhardinge Hancock and his wife lived at Congham Hall, midway between King's Lynn and Sandringham, which has now become a frightfully smart hotel. Hardy, as he was known, laid on boys' matches each year on his lovely ground for his grandson and, not only was it about as perfect a country ground as one could wish to find, it was also a lucky ground for me.

Hardy himself was the very epitome of an English gentleman and, like Brian Johnston later, he always seemed to be wearing brown and white co-respondent shoes on these occasions. Although he lacked a monocle, he had a strong look about him of P.G. Wodehouse's Galahad Threepwood. It came as something of a shock when years later I discovered that he was of east European stock and that Fitzhardinge Hancock was an assumed name. He had certainly found a winner and he had the appearance to go with it for he was small and dapper with exactly the right moustache, voice, instincts and all the rest. (Boys being what they are, it was not long before Hardy Hancock had been spoonerised with relish.) He gave us a wonderful time when we were small and he was kindness itself. When I later had a horrid accident on a bicycle at Eton and was incarcerated in hospital in Windsor, he made the effort to come and see me, although I fear at that stage I made little sense.

It was at another of these boys' matches, organised by Ruth Scott whose husband, Archie, was the first Old Etonian bookmaker, that I met the great Australian leg spinner and caricaturist, Arthur Mailey. My mother always told me that he took off his coat and bowled me a few balls on the outfield but I can't remember it. A few years later when I had made a hundred for the Public Schools against the Combined Services at Lord's, he sent me a copy of a small booklet he had written called *Cricket Humour* which he had embellished with some of his inimitable cartoons. The one on the front shows a bowler, Mailey himself, offering an umpire a five pound note which he is about to pocket. The inscription in biro on the inside reads: 'My best wishes for a successful cricket life. Saw you play at Runcton about three years ago and am very pleased about your progress. Arthur Mailey, '56.'

In 1952 I took Common Entrance for Eton and put all those with high expectations firmly in their places. I managed Middle Fourth which infiltrated me just above a dunce's cap and well below anything of merit. Going to Eton was another huge step forward and frightening but in a different sense from going to Sunningdale for the first time. I already knew a number of people at Eton, both from Norfolk and those who had gone before me from Sunningdale, and none of them had perished. Of course, those who were two years or more older than me were out of bounds socially for quite a time. Mark Nickerson, a next door neighbour in Norfolk who had bowled gallantly for Eton in 1953, was one of the senior chaps in M'Tutor's, as one's house was known. He gallantly put his reputation on the line by poking his nose round my door one evening to see if I was surviving.

The most frightening aspect of going to Eton was the knowledge that you were going into a sort of educational freemasonry which had its own language, its own rules, its own dress, and its own way of coping with the world. My family had been to Eton for a number of generations and John had finished there two years before I arrived and, blast him, had left behind a scholastic record I had no chance of equalling. The most alarming prospect was having to tie the daily bow tie for the first time. If you were over five foot two, you wore a morning coat with a white bow tie from the start and I just made it. If you couldn't manage five two, an Eton jacket, or bum-freezer as they were known, was the order of the day. Tying the bow tie was a simple operation but not until you had done it once and seen for yourself. Apart from the tie itself the essential piece of equipment was a paper clip which fastened one end of it to your shirt. My mother, with typical enthusiasm, had orchestrated a few rehearsals but, when I tried to go to sleep that first night, my big worry was whether I really would be able to manage to tie the wretched thing in the morning. When I got up and found that it worked, the relief was enormous.

My first few days passed in a blur as there was so much to learn. Apart from the names of the others in your house and the beaks (masters), there were a multitude of different caps which could be worn, depending on your prowess in the sporting field, there were the div rooms (schoolrooms) to be located, and the two sock (tuck) shops had to be found. It was surprising how easily it all came together. I was lucky because M'Tutor, Geoffrey Nickson, was unique. The greatest compliment I can pay him is that you would never have thought that he was a schoolmaster. He had a wonderful sense of humour and an impish sense of fun. He was strict when he had to be but without ever trying to make a fool of a boy – they did that themselves without any help from him – and he always talked to us as if we were sane and sensible human beings and not the ink-spotted horrors we really were. Sadly his successor, Martin Forest, who was in charge for my last three years, and I failed to get to first base. I felt he was a typical and rather humourless schoolmaster but people who were in his house for the full five years and therefore did not have any comparision to make, tell me I was wrong.

Everyone in the house loved GWN – all beaks were known by their initials – which was, in itself, remarkable. When some of us were caught playing bridge he exacted a penalty and then asked us to play with him in his study whenever he had the chance. One of his most endearing habits was to draw caricatures on work or order cards which told of your progress in school. I still have a splendid sketched caricature of W.G. Grace in red pencil which he drew for me the day after I had, as a fourteen-year-old, made

50 for the house against his scratch side. GWN himself bowled highly serviceable leg breaks and was impressed when I came down the pitch and slogged his googly over mid-wicket for four. He was sure that I had 'read' it and knew I was hitting with the spin. I had done no such thing and distinguishing leg breaks from googlies was an art I never mastered with any certainty. However I thought it would be better not to let on.

On the academic front at Eton I was thoroughly lazy, doing just about enough work to get by and concentrating everything on cricket. The general idea was that I should follow John to King's College, Cambridge where I would read history, the subject I specialised in after taking my O levels. I was going to take an entrance exam during my last half (term) at Eton, but it never happened although King's took me on trust without an exam, a decision I quickly made them regret.

I suppose Eton was in some ways still a fairly brutal school when I was there and corporal punishment was very much a fact of life. It was always reputed to be a hotbed of queerdom too, but in my five years I have to confess that no one ever tried to bugger me. The gentlest form of beating, to which I succumbed a number of times, was administered by the library in your house. The library comprised five or six senior boys who had their own private room, the house library, for daytime use. If one had committed some crime within the house, one was summoned to the library in the evening, after M'Tutor's permission had been given, bent over and given six or seven of the best. The hope was that none of the library were members of Pop (the Eton Society) for they were allowed to use a venomous weapon with sizeable knots at three- or four-inch intervals, known as a Pop cane, which could give the performance memorable lasting qualities.

Further up the scale came Pop tanning which was administered by the President of Pop after headmasterly approval had been forthcoming, for a serious crime such as smoking. The culprits were told to report to Pop room at a certain time on Sunday wearing an old pair of trousers, which gave it a bloodthirsty touch. I was present at one or two Pop tannings and it was rather a brutal performance. Swiping came at the top of this particular flagellatory ladder and was administered by the Headmaster or the Lower Master. You had to have committed a startlingly misguided offence to qualify for this, although certain people always did. The miscreant dropped his trousers, was held down by the school messenger, and was birched. Shades of Dotheboys Hall. At the time, we accepted it as the way of the world.

In my first summer half at Eton I played cricket for Lower Sixpenny, the under-fifteen side, which was supervised by the man who taught me more about the game than anyone else. Claude Taylor had been a prolific batsman for Westminster School and had then won a Blue at Oxford for four years in the twenties. He also played for Leicestershire while at Oxford. He loved the beauty of the game, had all the strokes and was a genius at teaching the mechanics to small boys. Cricket to him was above all a game of style and part of him was always caught up in the aesthetic nature of the art of batting. He was also an accomplished musician who taught the clarinet and for him cricket was a game which had all the subtle nuances of a musical score. CHT would sometimes stand behind the net when I was batting and if I played a stroke, be it an off drive or a late cut, that fitted his idea of how it should be played, he would purr his appreciation in his gentle, slow and slightly chalky voice. I always wanted to please him because it gave him such pleasure if I had listened and interpreted his advice as he had wanted me to.

If there was one thing more than any other that he taught me, it was the importance of footwork, which left one perfectly balanced to play each stroke. The one stroke which I particularly remember CHT teaching me, partly because I couldn't play it before I came under his wing, and partly because of the trouble he took over it all, was the on drive and the leg hit off the front foot which both come from the same base. He would spend hours halfway down the net with a box of six balls throwing me half volleys on and just outside the leg stump and coaxing me to open my left foot with the toe pointing to mid on which enabled me to bring the bat through alongside my foot. 'Even further across with the foot,' I can hear him pleading even now. And when I got it right: 'Beautiful stroke, beautiful stroke.' After a time I began to play the ball off the front foot through and wide of mid on pretty well and all those sweating bowlers will now know why I scored the majority of my runs on the leg side. It is no coincidence that CHT was the joint author of a book called *Cricket Dialogue* with David Macindoe who ran the Eleven at Eton when I played. It is a conversation piece which today would be considered fearfully old-fashioned because it extols the virtues of the proper way cricketers should deport themselves before, during and after the game.

It would have been impossible for me to have enjoyed my first summer half at Eton more than I did. I had a great piece of luck in that I was made captain of Lower Sixpenny the following year with Edward Lane Fox as my deputy which was a bit like keeping it in the family. On Sundays during the summer CHT would ask us to tea at his house at Willowbrook just over the Slough Road from Agar's Plough. His wife was the sister of Ian Peebles who had bowled his leg breaks with high good humour on thirteen occasions for England before the war, so the Taylors' household was steeped in cricket, with musical accompaniment on the clarinet. CHT remained a great friend through all my time at Eton and he was a wonderful influence if things were going wrong, just by the calming way in which he spoke.

In that first year in Lower Sixpenny, I had the luck to keep wicket to Simon Douglas-Pennant. He, Edward Lane Fox and I were all to play for the Eleven in 1955 and 1956, and Simon and I both went on to win Blues for Cambridge in 1959. Simon bowled at a lively medium fast left arm over the wicket and I had the greatest of fun standing up to him that first summer half. I never again had anything like the same number of stumpings off Edward, partly because the batsmen were better and also because I felt he now tended to bowl rather quicker and flatter.

After two years in Lower Sixpenny, I had passed fifteen and graduated to Upper Sixpenny, a club which was run by a delightful but rather intense Welshman called Ray Parry who had won a Blue at Oxford during the war. I was again captain and through the long winter evenings we plotted what I am sure would have been a most successful campaign. But when the time came, Edward and I were spirited away to higher things and found ourselves playing on Upper Club in the very top game in the school. I cannot tell you what a thrill this was. The captain of the Eleven was Clem Gibson, a tall, elegant stroke-maker when he remembered not to play across the line, and I cannot think of anyone who would have been able to make it as comfortable as Clem did for a fifteen-year-old who suddenly found himself thrust into such exalted company. The first school match that summer was against the Green Jackets and I kept wicket and batted well down the order at seven or eight, while Edward bowled his orthodox left-arm spin and batted some way above me. It all went reasonably well and the Fourth of June celebrations in honour of George III's birthday came along. The school played a two-day match against the Eton Ramblers (the old boys). Being a big Eton occasion, all our families turned up and the day used to end with a marvellous firework display down by the Thames. I had kept my place in the side and managed to slog a few runs in the second innings and after about another three or four matches, I received a letter from Clem Gibson in his immaculate handwriting, asking me if I would like to play against Harrow at Lord's. There are not many better moments in life than that and I need hardly say that I accepted with all possible haste. Edward, I am glad to say, had also got his letter.

The two-day match against Winchester came first and it was held that year at Winchester where Hubert Doggart, who played for England against the West Indies in 1950, had just taken over Winchester's cricket from Harry Altham who, with Jim Swanton, had written the definitive history of the game and served for years on the MCC committee. They were a strong side with Barry Reed, who later made a great many runs going in first for Hampshire, their best batsman. The next two weeks passed in a blur of unreality as the Eton and Harrow match approached. I found it quite extraordinary to think that on the Friday I would be changing in the dressing-room the England players had used for the Second Test against South Africa just under a fortnight earlier, the game in which Denis Compton had become the fifth batsman to score 5,000 runs in Test cricket. Eton always used the home dressing room which also provided shelter for Middlesex and England, although nowadays the teams swop dressing-rooms each year.

I was given a lift to Lord's by Richard Burrows who was one of our batsmen. His father, the general, had sent his car and chauffeur for two or three of us. I think it must have been a Rolls-Royce, at least I hope it was. Sweeping through the Grace Gates in a Rolls was not a bad way to make an entry in one's first game at Lord's. I don't think I have ever had a more profound and dramatic religious experience than I had when I went into the pavilion for that first time, hanging tightly on to my cricket bag. As I nervously climbed the first half flight of stairs I found myself talking in the sort of stage whisper reserved for church. The dressing-room was heaven and when I tiptoed outside and sat on the white seat on the balcony and thought for a second of the exceedingly distinguished bums that had sat there before me, I almost exploded with disbelief.

We got changed and the older hands who had done it the year before, did their best to assume a world weary air. Clem Gibson won the toss for us and we did not bat well on a decent firm pitch. The atmosphere in the dressing-room was electric and made more so by the sizeable crowd which was thick just down below us to our right on the concourse in front of the old Tavern where there were always a number of coaches of supporters of both sides who were both thirsty and noisy. We began well through Tom Pugh, at other times our loquacious first slip, who probably taught me something of the gentle art of conversation while I was keeping wicket beside him, and David Stoddart, but we suddenly found ourselves at 74/5 and there was mild panic in the dressing-room. I was batting at number eight and with two wickets having fallen at 74, there was a bit of a scramble to get ready. I sat on the balcony while Clem Gibson and Angus Wolfe-Murray put on a solid 36. We were all deeply worried about the way things were going but as far as I was concerned, at any rate, I am ashamed to say that a little bit of mental preening went on simply because I was sitting on the dressing-room balcony at Lord's with my pads on. Nonetheless, my heart was still in my mouth as every ball was played and when, at 110, Wolfe-Murray was bowled by Neame, life unfolded as if into an unbelievable dream.

I was vaguely aware of people wishing me good luck as I pulled open the dressing-room door and set off down the stairs, doing my best not to fall over my feet. I pushed my way into the Long Room which was alarmingly full and the average age would have been considerable. A few people turned and looked at me as I ploughed stoically on, turned right between the two long tables and there I was going out of the door and down the steps, through the gate which was held open for me by an attendant, and on to the grass. I suppose there was a good deal of noise going on because this was not a quiet match, but I heard none of it as I walked as quickly as I dared towards the players on the pitch, feeling smaller and smaller as I got nearer to the middle.

I arrived at the wicket at the Nursery End and found I was being given the sort of looks by the surrounding Harrovians that I fear they reserve especially for Etonians. I took guard, still in a dream, and suddenly came to my senses as Rex Neame, Harrow captain for the second time, started in to bowl his fine off spinners. I managed to get off the mark and at the end of the over Clem Gibson came down the pitch and had some encouraging words with me. I soon began to enjoy myself and after a time I felt I was playing in an ordinary game of cricket. The trouble was that it was easy to allow one's concentration to wander simply by looking round at where one was and thinking of all the other events that had taken place on this famous ground. We had put on 46 and I had played one or two half decent strokes. I was beginning to feel I could climb Everest, when I lunged and edged Neame to slip. I got quite a clap as I came in and I felt rather pleased with myself. But what an experience.

We were out for a most disappointing 161 in the middle of the afternoon and I could hardly wait to get down those stairs again and start in at the Harrovians. This time the Long Room felt a much friendlier place. When batting, I had not been too aware of the slope running down to the Tavern. There is a drop of something like nine feet between the north-west and the south-east corners of the ground and it made the job of keeping wicket rather awkward. Standing back at the Pavilion End, the ball went away appreciably down the slope outside the right-hander's off stump. To start with I found myself continually stretching to my right to take the ball when I was sure I was in the right position. I also had to stay down for longer than usual because the severe slope meant that the ball was not only wider than I had anticipated but lower as well.

Simon Douglas-Pennant removed two batsmen at 29 and then, 10 runs later, came a moment I shall never forget. Neame, who was a great threat, was beginning to bat pretty well. Scion of a well-known Harrovian family, there was an unkind rumour he had stayed on past his twentieth birthday to make sure of a fourth crack at Eton. He was facing Ian Sinclair at just above medium pace from the Nursery End and Ian had a deceptive action in which he gained a lot of pace from his shoulders in his delivery stride. Neame got in a tangle with one a fraction outside the leg stump and the ball flicked the inside edge before going through some way to my left. I was lucky that it was going up the slope as he was a right-hander and somehow, in crab-like fashion, I scrambled across and held on. To this day, Rex likes to pretend he didn't hit it, but I can only refer him to the scorecard. Edward Lane Fox then came into his own and took 5/33, although sadly I never had the chance to stump anyone off him, and Harrow were back in the Pavilion before the end of the first day for 105 which gave us a useful lead of 56.

Angus Wolfe-Murray and I stayed that night with Tom Pugh and we went to the Palladium to see Rosemary Clooney with whom Tom was madly in love. He was desperately keen to see her leave the theatre afterwards. When we got to the stage door she was getting into her car and showing just a bit of leg. We did not get to bed as late as events the next day may have suggested when Gus and I were both out first ball. For a time our second innings went entirely according to plan and at 115/4 we were 171 ahead. Then Neame removed Lane Fox and Wolfe-Murray in successive balls and again I had a frantic rush to get my pads on in time and was fastening the last buckle on my right pad when the roar from outside announced that Wolfe-Murray had gone. I walked out, took guard at the Nursery End and Neame came in to bowl and make history. Still thinking, I suppose, that quick runs were what we needed, I took a couple of steps to him, aimed a pull drive in the direction of the Tavern, missed the damned thing and my off stump went down. All hell promptly broke loose which I found mildly puzzling. In something of a daze, I started a walk back to the Pavilion which seemed never ending and encountered much jubilation in the Long Room, from Harrow supporters, I suppose.

When I went into the dressing room I must have been told it was a hat-trick, the first taken in an Eton and Harrow match since they began in 1805. This I had not realised for I had been getting my pads on and not watching immediately before I went in. Tom Pugh tells me that I then said, 'If I had known I was on a hat-trick, I would have tried harder.' The photograph certainly shows it was a somewhat extravagant manner in which to play a hat-trick ball. When I went round to Q Stand to see my parents my father said, 'You were a bloody fool to let him get a hat-trick.' Until recently, I thought that was the first moment I knew it was a hat-trick. Fortunately the last three wickets put on another 51 and we left them to score 223 in plenty of time to win. They began well before Simon Douglas-Pennant produced the spell of his life taking 7/33. Their downfall began when I caught Rex Neame for the second time in the match and he tells me he didn't like this one either. Typical Harrovian. We had an anxious time when the last pair of Harrovians put on 39, but with ten minutes to spare, Champniss gave Sinclair an easy catch at cover off Douglas-Pennant and amid terrific excitement we had won by 38 runs. What an introduction to Lord's it had been, but there was better to come.

CHAPTER

3

ON NOT MISSING THE BUS

In 1956 I was lucky enough to score a lot of runs for Eton and I managed to hang on to a few catches behind the stumps. Early in the season Walter Robins, who had captained England before the war, brought down a Forty Club side of eleven former first-class cricketers, including Denis Compton who had had a knee-cap removed during the winter and was playing his first game since. He bowled his left-arm spinners off one stride and, batting on one leg, played some amazing strokes before he was bowled for 72 by Edward Scott. Arthur Morris, whom we last saw opening for Australia at Lord's in 1953, was also in the side and, like Compton, perished to Scott who finished with 5/43. The other well-known members of Robins's side were Ian Peebles, Jack Young, Leslie Compton, Jack Parker and Harry Crabtree and we beat them by 4 runs. Soon afterwards Manchester Grammar School visited Eton for the first time and found the toffee-nosed inhabitants friendlier and more robust company and better cricketers than they had expected. They batted on for far too long, as I never stop reminding David Green who was in their side that day, and went on to play for Oxford, Lancashire and Gloucestershire. He is now one of the more venerable members of the cricketing press box. They left us well under three hours to make over 300 and the game was drawn. After a hectic start, I was out when my partner, David Barber, drove back a return catch to the bowler off a full toss which he dropped but deflected the ball on to the stumps when I was a long way out of my ground backing up. It was the only time I was ever out in that way.

David Barber was probably the most idiosyncratic opening partner I ever had in any class of cricket. He was bright, articulate and completely mad all at the same time and in the nicest possible way. He was also a great chum. Our frequent conversations in mid-wicket seldom had a lot to do with the cricket. He talked fast in a slightly high-pitched voice and was a genius at spotting toothsome blondes over the boundary at deep backward point. Sometimes I fear they may even have broken his concentration. He had a fine array of strokes and was determined to play them all as often as possible. There was almost nothing he wouldn't try and I know I never enjoyed opening the batting with anyone else half as much. He and I took issue on one particular subject only. He learned to run between the wickets at the school presided over by Denis Compton. I almost wrote Geoffrey Boycott but David distributed his favours equally and ran himself out just as frequently as his partners. Boycott boasts that he never ran himself out. I have no doubt that my former partner would have something libellous to say about my contortions between the wickets. This was what the *Eton College Chronicle* had to say about our running between the wickets in their account of this match against the Forty Club which was played on 31 May. It appears that I was not as generally innocent as I would have liked to think: 'Blofeld and Barber opened as usual, and once again they laid the foundations of a good score by putting on 51. But then, as we have come to expect, one of them was run out; this time it was Barber who made 44 in 25 minutes. Blofeld now leads 3–2 in this run out shambles.'

We had an extraordinary game against Winchester on a pitch on Agar's Plough which was soaked by a sudden storm a minute or two before the official start and, for a day and a half, it cocked a snook at everyone. Winchester won the toss and recovered from 89/7 to 151 all out. Their ranks included the fifteen-year-old Nawab of Pataudi who was already a class and a half better than anyone else. In the first innings, the prince tried to duck under a ball from Scott which would have barely missed the stumps and was hit in the face, although he returned later. Ian Sinclair, our captain, then chose the heavy roller which may not have been the wisest of choices and after seventy minutes of our innings we were 30/8 and the ball was exploding all over the place as if it was the Gabba in Brisbane after a tropical storm. At this point, Edward Scott was joined by Richard Burrows who had left the scene earlier after being hit a nasty one on the cheekbone. They put on 44 and the last wicket another 23, leaving Scott, who had shown remarkable skill, with 35 not out and in danger of regarding himself as an all-rounder – something he has still not forgotten. Winchester then slumped to 89/8 before an equally unlikely ninth wicket stand of 65 came to the rescue and, at the end of a wonderful game, we were 144/3, needing 213 to win. I had the satisfaction of catching 'Tiger' Pataudi in the first innings and stumping him in the second.

After a waterlogged Eton and Harrow match at Lord's, I was lucky enough to be chosen to keep wicket for the Southern Schools against the Rest for two days at Lord's early in August. Soon after receiving and accepting that invitation, I had another asking me to play for Norfolk against Nottinghamshire II at the end of the same week and against Kent II the one after. The first game at Lord's was really a trial match from which the Public Schools side to play the Combined Services over the next two days was to be chosen. I didn't make too many howlers behind the stumps and, batting down the order, I made a few runs before a declaration and was chosen for the Combined Services match. Wicket-keeping was my reason for being there and I found myself going in at number eight.

We batted first and I found myself galloping down the Pavilion stairs, through a now more familiar Long Room, down the steps and out into the middle with the scoreboard reading 71/6. There's always the comforting thought in those situations that you can't do much worse than anyone else. I found the bowlers, who almost certainly had eased off by then, none too demanding and had made a few when Mike Ainsworth, who was captaining the Combined Services, turned to the leg spin of Stuart Leary of Kent and the generously flighted left-arm spin of Raman Subba Row of Surrey, Northamptonshire and, later, England. I think I had a couple of full tosses early on which I managed to dispatch to the mid-wicket boundary and then I found the confidence to use my feet and I kept coming down the pitch to the spinners to take the ball on the full toss and runs came quite fast. I didn't have a plan or anything like that and simply hit the ball when it was there to be hit.

By the time the Commander (Ainsworth) decided this had gone on for long enough and brought back his quicker bowlers. My eye was well and truly in and, amazingly, runs still came at quite a pace. I reached 50 and didn't think much about it, except that at least I had done something I had been unable to do at Lord's on two outings for Eton. Then I just kept on going. I think I received much more than my fair share of bad balls. I well remember feeling a bit nervous as the hundred approached but luckily it didn't seem to get me down and I found full tosses in the nineties no less appetising than at any other stage. My hundred arrived and I should have felt ecstatic but I was rather dazed and bemused as many of the fielding side congratulated me and the smallish crowd did their best.

I had scored 4 more when our last wicket fell – what a lot I owed my partners – and I then really enjoyed the walk back to the Pavilion which went much too quickly, unlike the occasion a year before when I had seemingly traipsed back for ever, bowled first ball for nought. There weren't that many members sitting in the seats in front of the Pavilion when I came in but those that were there did stand, even though I didn't take it in until at least an hour later. When I say that it was an innings that just happened, I mean that, no more, no less. It was always a thrill to feel the ball going off the middle of the bat and this is what happened then. I know I didn't stand back every time I hit a four, preening myself and thinking that here I was at Lord's and this was the stuff to give 'em. I didn't feel any different from any other reasonable innings I had played. The next ball was the only thing that mattered. What makes it stand out was that the ground was Lord's, and only Peter May and Colin Cowdrey had performed a similar feat for the Public Schools. It felt fantastic in retrospect and by the time I had read some of the very nice things which had been written about the innings in the following day's papers, I did feel a touch pleased with myself, but I hope not too much.

My father, who had come up to watch the match, drove me back to Hoveton that Thursday evening where I almost certainly received a lecture from my mother about the importance of keeping my feet on the ground. The next morning soon after breakfast she drove me to Lakenham, Norfolk's lovely ground to the southeast of Norwich and, although I was somewhat insulated by my hundred two days earlier at Lord's, I was nervous as I approached the Norfolk dressing room for the first time. I need not have been. Peter Powell was our ever-cheerful and optimistic captain; Nigel Moore, tall, thickset, fair-haired and a golf Blue at Cambridge, the friendliest of men; Ted Witherden, once of Kent, was the county professional with an insatiable appetite for Minor County runs; Peter Walmsley, who took huge numbers of wickets, opened the bowling with his left arm; Arthur Coomb bowled at medium pace with Tom Cartwright-like accuracy; and Bill Thomas, bespectacled, left-handed, with an impish sense of humour and an irresistible chuckle – these were some of my colleagues in my first game for Norfolk.

We were presided over by perhaps the greatest character of all, Len Hart, our scorer and team manager who organised the logistics when we went away on tour. He had once been a leg spinner himself, and had played for Lionel Robinson, one of the game's great benefactors before the war. Lionel Robinson had his own ground at Old Buckenham, just outside Attleborough, where he entertained touring sides and many others besides. Len helped him to run the ground. When I met Len, he was tall, round, splendidly avuncular and full of good humour. I think he had lost most of his hair trying to corral the young Peter Parfitt, who had just left for Middlesex, and I fear my antics, after the close of play especially, when we were playing away, may have turned the rest even greyer. Of all the cricket I played, I think the relatively small amount of Minor County cricket in which I had the good fortune to take part was the most fun. When I played, Norfolk always had a side full of characters. We tried our guts out and won some of the time and in the sixties I was lucky enough to play under the captaincy of Bill Edrich who, as far as I was concerned, was one of the great men, and a genius at two-day captaincy.

In that first match, against Nottinghamshire second eleven, I opened with Peter Powell and I made an iffy single in the first innings. In the second, I seemed to carry on where I had left off at Lord's against some accurate seam bowling and I managed to make 76 in good time. In those days, Lakenham had a marvellous pitch for batting which was made with great skill for many years by Jimmy Field who looked after it on behalf of Reckitt and Colman, the owners. Notts were captained by Harry Parks who had played for Sussex and then gone to Trent Bridge as coach and looked after the second eleven. He was the younger brother of old Jim and uncle of young Jim who kept wicket for England in the sixties. I have mentioned earlier the small round tents which about a dozen of the members hired for the season. One always housed Mike Falcon who had been the patron saint of Norfolk cricket for much of the twentieth century. He never wanted to play first-class cricket but after four years in the Cambridge Eleven before the First War, he was an automatic choice each year for the Gents against the Players. He was the most successful bowler when Archie MacLaren vowed to bring a side that could beat Warwick Armstrong's unbeaten Australian side at Eastbourne when the Test Matches were over, in what was to be his final first-class match. He was as good as his word and Mike Falcon the old Harrovian took eight wickets in the match and Clem Gibson, the father of the Clem who captained Eton in 1955, took six. I can still see old Mike now sitting on the edge of his deckchair and clapping, with his hands up in front of his face, one of my pulls which went close past his tent for four.

What a week it was. I struggled to make 50 in the first innings of my second game for Norfolk, against Kent II. It was a grafting sort of an innings and at one point I played a defensive stroke to a ball which ended up in the crease beside me. I picked it up and threw it back to the bowler, whereupon John Pretlove, a Cambridge Blue and who has been a recent president of Kent, came up and told me firmly that fielding was the fielders' job and not the batsman's. I try and remember to pull his leg about it whenever I see him – although, of course, he was absolutely right. It would have taught me an even stronger lesson if Kent had appealed and I had been given out, as I would have been for handling the ball.

The only potential cloud on the horizon was the exam I was taking the following summer in order to try and get into Cambridge and I very much doubted I was going to pass it. During the winter my first sortie into journalism landed me in trouble. I wrote for the *Eton College Chronicle* an account of Eton second eleven of which I was captain and goalkeeper, visiting Bradfield and beating their second eleven at soccer. My account began, 'After a moderate lunch, Team B climbed a steep hill at the top of which they found a soccer pitch. After a long wait for the arrival of the referee, we eventually started.' And on it went in the same patronising vein. It earned me a not altogether friendly interview with my headmaster, Robert Birley, and I was told to write one or two letters of apology. Oh dear!

The spring of 1957 arrived and I returned to Eton for my last half which should really have been a triumphant finale for me. I was captain of the Eleven, I had a century at Lord's behind me, but after a pretty dreary start to the season, the Fates had an enormous kick in the pants awaiting me. The Fourth of June celebrations are always the greatest of fun and a chance for members of the Eleven to show off in front of family, girlfriends and thousands of other people. We muddled through the two-day match against the Eton Ramblers, captained, as ever, by Buns Cartwright who had played for Eton in 1907 and 1908. After gallantly surviving the First War, he put his legal training to spasmodic use and also became a professional Old Etonian. One of his most unlikely jobs was as ecclesiastical adviser to the first Lord Birkenhead, F.E. Smith, when he was Lord Chancellor, although history does not relate what he specifically advised him about. Buns was so heavily bewhiskered as to suggest that he might have been at any rate a minor member of the Bavarian royal family and was outwardly gruff, especially when the Eton Ramblers looked like loosing a match they should have won, which was often. He was now in his upper sixties and stood at mid off in thick dark blue gym shoes with which he tried to stop everything he could reach. These shoes were a sort of forerunner of today's trainers. He was one of the great eccentrics and, at heart, a kind man. When I had made that hundred for the Public Schools, I had a letter from Buns. It began, 'Well played indeed! A delightful knock which earned the high praises of Sir Don Bradman with whom I was sitting.' As good a throw-away line as one could have wished for.

The Fourth of June fell on a Tuesday and so we had played the Ramblers on the Monday and Tuesday. It had been a great personal occasion because one of the perks of the Captain of the Eleven at Eton is that he becomes an *ex officio* member of the *Monarch* which is the only ten-oared boat in existence and always brings up the rear in the Procession of Boats on the evening of the Fourth of June. My presence was unlikely because, to be allowed to go on the river, all boys had to have passed their swimming test. This I had never done because I had about six consecutive strokes to my name before I began to sink. So before that Tuesday, I had gone to the swimming pool with the appropriate masters and had shown that I could probably stay afloat long enough to be rescued. The old *Monarch* was a most sturdy boat and the chances of it going over were slender. We wore the most splendid old-fashioned clothes which precluded the use of a lifejacket, and hats which we waved to the multitude on the bank when we all stood up at the critical point of the procession. It was a long way from quanting round the Broad. My mother and father who had come to the Fourth of June set off next day for France for two weeks.

The following Saturday we were due to play Marlborough. On the Friday after lunch, I was bicycling up to Agar's Plough for nets, during which David Macindoe and I were going to choose the side to play against Marlborough. I had a rickety old ex-policeman's bicycle on which my father used to ride to church at Hoveton during the war. As Captain of the Eleven I was allowed a bicycle and so it was passed on to me. I was making good progress towards Agar's Plough and I was approaching the Finch Hatton Bridge just before crossing what in those days was called the Datchet Lane, when I passed Edward Scott, who was on foot, and had a conversation with him over my shoulder. What I had not appreciated was my proximity to the bridge and the Datchet Lane. I started to go straight across, still talking over my shoulder, when a bus reputed to be carrying a load of French Women's Institute ladies on their way to looking round Eton, bore down on me. I believe it was going faster than it might have been and I crashed straight into the front wheel and was thrown into the bus and then back on to the road by which time I was clearly going to be late for my net and maybe for all the others scheduled for me in the future. I was, of course, unaware of any of this as an ambulance turned up and ferried what was left of me to the King Edward the Seventh Hospital in Windsor.

That afternoon my mother and father were looking round Chartres Cathedral when, on an impulse, my mother stopped at a passing shrine, bought a candle and lit it. This was something she had never done before and, going back over it later, she decided that she had lit the candle at just about the exact moment I banged into the French Women's Institute. Anyway, it was all very French. It was a day or two before anyone was able to make contact with my parents and in their absence, and to the immense relief of the criminal classes, John came down, stayed in my room at Eton and coped as best he could.

I was not in the best of health. My skull had been broken much of the way round, a cheekbone had been squashed flat, my jaw was somewhat the worse for wear, a collarbone had taken quite a hammering and the perimeters of my right eye had seen better days. A good deal of sewing had gone on and I remained unconscious for quite a while. Then they had to fish all the splinters of bone out of my brain and surrounding territories, restore my cheekbone to something like its original position and I think they had to do some imaginative work on my nose. This doesn't account for its present size and shape as my genes had taken care of that some seventeen and a half years earlier. When I came round I was apparently anxious to get out of bed for I was determined to captain the school against Marlborough the following day. When that had all been sorted out, I made a remarkably quick recovery and went back to Norfolk quite early in July. The worst moment of it all came during the Eton and Harrow match when, as the official Captain of Eton, I had to listen to the lunchtime scoreboard on the wireless to find out what had happened during the first morning of the match. My job had gone, I am delighted to say, to my old friend Edward Lane Fox and after he had taken 4/14 in Harrow's first innings, they were on the run and it was only the weather which prevented him from masterminding a stirring victory.

My recovery continued apace, so much so that I was able to return to Eton for the last few days of what was, in any case, my last half. My entrance exam to Cambridge had fallen by the wayside, but apparently King's had made the rash decision to take me on trust. I suppose this probably had something to do with my father and John's impressive battles with the examiners. My last few days at school passed off without mishap and in some ways did my confidence a lot of good. But I encountered one massive problem. M'Tutor's had reached the semi-final of the house cricket cup and I was allowed to play, although I did not captain the side, a job which fell to Bill Legge-Bourke who, later in life, was not to be sneezed at as a progenitor. We were playing Nigel Wykes's house and their principal weapon was Edward Scott who was a trifle apprehensive about bowling full tilt at me. He shouldn't have worried because I could defend adequately but when, for example, the ball was dropped short and I wanted to hook, which was one of my strokes, I was completely unable to tell my feet to move. I knew what I wanted to do but my feet stayed put. This was infinitely frustrating and was soon to make me realise I was no longer half the cricketer I had once been. Looking back on it all now with the advantage of hindsight, I wonder if those concerned were not a little too optimistic about my immediate progress. I was told later that brain bruising, of which I had a nasty go, was likely to take as long as ten years to disappear and this was exactly what happened. The only time I ever again kept wicket as well as I had done while at school was when I toured Barbados with Jim Swanton's Arabs almost exactly ten years later.

In August I stupidly agreed to play a few games for Norfolk and was clearly far from ready and not even a pale reflection of the chap who had started quite well for them the year before. Then, it was up to King's early in October for my first term at Cambridge. This was another bad decision because it must have been palpably obvious that I was still not a very whole person after that wretched accident. Naturally, I was keen to do anything which seemed to indicate that the accident was not as bad as was at first thought and was eager to get on with life. But I cannot believe that today I would have been allowed to do as much so soon afterwards. My father had regarded Cambridge as the be-all and end-all of life and was anxious for me to go. I suspect also that he was doubly grateful to King's for giving me a place, as it meant that he did not yet have to decide what to do with me. Younger sons traditionally hotfooted it for the army, but the medical fraternity didn't like the look of me after my bang on the head, or the church which, although congregations were in decline, had not yet reached the stage where quite such desperate measures were called for.

There was a paradox about it all. If I had not had the accident, I do not think I would have gone up to Cambridge at all for I doubt I would have passed that exam for King's. My cricket would then have been intact but I would not have had the chance to get a Blue. If I had not gone up in October 1957, I suppose King's might have withdrawn their offer. I probably would have been a better cricketer and I would have got more out of Cambridge but I may never have had the opportunity. If they had withdrawn their offer, gone were my chances of getting the Blue, albeit an extremely bad one, which in view of what I was to do later, was the one degree that perhaps I needed more than any other. As a result, maybe the best answer was inadvertently found.

I was hopeful in my first year that I would make the Cambridge side. This did not take into account two things. The first was Chris Howland who was a better wicket-keeper than I was then, and the second was the unfortunate circumstances of my first game for the University. Through a Norfolk friend, Jane Holden, who had been at school with her, I had become great friends with Minnie d'Erlanger who went on to marry young Winston Churchill who had been at Eton at the same time as I had. She was coming out that year and had asked me to Queen Charlotte's Birthday Ball for debutantes at Grosvenor House and I had accepted. It now transpired that the following day was the first day of the match against Kent for which I had been selected. It was a bad moment and a dreadful decision. I almost certainly made the wrong one when I decided to go to the dance and hope we fielded first the following day. The milk train from Liverpool Street to Cambridge at the crack of dawn fitted in well with my schedule. That Ian McLachlan, an old Blue up at Jesus with our captain, Ted Dexter, was also on it, did not. Ian had been given the match off against Kent. A *Boys' Own* hero would have made a hundred and gone on to marry the girl as well. I made nought in the first innings and not many more in the second and never went out with Minnie again. As if that was not bad enough, word had crept around Cambridge as to the reason for that duck and my dedication to the cause was in doubt.

My second match was against Lancashire when I managed to make about 41 in one innings against Brian Statham and Ken Higgs, to say nothing of Roy Tattersall, and put on 78 with Dexter himself. I spent most of the morning session jumping out of the way of his straight drives and watching the slips jump to try and reach the ones which flew off my outside edge over their heads. Dexter was not an easy conversationalist at the wicket. Once he edged Statham on to his back pad which prevented the ball going into the stumps. In mid-wicket I had the temerity to suggest he had had a bit of luck. I was swiftly and resoundingly put into my place. 'Just occasionally, it pays to get your foot behind the ball,' I was told. It was several overs before I tried again. In those days, we were desperately lucky to be coached by Cyril Coote who had for years been the groundsman at Fenner's. He had one leg substantially shorter than the other and walked with a pronounced limp. In his time, he had been an extremely effective opening batsman for Cambridgeshire in spite of his handicap and was also a brilliant shot. He was a coach who had the ability to see in a moment a batsman's weakness and to know how to put it right. Cyril probably had much more to do with the University's outstanding record in the fifties than he was given credit for. He was also a brilliant groundsman who for years prepared perfect batting pitches at Fenner's. For those who knew Cyril, Fenner's will never be the same without him.

I failed my exams that year. They were college exams because History Part I takes two years and King's decided to give me another chance. When I returned in the autumn I was shown some of my written answers. They made almost no sense at all, which perhaps underlined that too much had been attempted too soon and that my college had been misguidedly charitable.

It was a family decision that I should try and earn a bob or two in the long vacation and I somehow persuaded Simpson's in Piccadilly that their sale of Daks trousers would take a considerable upturn if they acquired my services. I was thrust on to the first floor wearing a dark suit and, with a brand new measuring tape in my hand, I keenly awaited my first customer. He spoke almost no English but I sensed he wanted trousers so I whipped a tape measure round his waist and then made an attempt to measure his inside leg for which I got one out of ten and that was for going to the right place. He was a nice chap and there were no ill feelings, but he decided to buy a jacket instead, probably because he felt I was bound to do less damage with the measuring tape. Sadly, we never found one he wanted.

The following summer I made only a marginally better impression with the examiners and got a Special which was not enough to save me on its own. John Raven, the senior tutor at King's, wrote me a kind letter suggesting that we might try and work out a way of continuing our relationship. He went on to say that there were a number of his colleagues who felt that this was being too generous and implied that I would not be allowed to play cricket until after exams. It did not take me long to decide to fall on my sword.

On the cricketing front, things went a bit better. I made a few runs going in first with David Kirby, a Yorkshireman who felt that to score anything more than a single off any one ball in the two hours before lunch, was rather more than faintly immoral and required an immediate caution. I scored just enough runs to be awarded probably the worst Blue for an opening batsman since the Boer War, but there were splendid moments.

Soon after leaving Fenner's, we came to Nottingham to play the county at Trent Bridge. Reg Simpson who was maybe the best player of fast bowling produced by England in the immediate postwar period, was captaining Nottinghamshire and, to try and give the match some public appeal, he had persuaded Keith Miller to turn out for the county. I opened the batting without much success and stayed long enough to face Miller with the new ball and to receive one quick leg break. Keith made 62 in one innings and a hundred in the other when I dropped him off a skier in front of what was then the Ladies Pavilion at deep mid-wicket. Almost forty years later when Keith had been crippled by many of the afflictions of old age and the residue of an extremely athletic life, and was staying with Paul Getty at Wormsley, I gave Colin Ingleby-Mackenzie who was going down there, the scorecard of this game and asked him if he would try and persuade Keith to sign it. Back it came with the following words scrawled across the middle, 'Well dropped Henry, Keith Miller'. On the last day at Trent Bridge, I had been batting for quite a while for very few and was still in at lunch. I sat next to Keith and was moaning about my batting. 'You've got to ask yourself one question,' he said to me. 'Are you better than the bowlers? In your case, the answer is no, you're not. You've done well to stay in.' There was a lot of common sense in that.

I was asked by David Green, our captain, if I would be free to play against Oxford at Lord's after our match with Sussex at Eastbourne. I had scored a few runs in that game but another reason I remember it was that I was given my first bowl in first-class cricket. I bowled my first over to the Reverend David Sheppard on one of his outings for Sussex. He pushed forward to the one leg break which pitched on the spot and Chris Howland dropped the catch behind the stumps. Our next match was against the MCC at Lord's and their side included Denis Compton who had retired from county cricket the year before. We made 318/6 declared and bowled them out for 174, of which 71 were made in quite inimitable fashion by the Great Man. Neville Cardus saw his innings and, writing an essay about Compton for the *Playfair Cricket Monthly*, he said, 'The other summer at Lord's, his innings of 71 against Cambridge University was virtually a restoration, not to say a resurrection, of his genius, brilliant, original, happy.' You cannot sum it up better than that, even though he was by then playing virtually on one leg. When Cambridge batted again, we made 310/4 declared and I managed to score 138 of them in my only first-class hundred. The bowling may have been modest but it was still a first-class hundred at Lord's and we won by 50 runs. I had two chances of making another in our next match, against Oxford. Alas, I scored only 2 in the first innings and a snappy single in the second. In the first, I fended at a lifter from David Sayer which flicked my glove and was caught by Alan Smith, a future England wicket-keeper and chief executive of the Test and County Cricket Board. The appeal came and I stood my ground and it was Dai Davies standing at the Pavilion End, who gave me out. I should have walked but I did not and Dai Davies sought me out afterwards. 'Don't ever do that again,' was his terse advice. Different times.

My final cricketing adventure in that year, 1959, was with Norfolk. Bill Edrich had retired from first-class cricket the year before and had come back to captain the side with whom he had begun his career in the thirties. We had our best season under him the next year, 1960, and finished top of the Minor County table. We were then challenged by the runners-up who happened to be Lancashire II. We played the challenge match at Lakenham but with a very strong side which included Roy Tattersall, Malcolm Hilton, Colin Hilton, a tearaway fast bowler, Geoff Clayton, Peter Marner and Jack Bond, Lancashire won the match. Bill was a brilliant captain, the most delightful of men and a genius at keeping the other side interested until almost the end. If he had a problem it was that he wanted to declare for the opposing captain as well. If that turned out to be as determined an individual as Maurice Crouch of Cambridgeshire, bad blood could be spilled.

I remember catching Crouch off Arthur Coomb for his first ever pair for Cambridgeshire and even though the umpire gave him out, he was unwilling to leave the field. Bill was very persuasive from first slip and, with Maurice himself revealing an impressive range of expletives, all of us within earshot increased our repertoire.

My family and I now had to try and find something for me to do. It did not look like being particularly easy for it was not as though my qualifications were glaringly obvious. My mother's brother, Mark Turner, who was a big chap in the City, came generously to the rescue. He persuaded Robert Benson Lonsdale, the merchant bankers of whom he was a director, to offer me a job as a trainee at the princely salary of £360 a year. As that was the only offer on the table, I had little alternative but to accept it. My family were not certain about me disappearing into the world of commerce and gritted their teeth. The rest of the world, meanwhile, held its breath to see if one of the great financial careers of the twentieth century was about to begin.

CHAPTER

4

FIRST ASSIGNMENTS

I MUST HAVE LOOKED an awful idiot when, on the first Monday in October 1959, I strode down the Brompton Road to Knightsbridge underground station barely past my twentieth birthday. I was wearing a bowler hat which had been bought for me at Lock's in St James's, a three-piece dark grey suit and I was carrying a rolled up umbrella. Little Lord Fauntleroy could hardly have done worse. I didn't have the nerve to buy a copy of the *Financial Times*, but otherwise I suppose I must have thought I looked the part. I bought a ticket to St Paul's and changed on to the Central Line at Holborn. The train was packed and it was standing room only. Most people were reading a paper and the pink *Financial Times* was in demand. A great many were smoking, as was the custom in those far distant days when packets did not display a health warning and smokers were not considered to be modern-day lepers.

I smoked myself, a Turkish blend when I was able to pinch them from my father or afford them from Messrs Sullivan & Powell who ran their emporium at the top of the Burlington Arcade. When a customer entered that excellent shop, which is now extinct, he was immediately offered a cigarette by Mr Gardner which seemed the height of civilised behaviour. Mr Gardner presided over affairs from behind an elegant polished counter, rather darkly, as if he were plotting to overthrow Freiborg & Treyer who also sold Turkish cigarettes and had their foothold at the top of the Haymarket and, confident of its success, had just launched the invasion. I used to smoke a brand called Effendi and whenever I visited the shop, Mr Gardner always offered me a Sub Rosa which were the best. I couldn't afford either. If my father was guarding his cigarettes too carefully and I was short of money, which was a common occurrence, I settled for the Virginian alternative of Senior Service which my father always referred to as 'gaspers' and I was not allowed to smoke them at Hoveton.

It was a stampede at Holborn as one was swept along down the passages to another platform for the train to St Paul's. Then, it was a seven- or eight-minute walk to the other end of Gresham Street before turning left down to Aldermanbury Square where Robert Benson Lonsdale were housed in a small but modern block. On the other side of the tiny square, the foundations were being laid for the Brewers' Hall and behind that the traffic sped up and down London Wall. On my first day I had been told to report to Mr Lewis, to whom I had been briefly introduced when I came to see the General Manager three weeks earlier. Mr Lewis sat in a glass hutch at the end of the General Office and I immediately liked him when I discovered he was interested in cricket. He told me now, with the air of a man who was at any moment about to perform a high-class conjuring trick, that he had assigned me to Mr Sutherland who would teach me the subtleties of entering deals on the Stock Exchange for RBL's clients into large black ledgers. I just managed to stop myself jumping up and down with excitement. He took me to meet Mr Sutherland who was large, moustached and, if not a laugh a minute, at least an immensely reliable pillar in the affairs of RBL. A small chair was pulled up beside him and I sat down, while Mr Lewis wandered off to take a decision of immense importance in some other part of the General Office.

Mr Sutherland sat across the desk from Mr Mitchell, a small man who was the butt of a certain amount of office humour, but needed careful watching for he could suddenly catch fire and become incandescently angry. He also pored over more ledgers but for what purpose I am not sure for I never came under his tutelage. In his spare time Mr Mitchell was a racing bicyclist of considerable repute and was obviously extremely fit. This may

FIRST ASSIGNMENTS

have been the area in which he could have taught me most, although I rather hoped that my bicycling days were finally over. Mr Sutherland wrote in a regular hand and found a single-minded concentration which ensured his ledgers were neatness itself. But if ever a blotch or a mistake should happen, he had a bottle of an early equivalent of Tipp-Ex which he used adroitly for corrective surgery. To be honest, I was less than spellbound by this dizzy introduction to the gentle art of merchant banking and I felt sure that, try as I might, I would never achieve the level of skill shown by Mr Sutherland. I fear he, too, may have doubted that my heart was really in it. We soldiered on for a week or two before Mr Lewis once more appeared and whisked me away to give a helping hand to another cog in the huge and ever-rotating wheel of financial commerce.

I had a bit of fun when I joined Mr Langley who sat a couple of desks down the office from Mr Sutherland. As I remember it, he was the first in line to receive the details of any Stock Exchange deals which had been transacted by the dealing room just above our heads. He checked the figures and then made sure the different departments received the relevant information to enter into all the many ledgers. Mr Langley also had his own network of stockbrokers and was not averse to a bit of a plunge himself. This seemed to me to be a great idea and a way to try and ensure that a few more pieces of eight found their way into my bank account which was zealously guarded by the Aldermanbury Square Branch of Barclays Bank on the ground floor of the same building.

I became something of a hero for a short time when I was sitting beside Mr Langley and I have my mother to thank for that. Most weeks she would have her hair done by Gwen who had a small room, salon would be the wrong word, in one of the farm cottages on the main road, next door to Ingate. Gwen had worked on the farm as a land-girl during the war and gone into hairdressing after the Führer had been put in his place. She was doing my mother's hair one morning and told her that she had heard from one of her clients who had connections in the East, that a rubber stock called Jugra Land in Borneo or Sumatra or somewhere like that, was a snip at about ten shillings a share. The company, so she said, was going to be taken over. At the weekend mother passed the information on to me and on the Monday I let slip this bombshell and was extremely miffed to find that no one could have cared less. I put my money where my mouth was and bought a hundred or two and, lo and behold, over the next few days, the price began to creep up and one or two others also bought. This continued for a week or so and more people joined in. I was terrified the whole thing was going to blow up, which would have been highly embarrassing, but eventually the news came through that Jugra Land & Carey which was the company's full name, had indeed been taken over and we had all made quite a decent profit. My personal stock was high as a result.

From time to time while I was in the General Office, Mr Paine, the General Manager would walk down the open-plan passage which separated the two sides of the office and, a bit like a bishop minding his flock and on the look out for schism and doubt, he would stop and ask me how I was getting on in the sort of voice Alan Bennett would have used if he had been asked to be a high-ranking ecclesiastic. I assured him that I was learning fast and enjoying it or some other ghastly lie and he went on his way nodding his head like a benevolent guardian angel. After Mr Langley, I spent some time with the cashier, Timmy Ellis, who sat at the top of the office next to the glass partition which separated us all from Mr Lewis. Timmy Ellis was the nicest man in RBL, full of fun and good humour. He was really the office bank manager as people came from all directions for further supplies of cash. He was meticulously efficient and loved by one and all. I am not sure what he taught me, except that there was a lighter side to it all, because I had already learned how to cash a cheque a long time before I arrived in the City of London.

I enjoyed lunch, although the three-bob Luncheon Vouchers we were given on a daily basis needed a heavy subsidy. It was a great chance to see my chums who were either embryonic merchant bankers like me, though I think very few could have been quite so pulsatingly embryonic, or stock brokers, or chaps who were soon to be a powerful influence in the room at Lloyds where I suppose a great many of them went up in smoke about thirty

FIRST ASSIGNMENTS

years later. It was really a very jolly club if you liked that sort of thing, but I'm afraid that all I learned in my time in the City was that I had not the mind, the inclination, nor the aptitude to succeed.

I played cricket when I could over weekends in the summer. It was in 1960 that I was asked by David Fasken if I would like to play for his Arab side against the Crusaders at Cambridge. The invitation will of course have originated from Jim Swanton who ran the club in every detail. I was delighted and we played on the Clare ground which was somewhere on the left off Hills Road. It was a good pitch and we not only won the match but I also managed to score a hundred which will have secured my election to the Arabs, a club which was always the greatest of fun to play for, not least because Jim Swanton himself was such a splendid figure. Jim had been christened Ernest William but had been 'Jim' for longer than anyone could remember, and it was Michael Carey, one of his successors on the *Daily Telegraph*, who put it down to 'the importance of not being Ernest'. He was in his early fifties then and still liked to captain the side, which he did with a resounding authority. Disagreeing with his captaincy was a treasonable offence. Whether he was captain or match manager or merely the spectating founder, he was never pleased when the Arabs lost. Many is the Arab captain who lost a match, after Jim had finally retired, and was the recipient of a penetrative letter a day or two later telling him exactly where he went wrong and reminding him of one or two essential truths about the game of cricket and maybe one or two about himself as well. He was always a stickler for etiquette. There was the occasion when the Arabs were playing at Hampstead or Rye when an opposing batsman was felled at the crease and lay in a nasty heap spitting blood and teeth. Seeing this, Jim drove his Jaguar out to the middle with his wife Ann sitting beside him, but before they lifted the batsman into the car, Jim did not forget to go through the formalities of introducing Ann to the poor chap, which put it all on a proper footing.

In July and August I was able to play a certain amount of cricket for Norfolk but the trouble now was getting into some sort of form beforehand. While I was working for RBL, I initiated a two-day game in September between the Eton Ramblers and the Free Foresters which we played on our ground at Hoveton. I first persuaded David Thorne to run the Forester side. He bowled his left-arm spinners with great success for Norfolk while a regular soldier. His outstanding military career ended after he had played a leading role as a Major-General in the dismissal of the Argentines from the Falkland Islands. We both produced some good sides and they were closely fought contests on a pitch which can be best described as sporting. When David was stationed elsewhere and had to give up, Johnny Woodcock took over the Forester side and it was always the greatest of fun until the whole weekend became rather too much for my mother and father. We played the match for a time at a lovely ground near Amersham but in the end that ground became unavailable and the fixture stopped. I had always hoped that one day we would get it back to Hoveton but we all grew older and the temptation finally disappeared when the village decided to use another ground with more modern facilities, and John planted trees over some of the outfield to give more backing for the pheasants at Hill Piece.

After these epic contests, Monday morning in Aldermanbury Square had even less to offer. After a while, I left the General Office and moved on to the Investment Research Department where I am afraid I again left something rather less than an indelible impression, although it was undoubtedly more rewarding and interesting than the ledger run from which I had just come. I then had a spell in the Private Clients Investment Department which was run by a man I soon considered to be an imperial toad and I can only say that he viewed me as something which had a poisonous sting in the tail. I didn't last long with him.

In the summer of 1958, at a coming-out dance for debutantes, I had met Joanna Hebeler and we had fallen for one another. We both found ourselves at the same dinner party beforehand which was given by Judith Listowel who had a daughter engaged in the same pursuits. Our hostess was a formidable woman, married to Lord Listowel who became the Governor of Ghana or the Gold Coast as it was originally known. There were several people I knew at the dinner party and we went on afterwards to the Hyde Park Hotel where we danced the night away. Afterwards, all the men at the dinner party received a terse letter from Lady Listowel which ticked us off for not having danced with every girl at the dinner party. I remember the letter well because she had ended it, 'Yours Sinc Judith Listowel'.

Joanna and I were married in April 1961 in the parish church at Horsham, next door to the cricket ground on which Sussex still play a match or two each year. The deed was performed by Percy Herbert who had not long before retired as the Bishop of Norwich and had the best speaking voice I have ever listened to. He was a friend of my father and mother and would shoot with us every year at Hoveton. He was the most delightful man with a splendid sense of humour and if the Church of England could boast more like him, I am sure it would not be in the doldrums as it is now.

We were given the most wonderful honeymoon one could imagine by two Americans, Pat and Edith Kerrigan whom my mother and father met each autumn when they went to Florence. He was a senior partner of Merrill Lynch Fenner Pierce and Bean as they were then or 'The Thundering Herd' as they were colloquially known. One year, when Joanna and I were engaged, the Kerrigans came back to London with my parents. We met them before dinner one evening and in no time at all Pat had told my father that he would put us up in New York for a week of our honeymoon and suggested that my father sent us to Jamaica for a fortnight first which was not at all what my father was planning. He laughingly replied that surely Pat had a partner who lived in Jamaica whose house we could borrow. Pat said that indeed that was so and there matters had rested for a while.

Nearer the time, Pat rang from New York and said that he thought it would be unfair for us to have to deal with the running of the house and the staff and that he had arranged for us to stay in the principal suite at the Jamaica Inn in Ocho Rios which is as good as they get. Not content with that, he gave us spending money for Jamaica and more when we went back to New York for a week. It was all almost too much to take in and we eventually arrived at the Jamaica Inn, late one evening after we had almost landed in the sea at Montego Bay. Then, on the drive to Ocho Rios, our taxi's big end had given up the ghost and we had to cram into another which already had two people on board, to complete the journey. We were met by the owner, Gloria Elkins with her Dalmatian at her side. She told us that the couple whom she had to get rid of the day before to make room for us had been no other than Richard Burton and Elizabeth Taylor. I felt I had plenty to live up to that night. During the most luxurious two weeks of my life we met Ian Fleming and went to lunch at his house, Goldeneye, in Oracabessa. Noel Coward, who was full of bounce, also came to lunch. It was a long time before my feet again touched ground.

The Bond connection was carried further on only one occasion. A few years later, in the early seventies, I came back from Hastings by train after watching Sussex play a match on that delightful ground in the middle of the town which has since been grabbed by property developers and become a shopping precinct. By the time I arrived at Waterloo, it was raining hard and the taxi queue was long. There was nothing for it but to wait. I had hardly found my bearings when the most spectacular girl joined the queue just behind me. We started to talk, she in the most beguiling Canadian accent, and when we had finished with the weather and the likelihood of getting a taxi back to Chelsea where we were both bound, our conversation became bolder and more diversified. Her name was Lois Maxwell and she had also returned from Hastings after putting the finishing touches to an episode in *On Her Majesty's Secret Service*. She was, of course, Miss Moneypenny. I am ashamed to say I could not resist the most dreadful pun and suggested that we had a common Bond. She was polite enough to smile. She looked every bit as lovely as she did in the films and to my immense delight agreed to share a taxi with me. She had the most wonderful smile I have ever seen. When I dropped her in Draycott Avenue, she asked me to come up for a drink and I met her husband, Peter Marriott, an Englishman, who was not very robust and did not live for much longer. Lois and I sayed in touch for some time until, after Peter had died, she returned to Canada to live on

FIRST ASSIGNMENTS

property she owned in the back of beyond and alas I have never seen her again. She is the only reason I never miss a Bond film. Sadly, her moments are at best fleeting although well worth the wait.

It was bad luck on the wretched Robert Benson Lonsdale that they should have to put up with me after such a honeymoon. But when I returned to the City, their merger with Kleinworts had been consolidated and I was now used as the first RBL guinea pig who was sent over to their offices in Fenchurch Street to continue my traineeship. I strongly suspect that those at RBL were at their wits end to know what to do with me next at Aldermanbury Square and this was a heaven-sent opportunity to ged rid of me. If anything, I disliked the banking side of the business even more than the investment arm. I sat on the mezzanine floor in Fenchurch Street, bored out of my mind and spent most of the day running backwards and forwards to the betting shop by the Monument to listen to my chosen horses becoming inextricably entwined with the next race. I should explain that just before this, I had been taken to Royal Ascot for the first time and in two days' racing I had backed about eight winners, most ridden by Lester Piggott, and, just as I had done after my Stock Exchange success with Jugra Land, I felt it was easy. On both counts, I have been shelling out money ever since.

The time had come for me to decide what I really wanted to do with my life. I briefly considered the wine trade which would not have been clever because if anyone had been foolish enough to give me a job, I would almost certainly have drunk myself into an early grave. While my knowledge of the finer points of wine may have been slender, I had already acquired an attachment to alcohol which wasn't to be sniffed at. On the other hand, if I had joined the wine trade, I suppose I might have learned to spit at tastings which, as a willing amateur, I have always found absurdly difficult. I then decided after a long dinner with myself, a pen and a piece of paper, that the only thing I had ever been any good at in my life so far was cricket. I realised I wasn't good enough to go on playing it, but I didn't see why I shouldn't write about the game. I wrote letters to various newspapers and always received the same reply which was that I needed to gain some experience and when I had worked for a couple of years on, say, a provincial morning paper, I should try again. It was all rather depressing.

Towards the end of May 1962 the Arabs had a party at the Hyde Park Hotel and there I met Johnny Woodcock who had, since 1954, been the cricket correspondent of *The Times*. I told him of my plight and he listened sympathetically and told me, much as those to whom I had already written had done, that I must try and get some experience before tackling a national daily. But he did say that he would see if there was anything that he could do. I didn't think much more about it and was beginning to be resigned to slogging on in the City, realising that if that was so, I must pull my finger out and make more of an effort. The following Tuesday evening, Joanna and I had dinner with James and Sarah Cecil who were neighbours of ours in Dovehouse Street in Chelsea and he a fellow labourer on behalf of Kleinwort Benson – the difference between us, he would take over as chairman one day.

After an excellent dinner, at about a quarter past nine, I had to go back down the road to collect something from our house. On the floor inside the door I found one of those old-fashioned bright yellow telegrams. It said simply that I should ring Johnny Woodcock as soon as possible and gave his number. I rang at once and he told me that because Uel Titley – his father had been christened Sam and he used his son to complete the name – was unwell, they needed to find someone to cover the first two days of the match between Kent and Somerset which started the next day at the Bat and Ball ground at Gravesend. If I wanted to do it, I would have to go round there and then to *The Times* and meet John Hennessey, the Sports Editor, who would brief me and give me a press ticket. I could hardly believe my luck and told Johnny that of course I would do it. He said he would tell Hennessey. I shot back to the Cecils waving the telegram, a trifle more convincingly than Neville Chamberlain, I hope, and explained my predicament. They most kindly understood, the after-dinner bridge was aborted and I jumped into my car and set off for Printing House Square. There was not a minute to spare as Hennessey was about to leave for the night. I made it and, after many frantic enquiries, I was shown up to the Sports Room and met him. After shaking my hand and no doubt wondering to himself if this was really the chap Woodcock had spoken to him about, he told me to go to Gravesend the following day. He instructed me to ring up a number he gave me at half past three the next afternoon and ask how much they wanted me to write. He said I should ring again as soon after the end of the day's play as I could manage and no later than forty-five minutes afterwards, and dictate my copy to someone called Laurie Wayman. He then gave me my first-ever press ticket, shook me by the hand again and wished me luck.

I drove back to Dovehouse Street tremendously buoyed and excited by it all. Joanna was waiting for me and when my first flurry of excited chatter had subsided, she asked me quietly if I thought I would able to do it. I said I had no doubts about that at all, although of course I did and spent a virtually sleepless night turning it all over in my mind and wondering if I really would be able to describe a day's cricket. Before we went to bed, we decided that Joanna would come with me and after a quick search of the AA book, tried to find a pub in which to stay the following night in Gravesend. They all seemed to be full and after an age on the telephone, I managed to secure a double room in a pub in the main street in Rochester.

The next morning I rang up my office in the City and told them I had flu and at about half past nine we set off in the Cortina for Gravesend. It took a little longer than expected to negotiate south-east London but we still arrived at the charming old Bat and Ball ground well before the start at half past eleven. I had all the bubbling confidence of my first press ticket which I waved vigorously at all and sundry whenever we were stopped and it worked like a charm. I left Joanna in the car and set off to find the press box which proved to be a small tent on the other side of the ground not far from the pavilion. Clutching my first notebook, I introduced myself to the two or three others who were there and received muted applause. Kent won the toss and decided to field and I made my first note. The day progressed happily enough but, as the minutes clicked by, a dreadful gnawing feeling took hold of my stomach as I realised that before too long I would have to put pen to paper. Bill Alley, Somerset's ageless Australian who, the year before, had scored more than 3,000 runs in the season and is the last player to have done so, was in spanking form and hit 155 and, as was his way, a great many of them through mid-wicket.

The only discordant note to my first day was introduced by a colleague who asked me with an acid face if I was a member of the National Union of Journalists. I was very taken aback and told him I was afraid I was not as this was my first day, but that if things went according to plan and there were many more of them, I was sure that I would become a member. This was not nearly good enough and he launched into a tirade about the iniquity of jobs being given to people like me when there were starving members of the NUJ on every street corner. At least, that's what it sounded like.

I rang up *The Times* at half past three and was told they wanted 450 words which at the time seemed to be about the length of *War and Peace*. I was terrified. Soon afterwards the time came to write and, most uneasily, I opened my other notebook and searched desperately, as I have done so many times since, for my first intro. I have no idea how I found it, but I did and the piece was eventually written with a certain amount of crossing out, and, with my heart in my mouth, I found a telephone about twenty minutes after the close of play. Laurie Wayman, still the best copytaker to whom I have ever given copy, answered the telephone in a very pukka voice, but couldn't have been more friendly. He asked me to wait a moment while he prepared himself, and then he told me to fire away, although he didn't put it quite like that. I dictated and he took it down on a typewriter at breathtaking speed and suddenly it was all over. He asked me to ring back in an hour to see if there were any queries. I put the telephone down on a considerable high and found, as I have always done since, especially after one's last broadcast of the day, that I was full of pent-up emotion and adrenaline and with nowhere to go. I got back into the car with my long-suffering wife whom I had visited at lunch and tea. She must already have been thinking that being married to a merchant banker was infinitely preferable to this. I had come to the opposite conclusion.

We now struggled on to Rochester, stopping once on the way for me to call *The Times* and find out if there was anything wrong with my piece. Just for a moment, I was fearful that they might ask me to rewrite it. But no. When I spoke again to Wayman, he told that it was all right. I longed to ask him, how all right, but he had gone. I can't think why we didn't drive back to London that night. As it was, we had a filthy dinner of brown Windsor soup and very old mutton with underboiled potatoes. We then turned in and found that we were sleeping in the smallest double bed in Kent and probably in the whole of the United Kingdom. We also had the second noisiest room in the world with cars revving away from the traffic lights all night. I don't think I slept a wink, so nervous was I about what my piece would look like the next morning. I was up at about six o'clock striding through Rochester trying to locate a copy of *The Times*. The first two newsagents didn't have one, the third had 'already sold it', but the fourth came nobly to my rescue. In a frenzy, I tore the paper open and searched the sports pages and there it was. In one column my report stretched down the page and, as I read it, I realised they had changed scarcely a word. It was a marvellous moment. Of course, in those days, reports in *The Times* were anonymously written.

The second day came and went and, as it progressed, my jubilation and supreme confidence after my first effort gradually began to wane as I was faced with the prospect of having to do it all over again. But I did and it worked. I was back in the City on the Friday and, after such heady stuff, it seemed small beer indeed. Soon afterwards, Laurie Wayman rang me again and asked if I would do two more days for *The Times*, on the Wednesday and Thursday, at Portsmouth where Hampshire were playing Warwickshire. I leapt at it, rang my office on the Thursday morning and told them that the dreaded virus had returned and set off down the A3 to the south coast. Once again, through the admirable medium of Laurie Wayman, I found out each day the number of words *The Times* wanted, supplied them on time and had the satisfaction of seeing it all appear the next day.

This time, I encountered my first snag. On the Thursday Norman Horner, who opened the batting for Warwickshire, had one of those days when nothing quite worked. He couldn't time the ball to save his life, the few strokes he hit out of the middle of the bat found the fielders and he spent an awful long time over 85. I wrote that Horner was an 'unprepossessing batsman', which could not have been further from the truth because he was normally the most entertaining dasher. He was not at all pleased to read that he was unprepossessing and made sure that I was aware of this. I was most embarrassed and only hoped that no one at *The Times* had seen him bat as he normally did. It was a silly thing to write without checking up, for this was the only time I had seen him and it all too clearly revealed my inexperience. The sequel came two weeks later when *The Times* sent me to Nuneaton to watch Warwickshire play Middlesex and there was a raffle for Norman Horner's benefit. I bought some tickets and when he made the draw towards the end of the day, I won the bottle of gin and had to go and collect it from him. He gave me a bit of a look, too, when we shook hands.

The following Sunday, Wayman rang and offered me four days' cricket which, of course, I accepted. The next morning I rang the pious Mr Paine, the General Manager at Kleinwort Benson, and told him I had left for good. He said, 'What do you mean?' and I said, 'I mean that I am not coming in to the office again.' This caused him mild surprise to say the least because, as he then told me at some length, it was not the way it was normally done. Irregular was the word he used. I am happy to think that this initial sense of shock and maybe anger will soon have been overtaken by a much warmer, more comforting feeling of immense relief.

I had told my uncle, Mark Turner, about two months earlier that I was thinking of becoming a cricket writer and he had said, 'Go to it.' He was a trustee of the *Observer* and it was through him that I was able to make contact with their Sports Editor, the inimitable Clifford Makins who, more than anyone in Fleet Street, was a legend in his own lunchtime. Clifford could have played Jeffrey Barnard on level terms. Even if Mark he had not passed on this specific information to Paine, I daresay he will have inti-

FIRST ASSIGNMENTS

mated that there was a certain restlessness on my part. It's just possible that the General Manager will have had more devastating shocks to his system than my unexpected departure in the course of what I am sure was a long and blameless career.

So, while my chances of ending up as the Governor of the Bank of England had taken a severe knock, I was now setting off with not much more than bare feet and fingernails to climb the mountain at the top of which sat Cardus, Swanton and Woodcock. My sights were set not so much on the summit as the South Col of cricket writing. I never doubted for a single second which occupation would give me the most pleasure.

CHAPTER

5

PACKAGE TO INDIA

THE GREATEST character in the Cambridge side in 1959 was our Indian middle order batsman, Santosh Reddy, who lives in Hyderabad where I have no doubt that he exercises an influence over local affairs that is as far-reaching as it is jovial. At Cambridge Santosh had his leg pulled unmercifully and replied in kind. As a batsman he could be both dapper and punishing at the same time. He was small with a frantic way of running between the wickets which was invariably preceded by a series of frenzied yells. I next saw Santosh at the end of January 1964 in Calcutta during the Third Test Match between India and England. I was staying at the Great Eastern Hotel, no longer the hotel it had been under the British Raj, and Santosh took me out to dinner. His driving made his running between the wickets look like a solemn religious procession. He turned up in what passed for a car in that it had four wheels and miraculously started when he pressed the button. It not only propelled us through the streets of Calcutta, it did so at a fearsome speed with silencers which had long since departed this life. As a result, it made an appalling noise which was roughly comparable to the din that Santosh himself had made when calling his partner for a single. We had an excellent dinner, marred for me only by the prospect of the return journey which, I have to say, exceeded all fears and expectations. The only thing to be said in its favour was that we never actually established contact with any other solid object.

Some year's later, I was having dinner at Santosh's house in

PACKAGE TO INDIA

Hyderabad when he told me he had never come across any cricketer who had thought less about his game than I did. I answered, pretty arrogantly, that until the year before I had gone up to Cambridge, I had never had to. It had all just happened. I had played entirely by instinct and had got away with it. I had thought more about my wicket-keeping than about my batting, but by the time I met Santosh, my wicket-keeping was a thing of the past. At the time we played cricket together, his criticism was fair enough and if I had then tried to work things out more, I would almost certainly have made more of what I had been left with. If it is one's nature to play by instinct, it's a devil of a job to try and curb it. I wonder what Santosh's driving is like these days?

After those first few weeks writing about county cricket for *The Times*, I should have taken stock and thought hard about where I was wanting to go, rather that letting things drift as I did. My relief at escaping the ball and chain which the City of London had become was enormous. I was thrilled to be back again with cricket and, right from the start, I found the way of life that went with writing about the game strangely compelling. I have always enjoyed staying in hotels, eating good food and drinking decent wine and I suppose it was even better if someone else was paying for it. I've always been a gregarious chap and have very much enjoyed meeting people which I was now endlessly doing. Before I wrote my first word for *The Times* that day at Gravesend, I had no idea whether or not I could write. With fearful conceit, I simply imagined that I could. I suppose my instincts were right again and what I soon found was that I got great enjoyment out of trying to put down on paper what I had seen. Many people look at me in amazement when I tell them how much I have thrived on travelling round the world, and also round England in the summer, pursuing cricket. I feel exceedingly smug when I see all those chaps with the *Financial Times* under their arms rushing for the underground in the early morning or even clambering in behind their chauffeurs.

At the end of that first summer at least I had some solid experience of work in the field and therefore something tangible to offer. I should have then written a few more letters and tried to land something that was rather more permanent than sitting in vague hope on the end of a telephone line. But I was on a high, flushed by success, not that I had done anything more than keep my feet on the road, and I was confident something would turn up. Precious little did. I was sure *The Times* would greet me with open arms when they heard of my continuing availability. As it was, with some reluctance, they offered me the prospect of covering some school football matches, while the *Observer* hardly went overboard either and offered me the odd school racquets match on a Saturday. It was hardly the big time, although I was sure that professional football would follow on the heels of school football. I was absurdly optimistic. Unhappily for me, the winter of 1962/63 produced the longest and severest of freezes for many years. For week after week football matches up and down the country were cancelled and my days of gainful employment were few. As a result, dubloons in the Blofeld chest became fewer and fewer and the telephone and electricity bills bigger and bigger.

I was prepared to try anything to earn a bob or two and at one point I hired, for a considerable price, twelve cigarette machines which had been placed in cafés and staff dining rooms all around Fulham. The idea was to buy the cigarettes at wholesale prices from the people in the City who had rented me the machines and then to sell them at the retail price. I seemed to spend much of every day chugging around Fulham, filling my pockets with half crowns and refilling the machines with cigarettes. About six of the machines earned their keep, the other six were a waste of time. If it had gone well I don't suppose it would have significantly altered our lifestyle. It all came to an end when I turned up one day at the offices in the City to collect some more cigarettes and found the door closed and a note saying the firm had gone out of business. They had scarpered with all the loot I and many others had paid in order to rent the machines in the first place. For a while, I seriously considered trying to become a minicab driver and I think it was the problems I would have had insuring my car which knocked that one on the head.

During the 1962 cricket season I had made a lot of friends, both in and out of the press box. One of those, on the inside, was Christopher Ford who wrote about county cricket for the *Guardian*, although rugger was his first love and he was a powerful administrative force at Rosslyn Park. One day early in 1963 when all was gloom and despondency, the telephone rang and it was Christopher asking me if in the coming summer I would consider a job on the sports desk of the *Guardian* as a holiday relief. He told me it would involve spending a certain amount of time in the office, although I would get out to see some cricket. I jumped at the idea. At least it was fulltime employment for the coming summer which enabled me to mount something of a counterattack against my family who were busy being appalled at what I was doing, or rather at what I was not doing.

I started this job at the end of April and another who had joined the sports desk only a few days before me was John Samuel who had been Clifford Makins' predecessor as Sports Editor of the *Observer*. He had not held that job for long before he got badly on the wrong side of Chris Brasher who once was almost bracketed with Roger Bannister and Chris Chattaway and now had the reputation of being a somewhat strict overlord at the *Observer*. It was as foolish to mention Brasher's name to Samuel as it was later to mention Geoffrey Boycott's to Fred Trueman – unless you had at least a blank day ahead of you. John was one of the busiest people I have met. He burnt up kilowatts of nervous energy and was a blurr of perpetual motion. He was full of opinions expressed with energy and conviction, most of which were interesting and over the years he did a fine job in dragging the *Guardian* sports pages into at any rate the second half of the twentieth century. Later, when Sports Editor, he cut out a niche for himself as the skiing correspondent and, when he got on to the piste in the Alps, he was almost unstoppable. Later still he became the paper's motoring correspondent and, while testing an immensely powerful machine at considerable speed, managed to change from something like third gear into reverse with momentous and newsworthy results. Mercifully, he strode, unscathed, from the wreckage.

The *Guardian* had recently stopped calling itself the *Manchester Guardian* and was searching eagerly for a national identity which was inevitably handicapped by the Manchester office who saw themselves as the last upholders of a great tradition. In those days, for example, Rugby League was a vexed question. It was the life's blood of many old *Manchester Guardian* readers, while the softies in the south didn't know what Rugby League was. Of course, editionalising made sure that the right mixture landed on the right breakfast tables, but there was still something uncomfortably hair-shirted about the brethren in the Manchester office.

While I was working in the London office, an attempt was made to teach me the fundamentals of sub-editing. It is a good idea for journalists, who spend most of their lives outside the office, to know what happens on a daily basis inside and the sort of problems encountered after the men in the field have dictated their stories and put the telephone down. I was taught most of what I learned by Charles Harvey, a delightful and charming exhibit of the old school. He had worked for most of his life as a sub-editor on the *Daily Mail* which, in those days, was still a broadsheet. He now felt that it was his clear duty to atone for the days when he had been forced to let down his ever diminishing crop of hair in the interests of semi-popular journalism. Under his tuition my principal job each evening was to collect and collate the cricket scores which were then put together into a big rectangular box at the bottom of the cricket page.

It was a jigsaw puzzle that never quite worked and the odd filler was needed at the bottom of one or two of the columns so that the eventual satisfying symmetry could be arrived at. A filler was a small paragraph in tiny print which may have taken up not much more than a centimetre. Charles, a big man with a neat moustache, well-polished shoes, tidy creases in his suits and within hailing distance of seventy, was a stickler for etiquette when it came to fillers. Each day the agencies would send round brief flashes which were just the job. One day I subbed one which read as follows: 'F.S. Trueman, the Yorkshire and England fast bowler, will return to the Yorkshire side after injury for their match against Middlesex at Lord's on Saturday.' I put it straight in the basket for it to be sent upstairs and put into metal. Charles took it out and read it and turned on me with a sort of punchy avuncularity and showed me that he had changed 'the Yorkshire and England fast bowler' to 'a Yorkshire and England fast bowler'. I was suitably chastened.

I was in the office each night until at least ten o'clock, when I sometimes had the luck to be allowed home after the first edition had gone to press. Often, I had to stay to help change the page for the second edition. In those far distant days, the metal was put into the page by hand on the stone. In our present age of computers, it seems barely possible. I was let out of the office every now and then but not nearly as often as I had expected and wanted. One of the county games I was unleashed upon was played between Essex and Lancashire at Brentwood. On the first day, when Lancashire batted, I confused two members of their side, Brian Booth and Jack Bond. As one made 71 and the other 3, it was a painful confusion. The subs had not spotted it, which they should have done. Perhaps they thought an early roasting would take this young man down a peg or two. There was a fearful inquest which seemed to go on for days, but I managed to escape the chop. The Manchester office made a real meal of it.

In the summer we didn't see much of our Sports Editor, David Gray, because he combined the job with that of tennis correspondent. He spent more time, therefore, at such places as Roland Garros, Queen's and Wimbledon than he did at his desk in Gray's Inn Road where the *Guardian* perched precariously among the Thompson empire. On one of David's occasional appearances, I went with him up the road to the Yorkshire Grey which was the pretty dreary pub on the corner of Theobald's Road. Over a drink he gave me some good advice and told me I should be thinking of putting together a freelance package in order to go with the MCC, as they still were in those days, on their tour to India in the coming winter. He added he would be happy for me to cover the tour for the *Guardian*. A glass or two of wine with Clifford Makins in El Vino's in Fleet Street confirmed that Makins was also happy to let me cover the tour for the *Observer*.

Makins conducted an impressive amount of his business in that particular Fleet Street hostelry, usually from the table occupied by Philip Hope Wallace, the *Guardian*'s theatre critic. When

Philip died, a gold plaque was fixed to it which celebrated his long occupancy of that particular position from which he made serious inroads on the establishment's stock of claret. It was Gossip Corner and Philip delighted in all the latest tittle-tattle from Fleet Street. I was lucky enough to drink at that table several times with the two of them and it was an unending source of stories. Philip's *obiter dicta* were usually profound, always amusing and were expressed with an aristocratic enthusiasm together with a benign dignity. I well remember some years later when he had come back from a holiday in the Greek islands, he was describing his arrival by boat at the island of Lesbos. There were a group of local men standing close to the mooring and when Philip climbed ashore, he had said to his companions, 'There they are. Look at the lot of them. Lesbians to a man.' He chortled away happily for some minutes after that and repeated it twice for the benefit of new arrivals.

I still needed at least one more paper if the tour of India was to be even remotely financially viable which was not the least of its objectives. During these last two years, I had met and got on quite well with E.M. Wellings who wrote for the *Evening News* in London. He had the reputation, which he fully deserved, for being the most difficult, bloody-minded and cantankerous inhabitant of the cricketing press box. Lyn, short for Evelyn, had been an Oxford Blue for two years in the twenties and had also bowled with the seam for Surrey. He had never been a popular figure, not that this will have worried him in the least. He had a temper that made strong men quiver and he could be as offensively rude as anyone I have met. He was very thin with black swept-back hair and glasses worn at a militant angle. There was something slightly vulturine about his appearance and his prejudices fed upon the carrion of cricketers and their bosses. Nonetheless, he had a sense of humour, knew his cricket backwards and, as long as you were on the right side of him, could be an entertaining companion, although there was never a day on which he did not have some axe to grind.

When I told him that I was planning to go on the Indian tour he asked me if I would like to do the tour for the *Daily Sketch* which was in the same group as his own paper. It was a task which was likely to have fallen to Wellings himself if no one else could be found. It was just what I wanted, although I very much doubt it was what the *Sketch* wanted, even though Wellings persuaded them that I was their man. I was not well versed in the art of popular journalism. But I now had three strings to my bow.

With his wife, a formidable and substantially built lady who ran the organisation, Wellings had an interest in a travel agency just off New Bond Street. It was tacitly understood that if he collected the *Sketch* for me, I would make my travel arrangements through his firm. A clear case of industrial blackmail. Like everything else, he had firm ideas about hotels and usually took the view that his hotels were vastly superior to everyone else's. The result was that in India I found myself staying in hotels with only my travel agent for a companion while the rest of the press corps were billeted with the players which was, of course, where I should have been. He also tried hard to persuade me that I should adopt his views which he expressed most forcibly in the *Evening News*. He was most put out to find that my journalistic constitution was not yet strong enough for doses of high-octane vitriol.

The 1963 cricket season in England ended on a personal note of great happiness. On 1 September our daughter Suki was born at the Westminster Hospital. In those days, women preferred to do these things on their own, or maybe it was the way convention dictated. I remember that after taking Joanna to hospital, her mother and I took off to a delightful restaurant called La Speranza on the corner of the the Brompton Road and Beauchamp Place. It had been a family favourite for years, but sadly it closed down a long time ago. Their tournedos Rossini was worth the journey from Norfolk. My mother-in-law and I did ourselves pretty well before returning home and putting through a check call to the Westminster Hospital which revealed nothing startling. A call early the next morning told me that I had a fine bouncing daughter who has bounced her way through life at varying heights ever since.

A THIRST FOR LIFE

Suki was only just over four months old when I set off from Heathrow for Bombay in a Comet, an aeroplane which had had problems in the past. I was not, at that stage of my life, a good flier and I can still remember having the most uncomfortable thoughts through the night as we raced towards India at thirty-something thousand feet. I was apprehensive that the engines might cut out and I spent most of the night with the map from the BOAC booklet in my hand trying to work out if there was anywhere we could land in an emergency. It was not very rewarding and, in fact, we landed in Bombay exactly on schedule. Transfixed, I made my way for the first time, by taxi through the slums of Bombay, on the way to the Wellings-inspired Ritz Hotel which was soon to prove that there is only so much in a name.

It was the start of two months of almost constant excitement and adventure which sealed any doubts I may have had about the life I had chosen for myself. I had been injected to the hilt with every possible inoculation but it was not long before I was being reminded of the care one had to take about drinking only bottled water and the painful futility of being absurdly adventurous over food. Before leaving England, I had persuaded my doctor to sign a piece of paper confirming I was an alcoholic. I had taken this to the Indian High Commission who stamped my passport to this effect. It was only this way that one could neutralise the laws of prohibition which had India so boringly within its grip. Most hotels had a sort of inner sanctum where, after giving the password three times and waving one's passport in front of a policeman – who sat by the door and gazed at the passport for an unconscionable time before handing it back with the utmost reluctance – one was allowed to buy beer that was mostly liquid glycerine which did amazing things to one's stomach.

Another problem was getting our cables back to London. They had to be taken from the cricket ground back to the local GPO if a special facility had not been set up at the ground. The usual form when a page had been finished, was to wave your hand furiously and shout 'cable', whereupon a boy would come running to take it. What he did with it was anyone's guess. Some boys delivered it to the office at once, some ate their lunch first and I daresay others blew their noses on it. It was an inexact science. It was not unusual for one's copy not to reach England and this would mean the dreaded knock on the bedroom door some time in the early hours of the next morning. It would be followed by a slight rustle as something was slipped under the door. The light revealed a yellow envelope in which there was the discouraging message which said 'Why no copy?' or some such. This meant getting out of bed, dressing and taking a taxi to the cable office, which was open twenty-four hours a day. Then you would have the devil of a job trying to wake them up and persuade them to send your cables all over again.

The First Test of a boring series, in which all five matches were drawn, was played in Madras and we stayed at the Connemara Hotel. On the first or second morning at breakfast, Michael Melford who always seemed to pick up anything that was going, arrived in the dining room looking as if his life expectancy might stretch to five minutes if he was lucky. Johnny Woodcock was very solicitous and asked him what his night had been like. Mellers, as he had inevitably been christened by Brian Johnston, had an understated genius for one-liners and told us now that it had been too dreadful for words. He added: 'I went to the loo twelve times but I am not claiming a world record because I was wind-assisted.'

The Second Test was played in Bombay and might have been noteworthy for the presence of a member of the press corps in the England side. Injury and illness had seriously depleted the ranks to the extent that Colin Cowdrey and Peter Parfitt were flying out as reinforcements, but would not arrive in time. The day before the Test began, only ten players were fit and David Clark, the manager, asked me to stay behind at the end of a press conference that afternoon. He told me that unless one of the players made a remarkable recovery, someone from outside the party would have to be included. 'You and I are the last two to have played first-class cricket and you're a great many years younger than me. So, if it comes to it, you will be the man. Try to go to bed before midnight.' As you can imagine, I was thunderstruck, but I managed to say to him: 'I don't care if Cowdrey and Parfitt are flying out as replacements. If I make 50 or above in either innings, I'm damned if I'll stand down for Calcutta.' And we had a great laugh. As it happened, Micky Stewart, the vice-captain, struggled out of a hospital bed the next morning to make up the eleven, but was back in hospital after tea when Mike Smith lost the toss and England fielded first on an extremely hot day. It had been a near miss. There were only three fit specialist batsmen in the side and, thanks to an innings of great obstinacy and gallantry by Fred Titmus, the match was drawn.

The most dramatic moment of the tour came not on the pitch but before the start of the Fourth Test Match. The Kotla Stadium in Delhi had once belonged to the Maharajkumar of Vizianagram who had been an early captain of India. He had given the ground to Indian cricket and now was a radio commentator, although not a very good one. In addition to that, he wrote a daily column during the Test Matches for the *Indian Express*. When I arrived at the ground with Lyn Wellings early on the first morning, he was dismayed and infuriated to find that while he had been given not a very good seat in one of the lower tiers of the open-air press box, the entire back row had been reserved for Vizzi. Wellings began by moving his name tag from the place he had been allotted and sticking it on one of Vizzi's desks in the back row.

When Vizzi himself appeared with a considerable retinue sometime later, he was not pleased by this development and decreed that Wellings' typewriter should be moved to another table and his name removed and put back on his original seat. Seeing this, Wellings dissolved into a blind fury which contained much invective. This did not ruffle the Maharajkumar in the very least, which only infuriated Wellings still further. The exchange ended when Wellings picked up his typewriter, swirled it round and threw it at Vizzi's ample midriff. It did not make especially good contact and Vizzi's acolytes surrounded the expostulating *Evening News* correspondent, led him back to his original seat and made sure he did no further damage. He viewed Vizzi with smouldering hate from then on and never made any attempt to apologise.

I was the only other member of the English press on hand to see the whole drama unfold and soon received an invitation from the British High Commissioner, Sir Paul Gore-Booth, to go and have breakfast with him and tell him the full story. Official complaints had been made. We had an excellent breakfast and he presumably reported back to London. I believe the committee of the MCC seriously considered sacking Wellings from the club but in the end they decided to do nothing. Not for the first time, he had got away with a disgraceful piece of behaviour which, I am afraid, was typical of the man.

I was back as holiday relief for the *Guardian* in the summer of 1964 and this time I was allowed out of the office rather more. The following winter I was unable to put together a package so that I could go with England to South Africa, but by now the *Guardian* felt they were prepared to unleash me on professional football matches with safety. I very much enjoyed writing about football, although it was always a struggle at the end of an evening game to make sure one's piece had got through in time for the first edition. It often meant that one had simply to pick up the telephone and start dictating because there was no time to write. It was a long time before I got the hang of ad libbing and I must have driven the copytakers nearly mad. I was also asked to write about the odd game of rugger – with disastrous results. One day I was sent in the afternoon to Croxley Green to watch Hertfordshire play a county rugger match before moving on to Stamford Bridge to watch Chelsea do battle with another league side in the evening. In my first report of the day, I confused football's penalty area with rugger's twenty-five yard line, as it was in those days. Again, the subs failed to spot it and I was not asked to cover another rugger match.

When I first started with the *Guardian*, Frank Keating was a member of the sports-writing team and we had become good friends. By 1965 he had moved to television and had become a pillar of the sports department at Rediffusion, the mid-week London arm of ITV. In the spring of 1965 he and his boss, Graham Turner, organised a series of sporting programmes in the London area collectively called *Spring Out*. There were a couple of county cricket matches, some football, a game of hockey and some tennis. Frank suggested that I should become one of the cricket commentators and there were several others who were trying to get into television for the first time. One was Barry Davies who in those days worked for *The Times* and without whom no major footballing occasion is now complete. We all had to go along at different times to the Rediffusion building in Kingsway and do a commentary over a film of a recent England football match. I was told which match it was beforehand so that I was able to do my homework. The day arrived and I was led into a huge room and had to sit with a microphone in my hand in front of a big screen on which the match was to be shown. What was so unnerving was that not far behind were about eight or nine people sitting in chairs listening to what I said. It was really quite alarming but I managed not only to get through it, but to score few enough own goals to be asked to commentate on the cricket. We were also joined, for the match at Lord's, by Colin Cowdrey and intermittently by the ubiquitous Learie Constantine, the famous pre-war West Indian all-rounder, who had just been ennobled. George Duckworth, the former England wicket-keeper who had become the permanent baggage master on England tours, was our scorer.

Each broadcast was introduced by Desmond Carrington who turned hearts on a weekly basis in *Emergency Ward Ten*, a forerunner of today's multitude of hospital soaps. He spoke then, and still speaks to his weekend audience on Radio Two, with the soft unctuousness of a trickling chalk stream. Just before the series began, he came to Lord's for perhaps the first game of the season in order to check things out and get the atmosphere. Jim Swanton was on duty for the *Daily Telegraph* and I was talking to him in the old press bar at the back of the top deck of the Warner Stand when Carrington made his way in and stood quite close to us by one of the windows. I shall never forget Jim's face when Carrington proceeded to open the little handbag he was carrying and fish out a comb. He then carefully got to work on his eyebrows before attending to the rest of his make-up. Jim's eyes opened wider and wider and were within a whisker of popping out of his head. The only other person I ever knew to stop Jim talking in mid-sentence was the late Duke of Norfolk – but for entirely different reasons.

The following year, in 1966, I again worked for Rediffusion and this time my main colleague-in-arms was Crawford White of *News*

Chronicle and *Daily Express* fame. We were watching Surrey play Yorkshire at the Oval under a cloudless sky and during the afternoon when the match was in danger of going to sleep, I spotted a sunbathing figure in a deckchair on one of the balconies of the row of houses in front of the more southerly of the two gasholders. I could see through the railings of the balcony that the body in question had nothing on above the waist, and as I regaled the viewers with my discovery of this slumbering chap, the cameras zoomed in close and I looked back to the cricket. The next thing I knew was Crawford White saying on air, 'Be careful, Henry. That's the most beautiful man I've ever seen.' My eyes flashed back to the monitor just in time to see that the sunbathing figure had got up and stretched, revealing that its form was massively female. She and I were all over the front pages the next morning.

During that summer I did all I could to try and find enough work to justify my going to South Africa in the coming winter to watch them play Australia, but it didn't work out. Meanwhile, Jim Swanton had arranged for the Arabs to tour Barbados in January. Recruiting was still going on when I realised that South Africa was not possible. After a round-table conference, Joanna and I both decided to declare our availability for Barbados and happily the founder accepted our application.

CHAPTER

6

ARABS IN THE WEST INDIES

Our flight out to Barbados was delayed for a few minutes at Heathrow in order that we should not leave behind our captain, Colin Ingleby-Mackenzie. Rumour unkindly had it that he had come straight from the Claremont Club in Berkeley Square after a particularly testing night at the tables. If that had been so, I don't think that even Colin could have been as chirpy as he was when he fastened his seat belt early that morning. The luscious tropical dusk was beginning to fall when we landed in Barbados. We were photographed coming down the steps of the aeroplane and Colin was interviewed on television. When asked what he thought of his side, he replied with a straight face, 'We have no weaknesses except the manager.' As founder, manager and organiser, Jim Swanton was there to meet us with some of those who ran cricket on the island. Peter Short, a future President of the West Indies Board of Control was there with his vibrant moustache, Eric Inniss who was President of the Barbados Cricket Association was another and so was Everton Weekes, one of the famous Three Ws who, over the years, became a great personal friend. Our first rum punches were shoved into our hands and it was all too thrilling for words.

Our first net practice was scheduled for the following morning but on the way to the Kensington Oval we all went in solemn formation to Government House where, under Jim's watchful eye, we signed the book in the entrance lodge. This was an old-fashioned formality which was then still in vogue. The idea was that by signing it, you let the Governor know that a loyal subject was on the island and if he wanted to do anything about it, he could. We dutifully signed our names and then went on to Kensington to get down to the hard work.

I think the next four weeks were the most fun that I had anywhere as a player, not least because it was the only occasion when I managed to get my wicket-keeping back to something like it was before I had taken on the French Women's Institute at Eton. We began a couple of days later with a reasonably gentle warm-up match against a scratch side at Kensington which we managed to win. I opened the batting and made my only 50 of the tour, scoring many of my runs off Cortez Jordan who was the West Indies best-known Test Match umpire. He opened the bowling now at a most convivial military medium. In one over I hit him for three successive fours and at the end of it I cheekily suggested to him that he must have been glad of his white coat to help him take a few wickets. He grinned a trifle ruefully.

We played matches against most of the leading club sides who were too good for us. Most of them contained players who had represented Barbados and there was a smattering of Test cricketers too, such as Seymour Nurse, Peter Lashley and David Allan. When we played Wanderers at Darrells Road, we came up against Richard Edwards who was soon to open the bowling for the West Indies. He was too quick for us. Our last game was a three-day affair at Kensington against a Barbados Cricket Association Eleven which was captained by Everton Weekes. Everton played the most remarkable innings I ever had the luck to keep wicket to. On the first day we had a sudden, dramatic storm which almost flooded the pitch before there was time to put on the covers. The pitch became something of an old-fashioned 'sticky' and we were in all sorts of trouble before Colin Ingleby-Mackenzie declared when we were eight wickets down for ninety-something.

They did not then find it much easier, especially against the quickish off breaks of the Sri Lankan, Danny Piachaud, who had played three years for Oxford and was a fine bowler. He was able to make the ball turn and lift viciously. He picked up one wicket and then Everton came in and used his feet to get down the pitch and attack Piachaud in an astonishing display of batting. In the best of conditions he was quick enough through the air to make it difficult to use your feet to him, but in these conditions it was surely inconceivable to think in terms of anything except defence. Everton now proceeded to drive him through and over the covers from three paces down the pitch. He never played a single false stroke in making 70 or 80 and scarcely a defensive stroke either. It was the highest class of batting I ever saw at close quarters. What was so lovely about Everton was that it was all done with a smile. His judgement was as impressive as his footwork which went on putting him in precisely the right position to play all the strokes he attempted.

The pitch rolled out on the last two days and we managed to win by the slender margin of 4 runs after our one Bajan import, a fast bowler called Keith Walters, had bowled particularly well. No one was more pleased at this victory than Jim Swanton's chauffeur, Gibbons, who, in his quiet way, was another great character. He wore a dark homburg hat which he took off from the back in the most extraordinary manner as if he was making a belated attempt to strap hang in a bus. Gibbons had a splendid sense of humour, impeccable manners and the friendliest of toothy smiles under a moustache which, I felt, needed a good helping of fertiliser. Whenever you asked Gibbons anything and the answer was yes, he would always say with great profundity, after a considerable pause in which he weighed up all possible alternatives, 'That I do believe.' One of our leading strike bowlers was none other than the Earl of Cottenham who, off his long run, was a nasty proposition and had trials for Northamptonshire. He became a great favourite of Gibbons who, whenever he was passing on a message from his lordship, would begin by intoning 'The Lord says . . .' just as if he was reading the lesson in church.

During the course of the Arab tour, I had had the chance to talk to Jim Swanton about my job and where it was leading me. He seemed to be keen that I should change from the *Guardian* and write for his paper, the *Daily Telegraph*, and told me that, when he returned to England, he would have a word with Kingsley Wright, the Sports Editor. I had already begun to work for the *Sunday Express* on Saturdays and they were anxious to keep my name on an exclusive basis. So by the time the 1967 season began, I was writing for the *Daily Telegraph* under the pseudonym of Henry Calthorpe which is my second name. The *Daily Telegraph* reported all the first-class matches while the *Guardian* seldom covered more than three or four because of the limitations imposed by a much smaller space for sport. Even so, some of the games covered by the *Telegraph* were allotted very little space and there was nothing more frustrating than having to compress an exciting day's cricket into only 250 words. Another problem was that the first edition went to press ever earlier to make sure that readers in the Outer Hebrides did not miss out at breakfast. To make this possible, we were asked to submit the middle piece of our reports at teatime before top and tailing it at the end of the day. This meant effectively that one was writing a 400-word story in three different parts which was no great help to finding a seamless fluency, and I doubt it would have suited dear old Chaucer any too well. I stayed with the *Telegraph* for a few years, but it was not as much fun writing for them as it was for the *Guardian*. I was never entirely at home either using thirty-word paragraphs which was the formula us down-page minions had to stick to.

While I was playing in a match for the Arabs during that same summer, Jim Swanton told me he would like me to come out to the West Indies for the England tour the following winter. He was keen that I should cover the more minor matches for the *Telegraph* while he stayed in Barbados and then, when he turned up for the Test Matches, he wanted me to act as his dogsbody, although he did not quite put it like that. During a day's cricket, Jim would like to wander off to the pavilion and feel the pulse of the committee room and bend the ear of any figure of influence he might come across which would undoubtedly have included the England manager, Les Ames. While he was on these sorties, it was going to be my job to keep notes for him in the press box and be in a position to answer the many questions which would be fired at me on his return. It was never that simple because Jim always managed to find at least one question that I was hard put to answer. If, by way of practice, I had been able to do a stint beforehand for Alexander the Great on one of his more demanding days, it would have stood me in good stead.

A number of cricket writers and broadcasters had cut their teeth under the tutelage of Jim and a jolly effective, if slighty nerve-racking, training it proved. So far, I had managed to survive without him and this was my first encounter with him at close quarters. Jim could be an impatient employer, just as he found it difficult to put up with what he considered to be imbecilic behaviour on the cricket field. As his patience was tested, Jim would begin to click his fingers and his voice became more rasping. I thought we might have our moments in the Caribbean. Leslie Vanter, the amusing but mildly irascible Sports Editor of the *Sunday Express*, also employed me to do the lesser matches for his paper and to help Denis Compton during the Test Matches which was a more arduous task than I realised. Although Lyn Wellings pitched for my travel business, I moved to George Wareham who for many years looked after MCC and most of the press party. George, never less than impeccably dressed and unfailingly courteous, was the calmest of men in the most frenetic of professions. His bland manner never failed him and no problem or last-minute change of plan ever phased him. I always pulled his leg and once wrote him a letter saying that I thought there was no situation however bad that a few minutes of his time would not make irreparably worse. He still keeps the letter in his wallet and reads it when he feels the need for reassurance.

England were captained by Colin Cowdrey after Brian Close had been sacked for wantonly wasting time in a county match at Edgbaston, and it was the best Test series I have ever seen. The great West Indian side which Gary Sobers had inherited from Frank Worrell was in the process of being scuppered by old age. Wes Hall and Charlie Griffith were no longer the fast bowlers they once had been, the batting was more vulnerable and the fielding not quite so sharp. They were still the favourites to beat England. In the First Test at Port of Spain, which was in vibrant mood with the pre-Lenten Carnival celebrations building to a peak, England just failed to bowl the West Indies out a second time on the last day after Ken Barrington had made a typically resolute hundred, and Tom Graveney perhaps the best hundred I have ever seen. I remember John Thicknesse, who had succeeded John Clarke at the *Evening Standard*, asking Jim Swanton when Graveney had made 18, how soon in a Graveney innings could one be reasonably certain he would make a big score. Jim was noncommittal. In the end, Sobers himself and Wes Hall batted out the last session of the match. England had effectively won the Second Test in Kingston when the spectators rioted at the fall of the fifth West Indies wicket in their second innings. They were 204/5 still needing 29 more to avoid an innings defeat. It was agreed that the seventy-five minutes which had been lost would be made up on an unscheduled sixth morning. By then Sobers had made a remarkable hundred on a pitch with a horrid bounce and at the end of the most agonising seventy-five minutes I can remember watching, England were hanging on at 68/8 having needed 159 to win.

The visit to Barbados for the Third Test was given a bad start when, just before the match, Fred Titmus had four toes cut off when he caught his foot in the propellers of a speed boat. The match itself passed off uneventfully as a highish scoring draw on a flat pitch with John Edrich and Clive Lloyd making hundreds. We moved back to Port of Spain for the Fourth Test which was another unbelievable game. Hundreds by Rohan Kanhai and Seymour Nurse took the West Indies past 500. Then, after Cowdrey had replied in kind, Basil Butcher took 5/33 with his leg breaks in only his second spell of bowling in thirty-two Test Matches. West Indies led by 122 and Sobers then declared his second innings at 92/2, leaving England to score 215 to win in 165 minutes with Charlie Griffith unfit to bowl. Geoffrey Boycott and Cowdrey who, surprisingly, needed some persuading that the target was worth pursuing, steered England home by seven wickets with three minutes to spare.

The West Indies captain had to have a police guard when he arrived in Georgetown the next morning, for there were those who felt he had played with West Indian nationalism and were angry. He pretty well redeemed himself in the final Test which, as the series had not been conclusively decided, was played over six days. Sobers and Kanhai both reached 150 while Boycott replied with a hundred and Tony Lock, who had come all the way from Western Australia as a replacement for Titmus, scored 89 for England. The West Indies led by 43 on the first innings and after Sobers had made 95 not out in the second, left England to score 308 to win and, at the end of the sixth day, England's last pair of Alan Knott and Jeff Jones had to play out the last few overs. The two of them had met in mid-wicket before Lance Gibbs began the last over of the match to Jones. When asked later what they had said, Knott replied with a twinkle that they had sung the first verse of 'Land of My Fathers'. Somehow Jones survived and England had won the series. Phew!

The morning after the First Test in Port of Spain we had to catch a seven o'clock flight to Jamaica. I was out until all hours the night before listening to calypsos and was horribly late to the airport, incurring the extreme and rather comic wrath of Jim Swanton, even though the plane eventually left four hours late. As a result Jim barely spoke to me for a fortnight. At Montego Bay, the MCC followed on against the Jamaica Colts and the following weekend I wrote a piece for the *Sunday Telegraph* under the by-line of E.W. Swanton, at his written request because he was still too upset to speak directly to me. He sent me a message through another journalist that I was to write a piece for him. In Kingston, I paid the first of many visits to the Blue Mountain Inn and I still remember the exceptional banana flambé. On that dreadful last day of seventy-five minutes play, I stood in for Brian Chapman who was covering the tour for the *Guardian* as Bruce Barber in addition to the *Daily Mirror* as Brian Chapman. It was a ghastly performance which passed off unnoticed in Gray's Inn Road and enabled Brian to catch an early aeroplane.

By the time we arrived in Barbados, after a match against the Leeward Islands in Antigua, my relationship with Jim had recovered to a state of armed neutrality which was just as well as he and Ann had asked Joanna and me to stay with them at Coralita, the lovely house they had built not long before on the ninth fairway of the Sandy Lane Golf Course. Jim made stronger planter's punches than almost anyone and we drank them mostly round his beach hut and you can't get much more sybaritic than that.

Hospitality on the non-playing days was spectacular all through the tour. In St Lucia I remember a local mayor in his full regalia who dispensed rum and coconut water which had a decidedly more-ish sort of taste to it, and before the Fifth Test in Georgetown, being taken down the Kimune, a tributary of the Demerara River, to Santa Mission, the home of a tribe of Arawak Indians. I even tasted their homemade alcohol called *pawari* made from the cashew tree. I have never known firewater like it. They told us that if you swallowed two not-very-big glasses of *pawari*, every time you drank water over the next two days, you would again be drunk. We took a picnic which we ate not far from the landing stage in the shade of a big tree called a stinking toe tree. When it rained, the leaves produce a smell of extremely dirty socks. This was one of the most fascinating days I have ever spent anywhere in the world, in a country which is the West Indies and South America at one and the same time. In Georgetown that night we went to a concert given by the Mighty Sparrow and listened again to 'Mister Walker', the big Carnival hit that year. Towards the end, Colin Milburn gave a memorable rendition of 'The Green, Green Grass of Home'. I can still remember most of that tour as if it happened yesterday and, of all the many I have seen, this is the one I would most like to watch again.

The summer of 1968 in England has gone down in history for the dreadful mess the England tour selectors made of picking the side for the following winter's tour of South Africa. Australia came to England under Bill Lawry and comfortably won the First Test at Old Trafford and this was still the difference between the two sides when they came to the Oval for the Fifth Test at the end of August. I saw some of it because the *Telegraph* had given me a match off and most happily this had included the last day. In the run up to the match, Roger Prideaux, who had batted well in the Fourth Test at Headingley and done enough to have won a place on the winter's tour to South Africa, pulled out with an injury and Basil D'Oliveira was brought in. He made 158 in

England's first innings and with John Edrich compiling 164, England reached 494. Australia were then dispatched for 324 and England were bowled out for 181 in their second innings leaving Australia to make 352.

During the lunch interval on the last day, when Australia were 86/5, it rained in torrents and the ground was flooded. A hot sun came out but there still seemed too much for the groundstaff to do for a resumption to be possible. Then, suddenly, the crowd sensed this and, particularly from the area backing on to the Harleyford Road where I was sitting, came on to the ground to help the mopping up operations and I am delighted to say that I was one of them. Eventually the umpires decided that play should start at a quarter to five with seventy-five minutes left. For a while the pitch behaved itself much too well for England's liking, but with thirty-five minutes to go, D'Oliveira bowled Barry Jarman and when Cowdrey brought back Derek Underwood to bowl the next over from the Pavilion End, he removed both Mallett and McKenzie. He bowled Gleeson with twelve minutes remaining and then, with five minutes left, John Inverarity, who had defended with his life for 250 minutes, played no stroke to the ball which Underwood brought back with his arm and was palpably lbw. It was a perfect example of the excitement generated by an uncovered pitch and left the whole of England feeling cock-a-hoop.

Incredibly, the selectors then left D'Oliveira out of the touring party for South Africa and were roundly accused of having sold out to the South African government and its policies of apartheid. When, later, Tom Cartwright, a seam bowler, pulled out because of injury, D'Oliveira, a batsman, was chosen as a replacement. Now the South African government refused to accept him, saying he had only been picked because of anti-apartheid pressures in England and the tour was cancelled. This was effectively the start of the process which led to South Africa's sporting isolation until apartheid was abandoned twenty-two years later.

Having acquired a taste for touring and for Test cricket, county cricket could sometimes be a great anticlimax especially when a Test Match was being played in another part of the country.

During the 1968 summer, I had busied myself trying to find enough work to make it possible for me to go to Australia to watch them play the West Indies the following winter. Much as I had enjoyed both India and the West Indies, Australia was the country, above all other cricketing nations, which I wanted to visit. They had always been the main enemy and there was nothing to match a series between England and Australia. I remember so well listening to the wireless commentaries from Australia in the early mornings on Freddie Brown's tour in 1950/51. In those days, the atmospherics which caused much hissing and crackling, made it seem as if the broadcasts were coming from outer space and this gave them an extra dimension of excitement. Even if England were not Australia's opponents, I simply could not wait to see the game being played on those huge Australian grounds while listening to the barrackers and generally absorbing an atmosphere I had been reading about for at least twenty years.

Australia did not fail me. The tour began, as they all did in those days, in Perth which seemed a much more distant outpost then than it does now. The America's Cup had not yet arrived and Alan Bond had also not appeared on the scene. My initiation into the game in Australia took place in the old gold mining town of Kalgoorlie in Western Australia where the West Indies played a country eleven. The game itself was of little consequence, but Kalgoorlie was fascinating. I was taken down to a great depth in a gold mine; I paid a strictly non-operative visit, along with several others including the former England fast bowler, Peter Loader, and a well-known Australian cartoonist, Paul Rigby, to one of the state-sponsored brothels on Hay Street. Business was slack that evening and we drank rum and coke with some of the girls and that was all. The extremely wrinkled old madam with a face that looked like a road map of London, ran the establishment with a bark and never a shred of good humour. She had been in charge for more than ten years and I shudder to think how much money she must have made. I wondered what she spent it on.

The West Indies won the First Test Match easily at the Gabba where Lance Gibbs and Gary Sobers spun them to victory. My strongest memory of Brisbane was the night I spent with the head detective of the Queensland drug squad on duty in his police car. We arrested a fair number of people during the evening and even made an unscheduled visit to the city morgue. After that First Test, the Australians disappeared over the horizon with Bill Lawry, Doug Walters and Ian Chappell making huge quantities of runs. The West Indies were put in on a chillingly cold Boxing Day morning at the Melbourne Cricket Ground and destroyed by Graham McKenzie who took 8/71. After Lawry had made 205 and Chappell 165, Australia won by an innings. Walters was the centurion in Sydney when they won by ten wickets. Then came the best match of the series, in Adelaide, when, with one wicket left, Australia failed by 21 runs to score the 360 they needed to win. In Australia's second innings, when they had been given a marvellous start and seemed certain to win, Charlie Griffith became the second bowler in the history of Test cricket to run out a batsman who was backing up too far at the bowler's end without first warning him. He accounted for Ian Redpath in this way. The time-honoured practice is for the bowler to warn the batsman the first time he catches him taking an unfair advantage and to run him out the second. Twenty-one years earlier at the Sydney Cricket Ground, the Indian left-arm spinner, Vinoo Mankad, had accounted for the Australian opener, Bill Brown, in the same way. The incident in Adelaide produced a good story. Griffith had been roundly condemned by the entire press box with two notable exceptions, Keith Miller and Bill O'Reilly, who both wrote that Griffith was entitled to do what he did. Jack Fingleton, a contemporary of O'Reilly's, was sitting just below him in the tiered press box in the main stand and the next morning the following exchange took place.

Fingleton: 'You would never have done a thing like that in your life, Tiger.'

O'Reilly: 'When I was bowling, I never met anyone that keen to get up the other end.'

Australia won the Fifth Test by 382 runs, with Walters becoming the first player to score a double century and a century in the same Test Match, and the series by three matches to one. This was the final disintegrating moment for that once great West

Indies side and it was most disappointing to see the way in which some of the older players threw in their hands. The one vibrant spirit throughout it all was their manager, Berkeley Gaskin, whose friendly manner and urbane comments, together with his classical allusions delivered in an accent which would have had a prewar BBC newsreader looking to his laurels, turned all the West Indian press conferences into an educational delight. I shall never forget when, before the First Test in Brisbane, Gary Sobers had gone to Adelaide to meet his future wife who had just returned to Australia. The press demanded to know why he was not on parade. But Berkeley smiled his way through explaining nothing, while assuring all and sundry that Sobers' absence would be of great benefit to the side. By the end, almost everyone believed him.

Up until now, my only attempts at broadcasting on radio had come about when I had been asked to contribute diary items of about a minute to a minute and a half for the British Forces Broadcasting Service which operated from Dean Stanley Street in Westminster close to Smith Square and the Houses of Parliament. Gerald Sinstadt, whose masterly football commentaries can still be heard on the ITV network, presented the programmes and indeed commissioned the pieces which were done for him. My first-ever radio broadcast had been in 1966 on the same day that Joanna had taken Suki for a walk in her push chair to the children's playground in St Luke's Churchyard in Chelsea. As she was pushing Suki past the heavy metal swings, a boy ran past, caught hold of a swing and then let it go from a considerable height. As Joanna looked up it caught her a horrid blow on the bridge of the nose which effectively disappeared. She was rushed to hospital while I went in the other direction to Dean Stanley Street, my timing hopelessly awry as always. My mother-in-law was at a loss to know why I didn't cancel the broadcast. Looking back on it, of course I should have done, but at the time . . .

For some time I had been hoping to be given the chance to see if I was any good as a radio commentator and in the middle of the summer of 1969 I had my wish. The BBC arranged for me to do two twenty-minute periods of trial commentary during a county match at the Oval. Brian Johnston was covering the game for Radio Two and twice during the day, when he was not needed, I sat in front of the microphone. With the tape machine running in the background, Brian said, 'And now its over to Henry Blofeld.' I kept going for twenty minutes and never had any worries about what to say next as I described the events in front of me. I have forgotten who Surrey were playing. Once I was under way, I didn't feel at all nervous and in fact I rather enjoyed it. After I had done my second spell during the afternoon, I asked Brian how he thought it had gone. He told me that he never commented when people had trials. He said it was not up to him and he might easily disagree with the powers-that-be in Broadcasting House who were the final arbiters.

Two or three weeks later I had a telephone call from Henry Riddell's secretary asking me to come round to Broadcasting House one evening at about five o'clock. Henry Riddell was the assistant head of Outside Broadcasts and wanted to discuss the tapes with me. I was much more nervous about this meeting than I had been when commentating at the Oval. Riddell was small with a neat, precise voice and he was wearing a dinner jacket, which surprised me. I must have been with him for nearly an hour and he never explained why he was dressed as he was. I later heard that it was his habit to dine at his club in evening dress before catching the train to Brighton where he lived. He was friendly enough and talked to me about the art of commentary and how important it was never to be behind the action. He told me I must 'paint the scene', a phrase I have always remembered in my attempts to justify helicopters and buses and other forms of transport which roar through my commentaries. He told me that I must be my listeners' eyes and if anyone ever said to me after a broadcast that I had made them feel that they were there, it was the ultimate accolade.

We also listened to most of the two tapes, which I did not enjoy. I have never to this day liked listening to recordings of my voice. I always think I sound like the most appallingly pompous twit and that people in their right minds would be switching off as fast as they could. He finished the interview by saying that my name had been added to the list of BBC cricket commentators. I could hardly believe what I was hearing but he did go on to warn me that there were not that many opportunities. It still seemed too good to be true. About three years ago, when he was tidying out a drawer, Peter Baxter came across a short memo about me which had been written at the time by Robert Hudson, the head of Outside Broadcasts, and sent to Michael Tuke-Hastings, the cricket producer, whom Peter was soon to succeed. It was a sort of a little acorn.

I spent much of the summer of 1969 trying to organise enough work for me to be able to tour South Africa the following winter where they were playing Australia. I covered the series for the *Guardian* and the *Observer* and made some contributions to the *Sunday Express*. It was an extraordinary series because the Australian side which had thrashed the West Indies the year before were overwhelmed by perhaps the strongest side South Africa have ever had. This was the last series they played before they were excommunicated from international sport and it meant that I was lucky enough to watch the only four Test Matches in which Barry Richards played. South Africa's smallest margin of victory was 170 runs in the First Test, in Cape Town. The Australians' main excuse was that they had come straight from a gruelling series of five Test Matches in India which had taken its toll of the health of certain key players. Nonetheless, it was extraordinary that such a good batsman as Ian Chappell who had scored so many runs the year before against the West Indies, was now able to make only 92 runs in eight innings.

Of course, the South Africans bowled extremely well with Mike Procter and Peter Pollock leading the attack and having Eddie Barlow and Trevor Goddard in support. Their only weakness was spin with John Traicos, who later bowled his off breaks for Zimbabwe, playing in three Tests and Grahame Chevalier in one, but they were not really needed. The batting was immensely strong with Graeme Pollock, Richards, Lee Irvine, in his only series, and Barlow scoring hundreds. The hour after lunch on the first day of the Second Test in Durban produced the most amazing exhibition of batting I have ever seen. Richards and Pollock put on a hundred in this time and it is the only occasion when I have been lucky enough to see two great batsmen at their best in partnership. They were impossible to bowl at.

South Africa itself was an experience. It was easy to ignore all that was going on around you and have a great time. I played in a number of games for Wilfred Isaacs, a rich businessman who ran his own side. I opened the batting on two occasions with John Waite, who kept for South Africa in fifty Test Matches, and once with Russell Endean who played twenty-eight times for his country, which was a great experience, and I played an almost imperceptible role in two opening partnerships of over 50. But South Africa was not a happy country, divided into two by the odious racial policy of apartheid. Those dreaded signs, 'Nie Blanke' and 'Niet Nie Blanke' stared accusingly at you round every corner. There were some families in which some of the children fitted into one category and the rest into the other. It was enormously to the credit of those who ran cricket that they did as much as they could to break down apartheid, but within the framework of the laws of the country there was only so far that they could go. Of course, Ali Bacher who captained this formidable side against Australia, was the leading torch-bearer here. I think many visitors liked to pretend that apartheid didn't really exist and I suppose it was possible to shut your mind to it, but I don't see how you could shut your eyes to the system. It permeated its way through in every hour of every day.

The BBC had still not rung me for two full seasons when I went to the West Indies again, in 1971/72, to watch New Zealand play their first series in the Caribbean. It had been difficult to drum up interest in the papers in England because the perception was that New Zealand would be slaughtered. In as remarkable a series as any I have watched, New Zealand drew all five Test Matches and should have won the Third in Barbados where two dropped slip catches allowed the West Indies to escape. It will always remain a memorable series for me because, apart from the exciting cricket, it marked the start of my life as a Test Match commentator. The tour began in Kingston and we were there for ten days for two matches before going up to Montego Bay for a four-day game and then it was back to Kingston for the First Test Match. Radio New Zealand had sent their cricket correspondent, Alan Richards, to cover the series and, as usually happens, he was to join the local broadcasters in the Caribbean and their output would be relayed back to New Zealand. The arrangements had been made before Richards left Auckland.

What he was not aware of was that on each island there were two stations, one owned by the government and the other by Rediffusion. Both covered the cricket with a full ball-by-ball commentary. Richards had been asked to work for the government-owned stations on each island and soon after he had arrived in Kingston, he had been approached by someone called Winston Ridgard and asked if he would be free to commentate for his station. Alan said that of course he was. When it later dawned on him that Ridgard worked for Radio Jamaica, which was an entirely different station from the one he had originally promised to work for, he realised he was in something of a quandary.

We had dinner together that night at the old Courtleigh Manor Hotel where the visiting teams always used to stay, and he asked me if I had ever done any radio commentary. I immediately sensed a chance of something and, with all the confidence I could manage, I said yes I had, and, I suppose, strictly speaking, those two twenty-minute trial tapes constituted cricket commentary within the meaning of the act. Alan explained his predicament and I assured him that I was just the man he wanted. The next day he put me in touch with Winston Ridgard and it was all settled. The following day I was to join Peter Bailey who had toured England in 1939, and Jackie Hendriks who had just retired as the West Indies wicket-keeper. I was a little nervous but I had listened to cricket commentary since the age of eight and the BBC had accepted my trial tapes and I saw no reason why I couldn't do it as well as the next man. The Jamaica match went all right and so did the game in Montego Bay against the President of the West Indies Board of Control's Eleven where Glenn Turner made the first of his four double centuries on that tour. By the time we came to the First

Test back in Kingston I felt that I was in mid-season form and it all passed off without a hitch, so much so that Radio Trinidad asked me to perform for them during the Second Test in Port of Spain.

We had had enormous fun in the box in Jamaica and now, in Trinidad, I met one of the great West Indian characters. Raffie Knowles was a white Trinidadian who had played hockey for the island before the war and, although he was now getting on, he still ran Radio Trinidad's sports output, doing the commentary himself on everything from cricket to basketball to football and on to racing. His racing commentaries were unrivalled because he owned horses himself. Whenever one was running and Raffie was commentating, it appeared that there was no other horse in the race. His cricket commentary was eccentric too. He spoke with tremendous enthusiasm but his knowledge of the finer points somehow became lost in a general hysteria. The listeners will have known that something dramatic was going on, but quite what, was another matter. In Trinidad he was regarded as a saint by everyone, except probably his wife, because it was quite beyond him to grow old gracefully and young ladies still rang up. The last time I saw him, he gave me his Trinidad hockey tie which is a lovely memory to have of one of the great human beings.

Gerry Gomez, a former West Indies captain who toured England with that famous side in 1950, was another on the Radio Trinidad panel and masses of other old players came in to the box as between-over experts. In Guyana, the Raffie Knowles equivalent was B.L. Crombie. Although I worked with him for some years, I never discovered what those initials stood for. He had an English wife and chugged around Georgetown in an elderly Morris Minor which had a fraught digestive system, judging by the amount of smoke that usually came out of the exhaust pipe. Clyde Walcott, another of the famous three Ws used to join us in the Radio Demerara box. The only island to be curmudgeonly in its attitude to me as a commentator was Barbados. They refused to give me a work permit, although the following year when Australia were the visitors, they bit the bullet. It was all the greatest possible piece of luck for me and terrific fun too.

It meant that when I returned to England and made my first appearance on the BBC, I had already cut my teeth in the West Indies. It was a long time before I told anyone in the West Indies that it had all come about because of the outrageous lie I had told to Alan Richards over dinner that night at the Courtleigh Manor.

In the First Test of this series in Kingston, Lawrence Rowe who is a Jamaican, made 214 in the first innings and a hundred in the second in his own first Test Match. His strokeplay was so brilliant that it seemed then that he must go on to beat just about every record in the book. His temperament, which looked so secure at the outset, failed him later on and he also had problems with his eyesight, but it would be hard to imagine anyone batting much better than Rowe did in his first Test. The West Indies were frustrated by an heroic innings of 223 not out by Glenn Turner who carried his bat through the New Zealand first innings, and an obdurate hundred by Mark Burgess saved the match for them in the second. At Port of Spain, the West Indies were kept out by two remarkable innings by Bevan Congdon, a formidable all-rounder who was strangely underrated in world cricket.

In the Third Test in Barbados, the West Indies batted first and were bowled out for 133 by Bruce Taylor who took 7/74 on the first day. At medium fast with a high action, he found plenty of movement on a pitch with lots of early moisture. Batting became easier and Congdon, who had taken on the captaincy from Graham Dowling who was ill, made another hundred and Brian Hastings, an old friend and the nicest of men, chipped in with another and New Zealand led by 289 on the first innings. Big hundreds by Gary Sobers and Charlie Davis now saved the West Indies but both should have been caught in the slips by Terry Jarvis and Turner respectively and they were not the hardest of catches either. An opening partnership of 387 between Turner and Jarvis, doing their best to make amends on the flattest of pitches in Georgetown condemned the Fourth Test to a draw after Alvin Kallicharran had hit a hundred in his first Test. In the final game, back in Trinidad, it was only a brave eighth wicket stand of 65 in 106 minutes between Taylor and Ken Wadsworth on the last evening which prevented the West Indies from winning. A series of five drawn Tests may sound dull, but this was a wonderful series to start off with as a commentator and it was a staggering result for New Zealand.

CHAPTER

7

TMS DEBUT

I CAME BACK to England considerably pumped up and pleased with myself, but when I told people what I had been about, it didn't seem to me that it made quite the impact I had thought it would. I suppose these things get around, though, and I had, in the meantime, been brave enough to make one or two mildly enquiring noises in the general direction of the BBC. This was now my fourth year of waiting after that uplifting meeting with Henry Riddell. The 1972 season had not been in progress for long when at last they decided to grasp this particular nettle. I was asked by Michael Tuke-Hastings, the cricket producer, if I would be able to cover a county match for them on a Saturday at Chelmsford. It was another nerve-racking occasion for, although I had done all that commentary in the West Indies, reporting a match on a Saturday for Radio Two was an altogether different matter. The programme went on for at least five hours during the afternoon and a multitude of different sports were covered. Even in those days, county cricket was some way down the batting order, although the present all-exclusive obsession with football had not taken its stranglehold grip on proceedings.

During the programme I probably did not do more than seven or eight inserts and it was what I call stopwatch broadcasting. There would usually be four matches which were being reported on *Sport on Two* and when the producer decided that it was time to go round the cricket, he would allot, say, a minute for each match. If each of the first three reporters went on talking for one minute twenty seconds, there would be no time left for the fourth. So, as I quickly discovered, accuracy with the stopwatch was of much greater importance to my employer than the content of the broadcast, provided you didn't make a complete nonsense of it and get the players confused.

In those days, when Chelmsford was a ground of grassy banks and almost no permanent stands, we worked from a tiny wooden hut perched precariously on top of a BBC van which was parked near the sightscreen at the river end of the ground. I was honoured to have the august presence of Bill Frindall to score for me on that occasion. He had already been part of *TMS* for some years, so I was being thrown in at the deep end. There was also an engineer who had driven the van down from London and set up the technical side of things. I can't remember anything about the day's cricket, but I don't think I blotted my copybook to any great extent. I learned the pitfalls of the stopwatch. Quite early on, when the chap in the studio, who might even have been Desmond Lynam, handed over to me for a minute, I pressed the stopwatch and set off. After a couple of vibrant sentences I glanced down at the watch and, to my horror, found that I had not clicked it hard enough and the hands were still motionless at twelve o'clock. Of course, immediate panic set in and I stumbled my way on before ending on the score. I waited for a blast down the line from the producer for over-running but it never came, so I must have got it about right. The great rule was to hand back early rather than late.

One or two other Saturdays followed that first one and it was not long before I had a letter from Michael Tuke-Hastings asking me to commentate on two of the one-day internationals against Australia at the end of the season at Lord's and Edgbaston. I could hardly believe my luck. In those dim distant days, the radio commentary box was at the top of the Warner Stand at Lord's, between the press box and the television commentary box. It was for radio the worst possible position because one was looking over the head of third man or extra cover which made it extremely difficult to see what the ball was doing. But on this first occasion, those finer points missed me by miles. I was sharing the commentary box with John Arlott and Brian Johnston – a dream come true. The comments were being done by Jack Fingleton, the prewar Australian opening batsman who never missed a trick and, speaking in a slow Australian drawl, was always eager to have a dig at player and commentator alike. He was extremely kind to me but you had to watch your step. Fingo, suspicious of John Arlott's cricketing background, loved nothing more than to pull his leg. Arlott, in turn, regarded him with a fair amount of mistrust. The other summariser that day at Lord's was the former England captain, Norman Yardley, the friendliest and most charming of men, who had become a wine merchant and will, I am sure, have had many tasting sessions with John Arlott at which spitting rather than swallowing is unlikely to have been the preferred option. The final act on both these two one-day matches in the first one-day series to have been played in England, was Jim Swanton.

Although I thought I knew Jim quite well by now from my outings with the Arabs, to see him in action at Lord's was to see a Gladstone at the dispatch box. Jim had an extraordinary presence. He was a big man with a voice to match and he had never been hung about with self-doubt. It was in keeping with the man that one day at Lord's when the huge chimney some way from the ground behind the old Tavern began to belch smoke, Jack Fingleton should have told *TMS* listeners that Jim Swanton had been elected pope. One old adversary of Jim's was Rowland Bowen who wrote books but acquired greater notoriety by attempting to cut off his leg at the knee with a penknife and without an anaesthetic. He always referred to Jim as Pomponius Ego after the character in Mr Jorrocks. Jim entered the box shortly before the end of the day when he delivered those brilliant close of play summaries. It was quite a performance. When he came through the door it never seemed wide enough and the effect on those of us already there was rather as if the Lord High Executioner had just pushed his way in hellbent on making the punishment fit the crime. Jim insisted on a glass of whisky and water being ready beside his microphone and he would not be pleased if the ice was missing. He always began his summary by reading the full scorecard of the day and it was important, therefore, that the commentator who did the final twenty minutes play should not, during the last couple of overs, read it himself. Of course, as the end was fast approaching, it seemed the natural thing to do and there was more than one occasion when I was the last commentator and fell into the trap. This infuriated Jim who would mutter audibly in the back of the box. He would be even more upset if there was any noise around him while he was on air. He would then, as often as not, reprimand the culprit publicly in the middle of his summary. His intended punishment afterwards would almost certainly have been 'something lingering with boiling oil in it'.

Egos are hard to keep out of the picture in any commentary box and I know we are all as bad as each other. Jim perhaps deserved to have his leg pulled but this must never be allowed to take away from his skill as a writer and a broadcaster; nor does it in any way detract from his kindness all through his life to budding journalists and the young in and around the game of cricket. He was the most formidable and able of men. John Arlott once wrote a poem about him which went some way towards capturing the essence of the man. He left it on the table in the commentary box one evening at Lord's so that Jim would have been unable to miss it as he settled in for his summary. It went like this:

> Oh, stately is my manner
> And Swanton is my name,
> And in the *Daily Telegraph*,
> I write about the game.
>
> I was never at Oxford or Cambridge,
> But I think that my accent will pass,
> And, my dear Michael, I have a check suit,
> Which puts me right in the Bullingdon class.
>
> I dine out with all the best people
> And I thought I had made quite a hit.
> I cannot understand why mere cricket reporters
> All say I am such a big journalist.

TMS DEBUT

I think Jim saw it as his duty to look after the collective conscience of the commentary box. In the second of these games, at Edgbaston, I was in particular trouble with him. This match was the only occasion I ever broadcast with Alan Gibson who was later to become such a friend when he wrote so brilliantly and humorously about county cricket for *The Times*. He was an outstanding broadcaster in something of the mould of Arlott and often brought the most interesting line of interpretation to events as they unfolded. Like Arlott, too, he enjoyed a drink. In 1972 I scarcely knew him and, although some felt he could make life difficult for newcomers to the box, he never created any deliberate problems for me. However, at one point I inherited a bit of a teaser. When he was commentating, with Jack Fingleton as his summariser, they were trying to decide what it is that makes a cricket ball swing. Alan had had a longish correspondence on the subject with a learned professor at some university. It was fascinating stuff, even if they were unable to come to any conclusions and I am not certain they didn't end by making confusion worse confounded. Alan handed over to me soon afterwards and I said that while the reasons for swing may be difficult to pinpoint, one could say, having opened the batting on many occasions, that the ball undoubtedly did swing whatever the reasons. At the end of the game I got a frightful rocket from Jim Swanton because I had had the audacity to mention my own puny cricket career when I was commentating with Jack Fingleton who, among other things, had scored no less than six consecutive Test Match centuries.

If ever I have subsequently felt tempted to raise the subject of my own career, I have been quelled by the thought of Jim rising, sword in hand, in fury. Another interesting aspect of that conversation with Jim was why a writer of his standing was listening to the commentary in the first place. I always remember him sitting in press boxes with his earpiece in. The danger with this is that having heard the same viewpoint expressed time and again by the same commentator or summariser, it is difficult not to let yourself become brainwashed. That view then becomes your own view, not necessarily because it is what you feel but just because it has been constantly thrust down your throat. I know when I am commentating, it is often too easy to fall in with the consensus view which is being expressed in the box. It is, of course, *lese-majesty* of the worst possible kind even to have the temerity to allow the thought to enter one's head that Jim Swanton could have been brainwashed.

The following year Peter Baxter took over as cricket producer and is still with us, having grown old and grey in the job, although his athleticism between the commentary box and the engineers' room when something goes wrong, is still such that he needs no help from the handicapper. I went back to the West Indies the following winter when Australia were the visitors and I again commentated all round the Caribbean, as I was to do once more in 1973/74 when England were there under Mike Denness. For all that, I had to wait until 1974 before I was called to Test Match colours by the BBC. The First Test that year was against India at Old Trafford and I was asked to join a commentary team of John Arlott, Brian Johnston and Christopher Martin-Jenkins who had done his first Test against the West Indies the year before. Our summarisers were Trevor Bailey and the Maharajah of Baroda, with Jim Swanton giving the blessing at the end of each day's play. 'Jackie' Baroda had managed the Indian side to tour England in 1959 and was selected now as much as anything because there were no Indian commentators with the inflection which English listeners would understand. The etiquette committee at the BBC, almost certainly presided over by Brian Johnston, had met to decide what we were going to call the Maharajah on air. There was a feeling that 'Jackie', an assumed first name, was a touch too familiar for a royal personage. His own first name, Fatesingh, he himself had outlawed for ever-expanding reasons as he entered middle age. His Highness was a little too obsequious and so, after much scratching of heads, it was decided we would call him 'Prince' which satisfied all needs even if it made him sound like an elderly retriever.

By the time I came to commentate on my first Test Match in England, I already had three full series and some one-day internationals beneath my belt. Looking back on it now, I am surprised

TMS DEBUT

that I felt as nervous driving up to Manchester on a damp June Wednesday with my heart more or less permanently in my mouth. I suppose that in my mind, this was what it had all been leading up to: my first chance on *Test Match Special*. This was going to be the real test, when I was going to be finally and fully exposed to a home audience. I checked in at the *TMS* hotel and, as I decanted my luggage, saw through the window John Arlott passing by talking to Trevor Bailey. I had to pinch myself to realise that I was there on equal terms – well, more or less equal terms. Soon we all gathered in the restaurant with Johnners, as always, the life and soul of the party. Much wine flowed during dinner and John Arlott's first conversation with the wine waiter was along the lines of, 'We'll have four of the red and three of the white to start with.' I couldn't help wondering what the old hands must have thought about being joined by a brash, green newcomer. Whatever they thought, they could not have gone out of their way more to make a stranger feel at home. Brian told me not to worry about the next day as he knew it would go well, John wished me luck before I went to bed and so did CM-J and I was brought into every conversation. The Prince had found a different and much more luxurious billet, and we both wished each other luck when we met in the morning.

Imagining the most fearful calamities in the commentary box, I didn't sleep much that night and drove anxiously and slowly to Old Trafford through Altrincham and Sale in the days before the M56 and the M60. I parked my car on the practice ground, as we still do, and, after eventually convincing a lot of highly suspicious Mancunian gate attendants that my credentials were in order, I paid my first visit to the most antidiluvian of commentary boxes. It was situated at the Stretford End of the ground at the top of the red-brick building which housed the Board of Control and their guests. The tiny wooden commentary box was perched at the top of the stand alongside the scoreboard which made a terrible clatter every time the numbers were changed. Even an impressively agile mountain goat would have had a job to get there, let alone change positions inside the box with another mountain goat without making an unholy racket. But for me on that first day, the smallness and discomfort of the box and the gymnastic impossibility of changing positions, only helped to heighten the excitement of it all. I was the fourth commentator on the rota that morning and as the minutes ticked by the rats gnawed more and more at my tummy until eventually I heard CM-J hand over to me. As soon as I started, it all felt much better and by the time my first spell of twenty minutes had come to an end I found myself wishing there was time for another over or two.

The Test Match was memorable for nearly six hours of rain and for Geoffrey Boycott's last two innings for England before he embarked upon a three-year spell of voluntary exile from the side. He was ensnared in the first innings by Abid Ali who ran in to bowl at military medium a little like a motorbicyclist with a two-stroke engine, terrified that he is about to run out of petrol. In the second, his executioner was Eknath Solkar, who made his name by taking improbable catches at short leg, and opened the bowling with his left hand at an even more genial pace than Abid Ali, whereupon Boycott drove home and skulked in his tent for three years. He missed a bit of excitement along the way too. Dennis Lillee and Jeff Thomson blasted their way at a fearsome pace through England in Australia in 1974/75 and in England, in 1975, in the four-match series after the first World Cup. Then, in 1976, Andy Roberts, Michael Holding, Wayne Daniel and several others cut swathes through England's batting with what was almost an updated version of Bodyline. But, Boycott was still sheltering in his tent.

That Test at Old Trafford left me with three imperishable memories in the commentary box. The first concerned John Arlott. One day when the players were constantly in and out because of the rain, I heard at first hand his genius for plucking the perfect adjective out of thin air. The few spectators were huddled together in different parts of the ground and there was a group of them on the balcony with the iron railing on the first floor of the pavilion. The railing comes straight down for about eighteen inches before bulging out. Arlott encapsulated it perfectly when

TMS DEBUT

he described it as 'the balcony with the portly iron railing'. Portly instantly conjured up the exact picture. No one else would have come up with it.

The other two inevitably revolved around Brian Johnston. When India were batting on the third morning, Tony Greig was bowling to Sunil Gavaskar and Brian was on the air. Gavaskar played forward and Mike Hendrick fielded at mid on and returned the ball to Greig 'who, as he walks back, polishes the ball on his right thigh'. Gavaskar played forward to the next ball and again it went to Hendrick who threw it back to the bowler and now we were told, 'And now, to ring the changes, as he walks back Greig polishes his left ball.' At which point there was general confusion and much suppressed giggling. It was time for me to take over and all Brian could manage to say was, 'Over to Henry Blofeld.' It was a testing moment as I attacked the microphone, trying desperately not to laugh. My whole career was poised on a knife-edge.

I had only myself to blame for the next incident. I had been extremely apprehensive about the breaks for rain. It was the tradition of *TMS* to talk on about anything and everything when rain stopped play. I couldn't for the life of me see how I could contribute anything even remotely interesting. Well, of course, it rained like mad during the match and after lunch one day, when there was no play, Brian was presiding over the usual *TMS* chitchat and waffle when suddenly he looked at the clock and said, 'I'm now going to bring in Henry Blofeld.' I had thought about several things to say and I sat down and let rip for about seven minutes, bringing no one else in and feeling rather pleased with myself. Eventually I ran out of steam and turned to my right to get some help from the others. To my horror all the chairs were empty and there was just a single piece of paper on the table on which was written, in Brian's handwriting, 'Keep going until six thirty and don't forget to hand back to the studio.' I looked frantically round but there was no one else in the box and I began to stutter and stumble before the door burst open and they all came tumbling back in fits of laughter. What Brian had actually said to me in that note was, 'Don't forget, you're playing a team game.'

No blood was spilled but he certainly made his point and it was a lesson I have never forgotten. It had been quite a baptism for me.

CHAPTER

8

BOUNCERS, SLEDGERS AND THE PASSING STREAKER

THE LAST HALF of the seventies was as dramatic a period as any in the history of cricket, both on and off the field, and I was lucky enough to be in the thick of it. John Arlott was the cricket correspondent of the *Guardian* which was why we only saw him for the first half of the day in the *Test Match Special* box. After his post-prandial twenty-minute session, he gathered himself together and set off for the press box rather as though he were leaving to set up his base camp from which to conquer Everest. Any journey by Arlott at this stage of his life needed preparation as well as a Sherpa or two. It became quite an event and was almost always accompanied by much mopping of the brow with a voluminous and multi-coloured polka-dotted handkerchief. Huge beads of sweat gathered on his ample forehead at the slightest provocation. I am almost sure John would have sweated in an igloo. He did not like being cricket correspondent of the paper in the winter because he hated to travel unless it was a short haul to a beloved vineyard in France or Italy. For a few years it was my lot to cover the overseas tours for the *Guardian* while John contributed the occasional piece to put it all in perspective, either from Alresford where he lived in a retired pub which had an enormous cellar, or from Chateau Whatever in deepest Bordeaux from where the perspective will have been even sharper. It was an arrangement which suited us both.

In October 1974 England's cricketers set off full of hope for Australia. Dennis Lillee who had taken thirty-one wickets in England in 1972, a record for Australia, had threatened to give them the ascendancy for some while. He had in the meantime succumbed to a stress fracture in his back, the first time most of us had heard of this condition which was soon to become so fashionable and, although he was just beginning to bowl again, he was hardly likely to be much of a threat. Bob Massie, who had swung the ball like a boomerang when he had taken sixteen wickets in the Lord's Test in 1972, had never been able to recapture that swing and was out of it after only four more Tests. We had heard a little bit about a raw youngster called Jeff Thomson who had played one Test against Pakistan without taking a wicket. He had now moved from Sydney to Brisbane and we put all talk of him being the fastest bowler in the world down to typical Australian propaganda.

The tour began in Adelaide where, as luck would have it, Western Australia were playing a Sheffied Shield game against South Australia and we all rushed down to the Adelaide Oval to have a look at Lillee in action. He bowled well within himself and played with a dead bat at a press conference in the team's motel afterwards. We moved in gentle stages round to Brisbane for the First Test and, from the evidence of the game against Queensland immediately before, Thomson was quick with a violently physical slinger's action and questionable control. He bowled twenty-one overs in all, took a wicket in each innings and served up a plentiful supply of no-balls. Lillee and Thomson were both in the Australian side, but the England players had no reason not to be in excellent spirits when they arrived at the Gabba on the morning of the penultimate day in November. The only likely problem was the pitch. Eight days before the match, the Lord Mayor of Brisbane, Alderman Clem Jones, who was a member of the Trust which ran the ground, had caught the groundsman rolling the pitch sideways, something up with which he could not put and he promptly sacked him, assuming his duties himself.

BOUNCERS, SLEDGERS AND THE PASSING STREAKER

While the Alderman's rubicund vigour was admirable, his skill was more questionable and a two-paced surface with an uneven bounce was the product. Mike Denness lost the toss and watched Australia compile 309 after the last two wickets had managed to put on 80. Even this didn't seem much more than a minor irritation and on the second day Dennis Amiss and Brian Luckhurst strode out to open the England innings and in the press box I settled down to enjoy myself.

In the space of two overs all comfortable prognostications had been blown apart. Lillee was instantly recognisable as the bowler who had taken all those wickets in England two years before. I shall not forget the look of horror on Amiss's face when, in the first over, he tried to play Lillee off the front foot to mid on and the ball whistled away off the outside edge through the slips for four. The second over of the innings, bowled by Thomson, drained most of the colour from Luckhurst. Suddenly, England's opening batsmen were hanging on by their fingernails and the innings was only two overs old. The sea change in the press box had been almost as dramatic as that in the middle. The Australian writers in the front two rows were full of smiles and conversation with a bit of 'I told you so' thrown in. The Englishmen had gone quiet and there was much drawing in of breath as one thunderbolt after another bore down on the two openers. Lillee was classical and controlled and buzzingly venomous. Thomson was all brute force and muscular power as he bore down on the batsman like a most unpleasant prehistoric man sorting out his luncheon menu. In his third over Luckhurst started to play back to one which was through him before he knew it and he was caught behind; in his next over, Amiss had one which flew at his face from not so very short and lobbed off the bat handle to gully. Thomson had taken 2/4 in his first five overs. So much for his perceived lack of control. Both these bowlers should have written fulsome bread-and-butter letters to Alderman Jones.

A wicket might have fallen any ball and the England batting was dreadfully insecure. After twenty overs, the score was 57/4 and the realists must have known that the series was, to all intents and purposes, over. It was now that that most enigmatic figure,

A THIRST FOR LIFE

Tony Greig, strode out to bat, never a man to shirk a crisis or avoid a battle. I am not sure how much the Australians cared for him then. His haughty South African approach, and the vocal twang which went with it, may not have helped. It was ironical that eight years later on this same ground, against England, Australia were themselves to include a second option South African in their side. It was then that Kepler Wessels played his first Test Match and he, like Greig, also made a hundred. Greig, of course, had English parents and had come young to Sussex from South Africa where he was not yet that highly regarded as a cricketer. I had seen him play his first innings for Sussex, in 1967 when he had made 156 against a Lancashire attack consisting of Brian Statham and Ken Higgs, among others. A very tall man, he stood up straight and had driven the ball with great power off both feet.

Now, he stuck out his chin and took the Australian fast bowlers on. That evening, with John Edrich jumping and nudging and showing plenty of true Norfolk grit but little enjoyment, Greig threw his bat at anything at all wayward. At times, the ball flew off the middle to the boundary with a resounding and emphatic crack, at others it made a thinner, less convincing noise when it hit the edge and had the slips leaping about all over the place, although they grasped nothing more substantial than the sultry evening air. Greig was 34 not out at the end of the day. The next morning he square drove the first ball he faced, from Thomson, to the boundary and you could feel the stroke give him the boost he wanted. The night before his attitude had been opportunistic in a daredevil sort of a way. It was magnificent and heroic while it lasted but it had not even been tinged with permanency. Now, he took control and suddenly he was towering over the Australians as they shuffled off to the boundary to collect the ball. Lillee ran in with furious effort to bowl but he was straining too hard, the rhythm had gone and with it some of the menace. Wickets fell at the other end as the lower middle order scrimped and scraped desperately in pursuit of unlikely survival. We were watching different games at different ends.

Greig was 70 when the new ball was taken and this only seemed

BOUNCERS, SLEDGERS AND THE PASSING STREAKER

to heighten his resolve and his bloody-mindedness. He threw his bat at Thomson and the ball flew over the slips for four. Thomson, never one to show much emotion, turned and walked quickly back; Greig lent on his bat with a smile which will have infuriated the Australians. The roles had been reversed and Greig was the dominant force. The Australians in the press box had grown quiet again. Lillee now charged in, all calculated fury, and Greig smashed a full toss – drove is too mild a word – past mid off for another four. It was Lillee again and this time the ball was driven through cover with a searing finality and Greig himself was signalling a four when the ball was still twenty yards short of the boundary. It did one good to see and it didn't half annoy the Aussies. Four overs later, Greig drove Lillee through extra cover and then to the square cover boundary for the four which took him to his hundred. At first slip Ian Chappell stood still looking at the ground in front of his feet and Lars Porsena, who had spent a morning beside the Tiber watching the no less remarkable strokeplay of the brave Horatius, will have known exactly how he felt. It was inspirational batting and the only other comparable innings I have seen was Ted Dexter's 70 against Hall, Griffith and Sobers at Lord's in 1963. Lillee had the last word now when Greig was caught behind for 110. When he had disappeared from sight, the game and, for an Englishman, the series was submerged in anticlimax which lifted just fleetingly for a day or two in Melbourne immediately after Christmas.

It had been an innings of heroic proportions and of which only a handful have ever been played. It told, of course, of an extraordinary ability, but much more of the character of the man who had played it. The odds had been heavily against Greig but, like Horatius, he had stood his ground and given no thought for himself or his safety as he had taken the attack to the Australians. Earlier in the year, in Port of Spain, I had watched Greig bowl off breaks for almost the first time and he had taken 13/156 in the Fifth Test when he established an extraordinary psychological hold over the West Indies batsmen, enabling England to win by 26 runs and draw the series. Two years later, in Calcutta, I watched spellbound when he batted for 413 minutes to reach a hundred on a pitch especially prepared for the Indian spinners – an innings which effectively won the match for England. He was a truly formidable cricketer and you have to go to Gary Sobers to find another player in my time capable of turning in three such incomparable and yet disparate performances. He may have been born in Queenstown in Natal but no English oak had ever produced timber of greater resolve than this. Yet three years after this innings in Brisbane, Greig, as England's current captain, had signed for Kerry Packer's World Series Cricket. He had done so with as much conviction as he had batted that day against Lillee and Thomson. It still seems an extraordinary contradiction.

Back in Brisbane at the Gabba, Australia left England to score 333 to win and Thomson, bowling as quickly and ferociously as ever a cricketer can, cut through the batting as if he was a supercharged chain saw. I honestly found it frightening to watch him. He took 6/46 and I can see now the leg-stump yorker that accounted for Tony Greig. Tall men must always be vulnerable to the yorker for they have such a long way to come down, and Thomson produced the perfect ball. Australia won by 166 runs and England limped away from Brisbane with Dennis Amiss and Edrich nursing broken bones in their hands. By then, at one of those rather hairy *post mortem* press conferences, Alec Bedser, the manager, had announced that Colin Cowdrey, who was to be forty-two later in the month, was flying out as a reinforcement. Although eyebrows were raised, it made sense for he had the technique and also nothing to prove, while a young player could have been shot to pieces once and for all by the Australian fast bowlers.

Cowdrey arrived in Perth and found himself facing Lillee and Thomson at the WACA ground on one of the quickest pitches in the world only four days after he had arrived in Australia. The day he landed, he and Alec Bedser came to dinner with Johnny Woodcock, Michael Melford and me at the Weld Club where the three of us were staying. Colin was cheerful enough at what was in store for him but not having seen Lillee in his present mode or Thomson in any mode at all, may not quite have appreciated the peril he was in. He and Alec put it across Johnny and me at the snooker table after dinner and so we hoped we had done just a little for his confidence.

It was a gamble which nearly worked. Ian Chappell put England in to bat and the score had reached 44 before Luckhurst departed. Cowdrey, looking a little like Uncle Harry going out to bat in the fathers' match, came in to a rousing reception, and began to play pretty well. I am sure all of us watching were a great deal more nervous than he was himself. When he got up to the bowler's end, he said to Jeff Thomson, 'I'm Colin Cowdrey. How do you do?' and stuck out his hand. Thommo had not come across this situation before and was flummoxed. Cowdrey put on 55 with David Lloyd and had reached 22 when he was bowled round his legs glancing at Thomson who always gave him more trouble than Lillee. England were bowled out for 208 and then Doug Walters, between tea and the close on the second day, and Ross Edwards, made hundreds and Australia amassed 481. Luckhurst had been hit on the hand by Thomson in the second over of the match and was not able to open the batting in the second innings. Cowdrey immediately volunteered to take his place and he and Lloyd put on 62 for the first wicket before Cowdrey, who had made 41 and played some splendid strokes, was lbw shuffling across his stumps and trying to turn Thomson to leg. England were dismissed for 293 and lost by nine wickets.

During my many visits to Australia I have been lucky enough to stay at clubs like the Weld in Perth, either because they have a reciprocal arrangement with my own club in London, or because friends of mine in Australia have been brave enough to propose me for temporary membership. The Adelaide Club, the Melbourne Club, and the Australian Club in Sydney are all splendid institutions. The browsing and sluicing is excellent and I have always been made most welcome and comfortable. My original proposer for the Weld Club was Colin McDonald, a famous *Times* correspondent. He was for some years before the last war, their man in China, first in Peking and then in Shanghai. In 1937 when Japan and China were at war, he had two remarkable coups. He was travelling up the Yangtze River on board the American gunboat, the *Panay*, when they were bombed by the Japanese. He wrote a most moving account of the incident which appeared on 18 December 1937 and *The Times*, presumably at the behest of Geoffrey Dawson, the Editor, put his name on the story, even though in those days, it had a policy of strict anonymity.

Colin, a small wiry man who talked at a terrific speed and lived on double measures of nervous energy and anything else he could persuade his friends to buy him, retired to Australia in 1943. He lived for much of the next thirty-five years in the Weld Club where he busied himself making sure that visiting members were not ignored and telling intriguing stories about prewar China. He talked at length about the book he was going to write and always ended by quoting Hemingway as saying that the book you talk about the most is the one you never write. This one too remained unwritten. Whenever I now visit the Weld, I always expect to see Colin scurrying round a corner finishing one conversation at the same time as starting another while stuffing a passing cheese biscuit into his mouth at the same time.

The Third Test, which began in Melbourne on Boxing Day, was a marvellous game on a pitch which had an increasingly variable bounce. England were again put in and managed to make 242. Cowdrey once more almost did it but after batting 229 minutes for 35, he played back to one from Thomson which came on to him more quickly than he expected and was lbw. Australia were bowled out for 241 and, thanks largely to Greig and Amiss, England then made 244. This left Australia to make 246 to win and after a thrilling last day, they were 238/8. England had no answer to the Australian fast bowlers at Sydney and Adelaide and came back to Melbourne for the Sixth Test 4–0 down.

At this time, rest days were still a part of every Test Match. At Adelaide the rest day was always spent at the Hill Smith's Winery in Yalumba in the Barrossa Valley. Wyndy Hill Smith who had played for South Australia and Western Australia always laid on the most wonderful day for the players and those connected with the teams which included the media. It was a thirsty day, especially for those who took advantage of the tennis courts. One of them was Jeff Thomson who succeeded in pulling every muscle in his shoulder and was unable to bowl again in the series.

BOUNCERS, SLEDGERS AND THE PASSING STREAKER

It was the brave new world of Packer-inspired television in Australia which marked the departure of rest days. If the five days of a Test Match were played straight off, it meant that television equipment and crews did not have to hang about idle on the rest day and so money was saved. They would, I suppose, have disappeared anyway in the fullness of time as efforts were made to concertina tours into as little time as possible. It was one more change which has helped to alter the character of the game in modern times. Rest days, like many traditions, are not easy to defend when they are put under an objective microscope, but there were traditional rest-day activities which were as much a part of the scene as the cricket. The day at Yalumba during an Adelaide Test Match was the ultimate in rest days and it is marvellous that Rob Hill Smith, Wyndy's son, does his best to make sure that the teams and the immediate entourage get up to Yalumba some time before the match. The rest day in Port of Spain always meant a boat trip out to the islands organised by Jeff and Zara Stollmeyer; in Sydney, Peter Doyle, heavily chivvied by Diana Fisher who would probably win the prize for the most unlikely daughter-in-law an Archbishop of Canterbury has ever had, laid on his yacht for a lengthy journey round the harbour with those heavenly oysters washed down by gallons of chardonnay; in Dunedin, John Hislop, the cricketing surgeon and hypnotist arranged a boat trip on the Coutha River; in Christchurch, I went off to that wonderful ground, the Valley of Peace; in Georgetown, it was a flight by small aircraft to see the Kaiteur Falls, the tallest waterfalls in the world – even if not so vibrant as those at Victoria and Niagara. And on it went. Those clinical and cynical television people will have none of it, but I have not the slightest doubt that Test cricket is the poorer for the abolition of rest days.

The 1974/75 series ended up in Melbourne. Financial opportunism, or greed, was by then beginning to decree that a Sixth Test Match was a good thing in the most popular series of all. The reason for England's overall destruction was indelibly underlined. Thomson, as we have seen, was injured and, after bowling six overs in which he arranged the routine dismissal of Amiss, Lillee left the field with a bruised right foot. Mike Denness and Keith Fletcher made big hundreds and England went on to win by an innings and four runs and we all took off to New Zealand to burnish our clichés anew.

I helped cover this part of the tour for the BBC and joined the Radio New Zealand commentary team. During the First Test in Auckland, I was on the air when I saw the worst accident I have ever seen on a cricket ground. After another massive celebration of their release from Lillee and Thomson by Denness and Fletcher who made 181 and 216 respectively, New Zealand followed on and were nine wickets down in their second innings. Ewen Chatfield, who was not overplaced at number eleven, joined Geoffrey Howarth and promptly edged a bouncer from Peter Lever into his head. It was only mouth-to-mouth resuscitation by Bernard Thomas, the England physiotherapist, that saved Chatfield's life. He had already swallowed his tongue and it was very quick thinking by Thomas which saved the day. That evening in the hotel, Lever was almost in tears and promised at a press conference that he would never bowl another bouncer in his life. At the Whitsun weekend late the following May when Yorkshire were playing Lancashire, I read with amazement that Lever had been warned for bowling too many bouncers at the Yorkshire opener, Barrie Leadbeater. Such is life.

It was back to England for all the excitement of the inaugural World Cup. In comparison with what happens today, it was a pretty modest affair but it was an indication of the increasing impact of limited-over cricket since the Gillette Cup had begun in England in 1963. The six Test-playing countries – South Africa had been ostracised because of their apartheid policies – were joined by Sri Lanka and East Africa who had reached the final of the Trophy for the associate members of the International Cricket Council. This had been played the previous year in the Midlands and it had been a delight to go, for example, to the charming ground at Water Orton to see, say, Fiji play the United States of America. The World Cup final was unforgettable and although the West Indies were the predictable winners, Australia, needing 292 to win, reached 274 in a thrilling finish in the gather-

ptain of Eton in 1957. This photograph was taken only a few days before I was run over by a bus.

Aged nine in the nets at Norwich. F.G. Pierpoint (Surrey and Norfolk) shaping an early enthusiasm for the legside.

Reggie Cubitt, a cousin of my father's, Mike Falcon who helped bowl the Australians to defeat at Eastbourne in 1921, and my father watching cricket at Hoveton in the early sixties.

The dreaded hat-trick. Bowled by Rex Neame in the Eton and Harrow match at Lord's in 1955. I had a somewhat extravagant approach to the hat-trick ball.

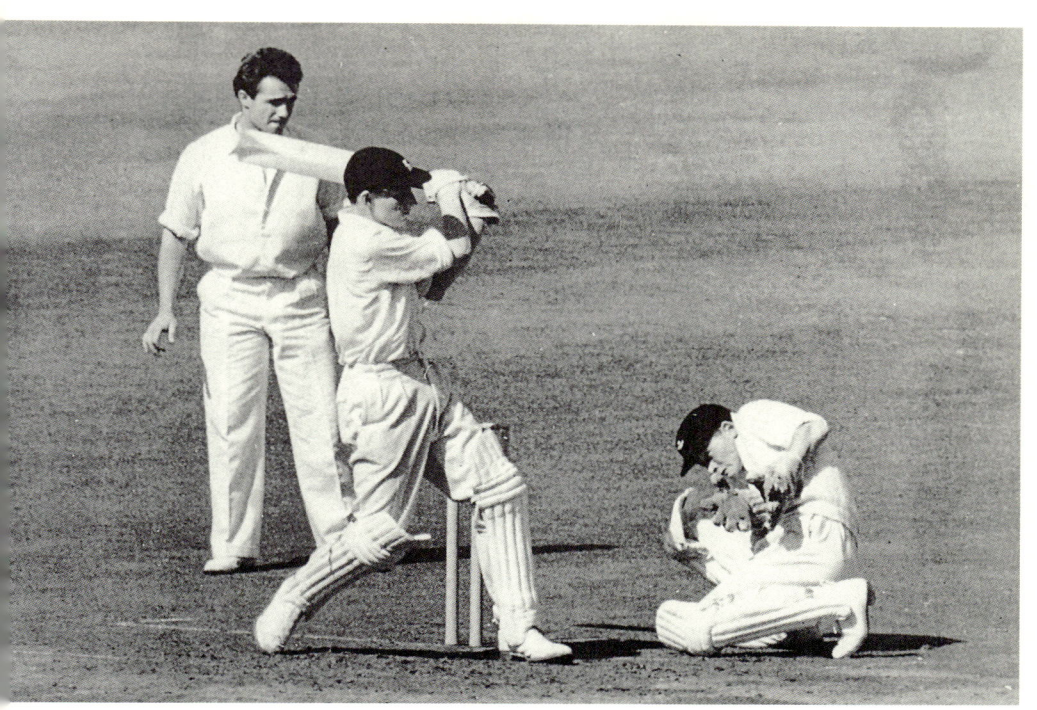

...tting for the Public Schools against the Combined Services while making 104 not out. Geoff Millman (...ottingham and England) is behind the stumps, Stuart Leary (Kent and Charlton Athletic) at first slip.

... second half in Pop. This group contains a future personal secretary to Prince Charles, a political ...umnist, a spy, a committee member of MCC, and a host of mega-successful businessmen.

Norfolk in 1960. The side, captained by Bill Edrich (Middlesex and England), finished at the top of the Minor Counties table. H.C.B. is second on the right in the back row.

The Arabs in Barbados in January 1967, inspired by Colin Ingleby-Mackenzie and presided over by Jim Swanton. We played hard and were not bad at cricket either.

I DIDN'T MIND BOWLING AT THE STATION MASTER OR — THE POLICEMAN — OR THE BUTCHER'S BOY

OR THE BUTCHER / OR THE PARSON / OR THE PUBLICAN

OR GILES THE FARMER

BUT WHEN THE LOCAL QUOITS CHAMPION HIT ME INTO THE NEXT COUNTY

TO HILLINGTON.

I THOUGHT IT WAS TIME TO RETIRE —

ARTHUR MAILEY.
"HILLINGTON". 1930.

g spinners need a sense of humour and Arthur Mailey, whom I met in the fifties at Runcton, certainly
d that.

An invitation issued by the patrons of the famous Hill at the Sydney Cricket Ground in 1978/79...

... which, of course, I accepted although I had not realised at the time that I had been that successful.

England's Christmas Day fancy-dress lunch on tour in India, presided over by the Colonel (Ken Barrington, the manager) on the right.

e slaps on the back were more threatening than the Australian bowlers. Ian Botham, 145 not out,
ops to shelter at the end of the fourth day's play in the famous Headingley Test of 1981. Ladbroke's
ting tent, made famous by Lillee and Marsh, is in the background.

e most infamous ball in cricket. Trevor Chappell, persuaded by brother Greg his captain, bowls the
ball of the match underarm and along the ground to Brian McKechnie at Melbourne in the 1980/81
rld Series Cup when New Zealand needed six to tie.

Ted Dexter, captain of Cambridge in 1958, my first year. I wonder if anyone has ever hit a cricket ball much harder or more dashingly.

ing dusk at Lord's. Viv Richards's fielding that day was superhuman and he ran out three Australians. I was able to compare this performance of Richards's with that of Colin Bland for South Africa in the Test Match at Lord's in 1965. The excitement of a World Cup final may have given Richards's throwing an extra frisson of excitement but, for me, Bland, tall, fit and athletic, remains the best fielder I have ever seen. He threw out Barrington and Parks in 1965 with direct hits from middle distances. There was something so calculating and pre-ordained about Bland. He was lightning fast across the ground, the two-handed pick up and perfect throw blended into almost the same movement, and the explosion of the stumps was the logical conclusion. Even Jonty Rhodes can't manage quite the consummate inevitability of Bland.

My first Test Match in the BBC commentary box at Lord's came later that summer when Australia stayed on after the World Cup for four Tests. They had won the first when Mike Denness miscalculated the weather forecast at Edgbaston and put Australia in to bat and they won by an innings. Tony Greig was in charge at Lord's which, like the last two Tests, was drawn. I think, like most people who saw the incident, the game's first streaker, so memorably immortalised on *TMS* by John Arlott, will remain my best memory of the match. This strapping young man, waving his hands above his head as if he had just caught sight of the promised land, appeared from under the Grandstand. He was a muscular merchant seaman from Marylebone who jumped over the stumps under the careful scrutiny of umpire Tom Spencer who remained motionless, prompting Brian Johnston's dreadful joke, 'He's over all right because umpire Tom Spencer hasn't signalled one short.' Arlott's commentary on the episode was measured and humorous and almost seemed to make it all worthwhile.

On the Friday night I went to the first of what used to be the annual dinner given for *Test Match Special* by the BBC in the Director-General's private dining room. It was a three-line whip affair, an evening of great bonhommie, considerable self-congratulation and the sort of speeches calculated to send us to the microphone the next morning fuller of zest than usual. The only drawback was the booze which flowed in a quantity which was almost too considerable. I suppose if you were entertaining John Arlott you had something to live up to and it wouldn't have done to have had him telling listeners the next morning that he had almost died of thirst the night before. There was no stopping Arlott. He arrived at the ground the next morning carrying two leather briefcases which held a total of seven bottles of claret. I know because he asked me to carry them both up all those flights of stairs to our commentary box. When he took them out of the briefcases he said memorably to anyone within earshot, 'Well, with any luck that little lot should see us through to the lunch interval.' He was a hard taskmaster.

Having become a member of *TMS*, I was in and more often out of the team, vying for a place with Chris Martin-Jenkins who was one year senior to me as a commentator, and with Don Mosey who liked to think he had got the nod with *TMS* before me but actually commentated on his first Test Match later in the same summer that I did mine. But he was a staff man so I had no complaints if he was selected before me. John Arlott and Brian Johnston naturally did all the matches and it was only because John moved over to the press box at the end of the first hour after lunch that four commentators were used. One was the overseas commentator who always joined our panel: Alan McGilvray if the Australians were visiting, Tony Cozier if it was the West Indies and Alan Richards if it was New Zealand's turn. So for these series there was only one place per match going begging. In the mid-seventies, CM-J succeeded Brian Johnston as the BBC's cricket correspondent but he did not get every Test, in order that Mosey and I should have a chance. At this time and through the eighties, I often did the number two job if I was not one of the commentary team. This meant sitting in the number two position, sometimes in a box which had the discomfort of a not frightfully upmarket rabbit hutch. From there, I did all the inserts through the day for the sports programmes and the news desks. It was not the most edifying form of broadcasting for it was difficult to make a twenty-second piece stand up and hit people between the eyes. But at least it meant that I could be at the match. At the end of a day doing that job, I was in much greater need of a drink than I was after a day's commentary.

I had made myself extremely unpopular during the summer of 1975 when I tried to arrange things so that I would be able to watch the West Indies play in Australia the following winter. I wrote round to various sports editors in the hope they might employ me to cover the tour for them if they were not sending a staff man. One of those I wrote to was Kingsley Wright who was still the Sports Editor of the *Daily Telegraph*. He wrote back saying that he had not yet made up his mind what he was going to do but that he would bear me in mind. I was then taken severely to task by Michael Melford, who did not often come out of his corner in this way, because he had been hoping to cover the tour for the *Telegraph*. He told me that I had weakened his position as his Sports Editor now realised that I would undercut him financially. He told me I should have written to him in the first place. I was horrified but fortunately the tour was covered for them by Jim Swanton who went on a final valedictory visit to Australia before he retired. In those days, newspapers did not often send staff men to cover neutral series, and I went along on behalf of the *Guardian* and the BBC.

It was not a particularly interesting series and Australia won by the convincing margin of five matches to one. Ian and Greg Chappell and Ian Redpath scored a huge number of runs and Lillee and Thomson proved too fast for the West Indies batsmen, including the young Viv Richards. He did not have a good time of it until he began to open the batting at the end of the series. There was one remarkable game, the Second Test in Perth, for which Johnny Woodcock and I were back at the Weld Club. Australia won the toss and thanks to an exceptional innings of 156 by Ian Chappell, made 329. Ian was not such an elegant strokeplayer as his brother Greg but if I had had to have one of them to bat for my life, I would have gone unhesitatingly for Ian. This was the best innings I ever saw him play and it was against some fearsome fast bowling, for Andy Roberts and Michael Holding were just beginning their famous partnership.

Ian Chappell was the most uncompromising cricketer I think I ever saw. He knew his own mind, would never let anyone else stand in his way and if he was the first captain who gave free rein to his players to have a go verbally at the opposing batsmen, he regarded it merely as one of the processes in the relentless pursuit of victory and not something to make an issue of. He was not a man who respected namby-pamby attitudes. He knew players had to be tough to succeed at this level and if they were not able to cope with what became, rather curiously, known as sledging, that was their problem. His attitude to the game was summed up when he was batting by his reaction to an appeal against him. He never walked of his own accord but stood still and looked at the umpire. If he was given out, there was never a visible show of discontent. He would take off his gloves and walk quickly and unemotionally back to the pavilion. With Ian Chappell, you got what you saw. He was an extremely incisive captain and a hard man to beat. On the first evening of this match he was past a hundred and not out and the BBC wanted me to interview him. I tiptoed apprehensively into the Australian dressing room, but he could not have been more helpful. He came and sat with me on the seat outside and gave me a good interview, even though there cannot have been many things in the world that just then he would have wanted to do less.

But even he was unable to prevent what happened in the remaining ninety minutes of the session, after he had led his players out on to the field the next morning in Perth. The tone was set when Roy Fredericks, the slightly built left-hander from Guyana, hooked at Lillee's second ball and it flew off the top edge over long leg for six. I have never seen a cricket ball hit as Fredericks managed to do that morning in Perth and none of it was slogging. He played scarcely a single defensive stroke before lunch and his partner, Bernard Julien, was only a sluggard in comparison to Fredericks. The 50 came in thirty-five minutes off 5.3 overs, Fredericks's own 50 in forty-seven minutes off thirty-three balls and at lunch, from fourteen overs, the West Indies were 130/1. We had none of us seen the like of it. Fredericks's hundred came from seventy-one balls and at the end of the day the West Indies were 350/4, Fredericks having gone to the first ball after tea when he had made 169 out of 258. They finished with 585, after Clive Lloyd had chipped in with 149. Australia were then bowled out for 169 in their second innings and Andy Roberts, so brilliant at working out a batsman's weaknesses, and now bowling consistently fast and accurately, took 7/54.

One evening during that match Johnny Woodcock and I sat down to dinner at the Weld Club and I said to him that, with a bit of luck, we would both be watching cricket in India in a year's time. He said that the last time England had gone to India he had wanted to drive from London with Brian Johnston and Michael Melford but that in the end the wives had put their feet down and said no. It was a journey he was still keen to make. I leapt at the idea and before the end of dinner we had decided to go ahead with what turned out to be the most exciting adventure of my life which we will come to in the next two chapters.

Meanwhile, I seemed to have been writing and broadcasting about short-pitched fast bowling for much too long. If it wasn't Lillee and Thomson, it was Roberts and Holding and when, after the series in Australia, I flew to New Zealand to watch them play two Test Matches against India, a young tearaway called Richard Hadlee was making the Indians duck and weave for their lives. He finished by taking 7/23 in the Third Test when India were bowled out for 81 in their second innings at the Basin Reserve in Wellington and New Zealand won by an innings. Even so, I was finding New Zealand an increasingly therapeutic place. It is the most beautiful country and the people are delightful and mostly shrug off the barbed insults which come their way across the Tasman Sea from Australia. When I had been in Auckland the year before, I had met Hylton LeGrice, an eye surgeon, who was looking after the medical requirements of the New Zealand team, although I hope short-sightedness was not one of their problems. Hylton is an excellent companion who has splendidly expensive tastes and loves the best things in life. His dining-room table is always weighed down with the best New Zealand wines. He was to become a director of Montana, the biggest wine producer in the country, and they have no one who does a more impressive public relations job for them. He turns up from time to time in

England for an extended stay, which usually coincides with a New Zealand tour, and he wears his immaculately knotted MCC tie comfortably and with a knowing look.

After tasting the improvement in the quality of New Zealand's white wines, I returned to England at the end of February and spent a wonderful month hibernating at Hoveton. I had moved into one half of a small house on the estate and it was there that I struggled with all the letters I had received while I was away. There is nothing I hate more than having to deal with three months' post for there are always some letters I wished I had not opened. The bills invariably exceed the cheques, but I have learned one excellent trick which I can't recommend too highly. If you put all the things which need dealing with in one pile and leave it for three months, it is amazing how many you then find you can throw away because they have answered themselves. The break at Hoveton was all too short and it ended well before the gulls had started to lay eggs in their usual profusion on the marshes. Hard-boiled gulls' eggs eaten cold with celery salt and brown bread and butter are one of the great delicacies.

Alas, it was soon time to watch the West Indies bowling far too many bouncers, this time at the Englishmen. The first two Tests were drawn and then we all descended on Old Trafford which was my only Test of the series in the commentary box. England's opening batsmen for that match were Brian Close, who was forty-five, and John Edrich, who was a mere thirty-nine. They had to contend with sometimes as many as four bouncers an over and the ambulance at the back of the pavilion kept its engine running all day. Roberts, Holding and Daniel, who took all twenty English wickets between them, were unrelenting in their efforts to decapitate as many Englishmen as they could and were nothing short of downright dangerous. The Australian, Bill Alley, who was one of the umpires, had said in my hearing shortly before the match that there was no way he was going to allow the West Indies to get away with such blatantly intimidating bowling as they had been doing up and down the country. Yet, when it came to it, he never once made a move to stop them. His partner was Lloyd Budd, the old Hampshire player, who was standing in his first Test Match and it was hardly surprising he was not prepared to act on his own. The West Indies bowling at Old Trafford was as nasty as anything I have ever seen and it was disgraceful they were allowed to get away with it. I wonder what Geoffrey Boycott was thinking in his tent when he saw Close and Edrich sweating it out, or maybe his television set was on the blink.

It is not easy to make a direct comparison with Bodyline. In 1932/33, the fast bowlers were allowed to have as many fielders as they wanted behind square on the leg side. With three backward short legs and two men back for the hook, it was impossible to play the ball with safety when it was pitched short and slanted in at the batsman's body. The only hope was to take evasive action but batsmen in those days had no experience against bouncers and were ill-equipped to do so. The West Indies had three fast bowlers on this occasion at Old Trafford but for most of the two decades that Clive Lloyd and then Viv Richards captained the side they had four and the attack was relentless. Lloyd claimed that it was just that they had four excellent fast bowlers and denied that it was a deliberate ploy to intimidate a whole generation of batsmen. I have no doubt the jury would find against him.

While the outer shell of cricket was being changed by the consistent use of short-pitched fast bowling, the game's inner mechanism was beginning to be tampered with too. It must have been somewhere in the second half of 1976 that the brains trust at the back of Kerry Packer's Channel Nine television network in Australia had come up with the thought that the exclusive right to televise international cricket in Australia was a sure-fire money-spinner. England, meanwhile, were planning for a visit to India and Sri Lanka and then a journey to Melbourne to play a Test Match in celebration of the centenary of the first-ever Test Match played at the Melbourne Cricket Ground in Jolimont Park in March 1877. Before any of this happened, Johnny Woodcock and I, and three of our more or less intrepid friends, set off in a 1921 Rolls-Royce and a new three-and-a-half-litre Rover to drive from

London to Bombay where on 21 November at the Taj Mahal Hotel we were to meet up with Tony Greig's England side at the start of their tour of India.

CHAPTER

9

IN THE ASSISTANT CHAUFFEUR'S SEAT

BY THE TIME Johnny Woodcock and I had got up from the table that evening at the Weld Club, we had not only agreed to drive from London to Bombay, but we had even chosen one passenger for the journey. Judy Casey, who lived in Sydney, was a particular friend of mine and Johnny also knew her and agreed that she was exactly the sparky sort of girl who would keep us all up to the mark. Judy, who is tall, blonde and the only glamorous mother of five spectacular children I know to have a pilot's licence, was quick to confirm her availability. Johnny and I had decided originally that we would do the journey in a Land Rover and so it remained for some weeks. I got on with the arrangements when I returned to England and by Easter our plans were coming along well. That weekend Johnny had dinner with a neighbour in Hampshire and one of the other guests was Adrian Liddell, a considerable farmer in the neighbourhood who had an impressive collection of old cars. He asked Johnny where he was going on his next journey abroad and when he heard that he and I were going to drive a Land Rover to Bombay, he said to Johnny, 'Why don't you let me drive you in one of my old cars?' Rather surprised by this, Johnny asked him if he thought any of them would get there. This piqued Ady who said most indignantly that indeed they would. Soon afterwards he nominated the 1921 Silver Ghost and it was settled.

I can't remember at exactly what stage we decided that a support car was essential or if Michael Bennett decided it for us – it was probably the latter. It cannot have been long after Johnny's conversation with Ady that early one evening I bumped into Michael, perched, as usual, on a stool at the corner of the bar in Boodle's, reading the evening paper with a glass of whisky to hand. His horn-rimmed half-moon glasses were, as always, precariously poised far down his nose. Another inimitable habit was a constant and energetic hitching up of his trousers around an ample girth, although he didn't often do this while sitting at a bar. He listened with interest while I told him of our plans. Then, in a decisive movement, he closed his paper, spun round on the stool to face me and said, 'Why don't I bring a car and come too?' It was not so much a question as a statement for that was the way with Michael. It struck me as a splendid idea and I was quickly on to the telephone to Johnny whose applause was rather more muted, but in essence he agreed.

The only slight sticking point was Ady's concern about taking a member of the distaff side with us. Johnny had assured him that Judy was as good an egg as could be found and Ady reluctantly agreed, having made sure that his worries had been recorded in the minutes. I, meanwhile, had been in touch with the AA who had sent me large folding maps of the road through Austria, Yugoslavia and Greece to Istanbul and then on through Turkey, Iran, Afghanistan and the Khyber Pass into Pakistan, down to Lahore and Delhi and on through Rajasthan to Bombay. The maps were so detailed that on the far side of the Bosporus every petrol station was marked, which was invaluable because the Rolls was enormously thirsty, hardly managing ten miles to the gallon – if only they had all had petrol. There were the details of what visas we required and what inoculations were necessary to be sorted out and gradually it all took shape.

When I stayed at Longparish with Johnny, I went over and met Ady and his family and saw the wonderful claret-coloured Rolls which had been earmarked for the journey. It made me think at once of Dornford Yates and all those splendid books about Jonah Mansell and Richard Chandos defying the ungodly, especially one called Rose Noble, and discovering hidden treasure in castles in Austria. They invariably travelled by Rolls. Ady had an infinite knowledge of the intricacies of the internal combustion engine on which he was prepared to discourse interminably in a vibrant voice. He also told me of his doubts about the wisdom of including a lady in our number and I assured him that he need have no worries.

Then Johnny came to London and met Michael who, although at his most bonhomous, had a forcibly expressed opinion on any subject that cropped up. He had never been laden with self-doubt. In real life he was a stock jobber who had just finished helping to put the London Stock Exchange on to computer. He was extremely bright even if, in his own mind, there were only ever two points of view: his and the wrong one. I think Johnny wondered about the wisdom of my selection but what had clinched it was that Michael was determined to bring a car and had bought a new three-and-a-half-litre Rover for the purpose which was a considerable contribution. I suppose I was naive for I was sure that when it came to it, everyone would pull together for the common cause.

The next meeting was in London when Johnny brought Ady up to meet Michael. It became clear then that while Michael was doing it for the hell of it and for a bit of fun, Ady was undertaking the journey simply to make sure that 'the old gal' as he called his spectacular Silver Ghost, arrived in Bombay in one piece and on time. Looking back on the journey now, I fear he will remember Komotini, Teheran and Delhi not for the marvellous dinner we had outside on the edge of the square, the Iranian crown jewels and the side trip to the Red Fort, but as places in which he was able to give 'the old gal' a thoroughly good service. For Michael, the old Rolls was never anything more than just another form of mildly inefficient transport.

Ady's head mechanic fine-tuned the Rolls in every detail. We had extra petrol cans tied to the two running boards, a larger than usual supply of spare tyres – this was a potential problem for a series of blow-outs could have left us stranded – at least a couple of drums of oil and everything the car was most likely to need.

The oil had to be checked every two hours or so through the entire journey and each time Ady had to get out of the car and lever himself under the engine on his back. Michael's yellow Rover was delivered on time – the Yellow Peril as it soon became known – and we set about getting a limited amount of sponsorship. Air India were keen to help and so too were Esso Petroleum and also, thank goodness, Long John Scotch Whisky who supplied us most handsomely in kind. We planned to leave on Wednesday, 6 October and, shortly before the off, Judy Casey flew in from Sydney in what I can only describe as spanking form. At this point, I have to say that she was my nap selection; by the time we had got to Bombay, I think we both felt that the odds had lengthened a touch. Her meeting with Michael was a great success which was a start. Then, I took her down to Hampshire and, with Johnny, we went over to have lunch with Ady. That was an encounter which I have to say might have gone better. Ady felt that his views about the folly of having a lady on board had been amply reinforced, while Judy was left muttering forcibly about his narrow-minded attitudes. I was still eternally optimistic it would all be right on the day, while Johnny bit his lip and put a brave face on it, but, I daresay, was much nearer to hoisting the red flag than I was.

Judy came down to Hoveton for a couple of days before we left and chuntered away about Ady before we drove back to London for one or two farewell parties, with the Rolls always voted 'old gal' of the match at each event. The makers of Long John gave a party in their office in Queen Anne's Gate and the Rolls left it fuller than when she arrived for it was at this point that our hosts had slipped a case or three of their inestimable product into the boot. There were cases of forty-ounce bottles and of flasks which were about a third of an ordinary bottle. These latter were worth their weight in gold because as we drove further east and the customs and immigration people became increasingly difficult, we would carelessly leave a flask or two visible in the car. When whatever official it was that we were having trouble with at the time saw the flask he would seize it and say gleefully, 'This is for me?' Who were we to deny him? It smoothed our passage no end.

IN THE ASSISTANT CHAUFFEUR'S SEAT

The day before we left London, we gave a dinner party on the ladies' side of Boodle's which was a great success. It was just after midnight when Michael made perhaps the definitive statement about the five of us. He said profoundly, 'I don't think I've ever gone off anywhere with a collection of people who are more conceited.' Strong stuff! The only two not to feel a trifle sluggish the next morning were the two cars who were tucked away in a big garage almost underneath the Albert Hall. We foregathered there at half past six and, after a last profound and collective hitch of the trousers, we drove up and out of the forecourt and into the rain where Patrick Eagar, the cricket photographer, was on hand to take masses of pictures and then we were away. Michael and Judy who struck a common cause in mild contempt of Ady's 'old gal', coupled with the name of the driver, were in the Rover. I sat beside Ady in the distinctly chilly assistant chauffeur's seat in the front of the Rolls, with Johnny stretched out in the back. The cars were all stuck about with stickers proclaiming Air India, Esso and Long John Scotch Whisky and I felt I needed a large shot of the latter almost at once. Sitting in the front of the Rolls, it was decidedly damp because the makers of the car had not wasted money worrying about the discomfort of the the assistant chauffeur or the footman. I began to feel a bit as Kenneth More and John Gregson had looked at times all those years ago in that lovely film, *Genevieve*, about the London to Brighton run for vintage motor cars.

Our road to the ferry at Dover took us through Sandwich and, as we had plenty of time on our hands, we decided to look in on Jim and Ann Swanton. Only Jim was at home, but the speed with which he made for the fridge and produced a bottle of champagne was impressive. With the high skill he was to show for the next forty-six days and nights, Ady coaxed 'the old gal' on to the ferry where they battened her down. When he drove her off a couple of hours later, it was on to the right-hand side of the road where she was to remain until we entered Pakistan thirty-two days later. When confronted by officialdom speaking in a foreign tongue, Ady would lean out of the open window, as he did now in Calais, and say in strident tones, 'I'm afraid I have no French.' There was a fine moment a few days later when we were on a steep winding climb in the mountains in Austria. We arrived at a road junction where a mechanical policeman, which looked like a sophisticated scarecrow, was automatically waving one arm. Ady brought the Rolls to a halt beside it, wound down the window and gave it a deafening, 'I'm afraid I have no Austrian.'

We went to Paris for a delicious lunch and a photographic and interview session on behalf of Long John at the plush offices of the firm that sold their product. During lunch, one of our hosts recommended an hotel in Sept Saulx in champagne country and we set off through the eastern suburbs of Paris. It was here that Ady made his only misjudgement of the journey and hit another car. Fortunately, the Frenchman was not as voluble as some of his countrymen can be and the bent bumper was pulled off the wheel and we were able to continue. I can't remember the rights and wrongs of the incident but it was a blow to Ady's morale and probably produced sniggers in the Rover.

Michael and Judy drove together in the Rover for most of the journey and Judy did some of the driving, although just occasionally she would spend a morning in the Rolls when she and Ady almost inevitably got on one another's nerves. After Sept Saulx, where we had our best dinner on the whole journey, we crossed into Germany and made for Frankfurt. We presented quite a spectacle on the autobahns and 'the old gal' was greeted with a good deal of hooting and waving. We were already developing a pattern, although the big days when we had to drive 300 or more miles lay ahead of us. The 'old gal' had two-wheel brakes and hardly did more than fifty miles an hour, apart from the oil stops, while the Rover was quite capable of more than double the speed. The three of us who did most of the journey in the old car made an early start and the plan was that the Rover caught us up sometime late in the morning. We conferred and decided on the town or village where we would like to have lunch. The Rover then went on ahead and had a look round and would either meet us at a particular restaurant which had probably been recommended by someone we had met the night before, or come back to intercept us and lead us to it. In Europe finding restaurants was easy; in

Asia it was more tricky. While we were eating lunch we decided where we would try and stay that night and again we would leave before the Yellow Perils who were allowed to linger over coffee and cognac – if they could find any. They would overtake us again later in the afternoon and go on ahead to book rooms before coming back to meet us on the edge of the town and lead us to the hotel. In the Rolls we liked to be at our next base before it was dark, not that we always were. It made Ady's job twice as difficult negotiating strange streets on the wrong side of the road in the dark.

The relief when we arrived at our planned destination was enormous and if the makers of Long John could ever have seen the gratitude with which we fell upon one of their spectacular bottles at the end of a day's march, they would have died contented men. The trouble was that, although they were forty-ounce bottles, they seemed to hold less each day. The combined thirst of the five of us made the consumption of the Rolls seem dreadfully faint-hearted. We started our daily *post mortems* full of good humour, but as the alcohol took hold it became progressively more sparky. Ady would probably say something which seemed harmless enough but would bring Michael or Judy out of their corners in a flash. At this point, Johnny or I would make our contribution in the hope of cooling things down, only to find it had quite the opposite effect on everyone. There were too many of us who never had the slightest doubt that what we said was right. They were lively evenings without a doubt.

It all began to feel just a little bit different now that we had left Central Europe behind. To start with, the lorry culture began. Once we were through the frontier into Yugoslavia we were soon on the main trunk road running the length of the country. At the frontier, there was a long queue of those enormous lorries making the journey, maybe from the north of England to Afghanistan or even beyond. There were one or two with which we continually leapfrogged and we would remain in contact with them for perhaps a thousand miles. As the staging posts became less frequent, we all stopped at the same places and a camaraderie of the road grew up. We heard stories of other lorries, while tales of our own progress were passed along and in some places people who had heard about our impending arrival were waiting to meet us. The further east we went, the stronger this sense of comradeship. Being British was a great common bond and much waving and hooting went on when we overtook or were overtaken by a GB plate.

Yugoslavia passed off uneventfully until, on the third day, we were plugging down the highway towards the Greek frontier and eventually Thessalonica, when one of the back tyres on the Rolls blew out with a report which made it sound as if the local bandit was making a statement. The way Ady caught the car and brought it under control was impressive and I think we took his masterly performance at the wheel too much for granted. He insisted on driving the whole way himself. We were leading at the time and, while Ady scurried about pulling a spare tyre off the roof and getting the car jacked up, the Yellow Peril hoved into view and pulled up behind us.

From time to time on the journey I was to make prearranged contact with the BBC sports room in Broadcasting House to give progress reports on *Sport on Two* on Saturday afternoons. Telephone systems generally were not what they are today and the following day I tried to get through from the Capsis Hotel in Thessalonica to dress up the blow-out into a life-threatening situation. Desmond Lynam was the unfortunate chap on the other end and I should think with all the interference on the line that it was completely unbroadcastable. I promised to be in touch again in a week's time from Erzerum in deepest Turkey. Ady was more successful and had a clear line on which to talk to his mechanic at home and arrange for him to send a couple of spare tyres out to Teheran.

Ady was in service mode in Komotini, a fishing village on the north shore of the Aegean where we stayed two nights in a small hotel overlooking the square, and came across the charming custom whereby almost the entire population took an evening stroll in the square, chatting among themselves while the sun went down. The children played and it was a delightful scene. We watched from one of our bedroom windows, saying farewell to yet another day through the good offices of Long John. I remember the evenings in Komotini as two of the best on the whole journey.

IN THE ASSISTANT CHAUFFEUR'S SEAT

It was as though we had had a nasty outbreak of peace and we managed to find an immensely jolly little restaurant overlooking the square where the wine was distinctly passable. Ady spoke joyfully of the service he had given the Rolls. Everyone said, 'How splendid', and we all looked forward to tackling Istanbul which was our next stop. But first, we had to negotiate the Greco/Turkish frontier which, not surprisingly, we found to be an area positively bristling with musketry of one sort or another. Tempers weren't any too good either.

The drive from Komotini to Istanbul was pockmarked by innumerable rather nasty accidents which was hardly surprising considering the diabolical standard of the driving. We crept into Istanbul together to compete with a rush hour which would have won prizes for awfulness. The Rover led the way and Michael and Judy showed a rare navigational ability while Ady's touch at the helm of the Rolls was as sure as ever. The Rolls received an amazing reception with people clapping and running alongside us as we went. It made me think of John Buchan's *Greenmantle*, in which this extraordinary eponymous figure dressed in turquoise mesmerised the people of eastern Turkey in the neighbourhood of Erzerum, where we would be in four days' time. The further we drove into Asia, the more 'the old gal' was held in awe and people were genuinely afraid to come too close and touch her. Nothing was stolen from the car during the entire journey which was not only the result of our attempted security.

We had no trouble finding the centre of Istanbul but then drove round in circles for nearly an hour before we finally located the Park Hotel which we made our base for two nights. Johnny, Ady and I shared a suite at the top of the hotel and that evening we sat in the window of the drawing room and had a drink looking out to the Bosporus to our left and the Golden Horn to the right with the start of Asian Turkey lying straight ahead of us across the water. There were a number of pretty sizeable ships, including a tanker or two, and white froth as the evening ferries chugged their ways to and fro, and I was able to pick up the outline of a couple of mosques. In the gentle flickering lights from the houses, it made a wonderful scene.

The next day I went with Michael and Judy to the Blue Mosque. It was huge and almost overwhelming in its magnificence. We found a student who spoke reasonable English and was keen to act as our guide. He eventually took us to a steep staircase leading to a throne-like platform which had been carved out of solid marble. Here, our guide stopped and spoke. 'The only two people allowed up there to the top are Allah and the Prophet Mohammed,' and then after a slight pause, 'and the electrician if the light bulb fails.' During the afternoon, somewhere in the purlieus of the mosque, Judy had optimistically bought herself a prayer mat, although some of us thought she had left it a little late for such a drastic measure. She then came within a fraction of spending £4,000 on a diamond and sapphire ring until Michael, with his horn-rimmed half-moons perched ever more dangerously on the tip of his nose, had stayed her hand. Michael's glasses were, by now, becoming a tourist attraction to rival 'the old gal' and he was a dab hand at extracting the fullest possible mileage out of them, and the hitching of the trousers did not go entirely unnoticed either.

In a sense Istanbul was the point of no return. The next morning, in heavy rain, the three of us left in the Rolls at seven o'clock. The first drama was almost the last. It was not fully light and just as we began to cross the bridge over the Bosporus, Ady, who had been fidgeting around for a while, asked me if I would hold the wheel for a moment or two. No sooner had I got hold of it than the car began to turn sharply to the right.

Mercifully, Ady was watching and seized the wheel just before we hit the parapet of the bridge and, who knows, he may have saved us from a watery death. No one would have been able to say for sure whether we would have died in Europe or Asia.

All the main political parties were holding conferences in Ankara and hotel after hotel told us that we had as much chance of finding a bed as a Greek restaurant. When we stopped in a traffic jam, we were adopted by a boy in his late teens who thought the Rolls was the most wonderful car he had ever seen. He gave us the names of several hotels to try and also his own telephone number and made us promise to ring if we were in trouble. After trying about twelve hotels, we were in trouble, and so Ady called him and we went round to his family's house. In the end his mother and father, who was a colonel in the Turkish army, said that we could spend the night as best we could with them. But first we joined the family in watching a football match on television between Ankara's number one team and Manchester United. I wish I could remember the result. This was typical of the kindness we met the further along the road we went. The catalyst had, of course, been Ady's car and, appropriately enough, it was Ady who was given the only spare bedroom and the rest of us had to make do with the floor which was a great deal better than sleeping in the cars.

After that we steered a wet and rather muddy path across Turkey and went for quite a way on unmade-up roads and once, between Ankara and Sivas, drove for three miles in thick mud. I spent more time in the Rover hereabouts as Michael was not well. He had been short of breath with a racing heart and one day his pills had gone on with his luggage in the Rolls which all added to the excitement. Judy did a good deal of the driving and the difference in approach between the two cars was glaring. Ady was hellbent on getting to Bombay as quickly as he could, driving as many miles as possible each day without looking very much to the right or the left. The people, the scenery and the food were really incidental to his main preoccupation which was the Rolls. In the Rover Michael and Judy could hardly have been more different. They wanted to enjoy it all, to take their time, to look at the country and to divert, if necessary, to see anything of interest and not to make too much of a business of it all. They were irritated by the aura which surrounded the Rolls. I could understand both points of view. Ady was doing it for a challenge, Michael for a bit of fun. I suppose the fault was Johnny's and mine for poor selection. We had a sparky evening in Sivas when Michael's complaint was that it was becoming too much of a marathon and Ady said he was fed up with always being told what to do and didn't much care for being shouted at – not that he spoke in a whisper himself. Johnny showed, day after day, that *The Times*'s gain had been the diplomatic world's loss.

The road was still not good and it was extremely difficult driving through the hills to Erzerum when we were, for most of the time, in the middle of a long queues of lorries. Erzerum is in the most beautiful setting and we were able to see it below us and in the distance for a long time before we arrived. The rather surprisingly named Kent Hotel did us proud and there was an excellent dinner, along the stuffed aubergine lines, in the restaurant across the street. The next morning I called the BBC from the local telegraph office and after an age talked on an unbroadcastable line to Chris Rea and said I would call in a day or two from Teheran. I thought it was a collect call, the local bandits in charge demanded payment but were no good at travellers cheques. I was forcibly kept there until Michael and Judy came to pick me up half an hour later and when they produced some cash everyone was suddenly full of smiles.

That day's drive offered some incredible scenery as we climbed higher and higher in ever tighter circles on the road to Agri. The views suggested that you could see to the end of the world and beyond. The huge lorries made it hard going on a road full of enormous potholes and loose gravel. Stones flew from under their rear wheels like rifle bullets and the windscreen of the Rolls became increasingly scarred and cracked. Every now and then, especially when the road wound its way up a mountainside, we came across one of the bigger lorries lying halfway down the hill on its side like a stranded whale. At the border, I spoke to a lorry driver, Phil, who lived in Derby and did the journey to China and back six times a year. He had now been stuck for three days with a fault in his gear box. He told me he wasn't frightened by the driving and if you knew what you were doing, it was not as dangerous as it looked. 'Those ones you see on their sides, they try to go too fast. It's as simple as that.' We had a picnic lunch which we ate that day in sight of the snow-clad peak of Mount Ararat in the far distance.

The Rolls had already eaten but they pulled in beside us and it wasn't long before another confrontation began. Ady said encouragingly and quite harmlessly that the Germans they had lunched with had told them we would have no trouble getting in

IN THE ASSISTANT CHAUFFEUR'S SEAT

at the Maku Inn about twenty miles the other side of the Iranian border. Michael said, 'Why?' rather as a marksman might fire a sighter and which to the uninitiated seemed querulous and disbelieving. Ady exploded saying that everything he did was doubted and questioned and it was really no surprise when Johnny told me later that evening that Ady was thinking of pulling out, although it would not have been the most convenient place to have made such a gesture. The Turko/Iranian customs looked discouraging because we found a two-mile-long queue of lorries but cars were allowed to jump this. Even so, it was four hours before we were through all the obstacles on both sides of the border. There was one lorry driver who told us he had already been there for a day and a half and expected to wait at least another two days as they were being obstinate. He also said, rather frighteningly, I thought, that it took only him twenty-one days to drive from Bristol to Kabul in Afghanistan and back, although I doubt this included a four-day wait at the Turko/Iranian customs. As Ady had said, we had no trouble in getting rooms at the Maku Inn.

Before dinner Ady helped Judy to her room with her case and they were away for some time which made the rest of us a trifle nervous. They had had a chat and apparently Judy had made a fulsome apology to him for having occasionally taken an opposite point of view to his. Dinner that night was fun and friendly and also rather good. Afterwards, we met a wild, red-haired Irish poet called Desmond O'Grady. He was the professor of English at Tabriz University and admitted to having written twelve books of verse. Whenever he looked at Judy, you could sense that he felt his thirteenth coming on. O'Grady, Judy and Michael had a highly involved conversation which soon slipped into argument, and of all things, the subject was love. I thought the time had come to go to bed when Michael began to take in vain the names of Abelard and Heloise, particularly while hitching up his trousers.

There is no public transport in Teheran, at least there was none then, and the traffic jams were of momentous proportions. Pahlavi Avenue, which seems to run from the top to the bottom of the city, made Hyde Park Corner in the rush hour look like one of the quicker Grand Prix circuits. Our first stop was at Air India to keep the sponsors happy and while there we learnt that finding accommodation was going to be extremely difficult. The problem was solved a few minutes later when Ady rang his friend, Fuad Majzub, who offered us all the full use of his house which was next door to the Shah's headquarters in north Teheran, the Saadabad Palace. Fuad himself lived in a smaller house not far from the Hilton, while his English wife and children lived in Worcestershire where he kept a collection of two hundred cars. Teheran was the halfway point in our extraordinary journey and I think it was fair to say that so far the cars had been easily the least temperamental members of the party.

CHAPTER

10

FROM THE SAADABAD PALACE TO BOMBAY

AFTER TWO DAYS in Teheran, Michael and Judy left for a brief convalescence at Babolsar on the Caspian Sea where we were to join them at the end of the week. Meanwhile Ady fossicked about with the Rolls and went and looked at Fuad's collection of cars just outside the city. We ate some excellent food with Fuad and his friends and one day, after Johnny, who has a way with these things, had successfully thumbed a lift for us into Teheran, he and I went and looked at the Iranian crown jewels which, if you know your crown jewels, are said to be the finest in the world. They were amazing and their reputation was easy to believe. Their glittering magnificence is impossible to describe. There was one moment of great excitement when an ear-shattering alarm went off and instantly the doors slammed shut and the whole place was immediately hotching with security men. For a moment, I thought they had at last caught up with Johnny, but it transpired that it was a false alarm and we were allowed out.

Fuad Majzub was clearly a man of many parts. He lived in close proximity to the Shah and the house in which we stayed did not appear to have a number or a name. It was just across the walls from the Saadabad Palace. Fuad, who was forty-fiveish, was an accountant who had amassed a great fortune. With rugged good looks, he was always charming and scrupulously polite but never said a word about himself. The nearest we came to being given a hint was one evening when we were dining at home. Fuad had rung and told me how to order dinner from Abrihim who was a gem and the closest Iran can ever have come to Jeeves. Fuad finished the conversation by saying he might come round himself later on, but wouldn't stay to dinner. He arrived at about a quarter to nine looking extremely smart in a dark suit. He stayed talking to us for an hour before leaving, he said, to have dinner with his mother and brother.

We began to eat dinner soon after he had gone and we had hardly finished the first course when there were two loud explosions just over the road. We rushed to the windows to see what had happened and found that the bangs had heralded the start of a firework display of astonishing proportions in the grounds of the Palace. Abrihim told us that they were part of the celebrations for the Crown Prince's birthday. We watched as rockets and every imaginable firework zoomed around us. The old Fourth of June fireworks at Eton were made to look like so many sparklers on wire sticks which we were allowed to have as children around the Christmas tree. We were certain that Fuad had left half an hour earlier to go to the firework party. The timing fitted and so too did his appearance. This was the last time we saw him in Teheran. I hoped that I would come across him in England when I felt I might have got round to quizzing him, but sadly I have never seen him again. Ady always said that he had strong royal connections. I felt that Fuad was much distressed by his wife's decision to live with the children in England and on one of his visits he said, most poignantly, that we had turned his house into a home again. I don't know about that. I had a large double room and for the only time in my life I slept in black sheets which somehow seemed to be the height of decadence, rather than domesticity.

Whenever we shouted his name, Abrihim came running from the kitchen area near the garage. If he was not there, his sister would come, at a rather more gentle pace, but that was a mixed blessing because, as Ady would have put it, she had no English. They were always accompanied by Lady, a huge liver-coloured Great Dane with only three toes on her left hind leg. She was a

FROM THE SAADABAD PALACE TO BOMBAY

heavenly dog as long you were not a stranger for then she admirably demonstrated her ability as a watch dog. The two of them were clearly delighted not to have to look after an empty house, even if only for five days. Abrihim's sister was an excellent cook and her *tour de force* was the Iranian equivalent of an Irish stew which was called abgoosht. But there was nothing even she could do about the goat Fuad had ordered to be killed for us on his farm. It was a very old goat and they didn't come any tougher.

While we were in Teheran, Johnny and I made contact with the British Embassy who had been warned that we were approaching. As a result, one morning we were taken to the Iranian Airways playing fields out by the airport where we watched a somewhat bizarre game of cricket on a football pitch. The Teheran Cricket Club side about to tour India were competing against the Rest and on a pitch which was ungovernably green they lost by six wickets. Ten minutes after the last ball had been bowled, the goalposts were up again and a football match was in progress. Johnny and I spoke at lunch afterwards at the Teheran Club, an imposing piece of Victorian Englishness, when we were put through our paces by an uncompromising north country contingent.

The worst part about leaving Teheran was saying goodbye to Abrihim who was in tears. The Rolls had been completely serviced the day before at Fuad's garage and now it had a new top half to the windscreen which greatly improved the lot of the assistant chauffeur. Michael had said on the telephone to Ady that the 150 miles to Babolsar had taken them six hours and we saw now that the snowline on the hills was pretty low. It was soon snowing and the conditions were most unpleasant. Johnny sat in the front because he had brought a raincoat with him, but the windscreen in front of him was completely covered with snow as there was only one windscreen wiper. Ady was magnificent, as if this was exactly what he had been tuning up for during those five days in Teheran. We ground our way remorselessly upwards and were passed, followed, led and almost drowned by the endless stream of lorries.

The snow was now settling and we began the most hair-raising and spectacular drive so far. The higher we drove, the more terrifying the sheer drop to the right of the car became. At the same time, the beauty was breathtaking and each corner seemed to produce something that was even better. The driving was made worse by the ultra-competitive instincts of our fellow drivers. The eventual descent from 8,500 feet to sea level was, if anything, more alarming than the climb as one hairpin bend followed another on an extremely steep slope. There had been a number of accidents and one empty bus was poised like a supernatural balancing act over an enormous sheer drop. When we had finished the descent we stopped for a badly needed drink and lunch at an excellent new roadside restaurant. We now had an easy forty-mile drive to Babolsar through fertile fruit-growing country, and caviar for dinner in a seaside hotel.

The next day we drove 328 miles through wonderful desert scenery to Bojnourd where we dined that evening with the locals at a barbecue by a roundabout on the edge of the town. It was marvellous food and we were able to drink vodka as long as we were discreet. Michael kept saying, 'This is exactly me,' and the only English any of the locals knew came from a large man who never stopped saying, 'We are brothers,' and every time he said it, he shook hands violently with Michael who had a terrible time preventing his precious vodka from spilling. In the morning, the local director of tourism came to oversee our departure and assured us that we were in 'the best hunting country in Iran. Wild boar, partridges, pheasants, sand grouse, a few leopard and a good number of bears, ibex and wild sheep.' When we next came through, he promised to fix it up for us. At lunch the following day, on the way to Mashhad, an old man wearing a colourful knitted skull cap, began to smoke opium through a hookah. There was much amusement when Johnny and I had a go and great laughter when we coughed ourselves stupid. The old man chortled away happily to himself, but I don't think he would ever have changed our habits from the alcoholic.

We had been warned that the Iranian/Afghanistan frontier was the most difficult of all. When I had picked up my visa at the Afghanistan Embassy in London, I had spoken to someone who seemed frightfully important. I asked him how difficult it would be to gain admission and he wrote a letter in Afghani script which

FROM THE SAADABAD PALACE TO BOMBAY

he told me to present to the customs as we arrived and as we left the country. Now I fingered it nervously. While waiting, we looked at the photographs of the ingenious places in which people who had been caught had tried to hide their drugs. While looking at them, Michael was accosted by a Pakistani whom he recognised instantly. Michael had a holiday house at Frinton in Essex and this Pakistani had been a guard at Liverpool Street Station who used to clip Michael's ticket on the train on Friday evening. The Pakistani was now driving home. I walked across the compound to the car park where there were any number of colourful Afghan lorries and began to take photographs. Anyone would think I had won the jackpot. Whistles blew, orders were shouted and soldiers surrounded me and pointed to the signs forbidding photography which of course I had not seen. I was forced only to expose the film.

When we had moved on to the Afghan side of things, it was even greater chaos, if that were possible. Our fate appeared to be in the hands of a twelve-year-old boy who decided whether our passports were to be stamped or another four-hour wait lay ahead of us. It was now that I brandished the letter from London. It not only got us through but also cups of tea were produced for Michael and me. If looks from our waiting fellow travellers were anything to go by, I wouldn't have lived the day. Goodness knows what can have been written in that letter, but it at least meant that Ady was able to drive most of the way to the hotel in Herat before it was dark.

From there we drove 250 miles to Kandahar through more amazing desert scenery. The big black tents clustered a long way back from the road made me think of Fuad's sheets. We had discovered in Mashhad that matches are like gold dust to these tribesmen and the children from the tents stand by the side of the road stretching through the desert hoping that some will be thrown to them from the passing cars. Michael, expansive as ever, promptly bought a hundred dollars' worth and, once in Afghanistan, we threw them to the children, and went on throwing, for a hundred dollars buys an awful lot of matches. In the summer months the tribesmen spend much of their time scouring the desert for wood which they burn to keep warm in the extreme cold of the winter. But they have no means of lighting the fires and so hence the importance of matches. I shall never forget the joy and disbelief on the faces of these small children when they realised what they had picked up. The journey from Kandahar to Kabul was less spectacular, although that day we drove 358 miles on a road built in slabs by the Russians which was the furthest on any day of the journey. In Kabul, soon to be bombed and shelled almost out of existence, we stayed for two nights at the Intercontinental Hotel,

The largely humourless Austrian manager arranged for us to watch a film of the game of Buzkashi, Afghanistan's only indigenous sport which we had been told about along the way. It turned out to be the most terrifying battle I have ever seen. A dead calf, which has been soaked overnight in water so that it becomes intensely slippery, is placed in a small circle in the middle of a field. The two teams who are on horseback and may number as many as thirty a side, start in their own circle at each end of the ground. The plan is for a rider to pick up the calf by a leg and to ride with it round a marker at their opponents' end of the ground and then to take it back down the field and drop it in his own circle. The first side to score three times wins the game. The rest of his side has to try and prevent the opposition from forcing the rider to drop the calf. It is a brutal game both for the riders and the horses. In a game of thirty a side, if a man comes off his horse in a mêlée, he will almost certainly be killed. The horses are highly trained and part of that training is to send them into the desert and leave them without water for three days to dull their minds. I was glad no one offered to take us to a game.

We spent half our second day in Kabul in Chicken Street buying Afghan coats to take home as presents. To hear Ady first of all trying to make up his mind what his children would like and then attempting to bargain with the shop-owner was worth all the deprivations we had encountered on the journey so far. Michael took a paternalistic overview and just stood or lent on anything and eternally hitched up his trousers as he presided over Judy's shopping. If there had ever been a gold medal for shopping, Judy would undoubtedly have finished on the rostrum and, left to herself, would have bought most of Chicken Street. As it was, she kept coming out of shops wearing every sort of coat and asking for our opinions which she preferred to coincide with her own. We all bought our fill and after hitching up his trousers for one last emphatic time, Michael even plunged in and bought something for his daughter, Vicky. We also visited the magnificent British Embassy set in spacious grounds which had been designed to suit Curzon when he had been Queen Victoria's man in Kabul.

We left Kabul in the Rolls at a quarter past seven one morning and I don't think any of us had any idea of the scenery and the views awaiting us, first in the Kabul Gorge, and then the Khyber Pass. This is a passage describing the journey which I have taken from the diary I was keeping on a daily basis.

> Then, quite suddenly, we found ourselves descending the Kabul Gorge. We had been told that it was more impressive than the Khyber and as I am writing this at the end of a day on which I have seen both, I can only say that this is right. My first impression was that I was sitting on the top of the world. The views were staggering. The sheer brutality of the rock-faced mountains, the drama of a narrow winding road perched like an uneasy gutter on the edge of an old house, the breathtaking views into the far distance, the look below us at two or three small semi-circles of road going round yet more jutting promontories of rock, each one below the other in an interminable descent and they were all part of our road. It was extraordinary too, to look upwards at the mouths of some of the short tunnels we had just come through and which were now above us. There was always yet another large lorry apparently skating along a piece of road far above our heads that we had driven over ourselves perhaps ten minutes earlier. And above that, the bright blue sky with not a cloud to be seen, and all the intriguing colours of sunlight and shade on the mountainside. Far below us, the stream at the bottom of the gorge frothed happily away and on each side autumn had turned the greens into rust and gold. Every corner produced a new sensation and with it came the disappointment that we could not go back and see it all over again.

The Afghan customs and immigration clicked their heels like nobody's business when I showed them the letter from the London Embassy and we were through in minutes. On the Pakistan side, the authorities could not have been more friendly and it was something of a shock to hear English spoken and to be back on the left-hand side of the road. The banks would not change money on a Sunday and so Johnny and I were led into a small shop which sold just about everything and would also change our Afghanis into rupees. The boss was a huge fat man with a perfect crew cut who looked exactly as Peter Ustinov would have done if he had been asked to play the part of a money-changer on the Afghan/Pakistan border. We had a rather indifferent lunch and from now on Ady was in trouble because he did not care for 'hot' food. Michael and Judy, a vision in yellow, then arrived and we went through the Pakistan customs together at Michael's insistence. A dapper moustachioed officer in a white uniform was delighted with the Rolls. He came over and looked at it and, amid much laughter, waved us through. Ady was brilliant at this sort of thing and once again he and 'the old gal' had saved us an hour or two.

We were then into the Khyber where we made the mistake of several times stopping to take photographs. The Khyber is in the middle of the northern tribal areas and the tribes do not live peacefully together. Even tourists can be in danger if they stop other than in the designated stopping places, but we did not know this. A bullet can be the penalty. There was one staggering view deep into Pakistan from a spot which had been officially named Look-out Corner. We went through a village where we were told we could buy almost anything we could ever want at duty-free prices and it is furnished entirely by smuggling. Down the hill, out of sight of the main road, there was apparently an enormous amount of weaponry for sale. I kept a careful eye on Ady and Michael. There was not much light remaining when we left the Khyber and emerged on to the plains and it was dark by the time we arrived at Dean's Hotel in Peshawar where we spent a comfortable night in old-fashioned colonial surroundings. This hotel was very much a relic of the British Raj. One old servant brought his hands together in front of his face and bowed when he saw the Rolls. After we had got out, he came over to me and said, solemnly but with a smile, 'I have not seen anything like it since the British left.'

It seemed strange the next morning to hear people talking about the Test series between Pakistan and New Zealand which had just ended with Pakistan winning by two matches to none. I know Johnny and I felt on home ground once we had passed over into Pakistan and not only because they spoke English which, of course, made life easier. The Rolls had had a puncture in Afghanistan and then between Peshawar and Rawalpindi the horn packed it in, but it was not long before we found a ramshackle garage on the side of the road. It did not take the chap in charge long to put the horn right. At least he coaxed a noise out of it, if not quite such a convincing one as it had in the first place.

Beds were hard to come by in 'Pindi and we ended up at the house of John Craven, a wing commander and Air Attaché at the British Embassy. He lived just across the road in the neighbouring city of Islamabad and he and his wife, Audrey, were about to drive home to England at the end of his last appointment before he was to retire and, so he said, run a pub. I think that between us we gave them some useful advice for their journey home, although we never heard how it all went. Michael probably advised them on how to run the pub.

On the way to Lahore we had another back wheel blow-out with which Ady dealt as if he had been changing Michael Schumacher's tyres at Silverstone with Murray Walker's stopwatch ticking away. If there had been an award for this sort of thing, Ady would by now have had the crossed spanners and at least three bars. Then it was the Indian border which, as it is closed to Indians and Pakistanis, takes no time at all.

It took us another ten days to reach Bombay. We had a hectic social life in Delhi where we stayed for three of the four nights in the officers' mess of the Border Security Force. One of Johnny's hockey-playing friends commanded the BSF and he looked after us wonderfully well. He also arranged for us to stay at Tekanpur, their headquarters, on the journey down to Bombay. While we were there we watched a remarkable exhibition of tent pegging.

Riders, going at full gallop, use spears to destroy the wooden pegs holding up a tent so that it collapses on top of its inmates. It requires great precision. We drove on to have fun with my old commentating chum from 1974, the Maharajah of Baroda, who entertained us in Delhi and later in Baroda where we spent our last night but one before arriving in Bombay. The Prince also arranged for us to spend the following night in the guest house of his cotton factory at Surat. In between these visits, we stayed at the State Hotel in Jaipur which was better than its name suggests, and in the Lake Palace Hotel at Udaipur which was built on a rock in the lake and had been one of the Maharani of Mewar's palaces and is just about the most romantic situation I have ever come across.

It was almost exactly three o'clock in the afternoon of 21 November when, after covering 7,867 miles in forty-six days and nights, the Rolls, to great acclaim, drew to a halt outside the front entrance of the Taj Mahal Hotel in Bombay. Ady had driven every inch of the way himself and we sat down to lunch a couple of hours later than we had originally intended while some of the England cricketers, who had arrived two days earlier, had a good look at 'the old gal' in front of the hotel. It was her finest hour.

After two days preening ourselves, we all went our separate ways except for Johnny and me. We set off round India with Tony Greig's England side. Judy flew back to Sydney and I am glad to say that any differences we may have had on the journey soon disappeared and her house is always my first port of call on any visit to Sydney. She remains the loyalist of friends. The two cars were shipped back to England with richly deserved campaign medals. Ady and Michael flew back to London but I doubt they felt any aeroplane was big enough to house the two of them at the same time. Michael retired from the stock exchange and sadly died not long afterwards on a visit to Kenya. Ady eventually sold the 'old gal' and still farms in Hampshire with quite a collection of cars. I doubt he has any more Austrian than he did when he spoke to that dummy policeman high in the Austrian Alps. *Anno domini* brought about Johnny's eventual retirement as cricket correspondent of *The Times* but there are still few Test Matches

FROM THE SAADABAD PALACE TO BOMBAY

around the world that are entirely safe from his presence. He remains the greatest of friends and is now a member of the committee of MCC. Every now and then he cannot resist the opportunity to light up the sporting pages of his old paper. He is as worth reading now as he ever was and is perhaps still the only one who is able to put earth-shattering events such as the current problems with match-fixing and betting into an immediate and sound perspective. My own progress since our adventure, is, I hope, reasonably well documented in the pages that follow.

CHAPTER 11

ENTER THE DEMON KING

I AM OFTEN ASKED which country I enjoy touring the most and people are surprised when I tell them it is India. Of course, Australia is fun and West Indian beaches are unique, to say nothing of the planter's punches, and is there anywhere more beautiful and enjoyable than Cape Town? And on it goes. India is different. The food, the culture, the conditions, the people, the history and all the incredible things to see make it so. If it had only the Taj Mahal, it would still be almost impossible for me to put any other country ahead of India. I know it is not everyone's idea of an ideal holiday. There's all that poverty to start with and there are many, I know, who have been put off India for life by the drive into the city from Bombay airport. If you are to survive, let alone flourish, in India, you have to learn to accept the desperate poverty and the smells that go with it. Those who are unable to do this will look at you in disbelief when you tell them that there is a bigger and richer middle class in India than there is in the whole of the United States of America. It is a country of dramatic contrasts and mind-boggling extremes.

It is difficult to reconcile the worst parts of that drive into Bombay with the magnificent palaces in which the maharajahs still live and indeed with the lifestyle of the mega-rich Indians. Yet this is one of the eternal fascinations of the country. On a more practical and personal level, I love their food. I have always

ENTER THE DEMON KING

got on extremely well with the Indians who, by and large, are a gentle race. It could hardly be more different from England and that, for me, is one of its great charms. Things move slowly, Indian time is late, taxi drivers never know where you want to go even if their old Ambassador cars don't break down, and they speak hardly any English. The country is riddled with the worst sort of bureaucracy – but who taught them that? The timetable of Indian Airlines, the internal airline, is more a work of fiction than a basis for negotiation. That may not be much of a recommendation, but I love it and have had an enormous amount of fun there over the years and I hope I have not finished yet.

Arriving at the Taj Mahal Hotel in Bombay, whether in a 1921 Rolls-Royce or a rattling, smoking taxi, is one of the great moments. The Gateway to India looms over one's shoulder, half the population of Bombay seems to be there as well, the splendidly beturbaned chap who greets the cars and opens the door would put any self-respecting peacock to shame. The only anxiety is to find out if you have been allotted the room you asked for in the old part of the hotel. That is a request which I have often found has left London but appears not to have reached Bombay and you have to be at your most persuasive if it has not. The old rooms are bigger and so much nicer than those in the huge tower block overlooking the Gateway. I was now out of luck as I settled in for the start of three unforgettable months with Tony Greig's side.

It is never easy to win a Test series in India. The pitches are prepared for the Indian spinners, the climate and the food count against the touring side and once things start to go wrong, the umpires get it in the neck as well. Now, miraculously, the England side overcame all these obstacles and to great Indian dismay, won the first three Test Matches. The First Test was played at Kotla in Delhi where I had not been since Lyn Wellings had behaved so extravagantly with his typewriter thirteen years before. After winning the toss and batting, Dennis Amiss made a big hundred, reaching it with a six which had always been Ken Barrington's favourite party trick, and took England almost to 400. This was John Lever's first Test Match and he now proceeded to take 7/46 and made the ball swing all over the place. He took three more when India followed on and finished with 10/70 in the match which in addition to an innings of 53 meant a useful first Test. The Second Test was played at Eden Gardens in Calcutta on a pitch which had been especially prepared for the Indian spinners, Bedi, Chandrasekhar and Prasanna. They were thwarted by that remarkable innings of 103 by Tony Greig which took him almost seven hours. He came in at 90/4 and with Roger Tolchard who was playing in his first Test, put on 142 for the fifth wicket. Tolchard made 67 and played a more valuable innings than some who have made a hundred in their first Test. He and Greig used their pads and every possible form of improvisation to keep out the spinners on a pitch where the ball was turning square. Greig, tall and oozing obstinate determination, contrasted strongly with Tolchard who was a smaller figure with a certain restless jauntiness. Tolchard scampered, Greig strode. Tolchard tickled, squirted and cut, Greig was expansively ambitious when he had the chance. Tolchard was a terrier wagging his tail hot on the scent of a rat, Greig was a Thoroughbred reining himself in. What fun it was and the Indians could not make head nor tail of it. The Indian spinners bowled 155 overs between them and took 9/269 when they must have expected to bowl England out for under a hundred. England won by ten wickets.

The Third Test was played on a seam bowlers' pitch at Chepauk in Madras and with Lever again in fine form, England won by two hundred runs, winning their first series in India since 1933/34 under Douglas Jardine. It was during this match that Bishen Bedi, the Indian captain, accused John Lever of using Vaseline to get extra shine on the ball. Traces of Vaseline had appeared on the ball and the England camp vigorously denied the accusation that it had been done deliberately. But the Vaseline had come from Lever. In order to stop sweat running from his forehead into his eyes, Bernard Thomas, the physiotherapist, had cut out strips of gauze impregnated with Vaseline, which he stuck to Lever's forehead just above his eyebrows to deflect the flow of sweat. Lever who always used sweat from his forehead to polish the ball, cannot have avoided getting some of the Vaseline on to his fingers and then on to the ball.

ENTER THE DEMON KING

On the rest day, the Sunday, there was a press conference I shall never forget in the team room in the hotel and this was all the Indian press wanted to talk about. At one point, Ken Barrington, the manager, who was taking the questions, was becoming flustered. Greig immediately stood up and said that as he was the England captain out on the field they should be asking him the questions. One could only admire the way in which he was prepared to stand up and be counted. Before even the first question came, he went on to say that the Indian press should not be taken in by a red herring like this. What they should be doing was writing encouragingly and optimistically about the future of Indian cricket. He told them it was a waste of time to go back over something stupid like this. He went on for some minutes and so persuasive was he that all the Indian writers did as he suggested and tried to write encouraging things about India's cricket in the next day's papers. It was a masterful performance by Greig who, as always, was plausible in the extreme and took in the entire Indian press corps who had been on the point of being given a good story by Barrington's reactions to their questions. During the tour, the Indian Board of Control gave a big dinner in Bombay for which the bigwigs of MCC came over. The next day, Gubby Allen spoke glowingly to Michael Melford about Greig's ability to say the right thing when it mattered. It was not long before he was going to be forced to revise that opinion.

The Fourth Test, in Bangalore, was won by India and was not without controversy. It was said one of the members of the Indian Board of Control had gone into the umpires' room before the start and had been heard to tell them that unless India won the Fourth Test, the Wankhede Stadium in Bombay would be virtually empty when it came to the Fifth Test. It was in this Test Match in England's second innings that I saw what I considered to be the worst decision I have ever seen in all the years I have watched Test cricket. Roger Tolchard was facing Chandrasekhar. He played well back to a ball and when it hit him on the pad, both legs were so far outside the leg stump that there was daylight between his feet and the stump. Yet the umpire's finger went up as if it had been the most clear-cut decision of the series.

England played four games in Sri Lanka, who were close to being elected to Test Match status, on the way to Perth where they had been allowed one game in which to try and acclimatise to Australian conditions before the Centenary Test began on 12 March. The WACA ground is never the ideal place for any side to try and acclimatise to Australian conditions. The pitch is faster than any other, with a steeper bounce, and is not going to do anyone much good when it comes to playing at Melbourne where the pitch is slow, with an increasingly low bounce. I am sure it was not part of an Australian plot, but not only did England gain little from it, they also had the worst of their match against Western Australia. They will not have arrived in Melbourne overflowing with confidence.

The Centenary Test was the first of the many centenaries and jubilees and so on which were celebrated around the cricketing world in the next few years, and it was much the best. Every England cricketer who had played for his country in Australia was invited by the Australian Board, as were the Australians who had played against England. It was a colossal gathering and a great honour to be even superficially part of it. A great number of old friendships were revived, the partying was non-stop, a huge amount of booze was drunk and, with one exception whom I will come to, a great time was had by everyone. The old Windsor Hotel in Spring Street, which was still the home of touring sides in Melbourne, was the centre of the social side while the MCG took care of the cricket.

I have always preferred the Sydney Cricket Ground to the MCG because it is essentially a cricket ground whereas the MCG is a vast stadium which was redesigned as the home for the Olympic Games in 1956. This turned it into a concrete jungle and of course it has a terrific atmosphere when it is full but, for all that, I don't think it has the true character of a cricket ground. The SCG has changed more recently, but has still managed to keep some of its old character, even though I hate the huge floodlight pylons with their ugly black stalks. The old Hill has gone but you can see where it was. That splendid scoreboard is still there on the old Hill behind the Doug Walters Stand. It is a protected building,

ENTER THE DEMON KING

as is the lovely Victorian pavilion which has not been touched, both tributes to a more gentle age when life did not move so fast and television was not all-powerful. There is no longer a grassy bank on the Paddington Hill either, but the spot is recognisable and the ground has not been suffocated by the dead hand of uniformity. The SCG, even in its modern guise, is more redolent of cricket than the Melbourne Cricket Ground. Thank goodness the 2000 Olympics has left the SCG well alone.

The invasion from England took Melbourne by storm. John Arlott, who never much cared for Australia, made an exception for the Centenary Test, both to commentate for the BBC and write for the *Guardian*. He had a somewhat turbulent journey out, travelling on the same flight as most of the old players. After a good dinner, washed down, I am sure, by a suitable vintage, he prepared for sleep and to discourage his neighbours or anyone else from talking to him, he left his headphones in his ears but made the mistake of not unplugging them. He was soon well away and this was noticed after a while by Bill Edrich who was himself conducting a robust party elsewhere on the aeroplane. Bill stopped by Arlott's side and turned the volume of his radio not only on, but up to the maximum, whereupon Arlott took off both metaphorically and physically. He just failed to hit the roof of the aeroplane but on landing back in his seat, he unwound a right hook of which he should have been proud and caught Bill somewhere on the face. Bill wore the scar proudly for the duration of the match. I wonder if Arlott had to have another bottle to get himself off to sleep again. He was not pleased, while Bill will have found it extremely funny, even allowing for any flow of blood.

I still have an old Windsor Hotel envelope on which I collected the signatures of Harold Larwood, Keith Miller and Brian Statham when I was having a drink in someone's room one evening – not a bad triumvirate of fast bowlers. For those few days in Melbourne, it was like walking through the pages of a dusty old Wisden. Every time I went up in the lift at the Windsor or walked round the corner to Collins Street I seemed to bump into never less than three world-famous cricketers. What was very noticeable was the camaraderie which had existed between the players on both sides in the old days. After the Bodyline tour, for example, Harold Larwood settled in Sydney while Tiger O'Reilly and Jardine became the greatest of friends.

The Centenary Test was an extraordinary cricket match, not least because of all that was going on behind the scenes. By then the formation of what became World Series Cricket was well under way – it had begun in mid-1976 – and the influence of Kerry Packer loomed large in the Pavilion at the MCG. There were players who had already signed for him, those who were still thinking about it and those who were hoping to be asked. It was during the Centenary Test Match that four England players were signed to play for Packer, although one, John Snow, had played his last Test Match the year before in England and was not part of the tour. The other three were Greig, Knott and Underwood and so both dressing rooms will have been on the alert during those five days as Packer's men flitted through the corridors.

England won the toss and Greig put Australia in to bat on a pitch which held some moisture and in forty-four eight-ball overs, Australia were bowled out for 138. It was an unbelievably good day for England and we all walked back across the Fitzroy Gardens, past Captain Cook's cottage, certain that England could count upon a more than useful first-innings lead. This did not allow for Dennis Lillee who, on a day on which the ball moved and swung, bowled superbly taking 6/26, as well as making enough of those extravagantly offensive gestures to infuriate the English and get the crowd going in that huge Southern Stand. His sparring partner was now Max Walker who, being a Victorian, brought the house down with each of his four wickets. No one managed more than Greig's 18 and England were out for 95 which gave Australia a crucially important lead of 43. Every night in Melbourne was party night and each morning there was quite a collection of sore heads in that cheerless old press box which even had electric heaters on the walls. I've been as cold there as I've been at any cricket match, although in March it was warm enough. The wind howls through the stands and a couple of sweaters are often a necessity for the Boxing Day Test Match.

ENTER THE DEMON KING

Australia lost three second-innings wickets that night but the next day their middle order flourished. Ian Davis and Doug Walters got into the sixties, David Hookes, who memorably hit Tony Greig for four successive fours, passed 50, while Rod Marsh became the first Australian wicket-keeper ever to make a hundred against England. Greg Chappell declared at 419/9, leaving England to make 463 to win. It was now that Derek Randall played the innings of a lifetime. The impish, loose-limbed, highly amusing character from Worksop, who had played his first Test on England's recent visit to India, strode to the wicket when Bob Woolmer departed with the score at 28. Lillee and Co. must have felt they could knock this curious looking chap over as soon as look at him. He talked to himself at the crease, calling himself 'Rags' which was short for Ragamuffin, and was the sort of character probably only cricket produces. There was always something boyishly cheeky about Randall at the crease and the longer Lillee bowled at him without getting him out, the more angry he became. Randall began to play his strokes from the start, several times early on bringing Mike Brearley down the wicket from the other end on a cautionary journey. It will not even have occurred to the Australians that they might lose, though the score reached 113 before Brearley perished, lbw to Lillee. Randall and Amiss now took root, Randall as cheerfully untamed as ever and Amiss looking much more solemn and studious, as was his nature at the crease. They had taken England to 191/2 at the end of the fourth day and it was good to see the Australians walk home scratching their heads as they went.

On the England batsmen went the next morning and when England had passed 250 with only two wickets down, even the most one-eyed Australians will have sensed they could just lose. At 279, Amiss was bowled by a shooter for 64, but Randall, who had now had a couple of lives, went on past 150. There was a lovely moment, in keeping with the occasion and all that it stood for, when Randall was 161. He played forward to Greg Chappell and was given out caught behind by Marsh who took the ball low down in front of him. Randall turned to go but Marsh held up his hands to indicate that the ball had pitched first and called him back. With such a tense finish building up, it took a great sportsman to do that. I can think of one or two who would have been all too happy to let him go. I wonder where Kerry Packer would have stood on that one.

The score had reached 346 when Randall played forward to the leg spin of Kerry O'Keeffe and was out to a splendid left-handed catch by Gary Cozier, who had not otherwise distinguished himself, at forward short leg. Randall had set a precedent he was never able to live up to. Anyone who had batted as well as he had then, should have played more than forty-seven Test Matches and have been a regular in the England side for a long time. He was the best English fielder of his generation, a brilliant humourist who communicated with the crowd, but for some reason, which was almost certainly psychological, he never fulfilled the talent we all saw on those two days. Greig and Knott both reached the forties but England had too much to do and were all out for 417. Australia had won by 45 runs which was the exact margin of their victory on this same ground one hundred years before in the match we were now celebrating. It was an incredible coincidence at the end of a great game of cricket.

There was one tragic figure at Melbourne. Clive Taylor was the cricket correspondent of the *Sun*. He could, and frequently did, write under a *nom de plume* for the broadsheets. He was not only a fine writer whose pen would have met any challenge, he also knew a great deal about cricket. He had been with us in India, and now in Melbourne he became seriously sick. He was in great pain but somehow managed to drag himself to the ground each day. He had an horrendous flight home and was rushed to hospital where his illness was diagnosed and treated as hepatitis. Actually, he was suffering from peritonitis, and three weeks later, just as the English season was beginning, he died at the ridiculously early age of fifty. He was an exceptional and charming man and one of the most able in the press box during my career. He had an excellent sense of humour and was always prepared to help anyone. Those of us who knew him still miss him very much.

By the time we got back to England to prepare for another visit by the Australians, none of us had any idea what lay just round

ENTER THE DEMON KING

the corner. With the advantage of hindsight there was the odd clue. It seemed strange that Lillee who had been at his best in Melbourne, and in six Tests that Australian summer had taken 47 wickets, was unavailable for the tour of England for health reasons. He had been told that the stress fractures in his vertebrae were in danger of causing permanent damage if he did not rest. In April, the South African press announced that four of their leading players had signed a lucrative contract to play matches round the world. No one had picked up on it. The first time most people heard what had been going on was on 9 May when Ian Wooldridge broke the full story on the front page of the *Daily Mail*. Thirty-five of the best cricketers in the world had 'secretly signed contracts to become freelance mercenaries'. They would play Test and one-day matches for the principal benefit of Kerry Packer's Channel Nine television network in Australia and it was his money that was bankrolling the venture. The game's establishment were dumbfounded, but it was the Australian Cricket Board that had prompted Packer's involvement by refusing to sell him the exclusive rights to televise all international cricket in Australia on Channel Nine. They had decided to stay with the Australian Broadcasting Corporation although Packer had offered them a great deal more money.

The players were being paid far more money than they would ever have earned from the establishment game and their fees ranged from A$16,500 to A$35,000 a year which, in 1977, was a lot more than it sounds now. The only player Packer wanted but was unable to get was Geoffrey Boycott, the last person I would have expected to have thrown away the chance to make a bob or two. There are a number of different stories about why this came about and one of them was that Boycott demanded to be made captain of the Rest of the World side which was to play six Super Tests and a number of one-day internationals against Packer's Australians. This would have been an unacceptable condition to Packer. Boycott said he had talked to Packer early in 1977 in Sydney when he was still in his self-imposed exile from the England side, and had agreed to sign. When he was later shown a copy of his contract in England, he apparently found that several things differed from the discussions he had had in Sydney. Always the odd man out.

Two highly respected Australian journalists, Peter McFarline and Alan Shiell, who had cleverly tracked down most of the story themselves, discovered that Wooldridge was about to break it in England. They therefore filed it to their own papers on the night of 7 May from Hove where Sussex were playing the Australians, for publication in Australia on Monday, 9 May. That evening, McFarline told his great friend, John Snow, with whom he was staying, what he had written and, with McFarline's permission, Snow rang Greig who was giving a party for the two sides. It would have been marvellous to have seen Greig's face as he heard the news and it will certainly have put a dampener on the party spirit. The next day Sussex played a Sunday League match against Yorkshire and I was there to cover it for the *Guardian*. When I arrived at the County Ground, I was unaware that anything was afoot, but in the press box I found just about all the number one cricket writers in Fleet Street and I was soon brought up to date. The original intention of the Packer camp had been to release the story either during or immediately after the Lord's Test Match towards the end of June, when Greig would already have been appointed as captain of England for the whole series against Australia. This would have made it difficult for the English authorities to sack him.

One interesting and amusing sideline to it all from my own point of view that day, was the difficulty I had in convincing the *Guardian* Sports Editor, John Samuel, that the story was authentic. He realised that if it was true, the implications were colossal. When I first told him, he asked me to ring him back in an hour. John Arlott was the cricket correspondent and he wanted to consult with him. I wrote a story for the front page and filed it but still Samuel was not wholly convinced. I stayed in Brighton that night as I was watching the Australians play Sussex the next day. At about nine o'clock, I rang the office to find out if they were happy with what I had written and Samuel again asked me if I was certain the details were correct. He had Arlott on another line who doubted it all because he had heard nothing about

ENTER THE DEMON KING

Packer, and being president of the Cricketers' Association, was sure he would have had some advance warning. Any doubts they may still have had were dispelled when they saw the first editions of the other papers. Only the *Daily Telegraph* failed to mention the story for they felt that too much was still up in the air.

The forthcoming series against Australia took second place to all of this and with both sides shaping up to one another, it was obviously a story that was going to run and run. I saw the Australians play Glamorgan at Swansea a week later when they almost lost and they were undoubtedly under great pressure because of this whole business. The media, to say nothing of their own Board, were constantly nipping at their heels. It was not long after this that I found myself back at Hove watching Sussex play Gloucestershire and the most significant spectator there was none other than Kerry Packer himself. He had just arrived in England and had come down to Hove to see Greig. I was asked by Greig to go to the captain's room at the top of the pavilion to meet him. Packer was unknown in England except from photographs which had appeared in the papers since news of his coup had broken. He was a big man with a huge head and had been labelled by Wooldridge as the man in the stocking mask, and it was just what he looked like. He was also phenomenally rich.

Kerry Packer was the younger son of Sir Frank Packer who had powerful interests in the media world. He had inherited when his elder brother, Clyde, had moved away from the family business. Greig had been at pains to point out to anyone who cared to listen that Kerry was a tough man who was used to getting his own way. He told us he was an extremely shrewd businessman who showed great loyalty to those who worked for him. When I met him now, he was accompanied by John Cornell, another entrepreneur, who had had the original idea of a cricket circus when he had been asked by his friend Dennis Lillee how he could raise more money for the top players. Austin Robertson, a journalist from Perth and a partner of Cornell's, was also in the room. Greig himself said very little. After some pleasantries about the weather, I asked Packer what he was doing at Hove.

'Watching cricket which I love,' he answered quietly. 'And I don't know many people with these facilities – the captain's room, I mean.' He and Greig laughed.

I asked him if he had come to see the authorities at Lord's. 'I am prepared to see the relevant cricket authorities at any time they wish to see me, but they have not shown any indication of doing so yet. I have not come across as a pressure tactic, though.'

The thirty-five players he had already signed consisted of eighteen from Australia and seventeen from the rest of the world. I asked him if he thought a constantly recurring series between Australia and the Rest of the World might not have a limited appeal. 'There may be other sides we can bring to Australia, and then we would have Test Matches between two countries. One thing I want to make clear is that there is no chance of us going away, just disappearing off the scene. We are here to stay, I can assure you of that. I know this will be good for cricket in both the short and the long term. In Australia the public are not getting the top-class cricket they want. Australia are playing India this year. Lillee and Thomson versus India will be a débâcle. Then there is the series against England next year which will produce good cricket. The following year Australia are in India and Pakistan and there are no Tests at home. Australia is the best place to play cricket, for crowds and money. And yet only one successful tour is planned in three years.'

Within a month, the full West Indies side had been signed.

'Cricket is short of money, and the organisation of the game is denying the best players in the world opportunities to earn what they deserve. This is not a panacea which will solve cricketers' financial problems overnight. It is, though, the biggest step taken by cricketers to try to find that solution. Where the benefit will come is that it will lift the payment for ordinary cricketers above what they are getting now.'

I asked him how, but he ducked this one and refused to come back to it.

'To go on with what I was saying. When top players start to do much better, as happens in any successful business, it gives the player at a lower level the incentive to work harder. He knows there are real financial rewards for him if he can succeed. We've just had the Centenary Test Match. It's taken the cricket authorities a hundred years to recognise the plight of cricketers; don't expect me to solve it all in twelve months. This is a big step towards it, and to making cricketers work harder and therefore to making cricket more attractive.'

He stressed it would not make the slightest difference to him if the authorities refused to talk for he had planned everything in considerable detail.

'How can they find out if we are going to benefit cricket if they are not prepared to talk to us? I think there is a suggestion in people's minds that we are trying to take over cricket. The reason I would like to have talks is to find a solution where we do not have to take over cricket. We don't want to. We would like to see it administered by the traditional authorities. That's why I would like to talk – not to have more influence, but to have less.'

Why did you not tell the authorities what you had done before you went public?

'In business you don't tell your opponents what you are going to do; you do it and let them get on with it. Whether you like it or not I have influence given to me by the top players in the game who thought they were getting a raw deal. If the authorities want a fight you would have thought they would have talked to me – if only to see how I fight.'

Packer had persuaded himself that, for public consumption at any rate, his objectives had changed since that thinktank had told him that exclusive coverage of cricket in Australia would make good television money. Cleverly, he had now made it appear that he had stolen the moral high ground when, in truth, his moral high ground was no higher than Channel Nine's profit and loss account. Although he had told me nothing that I didn't know, he had confirmed it all in a manner which brooked no argument. He was undoubtedly a formidable customer. I met him twice more that summer; once when he played for the Australian press against the English press at Harrogate on the rest day of the Headingley Test Match, and one evening just before that when I joined a dinner table presided over by Packer and Greig in the Ladbroke's Hotel by the station in Leeds where, in those days, the England team stayed. On this occasion, we were joined by Mike Brearley who had taken on the England captaincy when Greig had been deposed for signing with Packer. If they could have persuaded Brearley to join them, it really would have messed things up for the England authorities. Packer and Brearley spoke for some time and the gist of what Brearley said was that, while he had great sympathy with his plans and his wish to pay cricketers more, he would not be able to join him himself. Brearley had taken an intellectual approach to it all which may have been the one angle Packer, Greig and the rest had not explored.

No one was suggesting Brearley was one of the best players in the world, although he was to become the best captain. I am sure he will have realised why Packer approached him and he would not have wanted to have allowed himself to be used as a tool. He may also have felt that life as an opening batsman playing continually against the fastest bowlers in the world might not be as much fun as all that. Also, Brearley had other plans for his life.

Packer had realised by now that while it would have been all right if I had joined his side of the argument, I was really of so little importance that it did not matter. On the rest day at Harrogate he looked like a cricketer who had not touched a bat that often since leaving school but who had known a bit about it then. He will only have played to help get across the image of being a man who loved cricket deeply rather than someone who was now interested in it only because of the financial gain there was to be made out of it. There was a certain amount of irony that day in that Alan Shiell who, with Peter McFarline, had broken the story in Australia and was a strong opponent, was keeping wicket beside Packer who was fielding at first slip. I think he chatted mostly to his neighbour at second slip.

The drama going on in the background took a good deal of the gloss off the Test series in 1977 which was won by England under Mike Brearley's captaincy. The Australian dressing room was worse affected of the two and their manager, Len Maddocks, a splendid chap but perhaps not up to the level of intrigue around him, had a difficult few months with Packer players and non-Packer players in the same camp. Maddocks, a wicket-keeper, was

ENTER THE DEMON KING

Jim Laker's tenth wicket in the second innings at Old Trafford in 1956 and his nineteenth of the match. Perhaps the most noticeable point in the series came at Trent Bridge in the Third Test when Geoffrey Boycott decided, for whatever reason, to come out of his tent. I am sure the state of the Australian bowling had nothing to do with it. He made a hundred which took him a long time and he needed the inspiration of Alan Knott who made a superb hundred himself, to see him to three figures. At Headingley, in the Fourth Test, he went one better and became the first batsman ever to make his hundredth first-class hundred in a Test match when he made 191 and helped England to an innings victory and an unassailable 3–0 lead against a thoroughly demoralised Australian side. Maybe, at the eleventh hour, he was hoping Kerry Packer might think again.

Soon the dramas shifted from the cricket field to the High Court in the Strand. Kerry Packer and World Series Cricket had brought an action against the cricketing establishment for restraint of trade. By banning the players who had signed for Packer from taking part in cricket under their control, the establishment was effectively curtailing their earnings and preventing them from plying their trade. The cricket authorities were convinced of their own righteousness and, watching the trial through the newspapers, I felt it was as if they saw themselves as Empire against the infidel from the days when Queen Victoria was on the throne and justice may have been more about playing for the right side. The case was heard by Mr Justice Slade whose brother Julian, rather incongruously perhaps, had written the musical *Salad Days*. Packer's case was orchestrated by Bob Alexander who was reckoned to be the supreme advocate of his day and his skill undoubtedly went a long way towards winning the argument for Packer. It was ironical that when he gave up the bar, he was to become the Chairman of the National Westminster Bank, one of the game's main sponsors in England. He then went on to become president of the MCC. The High Court gave Packer all he wanted. The establishment were dumbfounded and after much consultation, decided not to appeal. The trial had cost the game dear, both financially and in terms of reputation. The nasty taste that was left in their mouths will not have been helped to disappear when it was rumoured that Lord Denning, the Master of the Rolls, anticipating an appeal, had decided to keep this case for himself. The inference was that he would have found for the cricket authorities. But then, maybe it was nothing more than spurious gossip.

CHAPTER

12

PACKER TRIUMPHANT

KERRY PACKER'S VICTORY in the High Court was the green light, if not the chequered flag, for World Series Cricket (WSC). For the next six months the effects of Packer's revolution reverberated around the cricket world and I was lucky enough to be in the thick of it. In Australia, both forms of the game were competing with each other. WSC was to be played in front of Channel Nine's cameras with the Australian side competing against the West Indies and the Rest of the World, while the Australia selected by the Australian Cricket Board was to do battle over five Test Matches against India in front of the Australian Broadcasting Corporation's (ABC) cameras. I flew into Melbourne on 22 November two days before WSC began their first match proper at the VFL Park at Waverley.

The Packer circus did not at first have permission to play on the regular grounds, so they had to hire venues like the VFL Park which was the new home of the Victorian Football League. Facilities for cricket did not exist there and John Maley, who had been the curator, as the Australians call their groundsmen, at the Gabba in Brisbane, was signed on some months before to prepare pitches in greenhouses. The pitches had to be lifted by giant cranes on to the ground and slotted into position. Considering the problems this posed, Maley was one of the outstanding successes of WSC's two years when they played in some strange places in opposition to the establishment game. The fastest bowlers in the World had signed for WSC and if they had been asked to perform on bad pitches, I dread to think what might have happened.

There was an air of triumphalism about the whole WSC outfit at VFL Park for this opening fixture. After all the talking that had gone on since John Cornell had had the original idea early in 1976, it was all about to happen. I went out to Waverley the day before the match to have a look round and found this huge stadium, which looked like a Wembley in the desert, hotching with security people. It was with the greatest difficulty that I was allowed on to the ground, let alone out to the middle to look at the pitch, although in the end I was successful. The players were all staying at the Old Melbourne Motor Inn where, in the days before the start, they had been subjected to a series of lectures almost as if they were the SAS before a particularly dangerous mission. Ian Chappell, the captain of the Australian side, and Richie Benaud who was in charge of the cricket, spoke on behalf of 'the cause', while John Newcombe, the tennis player, and Ron Barassi, perhaps the most successful Australian Rules Football coach of all time, spoke to them about what true professionalism meant.

I found Richie Benaud's involvement with Packer perhaps the strangest of all. On my first visit to Australia, in 1968/69, whenever I was in Sydney I stayed with Richie and Daphne in Bream Street in Coogee and they were wonderfully kind. Richie was very much an establishment figure. He was friends with all the influential members of the Board. Don Bradman was a great ally, and I doubt if, for example, anyone would have enjoyed the rest day in the Adelaide Test, always spent with the Hill Smiths in Yalumba, more than Richie. After retiring from the game, he made himself into cricket's best television commentator and came to England every summer, as he still does. No one in the game was a greater friend of the English establishment and the enjoyment was mutual. Rumour had it that Bobby Simpson was the first person to be offered the job which Benaud took on with World Series Cricket. Simpson was said to be unhappy about the future of WSC and declined the invitation. It was nothing if not an irony that the establishment in Australia then turned to him to captain their side against India and then the West Indies. I wonder if Simpson ever regretted the first decision he made.

Benaud first appeared with Packer when he visited Lord's for a meeting with the ICC. Hardly surprisingly, now that he was on the opposite side to many of his old friends, he looked a trifle sheepish in the photographs of him walking to the pavilion door at Packer's shoulder. But whatever the reasons that he joined Packer, he has been one hundred and ten per cent loyal to his employer. I have never heard it said that he has ever expressed doubts either about the future of WSC or about the wisdom of throwing in his lot with them or with anything that WSC initiated. He ran the cricket in the two years WSC played in direct opposition to establishment cricket and he was Channel Nine's presenter and leading commentator, jobs he has always done brilliantly. When he disappears from our screens we will all miss him for he will leave an enormous gap. I still wonder if, in his heart of hearts, he is glad he made the choice he did. I think many of his friends were surprised at his decision. One of them, Brian Johnston who was deeply opposed to Packer, told me he had made an agreement with Benaud which was that they would remain the greatest of friends but the subject of Packer must never be brought up.

There were less than four hundred spectators at the VFL Park when play began the next day and they were memorably described by John Thicknesse in the London *Evening Standard* as being 'scattered round the ground like confetti in a graveyard', which WSC did not enjoy even if it gave the rest of us a great laugh. But it was always unlikely that what was in effect a four-day practice game would grab Melbourne by the throat. It was difficult to be interested when the final result was so unimportant. Much the most significant happening during those four days was the news from the High Court in London that Mr Justice Slade had found for Packer. Apparently the great man had stayed up all night and when he heard the news by telephone, he immediately rang Tony Greig.

'I thought you'd like to know – we've stuffed them.'

The following day, Packer refused to give a press conference but let it be known he was happy to talk to journalists in groups of three and four. He was far from gracious in victory and was consistently rude and unhelpful to those who came to question him. He answered questions without any animation and every few minutes would complain, 'I want to watch the cricket. I suggest you do the same. That's what we're here for.' And later, 'You must remember there's nothing the cricket authorities can give me now. I have the players, the grounds and the wickets. What can they give me?' The group I was with had almost finished talking to him when we were joined by Johnny Woodcock and John Thicknesse. Packer was now at his most unattractively belligerent.

'Will you identify yourselves?' he asked.

'Woodcock of *The Times*,' was the reply.

'One of the enemy,' came back at once.

'It's true,' Johnny said slowly, 'I've been against what you've been trying to do. But I would nonetheless like sincerely to congratulate you on a considerable victory.'

'I can see from your face how sincere you are. I've read some of your stuff. You've never been prepared to give me a chance.'

'I don't know,' Johnny answered, 'I think I said that good might come of it.'

'Good might come of evil? I don't think that's much of a compliment.' He was no friendlier to Thicknesse and refused to answer any of their questions.

After that, Johny Woodcock and I drove up to Geelong for a limited-over game between an Australian Eleven, in effect their second eleven, and the West Indies Eleven. Rain ruined the day and the main point of interest for me was to see for the first time the thirty-yard circles drawn round the stumps at each end. For the first fifteen overs of the innings nine fielders, including the wicket-keeper, had to be inside the circle and after that, six had to remain there in order to stop sides going completely on the defensive and trying to shut the game down. This had already been happening in limited-over cricket in South Africa and had been adopted by WSC. It was an excellent rule which was soon to be used by every country.

I stayed on in Melbourne to watch the first of the much-heralded five-day Super Tests, between Australian and West Indian sides. The West Indians won in three days by three wickets and the biggest crowd, on the third day, was just under 6,000. To me, the cricket was bloodless. Although Viv Richards played a fine innings of 79 and produced some wonderful strokes against Dennis Lillee, it all seemed to be of no consequence. There was, of course, massive overkill on television which was the *raison d'etre* of the whole thing. Here Channel Nine may have been amazingly successful. It had been promoted for ever and when, the day after the match, I went round to see Richie Benaud at the Old Melbourne, he told me that the first viewing figures had been so extraordinary they had been sent back for rechecking. A few days later, when I was in Pakistan, I heard that no less than forty-four per cent of the Australian television audience had watched the Super Test. Packer would surely have enjoyed that statistic, but there were other figures going round which were nothing like so flattering. David Hill, who was in charge of Channel Nine's cricket and was later to start Sky Sport on the road to success in England, was the man who deserved the credit for taking television coverage of cricket into a new dimension. Much of what is today taken for granted, first came about because of the genius of Hill who is now one of the most powerful figures of all, apart from Rupert Murdoch, in Fox Television in Los Angeles.

While this was going on at the VFL Park, the official Australian side, captained by Bobby Simpson, who had retired from Test cricket ten years earlier, were playing the First Test against India in Brisbane. Simpson had heard the sound of the bugle and had returned to captain what, in all honesty, were the remnants of Australia. Packer's Super Tests had been scheduled on exactly the same dates as the official Test Matches, another sign of overwhelming arrogance. A most exciting game unwound at the Gabba and on the fifth day Australia won by 16 runs and they had played throughout in front of bigger crowds than we had had at the VFL Park. From one set of figures the television audience, helped no doubt by the novelty of WSC, had been overwhelmingly at Waverley; from another the ABC had just had the edge.

England were now due to play in Pakistan. When negotiating customs and immigration with Johnny Woodcock at Karachi airport took longer than it should have done, I found myself half-expecting Michael's punctuated bark issuing instructions and advice, interspersed with Ady's resonant, 'I'm afraid I have no Urdu.' But we found our way through unassisted and then on to a smaller aeroplane for the flight to Peshawar. The North-West Frontier Governor's Eleven were England's opponents and the first thing I had to do was watch Geoffrey Boycott bat through the first day for 115 not out. England went on to win their second victory in three tours of Pakistan by 212 runs. One of our journalistic colleagues who had not been on a tour before, went out one evening with various of the England players and began to tell Ian Botham that there was something wrong with his forward defensive stroke. In the taxi on the way home, strong hands had to prise Botham's fingers from round the unfortunate chap's neck. As a general rule, Test cricketers do not take kindly to advice from club cricketers – and I can't say I blame them.

The series was deadly dull and all three Test Matches were irrevocably drawn on flat, slow pitches which produced an inevitable stalemate. Just before the Third Test in a one-day game against the Governor of Sind's Eleven at the Gymkhana Club in Karachi, Mike Brearley had his arm broken in the fifth over of the match by a short one from Sikander Bakht. Brian Johnston was later to say that Sikander's Bakht was worse than his bite. Brearley's injury meant that Boycott was able to realise his lifetime's ambition and captain England. He was appointed for the rest of the tour in Pakistan and then New Zealand.

This last brief paragraph dealing with what was consummate boredom on the field of play, successfully conceals two high points of drama. On successive days in the First Test in Lahore, the supporters of the imprisoned ex-President Bhutto, led by his wife, used the occasion at the Gaddafi Stadium to riot. In Pakistan's first innings, their opener, Mudassar Nazar, was approaching the slowest ever hundred in first-class cricket. When he was 98, and I had just taken over the microphone from Don Mosey for the next spell of commentary back to England on *TMS*, he turned Geoff Cope to fine leg for a single. The crowd had been eagerly awaiting his hundred and, feeling sure that this was it, about forty boys could stand it no longer and raced on to the field to congratulate him. The police followed and set about some of the youngsters with their *lathi* sticks. One was hit a particularly nasty blow in full view of the big crowd who were infuriated and poured over the fence to give chase to the police. It was now that the pro-Bhutto element joined in. There must have been at least a hundred police and they were chased across the pitch and disappeared into the members section in front of the pavilion. They regrouped behind the pavilion but when they reappeared they were driven off again. This was the cue for the military police who were resentfully respected in a country under martial law. The spectators retreated, the ground was cleared of people and debris and with the players having tea, only twenty-five minutes had been lost. It all made for exciting and most unusual commentary which Don Mosey and I tried to make the most of. No sooner had play restarted than Mudassar reached his hundred in 557 minutes and, being on the air at the time, I was able to tell listeners that he had made 'a riotous hundred'.

The following day's riot was better organised and more sinister. Mrs Bhutto and her daughter Benazir visited the ground, although no one could remember either coming to a cricket match before. They walked round the back of the stands accompanied by a good many supporters. The trouble began in the Ladies' Stand, of all places, when some of their younger allies burst in and started throwing the seats and sofas and cushions over the wire fence on to the ground. The military police were summoned at once this time but, even so, thousands had come on to the ground by the time they arrived. They were forced to use tear gas to restore order and Don and I kept going through it all. Fortunately, the gas did not blow back into the pavilion as it had done at Sabina Park in 1967/68. We were sitting in the open air on top of the pavilion and Don Mosey, Brian Johnston's 'Alderman', short, irascible and going ever greyer, was looking more aldermanic than ever. The now well-known soubriquet originated in Brian's observation that Don was the spitting image of a civic dignitary. The Alderman now found all the goings on utterly preposterous and looked rather as though he was about to do something unpleasant to the rate of council tax. I am never sure that he enjoyed the East but he suffered it the best he could. He would rather have been back in his beloved Morecambe for he was the paradoxical Yorkshireman who had come to love Lancashire.

He had one nasty moment in this match when, after one day's play, he found that the bus for the English press had left for the hotel without him. There were no taxis and he had nothing for it but to leg it back to the hotel which was about two miles away. He was ridiculously irritable about this for some time afterwards. The Alderman was doing all the news reports and other bits and pieces for the BBC which, in those days, was an aggravating job because getting through to London on the telephone was a matter of complete luck. You put the call through to the exchange in Pakistan and waited, a process which often went on for hours. I shall always remember the Alderman pacing the hotel corridors between his room and the reception desk, seeking further information about the likely arrival of a call. His comments became more and more cynical which went far over the heads of those for whom they were intended, but provided innocent Anglo-Saxon bystanders with great amusement. New Zealand was the country in which Don was most at home and I think he would have liked to migrate there towards the end of his life. In New Zealand, he so far went native as to always wear shorts and stockings, confirming my impression that most knees look like underdone rock cakes and that Don would have made a bad boy scout. Underneath it all, he had a good strong north country sense of humour, but he was never the most contented of men and, indeed, wrote a book saying that *Test Match Special* was the contaminated preserve of public schoolboys. It made us all feel that he was the traitor within.

The riots were one distraction from the seriously boring business of this series, while Pakistan's attitude to their four Packer players was another and there was a strong move to reinstate them for the Third Test Match. The administrators were split on the subject.

Mushtaq Mohammad, Imran Khan, Zaheer Abbas and Majid Khan were a formidable quartet and would greatly have increased Pakistan's chances of beating England. Abdul Hafeez Kardar, Pakistan's first captain who had run the Board of Control for a long time afterwards, was now out of office but remained the most powerful cricket voice in the country. He was completely opposed to trying to bring them back for this series, while a former friend of his, Omar Kureishi, a commentator and the sporting director of Pakistan International Airline, was prepared to do anything to reinstate them. Packer himself said he was willing to release them, provided they were guaranteed places in the Test side. While this was going on, the England side, which contained four players who had turned Packer down, Boycott, Willis, Old and Randall, were most unhappy and threatened to boycott the match if the Packer players were selected. The ironical postscript to this was that when a replacement for Brearley was brought to Pakistan, it was Clive Radley who had been coaching in Sydney at Cranbrook School in a scheme set up by Kerry Packer.

In Pakistan, the new President of the country, General Zia-ul-Haq, had become involved and the situation became increasingly confused. Kureishi met Packer in Singapore and three of his players returned to Pakistan – Majid was still needed by Packer in Australia – to play in the Third and final Test of the series, in Karachi. It would have suited Packer if they had been picked for Pakistan as it would have meant that one Board of Control had been prepared to recognise World Series Cricket. The three practised for several days with the Pakistan squad and it was not until the night before the match that the new president of the Board, Chaudri Mohammed Husain, gave a press conference when he said that the Packer players would not play in this final Test. Initially, I thought that Zia-ul-Haq would have been happy to have had them back and had sent Kureishi to Singapore, although I had heard it said that Kureishi may have taken that initiative himself, having misinterpreted what the General had said. But, in the end, Kardar, who had the ear of Zia-ul-Haq, almost certainly won the day and presumably Husain made that statement after he had been told that the inclusion of the three Packer players was unacceptable to the President. During this Third Test in Karachi, these three players asked to see the General who had come to watch the third day's play. One of the General's aides asked the great man if he was prepared to see them. The General asked the ADC if any of them were related to him. When he was told they were not, he said he would see them. They had a short conversation which was begun by the General.

'Why do you want to see me?'

'We were brought back to play in the Test Match,' Mushtaq Mohammad answered. 'Why are we not playing?'

'That is your bad luck,' the General answered. 'Why are you not available to play cricket for Pakistan all the time? I have raised the fees of Test cricketers and I will guarantee you will get good jobs.'

'We are professional cricketers, and have lived abroad for a long time. And Packer is promoting cricket.'

'What Packer is doing,' the General said quietly, 'is *prostituting* cricket.'

When the series had finished in Pakistan, the England side flew on to New Zealand for three more Test Matches. I took the opportunity to go to Perth to watch two days of the fifth Super Test between the Australian Eleven and the Rest of the World. I flew with the team to Colombo and on to Singapore, where we went our different ways. On the first leg of the flight, I finished writing a chapter for a book, *The Packer Affair*, about all the goings on in Pakistan. We had to wait inside the terminal at Colombo and, with astonishing skill, I left the manuscript of this chapter and a book on my seat in the aeroplane. When we eventually returned to the machine, my manuscript was no longer there and had obviously been thrown away by the cleaners. The doors were not shut and I stormed up the aeroplane in a real panic and burst into the flight deck and forbade them to take off. It was a great piece of luck they were sympathetic and they got on the telephone at once. Inside the airport building people were dispatched to the bins where the cleaners deposited the rubbish and after a while my manuscript was found. It meant we were late leaving Colombo and, as the team had a tight connection in Singapore for the flight to Auckland, Ken Barrington, the manager, became understandably agitated. Mercifully, they found the script in the nick of time and the party made their connection.

The Weld Club was again my base in Perth and I watched two days' cricket which were as entertaining and vibrant as the three days of that first Super Test at VFL Park in Waverley had been boring. It was watched by a small crowd, although I am sure some, if not all, of the television figures will have made exciting reading for WSC. The match was being played in the middle of the trotting circuit at Gloucester Park which was the other side of the road from the WACA ground. Another of John Maley's artificially propagated pitches was being used. The Rest of the World decided to bat and on the first day they amassed 433/1 which was more a testimony to Maley's ability than a judgement of the Australian bowling. Barry Richards made 207 as only he could, dismissing the ball from his presence in his usual way and batting as if it was all a minor irritation and he would rather have been somewhere else. Batting in his gleaming white crash helmet, he looked as if he was about to jump on to his new Yamaha and have a go at the track record. Gordon Greenidge made 114 before he had to retire hurt and then Viv Richards and Clive Lloyd continued the assault, both chewing gum as if they were intent on beating some gastronomical record. With that batting line-up, the innings could hardly have failed to have been worth watching. By the end of the first day, Dennis Lillee was bowling off his short run and, to have found any enjoyment, would have had to concentrate awfully hard on the bottom line. The next day the Rest of the World reached 625 and Viv Richards made 177. At the close Australia were 73/4 and, as a contest, it looked over – which it was.

At the start of play two days later, I was sitting in the press box at the Adelaide Oval for the third day's play in the Fifth Test between Australia and India. The Oval was as beautiful as ever and on the previous two days the Australians had amassed 505 with Bobby Simpson and Graham Yallop having made hundreds. One of the great differences between the Adelaide Oval and Gloucester Park was that now, thank goodness, there was a complete absence of hard sell, not to say, overkill. While watching

WSC perform, there was no end to the number of minor WSC executives pinning you down and giving you handouts and then telling you that everything was the biggest, the best, the fastest, the most magnificent and, of course, the most skilful, and the players plunged into a massive exercise in self-justification. In the lovely Adelaide sunshine, it was a different world. There were none of those garish caps, just the baggy dark green and the Indian blue, and the soporific old cathedral seemed to be contentedly nodding its head in agreement on the hill behind the scoreboard. India replied with 269 and Jeff Thomson, who had been prevented from signing for Packer because of a previous contractual obligation with a commercial radio station in Brisbane, had taken two of the wickets. Simpson did not enforce the follow on and Australia were bowled out for 256 with Simpson himself gleaning another 51 in his usual assiduous way. India needed 493 to win and after four of their batsmen had contributed good half centuries, were out for 445. Australia had won the match by 47 runs and an excellent series by three matches to two.

Two days later I was back with the England side under the captaincy of Geoffrey Boycott across the Tasman Sea in New Zealand. In the First Test in Wellington, Boycott elected to put New Zealand in to bat and became the first England captain to lose a Test Match to New Zealand as Richard Hadlee took ten wickets on a green pitch and the left-arm seamer Dick Collinge, his opening partner, picked up six. In the first innings, England's gallant captain had made 77 in 442 minutes. The Second Test in Christchurch produced one moment of great amusement. After building up a lead of 183, England needed quick runs in their second innings for a declaration. This time, after two hours at the crease, their intrepid leader had managed just 26. Ian Botham had been promoted to number four to push things along and reckoned that one way of doing this was to run out his partner. He faced Ewen Chatfield, pushed the ball to cover and ran. Boycott said no, but Botham continued, going past the Great Man who was run out and there was hardly a dry eye in the house. It was a joy to see him walking off, a picture of such dreadful discontent. Not satisfied with this unexpected bonus, Chatfield then ran out Derek Randall for backing up too far without first warning him in the time-honoured way. It was the second time I had seen this happen – Charlie Griffith had administered the same treatment to Ian Redpath in Adelaide early in 1969. I can only imagine Randall must have been annoying Chatfield who was the last person I would have expected to behave like this.

During the course of this series, New Zealand found it was not completely immune from the attentions of Kerry Packer. After their Australian season, WSC were planning to pay a short visit to New Zealand and it was strongly rumoured that they were about to sign Richard Hadlee. In the end, he signed a short-term contract which enabled him to play for WSC on their short tour. Even so, it will have been no comfort to his father, Walter Hadlee, a former New Zealand captain and a strong figure on their Board of Control who had followed England in their opposition to Packer and his players.

A week after the end of the Third Test in Auckland I found myself watching the Second Test between the West Indies and Australia in Barbados. The West Indies with all their Packer players, had won the First Test, in Trinidad, by an innings and plenty and, at this point, it looked a mismatch. In the end, the Second Test went the same way after the first two days had produced some wonderful cricket. Australia were bowled out for 250 soon after tea on the first day and it was then that Jeff Thomson produced one of the greatest spells of fast bowling I have ever seen. On that first evening he bowled 6.5 overs and took three wickets for 40 and he was frightening as he tore in to bowl from the pavilion end. I never saw him bowl with greater rhythm than he did in those few overs and he remembers that spell as perhaps the best of his career. If he had had any luck he would have taken at least five wickets. The umpires were no help, his fielders did not cling on to all the catches and Richards was dropped before he scored. Michael Holding's famous spell at Geoffrey Boycott on the same ground is the one which most people remember and certainly Holding did not give away so many runs but he was not bowling at batsmen with the strokemaking capabilities of Viv

Richards, Gordon Greenidge and Alvin Kallicharran who were the three Thomson dismissed that evening. The West Indies won the match by nine wickets but long before the end politics were simmering behind the scenes.

The following winter the West Indies were scheduled to tour India and it was extremely doubtful that the players who had signed for Packer would be available for that tour. As a result, the five in the side who had not signed for World Series Cricket, Kallicharran, Croft, Haynes, Parry and Austin, had all been asked by the president of the West Indies Board, Jeff Stollmeyer, to give a verbal undertaking that, if they were approached by the Packer camp, they would not sign before the start of the Third Test on 31 March. By then the Board would have come up with some much-improved financial proposals for them. Meanwhile the Packer players had been asked to state their availability for the Indian tour. On the first day of the Second Test, two of Packer's representatives flew in to Barbados and the day after the match rumours circulated that more West Indies players had been signed by Packer's two men. At a hastily convened meeting in the team hotel, Croft, Haynes and Austin all admitted they had signed. Packer now had eighteen West Indies players and he will have been sure the Board would be obliged to do a deal with him unilaterally if they were going to be able to send any sort of a side to India.

The West Indies selectors now decided to use the last three Tests in this series to blood some young players with the Indian tour in mind. Clive Lloyd, the captain, was in agreement with this. When the selectors met to pick the side for the Third Test in Georgetown, they did so at the Pegasus Hotel in room 702 which happened to be next to mine. Our doors were adjoining but I thought it would be a trifle undignified to stand outside my room, key in hand, in case someone came along, with my ear to their keyhole. The best I could hear was the occasional muffled voice and an odd burst of laughter, not that they can have had too much to laugh about. By the time they had finished, in the early hours of the morning, Deryck Murray who had been Lloyd's right-hand man, Desmond Haynes who had passed 50 in each of

his master's feet. With Jim Swanton watching the English Press take on their Australian counterparts he Randwick Oval in Sydney in 1974/75.

C.B. with the Alderman (Don Mosey) commentating at Hyderabad in 1977/78.

Peter Parfitt, another loyal Norfolk man and the best of friends, batting for England against Australia at the Oval in 1972.

Cyril Coote was a coach supreme, fine opening batsman, brilliant shot and unrivalled groundsman, Fenner's in the sixties, seen here with H.C.B.

John Edrich, cousin of Bill and Norfolk to his boots, bats against Australia at Lord's in 1975.

…dfrey Evans, Don Bradman and Bill Edrich at slip – all in typical time-honoured pose at Lord's in …48.

…oup captain A.J. Holmes, chairman of selectors Norman Yardley, Bill Edrich and Denis Compton in …omewhat battered dressing room against South Africa at Trent Bridge in 1947.

Fred Trueman *in excelsis*, shirt sleeve unrolled, half scowl, hair dishevelled, giving his all for England.

matinee idols grow old. Keith Miller at Denis Compton's seventieth birthday party at Lord's in

No one has ever made batting look easier than Barry Richards, here playing for Hampshire against Lancashire with India's Farokh Engineer keeping wicket.

greatest of them all. Gary Sobers square cuts against England at Lord's in 1973 watched by Knott.

After the toss, Alec Stewart, in his first Test as England's captain, deals capably with my questions. Madras 1992/93.

his first three Test innings, and Richard Austin who, like Haynes, had been a Packer man only for a few days, were dropped. Lloyd, who was one of the selectors, felt this was taking things too far but was outvoted. Of course, it reeked of revenge and at three o'clock that morning the tall, bespectacled, lugubrious Lloyd, after, no doubt, burning up the telephone wires to Sydney, told the selectors he had resigned. For the next few days, it was chaos with no one knowing for sure what was happening except that Packer himself was now coming to Georgetown.

On the Wednesday I was talking to Clyde Walcott, one of the West Indies selectors but not a Board member, by the hotel swimming pool when we were joined by Fred Bennett, the Australian manager, Bobby Simpson, the captain, and Alan McGilvray, the commentator. Their fear was that Packer would manipulate the West Indies Board when he arrived. They didn't mind who they played against as long as it was a side chosen by the West Indies selectors and not by Packer. The possibilities were endless and rumours were flying everywhere. That evening I had been asked to dinner by Sir Lionel Luckhoo, the head of a remarkable legal family who had come originally from Lucknow in India. He was an extraordinary advocate who held the world record for the largest number of successive acquittals of accused murderers. At that time it stood at 209 and he told me that there were twelve more he was presently acting for and whom he hoped would increase the number. He was also the personal lawyer of Forbes Burnham, the Prime Minister of Guyana. The three Australians I had met by the pool were there, so too was my old friend Berkeley Gaskin, the president of the Guyanese Board and several others closely involved with the cricket. Gaskin had not stayed for long because he had had to go to the airport to meet Jeff Stollmeyer and Peter Short, another influential member of the West Indies Board. The speculation was endless and only brought to an end by a telephone call at eleven o'clock after which we were all asked to leave and were driven back to the hotel. Soon after we had left, Stollmeyer, Short and Gaskin arrived at the house and talked it all through with their host until the early hours.

A THIRST FOR LIFE

When I arrived back at the Pegasus, I ran into Alan Shiell who told me that it had been announced less than half an hour before that the five remaining Packer players had pulled out of the West Indies side in support of Lloyd. I stayed up until three o'clock waiting for a call to the BBC to come through so that I could relay the news to London. I was still in the lobby when Stollmeyer and Short came back from the Luckhoos, but I could get nothing out of them except the most amiable smiles.

The next day was even more fraught but it began with a moment of humour. At nine o'clock four of the Packer players had a meeting with some of the West Indies Board. Colin Croft turned up carrying his crash helmet, obviously fearing he was going to be subjected to plenty of verbal bouncers. Later, Lloyd complained the Board had come to Georgetown with their minds made up and there was no room for manoeuvre. Stollmeyer gave a press conference. Usually the most mild-mannered of men, he was now extremely angry as he went through the background to all that was happening. The West Indies Board had done more than any other to accommodate the Packer players and was the only one prepared to continue playing those who had signed for the Australian businessman because they were only too well aware of the poor financial rewards for playing for the West Indies. They had angered the other members of the ICC by being the only country to do so and Packer's gratitude for this had been to shove it back in their faces.

There was a great fanfare later that afternoon when an obstreperous Batman himself flew in with various of his acolytes, although not Robin, for Tony Greig had remained in Australia. At twenty past seven that evening the press again foregathered in the Pegasus conference room and Batman, looking larger than ever, came beaming into the room. I sat opposite him across a round table. He told us he had never had the chance to see Guyana and he also wanted to watch some cricket. Once this childish throat-clearing exercise was over, he and I had another brief skirmish.

'Would your visit to Georgetown and the West Indies be connected with the fact that the West Indies Board have asked your players to state their availability for the forthcoming Indian tour?' was my question.

'You always know more about my movements than I do myself. I have just heard you say on the BBC that I am intending to play at the White City before the World Cup in 1979.'

'No,' I replied, 'I said that I had heard that you were going to.'

'It didn't sound like that to me.' And here the conversation ceased. I walked out of the conference soon afterwards for I had heard all that he had to say several times before. Packer did not stay to watch the Test but remained in the West Indies in order to see some of the governments to try and make sure he could use the main grounds when WSC were planning to tour the West Indies the following year. He also had a big party at the Sandy Lane Hotel in Barbados for all his West Indian players and their wives and girlfriends. A gentle exercise in wheel-oiling, which Packer always enjoyed. He was now on his own in the Caribbean and had ensured that the West Indies Board fell into line with all the other Test playing countries with regard to World Series Cricket. I felt that evening that there was a sad similarity between events in Karachi a few months earlier and what had happened now in Georgetown.

The new West Indies side, captained by Kallicharran, somehow managed to lose the Third Test by three wickets on the last afternoon after setting Australia to make 359 in two days and removing three of the specialist batsmen for ducks. Australia's batting collapsed in a heap in the second innings in Port of Spain in the Fourth Test which gave the West Indies the series. Australia should have won the Fifth Test, which I did not see, but when the West Indies, needing 369 to win, had lost their ninth second-innings wicket for 258 and thirty-eight balls remained, the crowd rioted and there was no more play. There was an attempt to make the time up the next day, as had happened when England were there in 1967/68, but umpire Gosein from Trinidad refused to take part and no replacement could be found.

Packer and I had dogged each other's footsteps for almost six months and I was extremely grateful to be able to spend a few days away from him at Hoveton late in April. It had been an exciting winter but, sadly, all too little of the excitement had happened on the field of play. It was clear that even if a compromise was to be forthcoming, cricket would never be the same again.

CHAPTER 13

THE BESPECTACLED HENRY BLOFLY

AFTER SUCH A HECTIC WINTER I found something engagingly therapeutic about the start of a new English season. As usual, it was wet and cold, but that was all part of it. I always enjoy catching up with friends I have not seen since the previous September. It was all as evocative as the delicious scent of new-mown grass or the first sniff of the linseed oil which, when I was young, I used to put on my bat early in April – smells which told me the first ball was not far away. The first visit to Lord's at the start of the season made me feel I knew exactly what it must have been like for David to catch sight of Jonathan when he had been away for the weekend. It didn't matter that it rained for three days while Middlesex were supposed to be playing Hampshire. Nancy fed me on coffee and bacon rolls with her usual chatty gusto in the committee dining room and all the old familiar faces were in place. I watched a mix of generations doing their best on the real tennis court where their muffled shouts reverberated around the court rather as the chat of two jovial parsons bumping into each other in the vestry might have sounded. At the other end of the ground Don Wilson was busying himself around the indoor cricket school organising the latest influx of young hopefuls. The oilcoated groundstaff were moving benches on the edge of the Nursery ground and it was like coming home. What a merciful release it was no longer to be dealing with the dreaded Kerry Packer who, not a year before, had brought the modern face of cricket fleetingly to Lord's when he had come to try and compromise with the ICC.

It was not long before I had made the journey to Fenner's where the wind seems to blow straight off the North Pole, to watch Cambridge University play Surrey. This was a step back into my own past which hardly seemed more than a day or two ago when I was greeted by Cyril Coote, older and balder but still producing those excellent pitches and casting his knowledgeable eye over the newcomers, as well as bemoaning the lack of interest shown by tutors and examiners in University sport. The old pavilion had gone and a new, more compact, red-brick affair had been built at the Hughes Hall end of the ground. It was more efficient, more attuned to present-day needs but with a red-brick, bungaloid insignificance when compared to the more stately presence of its chilly and uncomfortable predecessor at the Hills Road end of the ground. I have no doubt the new pavilion makes much greater economic sense and the hot water works all the time, even if it is too contemporary for words. It was in the old pavilion that I saw the Test umpire, Dai Davies, when Cambridge were playing New Zealand in 1958 and my 9 in the first innings was the equal top score, stand on the table and sing 'Land of my Fathers'. One of the regulars at Fenner's was still a tall, elderly and heavily bespectacled don whose name I have forgotten but, tall and tweed-suited, he walked most deliberately round and round and round the ground. I never ever saw a single flicker of emotion cross his face in all the many days I saw him at Fenner's. We called him HH which stood for Hardly Human, but he loved his cricket and may have been less gloomy than he looked. Perhaps his ghost walks even now.

Series that summer against Pakistan and New Zealand were not the most exciting of prospects and both countries were dispatched with little difficulty. The First Test, at Edgbaston, marked the arrival of David Gower, who walked out to bat with the gait of a lounge lizard and an air of indifference. I was at the microphone when he took guard and then swivelled and hooked his first ball in Test cricket, bowled by Liaquat Ali, to the bottom of the Rae

THE BESPECTACLED HENRY BLOFLY

Bank Stand for four. He had so much time to spare that it looked as lazy and matter-of-fact as countless other strokes with which he was to entertain us over most of the next twenty years. He made it look like child's play, as he always did until his genius was wantonly discarded by those wretched bureaucratic and humourless minds who were running England's cricket in the last decade of the century. There was one much less pleasant moment in that First Test which I did not enjoy. In Pakistan's second innings, Iqbal Qasim, their left-arm spinner, had come in on the third evening as nightwatchman. He hung on for almost three-quarters of an hour the next morning, a job well done, until Bob Willis went round the wicket with his first ball. The lefthander was hit in the mouth by a bouncer which, from that angle, inevitably followed him, and he had to retire. It all seemed to have been done so deliberately and Iqbal Qasim was not the only one to have been left with a nasty taste in his mouth. Yet it was out of character for Willis to do this, although he was a great one for hyping himself up out on the field and bowling as if in a trance. Maybe, for some unknown reason, the iron had entered his soul that morning.

This was Ian Botham's second season as a member of the England side and I shall never forget the excitement as he destroyed both these two countries. I don't think I've ever seen a more compelling, irresistible cricketer. He was a big strong man with a tousle-haired, boyish enthusiasm about everything he did. Batting at number seven, he hit hundreds in both the first two Tests against Pakistan. I can't think of another English batsman who generated such excitement when he cracked the ball through the covers or drove it massively back over the bowler's head. They were strokes the caveman would have enjoyed every bit as much as the England selectors. This was only one half of the story, too, for he then picked up the ball and ran in to bowl with an equally devastating effect. No wonder he became a folk hero. After making a hundred at Lord's against Pakistan, he took 8/34 in their second innings, the best bowling figures ever in a Test at Lord's, and picked up thirty-seven wickets in the six Tests that summer. How the Packer lot must have wanted to sign both Ian Botham and David Gower. It was precisely in order to prevent further intrusions into English cricket by Packer that Cornhill Insurance had been persuaded to start their sponsorship of England's home series. The prime function of the money they brought to the game was to increase the rates of pay. The new England contracts must also have been worded so that it was extremely difficult for any of the players to sign for Packer. England had to hang on to Botham and Gower at all costs. They gave us all something to hope for and their best performances made the whole country feel better.

On the other side of the world, the conflict between Packer and the establishment was as ferocious as ever. The Australian Cricket Board were as intransigent and implacable as Packer himself and they have to bear considerable responsibility for what this whole sorry episode cost the game. If they had taken the trouble to do their homework on Packer the moment they first became aware of him, they would surely have realised that they had to react differently and have been prepared to go some of the way to accommodate him. It was now going to be a fight to the death, with the cards stacking up in Packer's hands. It was obvious that no one relished a good fight as much as he did and the Queensberry Rules most certainly did not apply.

In the winter of 1978/79 England were going to take on the Australian Board Eleven while World Series Cricket, who were as verbally pugnacious as ever, would be playing Super Tests and one-day matches in opposition. Before I left England, I had been rung up by Crawford White who had retired four years before as the cricket correspondent of the *Daily Express*. He had been called by a radio station in Perth, 6PR, and asked if he would be able to work for them during the forthcoming England tour. He obviously couldn't and kindly put them on to me. They wanted me to join their commentary team for the matches in Perth and to do some reports for them during the series. I accepted eagerly and this was the start of a good relationship I had with commercial radio in Australia until the early nineties. On that tour, Chris Martin-Jenkins did most of the work for the BBC and also joined the ABC commentary team. The BBC took their output through the night on Radio Three medium wave, which had the grave disadvantage of not reaching more than about two-thirds of the country but was the home of *TMS* in those days. I was also covering the tour for the *Guardian* for, unlike most of the wine he drank, John Arlott still did not travel, and for the *Sunday Express*.

In the old days, tours made a somewhat leisurely start in Perth before progressing along the south coast and on up to Brisbane for the First Test. Even before Packer, things had begun to change and now for the second time England's first port of call was Adelaide. The reason for this was that, from 1970/71, Perth had staged its own Test Match and, being so isolated, it would have added considerably to the cost if the touring side had had to make two visits to the west. I was staying in the Adelaide Club for the start of this tour, which was perfect for many reasons, not the least of which was that each day began with a lovely ten-minute walk down the hill past the Festival Hall over the Torrens River to the Oval.

A gentle opening first-class match against South Australia, who were not the strongest of sides, should have passed off without any problem, but it was the first time the Englishmen had come across Rodney Hogg. He was decidedly quick and was one of the main reasons that England lost by 32 runs. We were clearly going to see a lot more of him. In England's first innings, he felled Clive Radley with a nasty bouncer which hit him above the eye and he needed stitches. This blow effectively ended Radley's brief but successful England career for he never again played in a Test Match and from then on was extremely apprehensive against short-pitched fast bowling.

When I was sitting in the press area in the main stand on the first day, an old friend, Ron Mackenzie, who was one of the photographers from the Murdoch group of newspapers, came over and spoke to me. I had met Ron in England and the West Indies when he had been covering Australian tours and he was the most genial of men. He told me now that *The Australian* which was the nearest Australia came to a national daily, were keen to find an English journalist to write columns for them during the tour from the English point of view. He wondered if I would be interested and when I told him I was, he put me in touch with Mike Gascoigne, the Sports Editor. We agreed terms on the telephone and I began to write for them that same day, in conjunction with Phil Wilkins who was their main cricket reporter. I did not write a piece every day but only when Gascoigne and I agreed that there was a worthwhile story to be written. This was the start of a largely enjoyable relationship which lasted for more than ten years.

As the England party progressed towards Brisbane for the First Test, it was to the accompaniment of dark and deep rumblings from the Packer camp like a thunderstorm coming up from behind the Boggo Road Jail at the Gabba. It was their business to denigrate the England tour and the noisy battle created a great public awareness for the game and for the WSC side of the argument in particular because of its novelty value. This was reflected later in the television ratings. The razzmatazz and hype which went with WSC appealed to a new young audience which either switched on to have a look or went along to see what it was all about.

Just before the First Test began at the Gabba, I was approached by Peter Meares who worked for ABC television, and he asked me if I would be prepared to do a face-to-camera piece with him during the tea interval on each day of the Test Match. I leapt at this also, for it sounded good fun. It was one of the ways the ABC was gingerly expanding its coverage in response to Channel Nine's extravagant treatment of the Packer cricket. Channel Nine were using eight cameras instead of four and now there were cameras at each end of the ground and the viewer was no longer blocked by the wicket-keeper when the bowling was from the end that had no cameras. I find it amazing that it was not until the late seventies that someone had the genius to come up with this elementary idea.

The only incident of note in the First Test came after the match. I was one of those asked to pick the Man of the Match and I went for Derek Randall who reached the seventies in both innings. Another candidate was Rodney Hogg who, in his first Test, took six wickets in England's first innings, but only one in the second.

Alan McGilvray, a Scotsman by origin, but a fierce nationalist, was another entrusted with this job and he picked Hogg. When he heard that my choice had been Randall, he questioned my decision strongly and did not speak to me for the next eighteen months and only briefly then, for we were to have another altercation.

England were leading by two matches to one when the sides came to the Sydney Cricket Ground on 6 January for the start of the Fourth Test. There were almost 21,000 spectators and to their delight they saw England, who had won the toss, bowled out for 152. The big difference at the SCG this year was the presence of six huge black floodlight pylons which had been put up by Kerry Packer. The new government of New South Wales, led by 'Nifty' Wran, had installed a different set of trustees to run the SCG and they had agreed that Packer should be allowed to use the ground. The floodlights did nothing for its beauty. I was watching the first morning's play from the press box and after about an hour I looked through my binoculars at the bottom of the pylon on the Hill which was surrounded by quite a dense crowd. One of the characteristics of the Australian grounds are the banners the spectators stick up on the stands or hang over the boundary fence. Some of the comments are extremely pithy. There was a large one on the bottom of the pylon on the Hill and when I fixed my binoculars on it, I read the following message written in large red letters on a sheet stuck to the pylon: 'THE BESPECTACLED HENRY BLOFLY STAND'. It took me a moment or two to realise that it was intended for me, but soon the ribbing began. It was there again the following day and now, underneath the original sign, was another which said, 'COME ON OVER HENRY AND HAVE A PINT'.

I had been asked to lunch that day by the Cricket Ground Trust in their offices at the bottom of the Noble Stand. The invitation asked me to spend the whole day there if I wanted and I went down about half an hour before lunch. In those days these excellent lunches were presided over by the avuncular figure of Arthur Morris, the former Australian opening batsman, who was no longer quite the sylph he had been when I had played against him at Eton in 1956. No nicer man ever played cricket, but I knew the moment I shook his hand and he said, 'Welcome to Henry Blofly', that I was going to have my leg pulled unmercifully. No one made more of it than Jack Fingleton who was another lunch guest. I was wearing my I Zingari tie of orange, gold and black stripes, and with that cynical half smile of his, Fingo said to me, 'Blowers, you won't dare to go round to the Hill in that tie.' That was a challenge I could not refuse and so after lunch I set off on the walk to the Hill at the other end of the ground.

The only concession I made was to take off my jacket and undo the top button of my shirt, but the tie was still in place. After setting off behind the Bradman Stand, I had to walk the rest of the way through the crowd, from the Paddington Hill right round to the floodlight pylon. As soon as I appeared, the crowd were on to me and my journey was now accompanied by a considerable cacophony of shouting and cheering and a number of catcalls. It was highly embarrassing and even the England side, who were in the field, began to look round to see what on earth was going on. However, I kept going and, after what seemed like an age, arrived at the pylon where, if a batsman had hit a six, he would not have received a much bigger cheer. I was offered hundreds of stubbies (cans of beer) and I met all those who had been responsible for the signs. They were students from Sydney University and one, a marvellously pretty girl, threw her arms around me and said that she wanted to marry me. This was the most promising news I had had for a long time until she qualified it by saying that the man she was really after was Geoffrey Boycott. There have not been many times in my life when I have been lost for a word but this was unquestionably one of them.

I must have stayed there for nearly an hour before I began the long, noisy walk back. By then I had made them promise to give me at the end of the match the sheet which proclaimed 'THE BESPECTACLED HENRY BLOFLY STAND'. When England won, they streamed across the ground and handed it over, and I still have it tucked away in a bottom draw. The day after there was another sign saying, 'OUR HENRY CAN EVEN OUTDRINK KEITH MILLER' and Keith has still not sued for libel. The day after that, another read, 'OUR

THE BESPECTACLED HENRY BLOFLY

HENRY IS TO CRICKET WHAT TONY GREIG IS TO LIMBO DANCING'. I wasn't so sure about that one. It was a lot of fun and it went on for a few more years, but without quite the impact it had at the start. It was a great honour to have been singled out in this way and no doubt comes of having the sort of voice that to Australian ears goes with a bowler hat – I like to think maybe with one honorary cork dangling from its brim.

The series itself was not nearly as exciting as these sideshows. The Australian Board made the mistake of jettisoning Bobby Simpson. When asked to captain Australia again, he said he would only do so if he was appointed for the full series. The Board were not prepared to give this undertaking which did not seem to me to be much of a way to say thank you to someone who had come out of retirement to help them as he had. But Simpson had never been the easiest of men and maybe he did not put his case with as much tact as he might. It was not difficult to fall out with him and I have never met anyone so sensitive to even the mildest of criticisms. The Board appointed the Victorian, Graham Yallop, to do the job instead and with such a potential match winner as Hogg, who took a record forty-one wickets in the series, I felt that his lack of imagination and refusal to attack cost Australia dear. England won the series 5–1 in front of poor crowds and, as the Australian season continued, the popularity of World Series Cricket increased. The day/night one-day games played under floodlights were a tremendous success and they provided a wonderful spectacle. The longer the season went on, the more obvious it became that WSC and Packer were not going to go away and they were grabbing too big a slice of the game's income for the comfort of the Board.

During the previous summer in England, I had gone down to Eastbourne to watch the New Zealanders play Derrick Robins's Eleven at the Saffrons where almost twenty years before I had been awarded my Cambridge Blue. It was not the most exciting of games but we all stayed in an hotel which Derrick thought most highly of, in Herstmonceux, and a great time was had by all. Their cellar was severely tested as were some female inmates of a local college of physical education. During the evening,

Derrick told me that he was taking a side of young and promising county cricketers to five South American countries in late February and March. I said, 'I can think of nowhere I would like to go more.' Derrick's answer was, 'You'd better come along, too, as assistant manager and social secretary.' My old friend from Norfolk, Peter Parfitt who played thirty-seven times for England, was to manage the side and it all sounded too good to be true. The former England wicket-keeper batsman, Les Ames, a friend of Derrick's, was also in the party as a sort of managerial overlord and keeper of the collective conscience.

The countdown began as soon as I arrived back in England. I have been on an enormous number of cricket tours, but I have never been as excited as I was at the prospect of this one. There seemed to be something so unbelievably exotic and mysterious about South America. We left London one afternoon before the end of February and flew to Madrid where we changed over to an Iberian Airlines jumbo which eventually decanted us in Bogota, the capital of Colombia. The only thing I knew about Bogota was that it was where they had arrested Bobby Moore on a trumped-up charge of stealing jewellery before the 1970 World Cup finals in Mexico. Three of us, Derrick Robins himself, Kelly Seymour, our doctor, who had bowled his off breaks for South Africa on seven occasions, and I found ourselves billeted with His Excellency the British Ambassador which was not to be sniffed at.

The only problem was that kidnapping ambassadors was the current national pastime in Bogota and so elaborate precautions were taken for our safety and particularly that of H.E. We were hemmed in by bodyguards with telling bulges under their jackets and when we visited the Embassy itself, we went in through a secret entrance which, it was hoped, would fool the kidnappers. Another problem was the pickpocketing which obviously was given a place of great importance in the curriculum at Colombian schools. We conquered the Colombian side which had been reinforced by a former West Indian Test cricketer, Tony White, who played a couple of games against Australia in 1964/65 as an off-spinning all-rounder. Sadly, none of the opposition we met in South America was any sort of a test for the young players Derrick

THE BESPECTACLED HENRY BLOFLY

had got together. In the one match, in Rio, when I was asked to keep wicket and open the batting, we still won by a distance.

After Bogota we flew down to Lima, a most congenial city, and defeated Peru on the lovely ground at the Lima Cricket and Tennis Club. In the old days the British abroad always seemed to do themselves pretty well. In Lima they had appropriated several acres plumb in the middle of the most fashionable part of the city for their own amusement. It made me think of the British Embassy in Kabul with its spacious grounds, always supposing the Russians, the Mujahaddin or the Taliban have spared it since we were there in the Rolls. I was ill at the end of our visit to Lima and had to spend an extra night at the Hotel Bolivar where I had a desperate time trying to convince a Peruvian doctor whose appearance would have made Al Capone and the Godfather look like prospective Sunday school teachers, that I was allergic to penicillin. From the predatory manner in which he held the needle, I could see that he worshipped more than just occasionally at the shrine of the Marquis de Sade. When I told him about my penicillin allergy his grin widened and his plentiful black moustache began to vibrate. In a panic, I rang the hotel manager, who I knew spoke English, and he agreed to come up. I just managed to forestall the injector until the manager arrived. My problem explained, with renewed grins, the bandit plucked another phial out of his bag and bore down on me holding the syringe as if it was a bayonet. I shut my eyes and commended my soul to God and anyone else who was listening, had the injection and some pills, and paid a supersonically steep bill. The doctor was the emphatic victor on every count and my bum was sore for days.

Then it was Santiago and two nights at the Prince of Wales Country Club in the shade of the Andes and some excellent Chilean Cabernet Sauvignon which went down a treat and didn't appear to clash with my pills. I had an anxious moment at Buenos Aires airport when the customs opened my grip bag in which I had two tapes of *Evita*, strictly prohibited in Argentina. Fortunately, he was not the most thorough of customs officers and dived into the bag as though it was a lucky dip. He came up with my sponge bag which he examined very closely and with great suspicion, treating my after shave lotion as if it was a grave danger to human life, until with considerable reluctance he let me through. We spent the inside of a week at the Hurlingham Club and played three games of cricket, two at Hurlingham and one at Lomas on a lovely ground in the middle of the city which made me think of the Honorable Artillery Company ground in the City of London. I shopped at the Harrods in Buenos Aires and became quite an expert on Argentinian nightclubs most of which had a great deal going for them.

Then it was on to São Paulo for our first game in Brazil which caused the cricketers nothing like such a problem as they had later that night trying to tell a transvestite from the genuine article. I believe there were one or two quite interesting experiences. Rio was marvellous and we stayed with members of the expatriate British community. We bowled the Brazilian side out for 23 on the pretty ground at Niteroi surrounded by rhododendron-like shrubs. Derrick was furious that it wasn't for 19 because four byes had been let through. He was a hard taskmaster and a great competitor. We had an inhouse golf competition at Hurlingham and in the practice round, Graham Stevenson, of Yorkshire and occasionally England, was in unstoppable form. Overnight, the pairings were changed and now Derrick, having jettisoned his original partner, was playing with Stevenson, only this time, while he still hit the ball many a mile, it was almost invariably over cover point's head which was little help to his partner whose voluble protests gave us all a big laugh. I tasted fueijada, a delicious dish made largely with beans and lamb, for the first time. One of our number, who went on to great things, had a more interesting experience when he found the girl of his life on the Copacabana one evening and had foolishly failed to investigate her amateur status. When he woke up the next morning in a strange hotel room, he found that all his clothes were missing, which is a nasty one to have to sort out in a hurry and, much to Derrick's fury, he was late for the start of play.

It took me a while to get my feet back on the ground after all that. The second World Cup was played in England in 1979 and the West Indies again won the competition, beating England by the convincing margin of 92 runs in a final which never caught the imagination as their victory over Australia had done four years earlier. The Indians stayed on to play a series of four Test Matches which England won, but India, thanks to an innings of 221 by Sunil Gavaskar, one of the most brilliant I have seen, almost took India to an incredible victory at the Oval which would have drawn the series. They had been left to score 438 in 498 minutes and 15 were needed from the last over with the ninth wicket pair together and they could only find 6 of them.

I was tucked away in the cubicle next door to the main commentary box from where I supplied the needs of all the other programmes. As India came closer to victory, every producer in Broadcasting House seemed to want some of the action. When I did those inserts, the one that was the most fun was the PM programme in the late afternoon when I usually seemed to talk to Sue McGregor and we always had a good laugh. The most difficult chap to get on with whenever his morning programme came briefly to the cricket was Jimmy Young. He was obviously not a cricket lover and liked to try and boost his ego by having a go at whoever was sitting at our end. He usually did it with his last comment on the tail of the interview too, which meant you could not get back at him. Those of us who did the number two job seldom enjoyed our chats with Mr Young. While his septuagenarian bounciness still delights the housewives in their droves, we, at the Test Matches, badly needed to be wearing our helmets for these encounters. When we were in Pakistan, I can remember the Alderman, Don Mosey, having a most diverting exchange with the father of Radio Two. They could hardly have had more conflicting styles of broadcasting.

The most dramatic news of that English summer of 1979 was the announcement on 30 May by Bob Parish, the chairman, that the Australian Cricket Board had come to an agreement with Kerry Packer. It was effectively a complete sell-out to Packer who, through his promotional company, PBL Marketing, had taken over the running of Australian cricket with the Board being used only to rubber stamp their decisions. The ACB sought the peace and Packer, who by then was holding all the cards, was happy to oblige because he knew it would be entirely on his terms or not at all. The details of the financial agreement were not revealed at the time, probably because the Australian Board did not want to show the extent to which Packer had won the day. It came out later that the ACB were to receive a sum of A$1,150,000 each year although, astonishingly, this figure was not indexed to inflation. By 1986, inflation had taken such a toll and this figure represented such a paltry percentage of the income coming into the game that even PBL agreed it should be revised.

All the Packer innovations during the two years they played in opposition to the ACB were now to be used by the Board: coloured clothing, day/night matches and thirty-yard circles in the limited-over games. Then there was all the showbiz razzmatazz such as skydivers and cheerleaders, performing dogs and exhibitions of American Football. England and India had both accepted invitations to tour Australia in 1979/80 and the ACB were now instructed to ask the Indians to put off their visit for a year so that the West Indies could be invited. England and the West Indies both had to play three Test Matches and then there were fifteen limited-over games in a triangular tournament, followed by a final of five matches.

The humourless Parish, who looked like a chap in a Hitchcock movie, was hard to keep track of. He flew round the world making pathetic excuses for the ACB's policy of appeasement which had been greeted with horror everywhere. The ACB had been short-sighted and pig-headed when Packer had first tried to buy the exclusive rights to televise cricket in Australia in 1976. To refuse such a huge increase in rights fees in favour of staying with the Australian Broadcasting Corporation without even attempting to explore the possibility of compromise was unbelievably foolish. The ACB then made sure that all the rest of the Test-playing countries gave them the support they wanted. The front against Packer had been pretty solid across the globe for getting on for two years and then suddenly everyone discovered that the Australians had not so much sought a peace with Packer as made an abject surrender. Parish and Company must have been excessively naive if they were surprised at the near contempt with which they were then treated by the rest of the cricketing world. It is sad to have to write this as Tim Caldwell, small, thick-set and eternally cheerful, who had preceded Parish as chairman of the Board and was still a most influential figure, had become a great friend of mine and no nicer, more amusing man has ever lived. I went up to Orange in New South Wales to stay with him a long time after these events and he seemed to be in no doubt then that things should have been done differently. While I was there, he asked me to plant a tree in his garden next to one which had been planted by Don Bradman. It may not have been as good as batting with the great man but it was something, and, by all accounts, my tree flourishes.

From 1979 on there was an unmistakable them and us feeling about Australian cricket. To paraphrase Orwell, 'All cricketers were equal, but some cricketers were more equal than others.' It was the same in the commentary box. Channel Nine wore a nauseating air of smugness. I can understand it because the Packer lot had won an enormous victory and, having had so much calumny poured upon them, they obviously wanted to make the most of their victory. The man Packer appointed as head of PBL Marketing, Lynton Taylor, was one of the few people I have ever met whom I felt was utterly devoid of charm. I once gave him dinner at the Weld Club in Perth in the hope that we might move on from a position of permanent armed neutrality. He never smiled all evening, was aggressively bored and barely said thank you afterwards. The ACB, as I have tried to show, had only themselves to blame for their disastrous mismanagement of the whole business and so I suppose you could say they deserved each other.

The financial arrangements for the England tour to Australia in 1979/80 were conducted between Lord's and PBL, although the latter used the ACB as the go-between. It was a ghastly hotchpotch of a summer with one-day, four-day and five-day matches being indiscriminately intermingled. The public were not particularly receptive to it as far as the gates were concerned, but the television sets were being turned on all over the country which was what Packer and PBL were most concerned about. The Packer players felt they owned the world and could do what they wanted. Ian Chappell, who had come back out of retirement for the Packer cricket, had behaved so badly when South Australia played Tasmania in Devonport that he had been suspended by the ACB for three weeks. The day after the suspension ended, he captained South Australia against England and was again reported by an umpire who was standing in his only first-class match. This was the incident which brought about the retirement from the ACB of Sir Donald Bradman who was perhaps the only one of them able to see the whole issue in a clear perspective. A disciplinary meeting to deal with Chappell, and presided over by Bradman, was arranged in Adelaide.

'It was a set-up,' Bradman said later. 'The two other Board members cried off with feeble excuses and I had to sit alone in judgement. I heard the case; found Chappell guilty as charged, and suspended him forthwith for a period of six weeks. I sent my report to the Board who did not back me up. Chappell's sentence was suspended. I had no other course of action than to see the season through and not re-nominate again.' This was, of course, a considerable victory for Taylor, an opponent hardly worthy of Sir Donald Bradman.

In the First Test against England in Perth, Dennis Lillee put on the most appalling performance. He came to the wicket with an aluminium bat and, after he had scored 3 runs in four balls, Brearley complained to one of the umpires, Max O'Connell, that the bat was damaging the ball. Lillee had warned the Channel Nine television commentators that he was going to promote aluminium bats in this obscene manner and they made the most of it. O'Connell told Lillee to change his bat and now for eleven minutes his behaviour was too dreadful for words and, after much arguing with Brearley and the umpires, Lillee threw his bat twenty yards towards the pavilion before stalking off in high dudgeon and coming back eventually with one made of wood. He should have been suspended instantly but all that happened was that he received a letter from the ACB telling him it was not the way to behave. This was another good illustration of the way Packer was in complete control.

THE BESPECTACLED HENRY BLOFLY

England lost all three of their Tests, while the West Indies won two of theirs. In among the Test Matches, a triangular one-day competition was played for the Benson & Hedges World Series Cup. In the terms of the peace treaty, the ACB had guaranteed to play twenty one-day games each season: fifteen preliminaries and five finals. In this first year, they contrived to play only fourteen one-day matches and as a result were heavily fined by their 'joint partners', PBL Marketing. This must have been the last straw and it seems to me that it was a final demonstration of the approach of the Packer camp towards the ACB. Only a dedicated enemy would have refused to pick up the telephone at some stage in the preparations for the season and warn the ACB to watch their step. But the ACB had made their bed and now for some appreciable time they were going to have to lie in it.

CHAPTER
14

REST DAY

ON THE WAY HOME from Australia, England put down in Bombay where they played a Test Match against India to celebrate the Golden Jubilee of the formation of the Board of Control for Cricket in India – not the best of excuses for such a gala occasion. I was back at the Taj Mahal Hotel for an extraordinary match which lasted only four days and belonged almost entirely to Ian Botham. He set all sorts of records when he took thirteen wickets for 106 in addition to making 114 in the first innings, taking England to victory by ten wickets. Eight of his wickets came from catches behind by Bob Taylor, a sure indication that the ball was swinging, and Taylor's ten catches in the match were a world record. It was Taylor's misfortune that his career coincided with Alan Knott's. For years Taylor had travelled the world uncomplainingly as Knott's deputy. He is the most delightful and friendly person with an excellent sense of humour which he needed to keep him going for all those years. He was a brilliant keeper, although perhaps not quite the equal of Knott, who was five years the younger, nor was he such a capable batsman. After Knott had signed for Packer, Taylor took his place in the England side and went on to play fifty-seven Test Matches.

Even allowing for Botham, the main reason I remember the Golden Jubilee Test so well is for the total eclipse of the sun on what should have been the second day of the match. As a result, this became the rest day. The sun is a Hindu god and local superstition had it that it would be tempting providence to set foot out of doors on a sunless day. I was covering the match for the *Guardian* and I had to file a piece on that day. At that time, before computers ran the world, I had to take my typewritten piece by taxi round to the telegraph office in the middle of Bombay. This is a journey on which I usually reckon to see about half the population of Bombay in the streets, so packed are the pavements, even though it is, at most, a ten-minute ride. The traffic is always appalling with the old taxis belching black smoke, a nasty proposition if you are caught behind one in the inevitable jam.

I was surprised there were any taxis outside the hotel that day, but I suppose that even good Hindu religious principles falter when there is an excellent chance of making the odd rupee. The road to the telegraph office was eerie. The pavements, like the roads, were completely empty and we broke the record for the journey by about eight minutes. The telegraph office is also usually bulging with people but on this occasion there was no one except the operators and I was back at my hotel less than a quarter of an hour after leaving it. It was the first eclipse I had experienced and really it was a bit disappointing. During the crucial hour, Bombay was caught in a heavy shadow but there was no need for car drivers to put on their lights, although I suppose subcontinental umpires would have brought the players off for bad light. The next time I enjoyed an almost total eclipse was nineteen years later, in 1999 in London. There the pavements were full of people looking at the sun through pieces of smoked glass to protect their eyes. There was the same sort of shadowy light which would have had Dickie Bird in paroxysms of delight with his light-metre working overtime, but again I found I couldn't get worked up about it.

The previous September I had reached the age of forty and was getting on for the halfway stage of my working life and maybe this should have been the time to take stock, instead of just careering blindly on. During the drive from London to Bombay, when we had had that tricky time at the frontier between Iran and Afghanistan, another of those waiting a long time to get through had been a Welsh professor of linguistics called Ivor Lewis. He was getting on for seventy and spent half the year teaching in Bangalore in Southern India. We met him again, that evening at our hotel in Herat and, in his lovely rhythmical Welsh voice, he had tried to explain linguistics as the search for a spoken language of computer-like efficiency where there could be no misunderstandings. It was extremely complicated. Later, he talked to me about my job and the way of life which went with it. He asked me to tell him what I had done in the last year. I gave him a precis.

'You're just like my son,' he said when I had finished and there was a touch of amused despair in his voice. 'If you are to achieve anything worthwhile, you must stop moving around at such a frenetic pace and quieten down and decide what you really want to do.' He is not the only person who has said that to me and I suppose it was more or less what my mother meant when she said to me on many occasions, 'When on earth are you going to get yourself a proper job?' The professor made me think for most of that morning on the road to Kandahar before I tucked it away in the pending tray in the back of my mind and beyond, where it has remained ever since. Of course it would have been more sensible if there had been an overall plan to my life, instead of lurching from crisis to crisis. My excuse is that I have always been taken over and captivated by the present. I love writing and broadcasting about cricket. I love good wine and good food, just as I love the books of P.G. Wodehouse. I love Norfolk and North Farm and the dogs and so many more things on a hit or miss out-of-sight-out-of-mind basis, not in an unfaithful way but just because of my absorption with the present. When things move out of vision, I concentrate on what has taken their place. I have always regarded each day as an orange which needs to be squeezed dry of every drop of enjoyment.

I have never thought too deeply about where my job was taking me and the reason I am writing this chapter now is that at the stage I have reached in this book, I was still gallivanting around convinced that something would keep on turning up. I hoped someone would be inspired listening to my commentary and, smiting the brow, say that I was just the man for this, that or the other. I thought perhaps an editor of some newspaper might have

REST DAY

similar thoughts. Of course, nothing grand like that has ever happened but there have been enough things to keep me reasonably busy and on my toes. I am often asked whether I prefer writing to broadcasting, or the other way round. I think the answer would have to be that when I am broadcasting I prefer broadcasting and when I am writing I prefer writing. I have been lucky enough never to have struggled to find words in either capacity.

In writing an autobiography there are several temptations. One is to think you are in the confessional and now is the time to let it all come out. I don't think I'm much different from anyone else in that there are plenty of hidden corners of my life that I don't care to look back on, skeletons around which I have no wish to put back the flesh and blood and have no intention of doing so. Then there is the tempation to paint oneself as a thoroughly decent and law-abiding citizen with the highest possible standards. That's nonsense too. I have a genius for upsetting people for a combination of reasons. At times I can be extremely difficult and bloody-minded, I can be unreasonably unsympathetic to views that don't coincide with my own, I can be bombastic, I have always felt that the bottle should be finished rather than left for the next day, and I inherited – I shall pass on the blame if I can – a bad temper. This last has quietened down a bit as I've grown older, but if I mark out my long run, I am still capable of giving quite an impressive display.

There are any number of poor defenceless souls who incur my wrath, like telephone operators who think they know best, shop assistants who can't understand what I am after, headwaiters who present me with a bulging menu and then tell me that the first three things I want to order are off. Wine waiters get similar short shrift if I order a bottle of burgundy which is advertised in their list as 1995, a splendid year, and when it comes along it is revealed as being of a different, inferior year being sold at the same price. I find it extraordinary that when you ask a barman in a perfectly presentable hotel to mix you a dry martini with a piece of twisted lemon peel, the mixture that comes back is about as dry as a piece of Turkish Delight and once or twice a piece of lemon, not just the peel, has been squeezed into it. I can't think of the number of times I have ordered a steak not just to be underdone but to be blue and it has been put in front of me as a victim of the scorched earth policy. I have encountered wine waiters who have opened a bottle which is obviously corked and when I tell them to taste it themselves, have the nerve to say that I don't know what I am talking about. Then come the people I talk to who think they know what I am going to say and don't bother to listen to what I actually do say. Almost worst of all are the people driving cars for whom I stop in order to let them go by, either in London or on the single-track roads around North Farm, and they sweep by without giving me even the courtesy of a raised finger in thanks. You can see, I am afraid, what an impossibly intolerant chap I am although if you've got this far you've probably picked that up already.

An autobiography also gives the writer a wonderful chance of revenge. It provides the opportunity to put the record straight and give those who have wronged you a severe kick up the backside. In one or two places, as you will have gathered, I have fired a few volleys of shrapnel and my targets could hardly have expected to escape. There are some who have been lucky to get away with it, but litigious habits are nowadays widespread and one or two would, no doubt, be eager to race off to the courts at the first possible opportunity. This is a powerful deterrent, even to highly justifiable beastliness. My halo can be seen, therefore, more as a product of my publisher's expediency than of Christianity. In all honesty, there are not many I would love to lift my pen against, although the few that there are, and they don't only come from the world of cricket, will know full well from what I have not said, who they are.

Then there is the whole business of my love life and all that. I feel desperately sorry for my first wife, Joanna. She married a twenty-one-year-old embryonic merchant banker who turned, overnight, into a journalist and rapidly became impossible to live with. He also never had a weekend away from work. We married much too young but I have never regretted it for a single moment because, if we had not, my exceptional daughter, Suki, who we will come to later on, would never have been born. Most of the relationships I have had have been volatile affairs – screaming fun when all was right but with a dramatic downside when it went wrong. I have always been strongly attracted by women of fiercely independent character whom I thought I could steamroll into submission. It was invariably they who did the steamrollering. The more placid ladies soon became boring, if they hadn't run a mile in the first place. My second wife, Bitten, is beautiful, blonde and Swedish and the most unboring woman I have ever met, and we were married in 1990, but I am getting ahead of myself.

All through my adult life I have been continually asked what effect my accident at Eton has had on me. The answer is that I haven't a clue. I was desperately lucky to live, but perhaps the greatest luck I had was not to be left as a cabbage. In the early stages I suppose I tried my best to pretend it had not happened. I was eager to get on with life, which I attacked with as much enthusiasm as ever but too little sense. I don't think I was particularly sane when I went up to Cambridge and I dare say I wasn't that much better when I moved on to the City. My own feeling is that the accident made me more insecure than I need have been because, at an important point in my life, the only thing I had ever been any good at had been taken away from me. I had been left with precious little to hold up and show the world and I badly needed the confidence of my own success at something.

After scoring that hundred at Lord's for the Public Schools, I had been written about in glowing terms as a cricketer of the future. My whole life was cricket and I would have done anything to be able to continue onwards and upwards when I left Eton. Before my accident I might have been good enough to play firstclass cricket but it is stupid even to conjecture at anything beyond that. I think the most frustrating aspect of it all was watching cricket soon afterwards and knowing full well that if I had not had that blow on the head, I would surely have been able to do better than those two out in the middle. Pure conceit, I am afraid.

By the time I found myself writing about the game, I think I channelled everything I had into grounding my bat in that job. In one sense I was still in cricket, which was important to me, but it barely occurred to me that if things had broken differently, I might myself have been doing what I was now watching and writing about. I gave up playing cricket in my twenties which was ridiculously early but, as I was writing about the game seven days a week, I was unable to find time for practice, let alone for playing seriously. Having played the game to a reasonable level, I was not prepared to involve myself in what my father would have described as 'bumble puppy cricket'. If I had still been working like a good boy in the City, I am sure I would have kept on playing for as long as I could. As it was, when commentating came along to add to my writing, I was as concentrated as ever on my job. It was not until I arrived at about the age I have now got to in this book that I found myself looking back to that day in the Datchet Lane and wondering what might have happened if I had kept my eye on the bus. I soon realised that it was an entirely fruitless exercise and I was too far away from my days as a player for any thoughts of what my future might have been within the game to be anything but meaningless. It's hard enough sometimes to deal with life as it is without trying to complicate matters still further with what at best is hypothesis.

Insecurity has a lot to answer for. The main cause of it is almost certainly genes and, while that accident may subsequently have made me more insecure, the genes were already there. In their ways both my parents were insecure. Appearances were very important to them, as well as standards, although they are not necessarily quite the same thing. When I was young, at the Home Farm and then at Hoveton House, the invariable litmus paper test to any course of action I was contemplating was, 'What would Reggie and Christo think?', accompanied by much metaphorical shaking of the head and drawing in of the breath. It was not so much a question as a statement, for if the stage had been reached where this question had to be asked, the answer could be assumed to be no and therefore I had been found guilty. Reggie Cubitt, a cousin of my father's, was a landowner and farmer in neighbouring Honing. He was called Reggie by everyone, and that included small children. After his four older brothers had been killed in the Great War, Reggie inherited the family estate. He was the

REST DAY

very epitome of a First War colonel with the right sort of white moustache and a voice which would have been very much at home in the officers' mess and similar establishments. He was a bachelor and, as children, we regarded him as great fun, and this did not only depend on the size of his financial offerings at Christmas and birthdays. Christo Birkbeck was another farmer-cum-landowner. He lived at Rippon which was about the same distance from Hoveton as Honing. I well remember his love of my father's homemade sloe gin which, if he had the chance, he would have drunk out of a half-pint mug at the end of a shooting lunch. He too was great fun and once slipped me a sovereign before I went back to school at the end of the Long Leave (Eton for half-term) shoot in early November. They were both older than my father, but why they should have become the ultimate arbiters in good taste, I am not sure.

They shot and sometimes fished together and invariably had the same views on who was a cad and a bounder and generally beneath the salt. Every summer the three of them drove up to London to watch the Gentlemen and Players match at Lord's. They stayed at their club, Boodles, and most nights after dinner drank a second and maybe even a third glass of vintage port which was unheard of at home and would, as far as my father was concerned, have produced a certain matriarchal wagging of the finger. This was as close as they came to letting their hair down. If I was lucky when I was first working in London, I would be asked to one of these annual outbursts of extravagance. The conversation did not move far away from farming and Norfolk and when it did, it seldom reached a significant intellectual plateau. My father, like my mother, was highly involved in the art world and they were great collectors, but that was not one of Reggie or Christo's strongest points. When my father died in the summer of 1986, I was in Sydney making a television commercial for the following season's cricket in Australia. I flew home the next day and drove straight to Hoveton. My mother said to me that evening, 'It's all right, darling, Daddy's having the same coffin as Reggie,' and there was a great sense of relief in her voice. It would have been too awful for him to have been buried in the wrong sort of coffin. She discovered this, not by digging up Reggie, but by using the same undertaker.

The older I got, and the more the distance between childhood and adult life opened up, the better able I was to see and laugh at the foibles of my parents. They were both creatures of fierce habit, especially at home which, for their generation with people to look after them, was not surprising. For example, meal times were never a basis for negotiation. Breakfast was at half past eight sharp and my father was down ten minutes before that and made the coffee. No one in the kitchen could be trusted to make coffee that was strong enough. He worked on the admirable principle that if coffee was not so strong that it gave you nervous palpitations of the heart, it was not worth drinking. Breakfast was a feast which would have made a Trappist monk feel at home for it was conducted in silence. My father was best left to his pile of letters and the *Eastern Daily Press* at this time of day.

There was a glass of sherry in the hall at half past twelve and lunch was at one o'clock when a bell, which had once been tied round the neck of a cow in Switzerland, was rung vigorously and into the dining room we all trooped. Tea was pushed into the hall on a trolley at half past four, but when I arrived late for tea I was cautioned rather than censored. I remember my mother always insisted we finished the last quarter of the old cake which had become dry and crumbly before being allowed to tackle the new one which, as a result, became dry and crumbly before it was even begun. Dinner was at a quarter to eight and was preceded by another bell-ringing session. By then, I was expected to have had a bath and changed. My father always wore a smoking jacket and black tie for dinner and my mother a long dress or a long skirt. Even towards the end of their lives, when my mother hotted up whatever had been left for them on the Aga and they ate in the kitchen off the yellow Formica table, they still dressed for the occasion.

After dinner they sat in the hall, my father reading a who dunnit and my mother either doing her tatting, as she called her needlework, or reading. There was a television set in the hall but my father, like John now, loathed watching it, although the nine

REST DAY

o'clock news always got a touch. After the headlines, my father would lean over towards the set and say, 'I think we've seen enough,' which would produce an immediate protest from my mother. The news was left on and my father pointedly read his book until it was almost over. My mother would then say, 'All right, Tom, you can turn it off now if you want.' He quickly looked at his watch before replying, 'Now we've got this far, we might as well see the weather forecast,' by which he set great store. It was the same every evening.

One of the most entertaining set pieces of the day, which went on until my father died, came when it was time for bed. Again punctuality was paramount and ten o'clock should have been the time for that ritual to begin. At twelve minutes to ten, my mother would look up, yawn and say, 'It's time for bed, darling.' Whereupon my father would glance at his watch and say in horrified tones, 'It's not even ten to ten. We can't possibly go to bed yet.' They would return to whatever they were doing and another twenty-five minutes would go by. Then my father would look at his watch again and, half-rising from his chair, say with some dismay, 'Good God, Grizel, it's a quarter past ten. We should have been in bed hours ago.' And they would hurriedly turn out the lights and make an energetic dash for the stairs up which they would make a more or less stately progress in line ahead formation. That seldom varied either.

This was all done without any sense of humour, at least on my father's part, but he was able to laugh, especially when reading P.G. Wodehouse's latest offering. He could laugh at himself, too, and I particularly remember one such occasion late-ish on in his life. Over the years everything at Hoveton had been made over to my brother John or to the family trust or whatever – as the younger son, I was never let into details of any of these secrets. My father suddenly discovered when he was well into his seventies that there was one small road, Riverside Road, in Hoveton stretching from the middle of the village down to the River Bure which still belonged to him. It was not an especially prepossessing piece of road and it was liberally sprinkled with some impressive potholes. The first forty or fifty yards of it were always in use as they led to the car park for a new shopping precinct. One day my father was driving down Riverside Road in gingerly manner to avoid the potholes and somehow succeeded in completely blocking another car. Much hooting ensued and the other driver wound down his window and shouted angrily at my father, 'I suppose you think you own the bloody road,' to which my father replied after a slight pause, 'Well, as a matter of fact, I do.' He greatly enjoyed telling this one.

The one habit I managed to inherit, probably from some distant forebear, but certainly not from my parents, was my dreadful absent-mindedness and disorganisation. Whenever I leave my house, I have hardly got to the end of the lane or round the block before a frantic feeling of my pockets reveals my wallet is missing and back I have to go. When I start again I discover my mobile telephone is still charging in the kitchen and on it goes. I spread panic through the house in my frequent desperate searches for my glasses; my keys can be just as elusive. Whenever Bitten gives me a shopping list and points me in the general direction of a supermarket, I always manage to return home without the most crucial item of all.

The art of tidiness is something else I have failed to master. Like the pile of clothes on my dressing-room bed, the mountain of papers on my desk rises inexorably towards the ceiling until they all crash to the floor, where they remain undisturbed. Eating, too, has its moments and by the time I return home from lunch or dinner, it is often possible to determine the menu from a careful look at my shirt front. I have probably chosen the wrong job for someone who has all these problems. After all these years on the road, I should have learned to pack with considerably greater accuracy than I have. It starts with being unable to select the appropriate raw materials in the first place and then being quite unable to put them in a suitcase so that they arrive in anything other than a creased and mangled state looking like a used economy-class airline blanket. When I arrive at an airport it's always worth a bet that I don't have all the appropriate documents and, if I do, the chances are that I will leave one of them on some counter or other. I have a genius, too, for leaving things on aeroplanes, like that wretched chapter in Colombo.

By the time we arrived at the eighties, I found myself wondering before the start of a new English season if after the first day I would discover that I was bored to death with the whole business of watching cricket. Just occasionally I still ask myself this, but by now it is far too late to try and do anything else and so I instantly suppress any such thoughts. The extraordinary thing is that far from growing bored with cricket, I have found myself becoming more and more interested in the whole process. There have been some times, though, when watching county cricket in particular and the players appear to be doing little more than going through the motions, that I have discovered my threshold of boredom has noticeably risen. But I hope this has been the extent of any mid-life crisis.

CHAPTER

15

WEST INDIAN ANTICS

WHEN ENGLAND returned home from Bombay, Mike Brearley announced his retirement from the captaincy and it was an open secret that he recommended that Ian Botham should be appointed to succeed him. Botham was the most extraordinary phenomenon to hit English cricket for a long time. He had played his first Test Match in 1977 and he was only twenty-four at the start of the 1980 season in England. Events were soon to show that Brearley's endorsement of Botham as his successor was by no means his cleverest move as England's captain. It was interesting that the West Indies were to visit England in 1980 and that the following winter England were to visit the Caribbean. In Brearley's splendid career as captain of his country, he never played a Test Match against the West Indies, the one side against whom captaincy alone may not have been enough. Did his positive espousement of Botham's cause as his successor ease his own departure? I am sure these are unworthy thoughts and they would never have occurred to me if Botham had made rather a better hand of the job. As it was, I find it difficult to believe that a mind of Brearley's famed capability could have made such a bad misjudgement.

While all this was happening, I had gone back to Australia from Bombay because Derrick Robins had decided that I had been such a success as assistant manager to his side in South America, that he would give me another chance to prove my worth, this time on his tour to Tasmania and New Zealand. It was never likely to be as much fun as the visit to South America the previous winter as it was less of a journey into the unknown. Hobart and Wellington don't have quite the potential of Buenos Aires and Rio. This time the party was managed by the former England captain, Mike Denness, and Les Ames again came with us. It was a joy to have him with the party, not only because he was such a delightful man, but also because he was able to relate to the young players and always gave them shrewd advice when asked. He would never venture an opinion unless his advice was sought. I was surprised on both tours that the young county players were not more eager to seek his opinion and also the company of a man who played forty-seven times for England as a wicket-keeper batsman, and made a hundred first-class hundreds. Derrick's side was not as successful as it had been in South America, but the opposition, especially towards the end in New Zealand, was pretty good. Our activities off the field were considerably less flamboyant, too.

This Robins tour took place just after perhaps the most ill-fated tour of all time when the West Indies played three Test Matches in New Zealand and ran into trouble with the umpires.

In the First Test in Dunedin, New Zealand won a thrilling game by one wicket. The West Indies were loud in their condemnation of the umpiring. Twelve lbw decisions were given against the batsmen during the match, seven against the West Indies and five against New Zealand. When the match was over the West Indies players and their manager, Willie Rodriguez, the old leg spinner from Trinidad who in my view has to bear some of the responsibility for what went on, did not behave as tactfully as they might. They were particularly virulent in their comments about one of the umpires, Fred Goodall, who, admittedly, always liked to umpire as if he was staging a one-man play. He never settled for one histrionic gesture if two or more could be applied. It all came to a head in the Second Test in Christchurch when, in protest at his umpiring, the West Indies refused to take the field after tea on the third day. They asked for a change of umpire which was rightly refused and they locked themselves in their dressing room for a team meeting and emerged on to the field twelve minutes late. If Goodall and his colleague Steve Woodward had ruled that they had forfeited the match, it would have been fair enough.

The trouble had been sparked when the New Zealand captain, Geoff Howarth, survived a confident appeal for a catch behind by Deryck Murray when he was 68. He reached his hundred from the first ball after the belated restart and batted on through a most unpleasant last session when some West Indies fielders ignored balls hit in their direction. The West Indies threatened to go home and only intense diplomacy on the rest day ensured they finished the match and the tour. When play restarted, Richard Hadlee was given not out by umpire Goodall when there was a loud appeal for a catch behind. Colin Croft, the bowler, barged into Goodall as he ran in to bowl the next ball. The Second and Third Tests were both drawn and New Zealand won the series. When I interviewed Clive Lloyd for the BBC during his last Test Match, against Australia at Sydney in 1984/85, I asked him about this series in New Zealand. He told me how much he regretted it and it was the one thing in his cricketing life he would like to be able to have over again. Having been the best side in the world for almost ten years, the West Indies players probably felt that they could do as they pleased and get away with it.

The 1980 season was especially memorable for those of us in the *Test Match Special* box because at the end of it John Arlott hung up his microphone for the last time. He had turned sixty-five and was determined to go when still firing on all cylinders. For the last few years he had, in fact, been wearing extraordinary glasses with yellow lenses to help his vision and he had been having difficulty in identifying people. It had not yet reached the stage where it was noticeable, but maybe it was one of the things which prompted him to go when he did. His departure from the Test scene at the end of the Centenary Match against Australia at Lord's on 2 September was a modest and unemotional affair. I was doing the number two job for that match and was one of the many crammed into the main commentary box when he did his last twenty-minute session.

He had reserved for the occasion the striped shirt I shall best remember him by. He bought his shirts from the Van Heusen factory in Taunton and in my early days as a journalist, when we were both watching Somerset, he took me with him one morning before the start of play to collect the latest batch. In spite of the time of day, it was still accompanied by a glass or two, if I remember rightly, of something red and palatable. On those occasions he bowed to his priorities and did not mind missing the first ball. On that last day at Lord's, he did not say farewell to his listeners but simply came to the end of his last commentary spell and in those inimitably fruity Hampshire tones, said, 'And after Trevor Bailey, it will be Christopher Martin-Jenkins.' There was an announcement over the Tannoy marking the moment and this was followed by ringing applause all round the ground. The commentary box was swarming with television cameramen and interviewers but he dealt with their requests quickly and walked away without any fuss to go to the press box and write his piece for the *Guardian*. For such an emotional man it was an impressively low-key departure.

Although Arlott could be difficult with his likes and dislikes, I always got on well with him. I enjoyed his stories enormously, even if I had heard them three times before. He told them with such relish and delighted so much in the punchline you could see him anticipating it as the story unwound. I was never bored with listening to him, unless it was very late at night and yet another bottle of red wine had appeared and some of the old prejudices were beginning to surface. He could sometimes be short with those old buffers who come out of the cobwebs at most cricket grounds and tried and get him into a corner. He was essentially an anti-establishment figure and it may have been for this reason that colleagues including Brian Johnston and Jim Swanton held him in great respect but without much personal warmth.

Once, after a day's Test cricket at Old Trafford, I gave Arlott a lift back to Bucklow Hill and he insisted on taking me to see some friends of his on the way. They lived extremely close to the ground. We turned left out of the practice ground, left again at the roundabout and there we were. They were an elderly couple and they were more delighted than you could believe to see John who always brought a bottle with him on these visits. It was opened and we drank it in their sitting room. They were both full of all the things he had said on *TMS* that day and it was an animated, vigorous conversation. It was touching to see the joy his commentary had brought to these two who had organised their day around the wireless (not the radio) with sandwiches and frequent excursions for tea. They were polite enough to say they enjoyed my offerings – I think it made all the difference that I was a friend of John's whom they worshipped. When Brian Johnston's name came up, dark disapproval set in and, in a charmingly firm but gentle way, they shook their heads and felt he was too flippant and was unable to make them see things as John did. I have to say, I felt their views on Johnners had been aided and abetted by John on previous visits. We were there for an hour and they told us more about the day and our commentaries than we knew ourselves. What made it so extraordinary was that they were both blind and had been for most of their lives.

The Centenary Test Match produced another, far less pleasant incident. There was plenty of rain during the match and the light was seldom more than average and often a great deal worse. The two umpires, David Constant and Dickie Bird, were forever going backwards and forwards to the middle and peering into their light metres, as well as prodding two used pitches near the one being used for this match which had become extremely wet. They received a good deal of unkind barracking and when they returned to the pavilion from their fifth inspection on the Saturday afternoon, Constant was barged into and hit by some members standing in the passageway leading from the ground to the Long Room. On wet days some of the members of MCC, like many others, probably succumb to the temptation to spend too much time in the bar for there is nothing else to do. This was a bit like members of the old House of Lord's having a couple over the odds and giving Garter King of Arms and Black Rod something to think about just before the State Opening of Parliament. This incident will remain a sad blot on the escutcheon of England's most noble cricket club, even though the culprits were brought to book.

The main part of the summer had been filled by a series against the West Indies, the last for many years in which England were able almost to hold their own. They lost the First Test by two wickets in a thrilling finish at Trent Bridge. The other four were drawn, although England never looked much like winning any of them and were helped by the rain which caused four blank days in the series. Botham's captaincy had not been that impressive and the job unquestionably affected his form as both bowler and batsman, although he seldom produced his best against the West Indies.

I was back in Australia at the end of November 1980 to watch a short series against New Zealand who made little impression, losing two of their three Test Matches. After that, India played three Tests, losing the first easily and then surprising everyone including themselves by bowling out Australia for 83 when they needed 143 to win in the Third, and drawing the series. In the finals of the dreaded one-day competition, Australia beat New Zealand but only after one of the most pusillanimous incidents I have ever seen on a cricket field. When the two sides came to Melbourne for the third of the best-of-five finals, they had each won one match. At the MCG, Australia won the toss and made 235/4 in their fifty overs. When Trevor Chappell came on to bowl the last over of the match, New Zealand needed 15 to win with four wickets in hand, and with two left they needed 6 to tie from the last ball which was bowled to Brian McKechnie. Greg Chappell, the captain, came over and had a word with his brother Trevor and the upshot was that on one of the biggest grounds in the world, Chappell walked a couple of steps and solemnly bowled an underarm grub to McKechnie which he pushed back down the pitch. Small wonder that New Zealand's Prime Minister, Robert Muldoon, described this as 'an act of cowardice', and went on to say, 'It was appropriate that the Australians were dressed in yellow.' Greg Chappell later expressed considerable regret at what he had set in motion.

When the 1980/81 season had finished in Australia, I raced to the West Indies where England, under Ian Botham, were about to start an extraordinarily eventful tour. The fact that England lost the series was the least surprising of the events that were to unfold. After picking up some clean shirts in London on the way through, I found myself at the lovely Queen's Park Oval in Port of Spain six days after I had left Australia. England lost the First Test by an innings and 79 runs after Botham had become the first England captain since Bob Wyatt in 1934/35 to put the West Indies in to bat. The West Indies fast bowlers were too good for England who were themselves without Bob Willis, the vice-captain, who was injured and, after this match, was forced to return to England for an operation on his knee. Botham's captaincy had not been good. I wrote disparagingly about it in the *Sunday Express* and it was not long before someone sent him the piece to read.

Port of Spain in February is never the place to be gloomy. Preparations for Carnival were going on in top gear. The papers were as full of the antics of the leading Calypsonians, the Mighty Sparrow, Lord Kitchener and the rest, as they were of the cricketers. One evening after dinner, three of us, Patrick Eagar, without his cameras for once, Jane Morgan, a BBC radio producer, and I, went along to Frederick Street in downtown Port of Spain to listen to the Mighty Shadow, another premier league Calypsonian. We had a great time. There were some splendid calypsoes, even if the humour seldom rises above the belt. When it was all over, there wasn't a taxi in sight. We were not all that far away from the Queen's Park Hotel and when Jane asked me if it was safe to walk, I told her there were few safer journeys. After a couple of hundred yards, we turned left over a piece of waste land to cut off a corner. Suddenly there was a slight scuffle of running feet behind us and three or four youngsters scampered past. Once past, the biggest of them turned round to face us in a slight crouch and I could see a gleaming metal object in his right hand which looked remarkably like a gun. It was pointing unerringly at my tummy and then I saw that one of the others had a similar looking weapon in his hand. I was asked the next day if I was sure they were guns. I replied that I was in no mood to find out. They asked to see the colour of our money, and I won the first prize for cowardice by pulling out all the local money I had, which amounted to about thirty pounds' worth. They were so impressed by my obvious desire to help that they forgot about my watch and signet ring. Patrick also complied rapidly with their request, although he had rather more money on him than I did.

Jane had the worst of it because, when they took her bag, she asked them if she could have her passport back. They felt that this amounted to insolence on a grand scale and she was promptly hit in the face. It occurred to me that James Bond might well have had the answer to this, but mercifully they soon fled and so there was little to be gained thinking further along those lines, which was a relief. Someone called the police who were quickly on the scene. With the help of their torches, we scoured the ground and soon found Jane's passport and a few other bits and pieces they had emptied out of her bag. The police told us that with all the overseas visitors in Port of Spain for Carnival, it was the high point of the muggers' year. Not only that, but the best muggers in neighbouring Venezuela made a point of coming over for a short tour. When we had finished making statements, I spent about an hour in a police car driving through Port of Spain looking for 'suspicious characters'. I don't think I saw anyone who didn't look suspicious, but we never came across our lot again.

By the time we had reached Georgetown in Guyana where the Second Test was to be played, Robin Jackman had joined the party as a replacement for Willis. The party was encamped at the Pegasus Hotel and the first game was a one-day international up country in Berbice which the West Indies won by six wickets. By the time we had returned to Georgetown the next day, politics was threatening to end the tour. A radio commentator in Jamaica with a programme to fill had questioned Jackman's right to be in the West Indies because of his strong South African connections. He was married to a South African and spent the English winters there playing and coaching. The government of Forbes Burnham took up the issue immediately and declared Jackman *persona non grata* in Guyana which meant that he had to leave and would not be able to play in the Test Match. It took me back three years to the Packer problems in Georgetown and now, as then, Lionel Luckhoo's house in Bel Air Park was in the thick of it. Lionel Luckhoo was still Burnham's solicitor and had a better idea than anyone about the government's thinking on this issue. England obviously could not allow foreign governments to dictate to them who they should play in their Test team. As a result, we soon drove back down that dreadful road to the airport, which is full of some of the biggest potholes in the world, and flew out to Barbados where accommodation had been hastily arranged at the Rockley Resort on the edge of Bridgetown.

There were still three Test Matches to come and the Foreign Ministers of the three countries in which they were to be held, Barbados, Jamaica and Antigua which was about to host its inaugural Test Match, gathered in Bridgetown and held their discussions in another part of the Rockley Resort. After much talk, it was decided that the tour would go ahead. I would like to think that Antigua's Lester Bird may have been swayed by the fact that he was about to become a Test Match commentator. On past tours to the Caribbean, I had several times joined the local commentators in Antigua who had been gathered from both ends of the political spectrum. There was Lester Bird whose father was Vere Bird, Antigua's long-serving Prime Minister, who was generally to the right of things, while Tim Hector was a rabble-rousing Communist. Now that Antigua were about to host their first Test Match, Lester Bird would be at the microphone. Perhaps he felt that if he did not grasp the present opportunity, circumstances might yet prevent him from fufilling this particular ambition.

Four of us, Johnny Woodcock, Michael Melford, Robin Marlar and I, had decided some months before to rent a house for the Barbados leg of the tour. We had come up with a beach house called Kampala owned by Errol Barrow who was then the Prime Minister of the Island. It was in a good setting by the sea next door to the Paradise Beach Hotel where we had all stayed for the Arab tour fifteen years before. As the match approached, I began to feel pretty unwell with a more or less permanent headache and no energy and it grew worse. In the end a clever doctor from Hole Town realised I was suffering from a meningism which is a blood relation of meningitis and mercifully he prescribed the correct cure. I struggled to the match on the first day when the West Indies were bowled out for 265 after Botham had again put them in to bat. On the second day, the England batting collapsed in a heap and they were all out for 122. I was woken up early the next morning by Johnny who came in to tell me that Ken Barrington, who was only fifty, had died of a massive heart attack the night before.

As a player, no one had personified the true bulldog spirit of an Englishman more than Ken who played eighty-two times for his country. He had become England's permanent coach on tour, the players loved him and were loyal to him to a man because they knew he would never let them down. Crimp haired with a permanently sunburnt face and always smiling, Ken was everyone's friend. He was as good in the dressing room as he was at spotting and correcting technical flaws outside it. Ken had the most lovely smile and was the master of the malapropism. He was always urging his bowlers to keep to that length when the batsman cannot be sure whether to play back or forward, to keep them 'in two-man's land', as he described it. Ken was a partner in a garage at Bookham in Surrey where he lived, and for three summers I hired a car from him. When I picked it up in April, I would stay and have lunch with him before driving back to London. This happened three times and I wouldn't have missed any of them. He was so amusing and full of good sense and when we talked of other people his comments were always extremely perceptive. Known to the players as the Colonel which was his regular guise at the Christmas fancy-dress party when on tour, Ken was a dear man and his early death was a great setback for England's cricket.

Ken, who was a great worrier, had been especially upset by England's poor batting on the second day at Kensington Oval. He and Anne, his wife, had gone out to dinner and when they returned to the Holiday Inn, they had gone straight upstairs. Ken had lain down on his bed while Anne went into the bathroom and when she came out a few minutes later he was dead. Bernard Thomas, the physiotherapist, and Alan Smith, the manager, did their best to resuscitate him but it was too late for that. It must have been extremely difficult for the players to continue with the match the next day and in spite of a brilliant 116 by Graham

Gooch in England's second innings, the West Indies won by almost 300 runs. I shall never forget the devastating sense of loss and hopelessness in the three days after Ken's death. He was such a friend to all of us.

The inaugural Test Match in Antigua was almost hijacked by Viv Richards' wedding in St John's two days earlier. The bridegroom became the first West Indian to score a hundred in a Test Match on the Recreation Ground on what should have been the third day of his honeymoon. The wedding was a wonderful occasion and the streets were packed almost as if it was a royal wedding which, as far as Antigua was concerned, it was. I watched with Robin Marlar, hemmed in by the crowd on a street corner opposite the cathedral. Ian Botham was his best man and a number of the Somerset players had come over for the occasion. Some of the hats worn by the local ladies would have brought out the milliners of Paris and London in a cold sweat.

Finally, at Sabina Park in Kingston, a Herculean effort by David Gower who batted for seven and three-quarter hours at the end for 154 not out, saved England after the West Indies had gained a first innings lead of 157. We had to wait for more than a day for our aeroplane, taking off for England the following evening. There were several tired and emotional figures aboard that British Airways jumbo. Botham was wearing his blazer which he would need for the press conference at Heathrow the next morning. At some stage on the first leg of the flight he went through his pockets and found the cutting of the piece I had written severely criticising his captaincy during the First Test. He mulled it over with his next door neighbour, Graham Stevenson, one of Yorkshire's true intellectuals, and they decided that retribution must be sought during the stopover in Bermuda.

Six rows further back, I was unaware that any of this was happening and when we landed I decided to leave the aeroplane and stretch my legs. Inside the in-transit lounge, I found the loo and spent a penny. When I came out Botham was standing outside the door and said something I did not hear, but I heard Bernard Thomas, the pysiotherapist, tell him to be careful. Not long before we were due to rejoin the aircraft, Botham came over to me and said that he wanted a word and suggested that I accompanied him to another part of the lounge. By now I had realised what it was all about and, as politely as I could, I declined the invitation. He began to express himself forcibly about the piece I had written. He went on to make some more general comments about me which were less than complimentary. As he spoke, he began to prod me in the chest with his right index finger. Soon the fingers curled into a fist and the prodding passed over the dividing line into punching. The situation was becoming more fraught by the second until Thomas and Dudley Doust, an American who worked for the *Sunday Times* and was writing a book with Botham, came up behind him and led him away. He went, full of resentful reluctance. But within minutes he was back and pushed me hard into some chairs standing against the wall. I fell into one of them and stayed put while Messrs Thomas and Doust returned to try and persuade him it was time to reboard the aircraft.

When we were safely aboard, I suddenly found Botham standing over me again with his arm raised. I quickly took off my glasses and, without looking, pushed them sideways to my neighbour where they encountered soft resistance. After a little bit more soft resistance, she leapt to her feet with a loud, 'Do you mind!' because unwittingly I had been pushing them into an impressively ample right boob. A steward now arrived to steer the England captain back to his seat and peace returned. During the flight there were a number of journalistic conferences and we decided not to write anything about the incident. We arrived back in London on the Saturday morning and I went immediately up to Norfolk. Eight days later, on the Sunday, I drove to the village to buy the papers and I saw Botham's name in huge letters on the front of the *People*. I bought a copy, along with the others I wanted, and when I got back to my car I discovered the story had been well and truly leaked. I believe one of the journalists on the aeroplane had spoken a trifle loosely in a Fleet Street pub. It was the second time I had made that august journal's front page which for a decent law-abiding citizen was not a bad effort.

I can well understand Botham's feelings, but even so the law of the jungle should not really be allowed to apply. I like to think that on another day he might have acted differently. The following month when Somerset played against Hampshire at Southampton, he and I had a well-publicised drink together in the pavilion bar. We are now reasonable friends and from his lofty position in the Sky commentary box, he has become my spread-betting adviser. His advice is not difficult to follow for it comes down to one thing: sell England when they bat.

CHAPTER

16

THE BOTHAM PHENOMENON

I HAD FIRST SIGHTED the eighteen-year-old Ian Botham at Taunton, one of my favourite county grounds, on 12 June 1974 when Somerset were playing Hampshire in the Benson & Hedges Cup and he made the headlines for the first time in what we were soon to know was the typical Botham manner. I was reporting the match from the press box and there is nothing better than seeing an exciting young player emerge, although it was some time before we knew quite what we had seen. I even remember Eric Hill, who had batted for Somerset immediately after the war and had kept a wary eye on the county's fortunes from this same vantage point with wry good humour ever since, being more optimistic than usual about this young all-rounder. Hampshire were bowled out for 182 and Botham took two wickets, including that of Barry Richards which was not a bad first strike.

He then found himself walking in to bat in the fortieth over when Somerset were 113/7 which was to become 113/8 later in the same over. It was not long before he tried to hook Andy Roberts, the best of all the West Indies fast bowlers over this period. Botham was late with his stroke and the ball hit him full in the mouth. There was plenty of blood about and it was an injury which would have ended most batsmen's day. Botham refused all offers of sanctuary, received some first aid from the dressing room, shook himself both mentally and physically and buckled down to the job in hand. Runs came fast. Hallam Moseley, another West Indian, made him an excellent partner until a perfect yorker from Roberts ended his involvement. He and Botham had put on 63. Already, the power of Botham's strokeplay was irresistible and two sixes soared out of the ground. The last man was Bob Clapp, whom I had once caught on the square leg boundary at Fenner's, and his batting had not improved significantly since. A searing drive through extra cover by Botham a few minutes later saw Somerset home by one wicket. He had let the world know there was a pretty exceptional talent lurking down there in Somerset.

Three years later he was chosen to play for England against the Packer-infected Australia at Trent Bridge and it was his presence rather than Geoffrey Boycott's return from the wilderness which was responsible for the general feeling of anticipation. Australia won the toss and batted and Botham took the first of his twenty-seven hauls of five wickets in a Test innings. He then made 25 useful runs and we all know how it went on from there. Of course, Botham was his own worst enemy and that was part of his charm. He was a creature of passion, he got carried away by the excitements of life, he drank too much, he was prepared to give anything a go, he played too hard (off the field), but, my word, he produced the goods on it. Whenever I drove to watch Somerset or England play knowing that Botham would be in the side, it enormously beefed up my expectations. It must have been the same after the war in any game in which Denis Compton was playing and a long time before that, it was important not to miss the first ball at the Oval if Jack Hobbs's name was on the scorecard. There are not many players who have this effect on people.

Botham is the most open and likeable of men. I have always likened him to an excitable and enthusiastic young Labrador who vigorously wags his tail and has not been able to help knocking a few valuable ornaments off the table. He had an enormous God-given talent with either a bat or a ball in his hand. He has always liked and got on with his fellow human beings – unless they had the temerity to criticise his captaincy, although our run-in did not last for long. There may have been times in his life when he was too easily led but I never found there was ever anything devious

...o considerable pen pushers. Johnny Woodcock (*The Times*) and Jack Fingleton (the *Sunday Times* and ...ny Australian papers) debate their thirst at the Longparish cricket ground when Johnny's side was ...ying the village.

...hael Melford (*Daily Telegraph*) in white hat, H.C.B. (the *Guardian*), Alex Bannister (*Daily Mail*) ...h Peter Laker (*Daily Mirror*) behind, compiling their peerless prose at the end of the day in India.

A pivotal figure, Basil D'Oliveira was a formidable cricketer and is a great man.

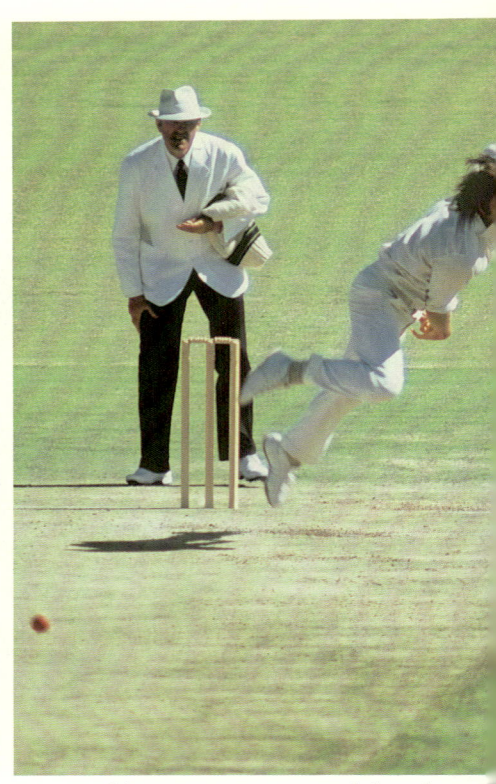

Nature seldom gets more primeval than this. Jeff Thomson at his ferocious best against England in 1974/75.

Perhaps the greatest one-day innings of all. Viv Richards drives Bob Willis over extra cover for six on way to 189 not out against England at Old Trafford in 1984.

...wearing his inevitable brown and white 'co-respondent' shoes, Brian Johnston awaits his next spell at the microphone at Old Trafford.

...the bowler's Holding... . . . the batsman's Willey.

A traffic jam in Afghanistan. The worried driver, Adrian Liddell, searches for a way through.

Rolls-Royce, boys and beasts of the field, on the subcontinent they all shall equal be.

...nny Woodcock and H.C.B. at an early stage in Europe on the drive to India. The Rolls was well
...epared for punctures.

...e drive intrepidly on into Afghanistan looking spectacularly out of place.

John Arlott, the greatest commentator of all, takes a breather after another good lunch.

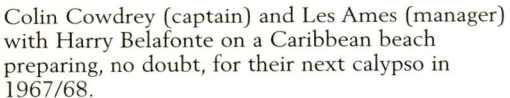

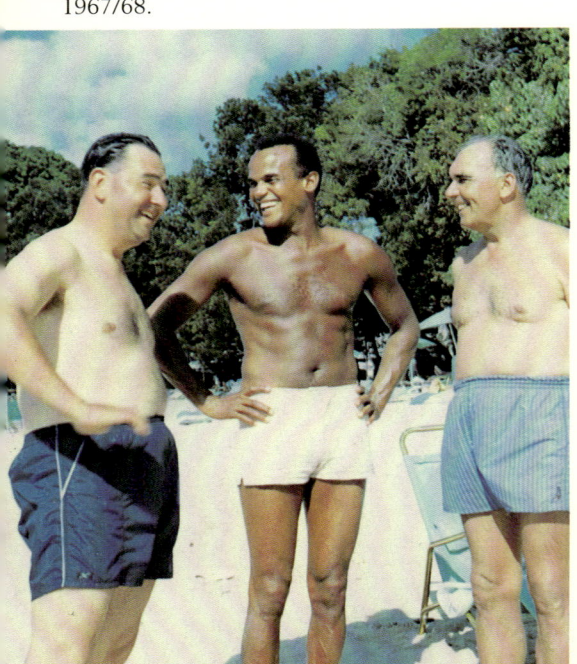

Colin Cowdrey (captain) and Les Ames (manager) with Harry Belafonte on a Caribbean beach preparing, no doubt, for their next calypso in 1967/68.

Tony Greig – an urbane look, a fine all-rounder, ultra-competitive and inexplicably enigmatic.

A most compelling trio in the West Indies in 1967/68 – Keith Miller, Denis Compton and two-time Derby winner, Scobie Breasley.

Everton Weekes on his way up to enlighten and entertain with his knowledge, his wit and his [ch]arm in the commentary box at Kensington [O]val, Bridgetown.

At the microphone with Imran Khan at Bourda, Georgetown in 1992/93.

[A] formidable trio. Peter Lashley (*left*) who played in the tied Test at Brisbane in 1960/61, the [Co]mmander (Arshed Gilani) and Raman Subba Row (match referee) at Kensington Oval 1992/93.

23 October 1990. Bitten and I clink our first post-nuptial glasses of champagne at Mortons in Berkeley Square.

THE BOTHAM PHENOMENON

or calculating about Ian Botham. You got what you saw. He lurched from one agent, Reg Hayter, who was very experienced and did his best to protect Botham from himself, to Tim Hudson who had made money as a disc jockey in California and wanted to take Botham to Hollywood and turn him into a latter-day Errol Flynn. It was too big a step. Hudson was obsessed with the idea, but only a few seconds thought should have told him that Botham's heroic future lay where it was. The only successful role in which Botham was ever likely to be cast was playing himself on the cricket field. Although I am sure Hudson's intentions were admirable, with the best will in the world, I don't think he was the most benign influence Botham could have found. There could hardly have been a greater contrast between Hayter and Hudson. The former was perhaps too conservative for his man while the latter was undoubtedly an over-correction.

Botham was cut out to be the hero at the pitface and I was lucky enough to watch many of his most dramatic performances. He played the game the same way as he lived life, which was by instinct. He buckled on his pads or grabbed the ball and it all happened. Those who play the game by the light of nature do not have to think about it or try to work it out for themselves. They never have to strip down the engine and reassemble it and find out how the mechanism works. He had difficulty therefore in appreciating the problems that affect ordinary mortals who have not been as lucky as he was. I am sure this was why captaincy did not come easily to him although I am confident he will not agree with me.

Botham returned to England from the West Indies with two poor series behind him, both as a player and captain. He kept the captaincy for the start of the series against Australia in 1981 and lost an exciting First Test at Trent Bridge by four wickets. I had the feeling as I watched from the press box that if Brearley had been in charge, England might have won for he would have made life harder for the Australian batsmen on the last day. When we came to Lord's for the Second Test, Botham, who had been appointed for the first two matches only, was under great pressure to handle his side more convincingly. In ten Test Matches he had not done much to suggest he had a great tactical grasp. He made the obvious bowling changes and otherwise stood in the slips and waited for something to happen. There was no flare or imagination about any of it. Things did not improve at Lord's and he made nought in both innings. After he had been bowled first ball in the second innings playing a crude sweep at Ray Bright, I shall never forget the embarrassing, almost eerie, silence which greeted his walk back to the Pavilion. A huge man, he seemed to diminish and shrink with each stride and by the time he reached the Pavilion gate, he looked as if he was the central figure of one of H.M. Bateman's 'The man who . . .' cartoons. It was no surprise when the news came through to the commentary box on the last day that he had resigned the captaincy only minutes before Alec Bedser, the chairman of the selectors, was to have told him he had been sacked.

It was a brilliant idea to recall Brearley who was almost certainly the only person who could have mentally rehabilitated Botham so that he was a competitor for the rest of the series. Brearley will also have insisted that he remained in the side as a player. This was the scene as the two sides foregathered in Leeds for the Third Test Match and I had the luck to have been selected for the commentary box. It was the most incredible Test Match I have ever seen and has been written about *ad infinitum*. England followed on 227 runs behind and, when they had lost their seventh second innings wicket for 135, were still 92 adrift. In the next eighty minutes Botham and Graham Dilley, tall, fair-haired and left-handed, put on 117; Chris Old, tall, wiry and also left-handed, then helped him add 67 for the ninth wicket and when England were all out for 356, Botham was 149 not out.

I shall be surprised if I see another innings to compare with it. He had come in at 105/5 and played normally for a while, but as wickets continued to fall and the hopelessness of the situation became ever more apparent, he took his life in his hands. It began as a form of black humour because for some time it was nothing more than the defiant firing of the last few rounds before the ammunition finally ran out. Botham used a heavy bat and the ball kept coming out of the middle with a decisive and imperious

THE BOTHAM PHENOMENON

crack. It was a wonderful display to commentate about but every soaring stroke was followed by the inevitable caution that it was not going to change anything. It was too early to tell that it was brave Horatius all over again and this time with a touch of D'Artagnan thrown in. All of this came from a man who had been down and out at Lord's less than a fortnight before – and he had already taken six wickets in Australia's first innings and then made 50 in England's first innings. At the second attempt Botham had played the innings of a lifetime and maybe it was Brearley who had made it possible. I shall always remember one stroke. After Dilley had been bowled by Alderman, Botham's immediate riposte was to stamp that enormous left boot down the pitch and straight drive Alderman for a low, raking six. It was awe-inspiring. When Old was later bowled by Geoff Lawson, England were still only 92 runs ahead. Bob Willis, who had once come out to bat in a Test Match at Edgbaston and found when he reached the middle that he had forgotten to bring his bat out with him, was not so absent-minded this time. He and Botham had put on 32 by the close that evening and when Willis was caught in the slips the next morning, Australia needed 130 to win.

It was during the ten-minute break between innings that Lillee and Marsh got wind of the news that Ladbroke's, prompted on these things by that famous crystal ball gazer Godfrey Evans, the old England wicket-keeper, were offering odds of 500/1 against England. Apparently, they persuaded the man who was driving the Australian team bus to go round to the betting tent and put a tenner on England for each of them. In the evening they probably sent him back with his wheelbarrow to collect. With England winning, these bets naturally received great publicity and I certainly never came across anyone who thought that it was anything other than a bit of good fun by two fiercely patriotic Australians. In the prevailing climate nearly twenty years later, it might easily have been suspected of being the first modern incident of match-fixing.

Of course, the first Australian second innings wicket fell to Botham. Then Willis, who had come on as first change, moved from the Football Stand end to the Kirkstall Lane end and bowled like a man possessed. He removed Trevor Chappell, Kim Hughes and Graham Yallop for two and it occurred even to Alan McGilvray that it was still some way from being over. I hate being partisan on the air and when I had that first meeting in Broadcasting House with Henry Riddell, he told me that if I ever referred to England as 'we', I would be doing my last broadcast. It was impossible not to get outrageously excited though, and the listeners in Australia will have badly needed McGilvray to restore the balance. A little later Australia capsized to 75/8 before Ray Bright and Dennis Lillee kept us all guessing. Runs were beginning to come too easily before Lillee chipped Willis low to Gatting at mid on. I had the great luck to be on the air when, one run later, Bright was comprehensively yorked by Willis and England had won by 18 runs. I was hoarse by the end of it and I had letters telling me that the last wicket caused such excitement up and down the country's roads that the best interests of the Highway Code went by the wayside. I have never seen a game of cricket which has so perfectly illustrated all the many advantages that a two-innings match has over the intensely fashionable and all-too-predictable one-day affairs. I feel almost as breathless writing about it twenty years on as I did watching and describing it at the time.

In the Fourth Test which began nine days later at Edgbaston when I was perching in the calmer atmosphere of the press box, England's margin of victory was 29 runs. This time Australia had needed 151 to win and had reached 105/4. For some strange reason Botham was now extremely reluctant to bowl when Brearley wanted to bring him back, but Brearley won that battle. In 28 balls Botham proceeded to take five wickets for one run. The next weekend but one, up at Old Trafford, he made 118 in England's second innings and, technically, this was an even better knock than the one at Headingley. He reached his hundred in 86 balls, hooking Lillee into oblivion. England won by 103 runs and hung on to the Ashes as a result.

Botham wasn't the only reason I remember that match. England had lost their first five second innings wickets for 104, at which point an Australian victory was more than possible. Then came Botham's extraordinary innings and some time after he was out,

THE BOTHAM PHENOMENON

I was on the air, not long before the close on the third day. I was telling listeners how Australia had come so close to bowling themselves back into the match before the arrival of Botham, at which point John Emburey snicked Terry Alderman through the slips for four.

'That must seem like the final nail in the coffin for the Australians,' were my next words. I then heard a gruff and slightly testy Australian voice which belonged unmistakably to Alan McGilvray, who was standing in the box behind me.

'We're not dead yet,' was what he came back with. I said that while Alan McGilvray didn't agree, that was the way it looked to me. I continued until the end of the next over and handed over to Brian Johnston for the last twenty minutes of the day. Then I began the immensely tricky process of squeezing myself through the tiny door of a commentary box which had been designed by someone who had been singularly struck by the Black Hole of Calcutta. McGilvray was standing almost in the door which made the job of extrication even more complicated. He spoke as I tried to squeeze past him.

'You'll be all right, Henry, when you learn to grow up.'

I imagined he was pulling my leg and gave him a somewhat careless, 'I wish I had the same high hopes for you.'

When I glanced up at his face, I saw to my horror that I had entirely misjudged the situation and we didn't speak again for another eighteen months. This was sad because it was only a few weeks earlier we had finally got over the Derek Randall incident in Brisbane. It was just as well I was not in the commentary box for the last Test at the Oval which was drawn, although even then Botham took ten wickets in the match.

I went to Australia every English winter during the eighties where I was working for *The Australian* and the assembled company of commercial radio stations and I usually had a reporting job to do for the BBC. I had a watching brief, too, for the *Guardian* and *Sunday Express* and so I was kept fairly busy. I enjoyed Australia enormously, although I don't think I was the only person who found the cricket hopelessly confusing. For the first three years after the 'peace' treaty two visiting sides played three Test

Matches each season. Then there was the eternal merry-go-round of the one-day competition which grabbed the public imagination and had people turning on their television sets all over the country. This was Packer's main vehicle for making money out of the game in Australia. I have to hand it to him because he was extremely successful in this, although it helped to have struck such a one-sided deal with the Australian Cricket Board. At first, the Test Matches and the one-day games were intermingled which was hopeless for everyone. The cricketers were constantly having to try and adjust from the five-day game to the one-day game and back again and it must have been just as confusing for the public. The wear and tear for everyone was painful except, of course, for Mr Lynton Taylor, who, as the years went by, presented himself more than ever in the image of Mr Kerry Packer as he busied himself about keeping what he must have considered to be the recalcitrant authorities up to the mark.

When one-day internationals began to be played in such numbers, I found my memory started to play tricks on me. It was impossible to remember one-day games in the same way as Test Matches and individual performances in these games didn't seem to stick either. On these interminable tours of Australia I needed more than ever the supply of P.G. Wodehouse paperbacks I always carried round with me to provide some light relief at the end of the day. A problem I always had with the day/night matches was that by the time I got back to my hotel, the only hope of dinner was room service which I always think is the most deathly way to finish off any day. If it has been a good day, I want to celebrate; if it has been a bad day, I want cheering up. I find eating in my bedroom, which then stinks of food, is just about the most indigestible operation I know. The room service lot never get my order right either. Kerry Packer really has an awful lot to answer for. But there aren't many better ways of ending a day than eating in a decent restaurant with a good bottle of wine and the adventures of Bertie Wooster and Jeeves or of Lord Emsworth and the Empress of Blandings, as companions. P.G. Wodehouse has been a favourite author of mine since my father introduced me to Jeeves when he read to me in the drawing room at the Home Farm before I went to bed all those years ago. It was about now that I began to try and collect his English first editions which gave me enormous fun, although it is an expensive hobby. I was to find the secondhand bookshops of Australia and New Zealand the most excellent hunting grounds.

In 1981/82, Pakistan and the West Indies came to Australia and Pakistan lost while the West Indies drew their Test series. The most lasting memory of that season comes from the First Test against Pakistan in Perth which Australia won with ease. In Pakistan's second innings, Javed Miandad, in his first bout as Pakistan's captain, pushed Dennis Lillee out on the off side and set off for a run. As he approached the non-striker's end, Lillee appeared deliberately to get in his way. Miandad, never a man to be treated lightly, ran into him and then Lillee aimed a hefty kick at his adversary. Miandad's immediate response was to lift his bat above his head as if he was about to use it to decapitate Lillee, a man who usually aroused strong emotions. Umpire Tony Crafter, the pleasantest and most even tempered of men, who was standing at what was the old pavilion end, realised he couldn't let it go any further. Commending his soul to God and keeping his fingers crossed that his life insurance premiums were all up to date, he stepped in between the two adversaries who both looked, just for a moment, as if they might turn their attentions to him. It was a little like having to come between Muhammad Ali and Joe Frazier just when it was getting interesting. Otherwise, Larry Gomes hit two centuries for the West Indies in his usual effective and acquisitive style. When we were in Adelaide for the final Test against the West Indies, I was taken to visit the Bridgewater Mill which is the base of Petaluma owned and run by Brian Croser, one of Australia's best and most influential winemakers. I am delighted to say we drank a great deal more of the delicious Cabernet-Merlot blend than we should have done.

England in India under Keith Fletcher had been beaten and it was Geoffrey Boycott, in ever restless pursuit of the mighty dollar, who made the news. All the time the tour had been in progress, he had been quietly helping to organise a rebel tour to South Africa. Towards the end of the tour, Boycott was not fit enough to play in the Fifth Test in Madras. He was then located in active participation on a neighbouring golf course in another impressive display of altruism. He was sent home by Raman Subba Row, the manager, which, of course, gave him all the time he wanted to organise his South African venture.

I met up with the England party when they arrived in Colombo for Sri Lanka's inaugural Test Match. After some years of trying, they had just been elected as full members of the ICC which brings with it Test Match status. I have always enjoyed Sri Lanka and staying at the old Galle Face Hotel, once an institution of great splendour, gave me the chance to have a somewhat crumbling glimpse of a vibrant colonial past. Visits to Sri Lanka have also given me the opportunity to meet up with Ian Pieris with whom I played a few games for Cambridge in 1958. He virtually ran Sri Lankan cricket for a number of years and had himself been a most capable all-rounder.

England were being captained by Keith Fletcher who, after Brearley, was the best of the county captains. He and I had been on many tours together and he became a good friend. The previous October he had come up to stay with me at Hoveton to flight some duck and on an excellent evening for it, with cloud and a fierce wind, I don't think he missed. It's not the easiest form of shooting, especially when it gets dark and the duck are upon you so quickly and without warning. I could see how his reflexes enabled him to hang on to those difficult catches in the slips. He made me look embarrassingly bad. Keith had a good sense of humour and when I met up with him in Colombo, I pulled his leg about England's dreadful over rate in one of the Tests in India when Derek Underwood and John Emburey had managed to bowl only nine overs in an hour. Keith had the perfect answer:

'Good heavens, Blowers, if we had been trying we could have got it down to seven.' There are admittedly constant interruptions to a day's cricket in India, but not that many.

England won a largely uneventful Test Match in four days on a turning pitch. During the course of it, I managed to lose my wallet with all my credit cards in it and by the time it was found behind the commentary box, I had, of course, cancelled the lot.

THE BOTHAM PHENOMENON

I remember, too, a good verbal contest in the box – we were commentating back to England on Radio Three medium wave – between Don Mosey and Peter Baxter, our much put-upon producer. The Alderman seemed to think he did not need the summariser he had been given and argued the point vociferously. When he dug in his toes, there were never any half measures and he invariably shoved in the whole leg up to the knee, just for good measure. Our producer, I am glad to say, rose splendidly to the challenge and gave of his best. The decibel level came close to beating the all-comers' record in Colombo.

In 1982 Peter May took over from Alec Bedser as chairman of the selectors and made an immediate attempt to stamp his own mark on things by sacking Fletcher from the captaincy. I have always thought this was an empty gesture. Another year or two of Fletcher, who had a great knowledge of the game and its tactics as well as its technique, would, I am sure, have been good for the side. There were some who felt that, while Fletcher was thoroughly at ease in the smaller environment of Essex, he was out of his depth in the bigger role. I think this was unfair because he didn't do that badly in India, a difficult country in which to win, and I am sure he would have grown with the job. I still wonder if someone succeeded in undermining him from within. May plumped for Bob Willis who was later to become a good friend of mine, especially when we both worked for Sky Television. In 1991 we spent our lives in the same car driving up and down the motorways and enjoying some decent wine at one or two excellent hotels. It was important to keep the Arlott tradition alive. When he was playing, Willis was so bound up in the world of his own bowling that it had to be a handicap to him as a captain. To listen to May trying to justify what he had done, one would have been forgiven for thinking Willis was another Brearley. Nonetheless, he was able to dispatch both India and Pakistan in 1982 with considerable help, of course, from Botham. At this point England's cricket was still holding its head up against the lesser sides, although they were now no longer quite so lesser as they had been.

At the end of the English season in 1982 there was not much

more than a month before it was time once again for Australia. It's lucky that I've always enjoyed travelling and I find even now that a journey to Heathrow, or any airport, sets my adrenaline running. I like aeroplanes, and I am one of these hopeless people who can be quite happy sitting for hours on an airport roof watching whacking great jet aeroplanes take off and land. I feel desperately sorry for those people who are terrified by the thought of flying and have the most frightful struggle forcing themselves on board. I was about twenty when I first took to the air in the gentlest of fashions. Before we were married, my first wife, Joanna, and I flew in a sort of reverberating pantechnicon which lumbered across the English Channel with much shaking and a great noise, from Lydd to Le Touquet. My car was also on board and I know I was jolly glad when we had all touched down on the other side, but it wasn't too bad.

The next time I flew was on our honeymoon in 1961 when we were in the nether regions of a Boeing 707 which took us to New York. We flew in another down to Montego Bay the next day where the landing didn't go at all according to plan. We touched down but never seemed to stop and in the end, when we pulled up, we were off the end of the runway with the Caribbean almost lapping at the wheels. I don't think we realised until later how close to a sticky end we had come. I can still see the large, toothy Jamaican taxi driver who had been sent to pick us up and take us to the Jamaica Inn at Ocho Rios. When we came through customs, he was waiting for us with our names on a large piece of cardboard. He had obviously watched us land and when he took my trolley, he said in a marvellously throaty Jamaican accent, 'Man, Ah just prayed,' and then he grinned from ear to ear. For a time after that I was a trifle apprehensive and when I flew by Comet to India two years later, I feared the worst. Luckily I quickly grew out of this rather gloomy approach and, although I never much enjoy it when the thing buckets about in the sky, I nearly always look forward to flying. I must confess though, to certain misgivings about domestic flights on the subcontinent. Most of the locals there seem to take everything, including the kitchen sink, with them on to the aeroplane which, as a result, is probably a great deal heavier than it should be which does not inspire confidence when it begins to lumber down the runway.

So flying to Australia was a doddle, but sadly for Willis, not even Botham could find his true touch in 1982/83 in Australia and England narrowly lost a series they should have had an excellent chance of winning, especially as Dennis Lillee was fit to bowl only in the First Test. For the first time in Australia, the BBC did not take the local commentary and mounted its own operation. Chris Martin-Jenkins, Tony Lewis, who was writing for the *Sunday Telegraph*, and I formed the basis of the team, while others flitted in and out as commentators or summarisers. At each ground they found us a makeshift position from which to operate. It was never ideal and usually pretty uncomfortable, but with the help of Peter Baxter, who managed to combine his roles of engineer, producer and commentator at the cost of several more grey hairs, we got by. There was something exhilarating about commentating back to England from overseas, especially from Australia. This was probably because my earliest memory of commentary was the unbelievable excitement of waking up at six o'clock in the morning to tune in to the 1950/51 tour of Australia. It was difficult listening in those days because of the dreadful interference on the line. I so well remember the wonderful feeling when England were doing well and I longed now to bring good news to those enjoying the last few minutes in the warmth of their beds. The news from Perth, Brisbane and Adelaide had not been good, but in Melbourne it was to change.

Just occasionally a Test Match has the feel from the very first ball that it is going to be close and exciting and this was one of them. England, who were put in, made 284 and on the second day Australia were bowled out for 287. England then made 294 and Australia were left to score 292 to win. It was all nicely symmetrical. Norman Cowans, who spent most of his career being his own worst enemy, now had the day of his cricketing life. He took six of the first nine Australian wickets, reducing them to 218/9 when Allan Border was joined by Jeff Thomson. It should have been a formality for England to finish it off. Willis now decided that in order to get at Thomson, he would let Border have a single whenever he wanted off the first four balls of an over with the fielders spread out. With the pressure off like this, Border found on this huge ground that he was able to push the ball into the gaps and run twos as well as hitting the bad balls to the boundary. Thomson is no mug with the bat either and defended resolutely, picking up 21 runs of his own. By the close of play on the fourth day they had taken Australia to 255/9.

There was a good crowd in place the next day when Cowans bowled a maiden over to Thomson. Still Willis persisted with his tactics from the night before and I haven't often felt as frustrated as I did watching that morning. The two Australians were never in any difficulty and, with raucous support from the crowd, they crept closer and closer to their target and I am afraid our voices on *TMS* were full of despair. I took over the commentary when only a handful of runs was needed. We were sitting in the open air in the front row of the top tier of the pavilion in front of the Channel Nine and the ABC radio boxes. England's position was as exposed as our own and it seemed hopeless. Australia now needed 4 to win and Botham was bowling to Jeff Thomson. The ball was short and lifting outside the off stump, like many others which Thomson had left alone. Now, the pressure was getting to him too, and he followed it with his bat hoping to pick up a single to third man. The ball hit the outside edge and flew at a comfortable catching height to Chris Tavaré's right at second slip. He got both hands to it but the ball hit him on the heel of one of them and popped out. Before England supporters even had time to draw in their collective breath, Geoff Miller was running behind Tavaré from first slip and the ball lobbed gently into his hands. England had won by 3 runs and none of us could believe it. It was almost inevitable that this was Botham's hundredth wicket against Australia to add to the thousand runs he had already scored against them. I think that listeners in England could have heard my commentary even if I had not been using a microphone.

England could only draw the last Test in Sydney and so the Ashes were once more back in Australian hands. On the last day of the series sitting in Radio 2UE's commentary box at the top of the Brewongle stand, I did no less than sixty different reports, in addition to five spells of commentary for the BBC. I had to write a couple of pieces as well and after a day like that I felt I had earned a good dinner.

The collective wisdom of PBL Marketing and the Australian Cricket Board had decided at long last that the one-day internationals should not be intermingled with the Test Matches but played when they had finished. We then embarked upon a relentless series of fifteen qualifiers but mercifully the finals had been cut down from the best-of-five to the best-of-three. England made no sort of a fist of it and Australia beat New Zealand in the first two matches of the finals and to our great relief, that was that.

In Sydney for the Fifth Test Match, I had stayed for the first time at the Sheraton Wentworth. It was there that I met again a great character with whom I was to have a good deal of fun on my future visits to Australia and who became a close friend. Tony Facciolo was born in Venice shortly before I was born in Hoveton. After a spell as a trainee at the Savoy, where I bumped into him in the days when I was cutting my teeth in London after dark, he gravitated to Australia where he became the chief concierge at the Sheraton Wentworth when it opened in the sixties. In those days he positioned himself at the end of the large entrance hall in something that looked like a pulpit without the steps from where he presided over the phalanx of porters and receptionists with a firm but light touch. Facci is the greatest Mr Fixit of all times. There is no one of any importance in Australia he does not know, and almost always on first-name terms. The concierge network runs through the world and wherever I want to book a hotel, Facci invariably knows either the general manager or the concierge and if, going through the normal channels, the hotel appears to be fully booked, it never is when the request comes from Facci. He is the best salesman the Sheraton group has. He was the first person I met when I switched my allegiances in Sydney.

The second was Peter Thomson, an Ulsterman. He was then the General Manager of the Sheraton Wentworth and married to Marie-Louisa, a Cuban lady to die for. I don't think it would be possible for Peter to run a bad hotel. His instinct is always right, he knows what people want and does everything he can to provide it. He knows every member of staff by his or her first name, which is not a bad effort considering there are more than five hundred of them, and under his genial eye the whole operation is well oiled. I was staying in the Sheraton Wentworth in early July 1986 while making a commercial for their next summer's cricket, when England were touring. When I got back to the hotel after dinner on my last night before returning home, I discovered that the night-manager was on the look out for me. She told me quietly that there had been a telephone message from my sister saying that my father had died. She was simply sweet about it and the next morning the entire staff seemed to be at my disposal. Peter came to my room to say how sorry he was. I shall never forget how kind and thoughtful they all were. It may not seem, given the circumstances, to be much beyond the normal call of duty, but I can think of many big hotels in which I have stayed where I might have received a couple of metallic I'm sorrys and that would have been the end it.

Facci told me some hair-raising stories of world famous guests (names withheld, of course) who relied upon his offices to satisfy all sorts of eccentric needs and obsessions. I daresay there is little he does not have at his disposal at the end of a telephone. He is also a great connoisseur of wine. There was a brief but solemn period of his life when he was married to a lady who did the dirty on him in some style. Apart from that short time in blinkers, he was an active admirer of the collective beauty of Australian ladies and if the sum total of his girlfriends were laid end-to-end they would stretch across the Sydney Harbour Bridge and most of the way back again.

The headquarters of the Sheraton Hotels has now moved on from the Wentworth just up the road to the Sheraton-on-the-Park where, as group concierge, Facci is installed, appropriately enough, at an antique Sheraton table in the big front hall. These he manages to look both stately and benevolent. Facci has dark hair, a huge behind and a waddle to go with it, an enquiring face that never rests, and fluent English heavily disguised by a Venetian accent. His Italian blood ensures that he talks fast and passionately.

When I see him in close conversation with someone at his desk, it is as likely to be a Prime Minister, or a member of some royal family, or Rupert Murdoch as it is a punter with a hot tip or the head detective in the New South Wales police force. You may be sure they will both learn something to their mutual advantage. It is Facci who has made certain that I have remained with the Sheraton group in Australia and he will crop up again before the end of this book.

CHAPTER

17

TRANSPORTED IN PAKISTAN

Any dedicated follower of cricket is going to have to put up with an awful lot of time on the road. The longer journeys between countries and, in most of them where the distances are big, between cities, are mostly made by air. England is the only country where cricketers and their entourage are forced to rely upon the motor car. It doesn't make sense to fly from, say, London to Birmingham or Manchester, because if you time yourself from door to door it almost certainly takes longer than if you had gone by car. When a side has a match at Taunton, followed by one at Canterbury and another at Derby, aeroplanes can't come into it. There have been many summers during which I have done more than fifteen thousand miles on the road driving round the county circuit. I find the driving is all part of the enjoyment and using my car means that I am in a position to be able to stay out in the country rather than to fester in a dreary hotel in a town or a city. Over the years, I have built up a network of hotels which suit me for the main grounds in England and my annual visits are one of the most enjoyable features of my summer.

After coming back from those three one-day matches in New Zealand, which were all won by our hosts, it was time to get ready for the third World Cup, a competition which had still not set foot outside England. A World Cup means even more travelling than usual and also some uncomfortably long and late journeys, say from Manchester to Tunbridge Wells, to be in position for the following day's match. I had a very amusing experience quite early in the competition when I drove up one morning from London to Nottingham to commentate on Australia's first qualifying match against Zimbabwe at Trent Bridge. Zimbabwe were one of the two sides to qualify from the ICC Trophy played the previous summer. They had seen Sri Lanka gain full membership and Test Match status and were hoping it would be their turn soon. They had a useful side, although cricket was predominantly a white man's game and there was no great depth to it. This match was played in the middle of the miners' strike when Arthur Scargill had his day in the sun. When I got to junction 25 where I turned off the M1 for Nottingham, there was a considerable tailback. The nearer I crept up the slip road to the roundabout, I was able to see policemen bending down and talking to the driver of each car. It occurred to me that it must be something to do with the strike because the road to Nottingham almost at once went past the Radclyffe-on-Stour power station and there had been great excitement about secondary picketing. Eventually I got to the top of the slip road and a young policeman stuck his head through my open window and asked me if I was a picket. I gave him a booming, 'My dear old thing', and I think that effectively answered the question for him. He stepped back and waved me on. That moment was, I suppose, the nearest I ever came to the dreaded Scargill and when I got to the commentary box I foolishly told the story to Don Mosey. It was a long time before I was allowed to forget it.

Eventually, we settled down to describe a wonderful game in which Zimbabwe beat Australia with something to spare. It was a great day for their cricket, although they were soon brought back to earth when the West Indies beat them at Worcester and Edgbaston. For the Zimbabwean matches in this competition we were joined by their own commentator, Bob Nixon, who was a dentist in Bulawayo. He was a delight to share a commentary box with, although he and his wife had just been through the most ghastly time. Their daughter had been murdered in Bulawayo. In the end they came to England and settled in Stowmarket, but eventually the climate got to them and they now live in Cape Province in South Africa where Bob finds that his short-sleeved shirts are again of some use to him. He is a fine upstanding man with an excellent sense of humour and was an entertaining and generous commentator.

This World Cup produced the most splendid final when India, who were very much the underdogs, managed to beat the West Indies by 43 runs. When India were bowled out for 183, it looked as if the West Indies would saunter to their third successive World Cup triumph. This did not allow for some careless West Indies batting, allied to some fine bowling, especially from Madan Lal. I shall never forget the noisy West Indian crowd being silenced by Madan Lal. He bowled one which was not quite as short as it looked to Viv Richards who had sauntered in to bat with the air of indifference of a man who felt he only had to go through the formalities. Richards went to hook it and succeeded in skying the ball off the top edge. At mid wicket Kapil Dev circled under the ball before holding one of the more important catches in the history of the game. It was as if Julius Caesar had been tripped up by Ethelred the Unready and the West Indies went on to be bowled out for 140.

My other cricketing memory of 1983 comes from the Second Test against New Zealand at Headingley when New Zealand won their first Test Match in England at their twenty-ninth attempt. The only surprise about it was that Richard Hadlee did not take a wicket and their main executioners were Lance Cairns who took ten in the match with his in-swingers bowled off the wrong foot, and the underrated Ewen Chatfield. The New Zealand delight was a joy to see and I so well remember going over to the pavilion balcony after they had won to interview the two captains and Cairns who was Man of the Match. They had scored the 103 they needed to win for the loss of five wickets and until the last run had been scored, there were some who felt that a hobgoblin or two might appear from around some unseen corner. I shall never forget the disbelieving happiness of Walter Hadlee, the father of Richard, who had first come to England in 1937 and captained the side in 1949. England went on to win the four-match series by 3–1.

The dramas in Australia in 1983/84 began with a leisurely and entirely comfortable and orthodox journey by car from the middle of Perth to the town of Northam where Pakistan were playing a one-day game against a Country Eleven. We all went that day because the successor to Greg Chappell, who had resigned from the captaincy, was to be named. When I arrived in Australia, Rodney Marsh seemed to be the clear favourite, but Kim Hughes, a player who was much disliked and distrusted by the Packer lot, had growing support. Hughes made the journey to Northam and soon after he arrived it fell to him to read out the Australian team for the First Test in Perth. Hughes is a chap who seldom looks as if he has just backed a 33–1 winner and now he gave the strong impression that he was about to announce his own execution. He read the names in alphabetical order in a flat monotone and after reading out 'Hughes', he added in the same expressionless voice 'captain', which gave us all something to write about. That evening at a benefit dinner for Rod Marsh at the Sheraton Hotel those of us who spoke in praise of him had to be content to describe him as a great Australian wicket-keeper batsman. The beneficiary himself was in something less than mid-season form after the earlier news.

The Pakistanis got the series off to the sort of start that only they seemed to be able to manage. Imran Khan, who arrived as captain, was prevented from playing in the First Test because of his back. Zaheer Abbas took charge of the side which had as weak an attack as I have seen in a Test Match and they were beaten by an innings. The next thing I heard was that the news had come from Pakistan that Zaheer had been appointed as the official captain. This directive was almost immediately cancelled by the President of the Pakistan Board, the urbane and charming Air Marshal Nur Khan who had appointed Imran in the first place. It was what I can only describe as a priceless Pakistani cock-up, although I know it will not have been the Air Marshal's fault. Their cause had not been helped either by the decision to leave behind Sarfraz Nawaz, a fine seam bowler but an awkward chap. As soon as Zaheer had been officially appointed captain, he summoned Sarfraz who, after a three-day search, had been located in Bombay.

After the announcement that Imran had been reinstated, he graciously consented to Sarfraz's inclusion. I can't think what all this will have done for the morale of the party, but it gave us all a great laugh and provided wonderful copy.

When we were in Adelaide for the Third Test, I joined the commentary team of Radio 5DN which supplied the citizens of Adelaide and I daresay all of South Australia as well. The commentary was presided over by Ken Cunningham (KG to the entire population of Adelaide). For many years, he had played cricket effectively but a trifle dourly for South Australia. He commentated with great enthusiasm and much laughter and he was fun to work with. I have always felt that the Australian commentators who were not biased were the exception rather than the rule and KG was as one-eyed as anyone. It was during this Test against Pakistan that I heard him telling listeners that 'Lillee had the superb figures of 4/168' and a little later he regaled us all with the news that Pakistan were 'in the quite good position of 5/580'.

I had first worked with KG the year before when, from the middle of the open members' stand, we had sat at a bench and Derek Nimmo was our inimitable companion. What made this occasion so memorable was that our brief was to talk about anything and everything except the cricket. The contractual obligations of the Cricket Board meant that we were not allowed to commentate on the actual cricket. It was hysterically funny and I am sure Derek regarded it all as a net for *Just a Minute*. He had the knack of being able to discourse in a wonderful schoolmasterly voice with great tongue-in-cheek authority on any subject that came up. I met him in a restaurant in Chelsea's Draycott Avenue not all that long before he died, just before he was flying off to act in Singapore and Kuala Lumpur, and we had a great laugh about that time in Adelaide and KG's attempts to call us to order.

For this series, which Australia won comfortably and without any great cricketing excitement, Channel Nine introduced an actress, Kate Fitzpatrick, into their commentary team. This was another of David Hill's ruses and one of the very few which did not really work. It was no fault of Kate's but was because her role was never clearly enough defined, either to her or to her fellow commentators. It was no good expecting her to talk about cricket as Ian Chappell did and he was not the ideal foil to ask her all about which of the Pakistani players had the greatest sex appeal. I would have been surprised if it had taken her long to answer this question. She a wrote a weekly column in the *Sydney Morning Herald* and produced a long in-depth interview with Imran Khan in which she caught the distinct flavour of her victim whom she seemed to have come to know pretty well. In the New Year, in Sydney, Kate returned from the commentary box to the theatre. She opened at the Opera House in a play called *Insignificance* in which she played the part of Marilyn Monroe. She was brilliant and the theatre was where she belonged. While she was playing Marilyn, Messrs Greg Chappell, Lillee and Marsh all decided to retire after the Fifth Test in Sydney in which they had all turned in their own final *virtuosi* performances.

I am writing this at a time when Donna Symmonds, the highly articulate barrister from Barbados with a good knowledge of cricket whose family was great friends with Sir Frank Worrell's, has habitually been joining *Test Match Special* where she has a good following; Sybil Ruscoe has turned out for Channel Four in a role as similarly undefined as Kate Fitzpatrick's; and Eleanor Oldroyd is lending her skills to *TMS* although her job as a roving reporter has been thought through and is more successful as a result. I feel all this has much more to do with political correctness than anyone who made the decision to employ them would care to admit. No one enjoys having them with us more than I do, and I daresay it makes us all raise our game, but no one has yet convinced me that they add more to the commentary than we already have. It is perhaps another example of women striving regardless to do anything and everything men used to do on their own and I've no objection to that, provided they can add something to it. I know I shall take an awful lot of stick for saying this and be generally labelled a male chauvinist pig. I suppose this may be just another example of why I am rapidly becoming one of the day before yesterday's men although if the ladies increase our audience, fair enough.

When Australia was over, I hotfooted it to Pakistan where England, who had just lost another series in New Zealand, had come to play three Test Matches. As we will see, they had left an unfortunate reputation behind them in New Zealand. Before that came to light, Pakistan won the First Test in Karachi by three wickets after being left to score only 65 to win. Nick Cook, a most vociferous left-arm spinner from Northamptonshire, gave them a nasty shock when he took five wickets for 18 runs. We were mounting our own commentary for *Test Match Special* during this series and at this match in Karachi one of the most bizarre incidents, even by *TMS*'s standards, occurred. We had a lofty vantage point at the pavilion end and to our left I could see a very smart house perched delicately on a hill surrounded by a plentiful supply of extremely good-looking palm trees. During the commentary I told listeners about the house and speculated briefly on who might live there, plumping in the end for a government minister. The next morning I had a cable from Peter Richardson, the former England opening batsman whose nickname is Pakis, short for Pakistan Pete, which he had acquired on a tour of Pakistan in 1961/62. The cable read, 'Beautiful house surrounded by palms always owned by Sahib in charge of tickets.' It was signed 'Pakis'.

During the commentary we were joined at intervals by the various news bulletins from London for the latest score. When this happened, I would hear a voice in my ear from London, in those days usually belonging to Peter Baxter, at ten minutes to the hour saying, 'Nine o'clock news joining in ten minutes.' Ten minutes later, he would say to me down the line, 'Nine o'clock news joining now,' and I would then hear the newsreader hand over to me, at which point I would pause for a moment in my commentary, give the score and perhaps a couple of brief details before pausing again and going on with the commentary. It probably sounds more complicated than it was. On this occasion, Peter never came through to me and I thought there must have been a lot of other news and they had decided to give the cricket a miss. It so happened, a few minutes later, that I was telling listeners about the cable I had received from Peter Richardson and I sent him our greetings and added, 'And I would like to send our love to his lovely wife Shirley.' What had actually happened was that the line from London to Karachi had gone down without Peter Baxter knowing it and while he could hear us talking, we could not hear him. He gave me his ten-minute warning and then when the presenter, Richard Clegg, was about to come in, he gave me the final warning. With the line down, I heard none of this and at the precise moment he threw to me in Karachi, I had just got round to Peter's cable before sending our love to Shirley which was all that those listening to the nine o'clock news will have heard that morning from Karachi. A lot of bemused people in the studio wondered what on earth I was up to, to say nothing of the listeners.

Then it was on to Lahore where I was staying with Sarfraz Nawaz who, over the years, had become quite a chum, and Rani, his beautiful and cuddly film star wife whom I had never before met. The morning after I arrived I had had considerable difficulty trying to persuade Ashraf the Elder who was Sarfraz's chief of staff, that I wanted tea which was black and weak and that I preferred fried eggs which had been incinerated rather than cremated, although the fresh orange juice was breathtaking. After breakfast, Sarfraz's Uncle Malik, who had been appointed my chauffeur, took me to the Gadaffi Stadium. There I found the entire English press corps with pursed lips which did not bode well for the immediate future. That morning in London a story had appeared in the *Daily Express* saying that some of the England side had been smoking pot in New Zealand; not only that, but the *Mail on Sunday* had got wind of the same story and had sent two reporters to New Zealand where they had collected some sworn affidavits. They had now arrived at the Lahore Hilton, the team hotel, to confront the players and the management with what they had found. The rumour was that six players were implicated and the story would appear in two days' time on the Sunday.

Johnny Woodcock came to dinner that night at Sarfraz's and there were one or two local journalists as well. The issues were debated at length and Sarfraz electrified us all by saying that hashish had been made available to the England players while they had been in Karachi for the First Test. He was later to say this in public. The following morning, after two of Ashraf the Elder's unforgettable fried eggs, a hectic day began. I eventually ended up in mid-morning with Sarfraz at the Hilton where I learned that the England manager, Alan Smith, was soon to give a press conference. While we were waiting in the passage outside his room, a grim-faced Ian Botham came out of a neighbouring door and walked past us with an expressionless face. Soon afterwards we trouped into the team room and Alan Smith who, on these occasions invariably became a caricature of himself, launched into it after the customary sharp drawing in of breath.

'Ian Botham is going home injured. He has a continued degenerative condition of the left knee. Further medical advice is essential and an operation is virtually certain.' He vehemently denied in front of a BBC microphone that there was any connection between Botham's return to England and the pot-taking allegations from New Zealand.

I was driven by Sarfraz to the Gaddafi Stadium where Uncle Malik was waiting beside his motor scooter. He drove me back to Sarfraz's house where I wrote my various pieces about Botham's return to London. I had just finished my story for the *Sunday Express* when the telephone rang and miraculously it was Leslie Vanter, the Sports Editor. He wanted to talk about a feature I had written earlier in the week before handing me over to the news desk. the *Mail on Sunday* had been advertising their scoop with the drug story on radio and television and the *Sunday Express* also badly wanted the story. I told the news desk all I knew and was not much help, but I promised to have my story, such as it was, on the telex in just over an hour. I wrote another paragraph or two and was ready to go to the telegraph office when I suddenly found I had an almost insoluble problem. How was I to summon a taxi?

I was on my own in Sarfraz's house with his plentiful staff all of whom spoke as much English as I did Urdu – which was none; nor did I know Uncle Malik's telephone number. The solution came to me at once. I had several times met the manager of the Hilton with Sarfraz and all I had to do was to ring him and ask him to send round a taxi. I rang the Hilton and was told the manager, Tariq Saeed, was in a meeting. I was put through to his assistant who first of all unleashed a torrent of Urdu in my ear and for a dreadful moment I thought he had rung off before I could state my case. It turned out that he spoke enough English for my purposes, even though we had to go slowly. He seemed to understand that I urgently needed a taxi but kept asking me something else which I did not at first understand. Then I got it. He wanted Sarfraz's address and of course I didn't know it. With one of Sarfraz, Uncle Malik, Ashraf the Elder and Ashraf the Younger (father and son) in almost constant attendance, I had never bothered to find out where I was staying. I asked the assistant manager if he could try and find out if his boss knew where the eminent bowler lived. But first, he said he would hold on while I had one last try at my end.

With the hands of my watch moving round much too fast, it was now panic stations. I burst out of the front door and found an old lady, one of Sarfraz's entourage, sitting on the edge of the top step of the terrace with a small child on each side of her. She was extremely surprised to see me and even more perplexed when I enveloped her with a torrent of English spoken faster than she had ever heard anything spoken in her life. Even if she had been able to understand what I was asking, which was the address of the house, there was every chance she would not have known the answer. She rose somewhat ponderously to her feet and looked at me with an expression which was not helped by two formidable front teeth, and seemed to suggest that I was an obvious candidate for a loony bin. I now ran to the drive gates, unbolted them and went out into the road. The staff were becoming flustered and began to shout to each other, sorting out, no doubt, which of them was going to ring for the strait jacket. Meanwhile I looked round frantically for a number on the gate and then for a sign at the side of the road, but couldn't see either, although I was later shown where they were. Fleet Street and the *Sunday Express* seemed further away with each passing second.

I decided to change my tactics and ran into the middle of the road frantically waving my arms to stop a passing scooterist. He stopped hurriedly and looked at me as if I had had too much sun.

He, too, had no English and nor did the startled bicyclist whom I now waved down, but he was so alarmed he was unable to get out a word in any language. When I went back through Sarfraz's gate, the number of staff had increased noticeably and they seemed to be regarding it all as the best morning's entertainment they had had for years. Ashraf the Younger came up to me in some agitation and I could sense his eagerness to help. He clearly thought he had found the answer to my problem and made his points with great emphasis but it would only have been any good if I had spoken Urdu. Then, I remembered that the assistant manager of the Hilton was still holding on and so I shot back through the front door and rushed into Sarfraz's bedroom to the telephone. When he had listened to my sorry story, he promised to ring me back when he had spoken to his boss. I took to pacing round the reception room while Ashraf the Younger hovered in the doorway not knowing what to make of the English sahib's extraordinary behaviour. He got lots of marks for effort but I was inconsolable.

Then the telephone rang and I rushed back to the bedroom. It was Tariq Saeed from the Hilton and of course he did not know where Sarfraz lived, but with great composure he solved the problem as I knew he would. He told me to put Ashraf the Younger on the line. When I began to beckon at Ashraf the Younger, he wasn't at all sure about it and advanced cautiously as if expecting me to start frothing at the mouth at any moment. At last I got him to the mouthpiece and the conversation went on for long enough for me to think it highly unlikely that Ashraf the Younger knew the address either. He handed me back the receiver and after a brief pause I found Tariq's number two on the other end. He told me he had instructed Ashraf to go out and find me a taxi. Nearly an hour had already been lost when Ashraf the Younger set off up the street at the double. I did some more pacing up and down and another twenty-five minutes went by before I suddenly heard an angry mechanical buzzing at the front of the house. It heralded the arrival of an auto-rickshaw. Ashraf the Younger came through the gates with the sort of smile which suggested he had won the lottery while I leapt out of the house with my story in one hand and my cable credit card in the other. Now we had to tell the driver where I wanted to go. I looked at Ashraf and said as firmly as I could, 'The GPO.' Ashraf repeated this no less than eight times and even then I was not confident the driver, who was already revealing mulish tendencies, had understood.

The auto-rickshaw is a favourite means of transport on the subcontinent. There is a tiny perch of a seat at the front for the driver who holds one end of the steering bar in each hand. The passenger somehow squeezes in behind on a hard metal seat which has token padding and there is just about enough room for an athletic dwarf who is something of a contortionist below a thin metal roof painted in exciting colours and patterns. My chariot that day had a predominantly green roof with some engaging flashes of silver thrown in. A horizontal bar runs across the rickshaw in front of the passenger which he hangs on to for dear life to prevent himself from being catapulted out to an early death. It has an engine which makes about three times as much noise as any motor scooter I have ever heard and interior springing is considered to be an unnecessary luxury. That brings us to the driver. Without exception in my experience auto-rickshaw drivers are the most competitive men on earth. Also, as a breed, they appear to have been born without a trace of fear, together with an urge for self-destruction which is not to be sniffed at. Johnny Woodcock once made a serious effort to import an auto-rickshaw so he could drive himself from where he lives in Longparish to the Plough, which is not a monumental journey. Our blessed bureaucrats stopped him, which may have been just as well, otherwise he would probably have changed character, although the traffic in Longparish would have been rather less demanding than it was in Lahore.

On first acquaintance my driver seemed sensible enough. He was young and marginally less villainous in appearance than most of his colleagues, although he had a small and particularly nasty-looking moustache. He also had a red and white scarf wrapped carelessly round his head in a debonair sort of way. It was a journey I shall take to the grave with me. I was still getting into my seat when he let in the clutch in a manner which suggested he had taken against me. It was all I could do not to fall out as we raced down the road at breakneck speed in and out of every pothole on offer and as far as I could make out in the wrong direction, at least from the way Ashraf the Younger had been pointing. There was nothing I could do about it except sit back and try to enjoy an unofficial attempt on the record from wherever we had started out to wherever we were going.

I can barely describe the next twenty-three minutes. At the end of Sarfraz's road, which was being dug up, we screeched right in the teeth of the oncoming traffic and never once did the driver use anything but full throttle. Taxis swerved out of the way, brakes (never our own) howled, huge lorries which I could easily have touched as they thundered past not much more than a foot from me, appeared not even to have seen us and we were engulfed in pretty well permanent clouds of dense black exhaust smoke which promised instant death on its own. Bicycles loomed up and vanished, pedestrians cavorted this way and that and seemed to give the driver a target to aim at. How I managed not to fall out I shall never know. My driver carried on as if he hadn't a care in the world. Policemen came and went, some just stood there in the middle of the road as if resigned to their fate, one or two jumped nimbly out of the way before blowing their whistles furiously at no one in particular, rather as if they felt it was what was expected of them. An enormous petrol tanker suddenly appeared from nowhere and I shut my eyes because I was certain we were about to try and go underneath it.

Red traffic lights posed no problem for the simple reason that he chose to ignore them. In any case, a red light in Pakistan does not prevent the traffic from turning left, although it is a sensible precaution for the driver to have a look to the right before making a move. This picture of chaos was accompanied by the non-stop blaring of horns. I was numb with fear and kept thinking that the whole of my life should be flashing in front of my eyes, but all that flashed before me were the tailboards of lorries and the most noisy and smelly parts of the anatomy of the internal combustion engine. Although I had no means of knowing, I presumed that we were getting on for the middle of Lahore when the road widened to allow five lanes of traffic to move in the same direction. At the lights in front of us we had to turn left. We were in a queue in the inside lane when the driver suddenly saw that if he was in the right-hand lane, which was empty, he could get right up to the lights. Being the opportunist he was, he turned across the middle three lanes without waiting or looking and, like the Red Sea, a pathway suddenly opened up in front of him. Now we were in the front row of the grid but the only snag was that we had to turn left and there were four lanes of traffic on our inside. The lights were red and standing foursquare in front of the five lanes of traffic with his back to us was a policeman. The cars and lorries on our left were expecting the lights to change and the policeman to move because they were revving their engines in anticipation. My chap solved the problem instantly. Without a thought for his safety or mine, he turned left across the front of the four lanes of traffic and behind the back of the policeman and buzzed his way across as if this was what he did on a daily basis and thought little of it. If the policeman had moved back as much as six inches he would have received a nasty one up the backside. When he saw what was happening, he reached for his whistle before having second thoughts, so may be it was a frequent occurrence. Daniel would have opted for the lions' den.

It required a certain genius on the part of my driver not to have established contact with a single solid object during that journey. The only casualty was my head which made frequent contact with the roof of the rickshaw as we bumped our way across Lahore. I had almost forgotten about the need to dispatch my copy to London when the rust-coloured stone of the GPO building loomed up ahead of us. We stopped and my driver gave me a big grin and asked me for ten rupees. I handed him what I thought was a ten rupee note and was then somewhat alarmed when he appeared to want to embrace me. I had given him a fifty rupee note by mistake and I hadn't the heart to ask for it back. He deserved it. I found the telegraph office and sent off my stuff and I wondered what the readers would think if they had any idea of the journey those words had made before arriving on their breakfast tables. I took an orthodox taxi to the Hilton and caught up with the latest goings on in the whole drug saga. The players were denying most of the story which had appeared in the *Mail on Sunday*. Then two men, who made cricket equipment in Sialkot and had been sent by Sarfraz, arrived to give me a lift back to his house and when I got there I was shown the small plaque in the garden which said '143A New Muslim Town'. But think of the fun I would have missed if I had seen it in the first place.

The whole business about the drugs in New Zealand turned out to be rather a non-event. The story in the *Mail in Sunday* dealt a good deal in innuendo and when, for example, Allan Lamb was accused of having a woman in his room, it turned out to be his wife and even the draconian cricket authorities could have no serious objection to that. Botham, meanwhile, electrified everyone by saying, after he had an operation on his knee in Birmingham, that Pakistan was a dump and the sort of place that mothers-in-law should be sent on an all-expenses-paid trip. It did not endear him to a number of people, including my host, Sarfraz, who was a fierce Pakistani nationalist and now went through all sorts of convolutions in trying to get one back at Botham. In the end, Botham was forced to make an apology and claimed that he had been speaking under a post-operative cloud. The authorities at Lord's fined him £1,000 for his temerity. Staying with Sarfraz was hectic because when he wasn't issuing statements, he was taking either official or impromptu press conferences. In the end he had his own back on the field of play when he made 90 going in tenth in the Third Test in Lahore. He and Zaheer put on 161 for the ninth wicket, but England saved the match after some disgraceful time-wasting tactics in the field on the last afternoon.

Before that we had driven to Faisalabad for the Second Test and I found the means of getting from Lahore to Faisalabad and back infinitely more exciting than the cricket. We set off for the outward journey in a convoy of buses from where I was able to marvel at the standard of driving, the state of the roads, the longevity of motor horns in Pakistan and the agility of the pedestrian population. Our journey was made more exciting when one of the two team coaches broke down and the passengers had to cram into the other which did not apparently make for comfort. A friend whom I met in Karachi had promised to fix rooms in the Ripple Hotel for Johnny Woodcock, Tony Lewis and myself while the majority of the press settled among the rather less obvious comforts of Ray's Hotel which was positioned in an outstandingly noisy Main Street. When we arrived at the Ripple, a shifty receptionist told us the rooms had not been confirmed and they had been let go. Our friend in Karachi blew a sizeable gasket on the telephone to the receptionist. In the end, he arranged for us to stay in the Crescent Textile Guest House which we were told was the most comfortable accommodation in Faisalabad and I wouldn't want to dispute it. We had six delightful nights there.

After David Gower had come out of his first Test Match as captain of England with a draw – Willis was unwell – the three of us at the guest house set off in a taxi for Lahore. This journey was a forerunner of another which took me down this same road twelve years later when we ground to a halt in the middle of Faisalabad and Geoffrey Boycott tried to direct the traffic and sort out a major jam. On this occasion, trying to nip out of Lahore through the back streets, we fell foul of a level crossing which stayed shut for an unconscionable time before a seedy looking train arrived. By then the gatekeeper had gone missing and we had to wait another ten minutes before he was found and the gates were opened. The traffic on both sides of the crossing had built up to bursting point and when the barriers lifted, cars and lorries and sundry animals from both directions were furiously jostling for the same bit of the road. It was more than exciting and our driver, to say nothing of his passengers, should have been awarded a Victoria Cross.

The Lahore Test was made notable for me by an enormously enjoyable and amusing day I spent with two cousins of Imran Khan's trying to shoot wild boar. We met at a quarter to seven at Javed Zamaan's house in Zamaan Park after I had spent quite a time trying to persuade Sarfraz's minions that I was eager for them to unlock the gates and let me out of the house. We drove for about an hour out of Lahore and then we set off. I had borrowed a twelve-bore from a fellow participant who was big in carpets. Lots of exciting things happened. For the first drive of all, when the boar were apparently being driven towards us, we found after half an hour that we were facing in the wrong direction. Spasmodic shots announced the presence of a few boar and later a beater was gored in the leg by a charging boar but happily was not badly hurt and was much braver than I would have been. I never fired at a boar but I managed to down a partridge with my first shot of the day before missing a couple of others. When it was time to go home, the boar population had lost a minor skirmish and the tails of the five boar that had been killed were collected on reeds, because no good Muslim was allowed to touch a pig, and taken to Lahore. The government paid seventy-five rupees for every dead boar and the tails were needed as evidence. Our transport this time was the next best thing to a Land Rover and the journey was less fraught than most. As I remember it, some excellent cold beer was most hospitably laid on at lunch for the one infidel in the party. No wonder I took a very different view of Pakistan from Ian Botham – and maybe of their transport, too.

CHAPTER

18

GOWER TO GATTING

I FOUND THE EIGHTIES galloped by. Apart from a couple of good series against Australia, England's cricket became progressively more dismal but the pace of life quickened for me off the field. I had to move cottages at Hoveton because my brother John had become a County Court judge and, as his area of jurisdiction appeared to be mostly East Anglia, it suited him to return home. The house I had been living in at Hoveton Green was, when the other half had been done up, more suitable for him and Judy and the three children as a permanent resting place. I swopped with him and moved down to Haugh's End which is a delightful amalgamation of two tiny sixteenth-century cottages with a thatched roof on the edge of Hudson's Bay, the prettiest piece of water on the estate. It is in the most heavenly setting, marred only in the summer by the River Bure which is not much more than two hundred yards away behind the alders on the far side of Hudson's Bay. When the Broads were in full swing, the sounds of music and general jollity from the passing boats is a little too close for comfort.

John had another sadder reason for coming back to Hoveton, too. Our father, who was then into his eighties, had spent most of his life trying to put Hoveton back on to a firm footing after his own mother had steered rather an unsteady course when my grandfather had died in 1920. Now, in his old age, my father, with the best possible intentions, had allowed costs to spiral and had generally taken his eye off that particular ball and John had

had to come back to launch a rescue operation. It was sad but inevitable as some of the old familiar faces, who were few enough by then, were put out to grass and Hoveton became part of a combined operation with one or two other neighbouring farms. When I was young, it had been predominantly a fruit farm but as that had become uneconomical, the fruit trees had been pulled up, a good many hedges had been bulldozed in the interests of prairie farming and fewer men were needed to keep it going. At least I still used to know who the chaps were driving the tractors, but now even that was to change as the amalgamated farms pooled their resources. It took away the personal touch and it meant that Hoveton was no longer the happy family it had once been. This was before the thinking classes of Islington and such places became hellbent on destroying rural life as it was, and every dictat from Brussels caused yet more inconvenience.

I became ensconced by the side of Hudson's Bay in September 1984 and the view looking across the water was the perfect therapy for the 5–0 walloping England had just received from the West Indies. Canada geese and greylags honked away, mallard, teal, shoveler, wigeon and occasionally pochard and tufted wheeled in and landed on the water or were quietly swimming under the lea of the trees on the far side. There was the odd coot with that curious bald piece of bone going back over its head, and hence the simile, a few agitated moorhens, the reeds and some waterlilies. Of course, they were never all present at the same time, although there was usually a reasonable representation. The best sight of all came when, quanting through Hudson's Bay, a kingfisher would dart low across the water in front of the boat, jinking and darting rather like a tiny snipe and showing off that streak of brilliant blue on its wings which is so vivid I always have to look twice to make sure its real. When I was young, there might have been the boom of a bittern as well, but now they are very much an endangered species. Each spring, a swan nests on a tiny promontory jutting out on the other side of the water, just across to the left. The swans had nested in that same spot all my life until, a year or two ago, they moved a few yards to their left where they seem to have easier access to the water. I could see all this from the windows at the front of the house, although I had to look out between the trunks of three poplar trees on the edge of the garden with their toes lapping in the water. They were like three huge deciduous cricket stumps.

I had to tear myself away from all of this to go to Australia to watch them being thrashed by the West Indies. There was high drama at the end of the Second Test Match in Brisbane. Kim Hughes was appointed captain for the series but questions were being asked when Australia lost the First Test by an innings and Hughes had not helped himself by hooking Michael Holding down long leg's throat. Before the Second Test began in Brisbane Greg Chappell, the senior selector present, gave a particularly tough talk at the dinner the night before the match. He also spoke strongly to Hughes. All through the weekend pressure built up on Hughes to resign the captaincy and he continued to do himself no favours by again being caught at fine leg playing the dreaded hook. When Australia were beaten in four days, Hughes came into the players' dining room for a press conference accompanied by Bob Merriman who was the team manager and, I always thought, a most enigmatic figure in all of this. Merriman had been a trade's union arbitrator and was by nature a conciliator, but he didn't conciliate any too well between Hughes and Chappell. At the end of the conference, Hughes produced a piece of paper and announced that he had a statement to make. He started to read his resignation but it all became too much for him and he choked, leaving Merriman to finish the reading. This was to leave the way clear for Allan Border's long reign to begin.

On Sydney's usual spinning pitch, Australia won the toss and, with Bob Holland and Murray Bennett in the side, spun the West Indies to an innings defeat. This was Clive Lloyd's last Test Match and in the second innings, when the West Indies had followed on 308 runs behind, he emerged in that slightly improbable way of his, peering through his glasses as if he had just come out of a darkened room. He produced some wonderful strokes in this last knock, crashing the faster bowlers through the covers and lifting Bennett on to the Hill. Just when it seemed he might be about to score the hundred which had always eluded him in a Test

Match at the SCG, he drove McDermott to Border in the covers and departed chewing lugubriously and looking more than ever like Paddington Bear.

In Melbourne I transferred my allegiances from Radio 3UZ to Radio 3AW, a station which was run by Brian White, a delightful man and a brilliant broadcaster, who was to become a good friend. They were the number one station when it came to Australian Rules Football and their principal commentator was a most idiosyncratic performer called Harry Beitzel. He had been one of the best referees and now that he had retired from active participation, he had moved behind the microphone. He had a raucous voice which the populace of Melbourne seem to adore and, as a result, Brian had given him the job of masterminding the cricket commentary when 3AW won the rights.

One year Harry persuaded Brian White that the Victorian public were not over-impressed with the normal fielding positions and that they were completely indifferent to the claims of fine leg and third man, to say nothing of silly point and forward short leg. He came up with the idea that he would call the fielding positions in accordance with the hands of the clock and Brian eventually agreed. The bowler would be at midday and the batsman and the wicket-keeper and six o'clock. I don't think it would have been much of an idea, even if Harry himself had been able to tell the difference between half past four and half past eight. As it was, it became almost totally incomprehensible. On one occasion, Harry described a good catch at mid off at high decibel content and spent a second or two debating with himself whether it was at one o'clock or half past one or maybe even a quarter to two. He then handed back to the studio for a news bulletin. The reader thanked Harry effusively for his brilliant description of a catch at a quarter past one or was it a quarter to two before telling listeners he was about to read them the deep square leg news.

There was one ugly moment at the Melbourne Cricket Ground on Boxing Day that year which was inevitably given too much publicity over 3AW's airwaves. Boxing Day was the fourth day of the match and I had woken up with something of a hangover.

I left it as late as I could before clambering out of bed and after a brisk walk through the Fitzroy Gardens past Captain Cook's cottage, I only just made it in time for the first ball of the day. After I had done my first stint of commentary, I walked down the passage which led to the pavilion to collect my sandwiches for lunch. When I arrived at the glass door which would have let me into the Long Room, the attendant, whom I knew well, stood in front of me with a big grin on his face and refused to let me in. 'You can't come in here wearing jeans, mate,' was his explanation. I had a quick look down at my legs and, sure enough, I had put on a pair of jeans. I beat a hasty retreat and back in the press room I foolishly told one or two people. Later in the afternoon during a drink interval, the big screen flashed up the legend, 'Blue jeans Blofeld'. Tom Prior, an old friend of mine who wrote a column for the *Sun*, also got wind of the story and used it for his column the following day. Tom, who has now retired, was an able performer. His main claim to notoriety was that he had the unpleasant duty to be present as a witness at the last execution in Victoria. As a young reporter, he had been standing outside the prison gates when one of them opened and one of the prison staff came out looking for someone who could act as a witness. Tom found he was selected.

PBL reckoned that they and Channel Nine were on to a goldmine. After the eighteen matches for the World Series Cup which was won by the West Indies, they had arranged for a World Championship of Cricket to be played in a series of thirteen matches between the seven Test-playing countries. It was being held to celebrate the 150th anniversary of the founding of the state of Victoria and the matches were being played in Sydney and Melbourne. A diet of thirty-one limited-over internationals in succession, in the space of ten weeks, was more than any of us could put up with. Much to the promoter's fury, India and Pakistan reached the final and India won by eight wickets. The competition produced only one good laugh, which was all too sadly predictable. Mr Lynton Taylor, the inestimable boss of PBL Marketing, had not appeared all season which may have been why some of the cricket had seemed less of a drag than usual. He had clearly been saving himself for the World Championship of Cricket where he gave of his best. In a matter of moments he was up on his soap box, even though that still made him scarcely visible because the Almighty had been less than fair to him in the matter of elevation. He assured us that far from there being too much limited-over cricket, there was a possibility of even more but, happily, not this season. He told us that the complaints about the Australian season had come from English administrators who were jealous they had not been able to do a deal with Packer; presumably, so that they could have sold their birthright just as the Australian Board had sold theirs. What a little beauty he was. It was interesting that there was never a squeak from the Australian Board or its chairman, Fred Bennett, to say that they thought they ran the cricket and not Mr Lynton Taylor. Perhaps they had at last realised they did not.

All was not lost, however. Three days before the start of this jamboree I had left for a visit to Hamilton Island on the Great Barrier Reef. An Australian entrepreneur who had made a fortune redeveloping part of Queensland's Gold Coast, had rented Hamilton Island for ninety-nine years from the Queensland government and was in the process of trying to turn it into what he considered to be the last word in holiday resorts. The trouble was that he did not know when to leave well alone and, after building an airport for jets, he went on and on until it began to feel like Malaga or Torremolinos and not the tropical hideaway I had been hoping for when I bought an apartment there. The one invention I did rather care for was the booze-mobile which chugged its way to all the nooks and crannies of the island dispensing excellent liquid refreshment. In the end, I expect that, too, will have been overwhelmed.

In the meantime, a good deal of excitement had been taking place on the other side of the Indian Ocean. The England side, under David Gower, had only been in Delhi for four hours at the start of their tour when the Prime Minister, Mrs Gandhi, was gunned down by her Sikh bodyguards. For the next two days the players were marooned in their hotel as a wave of violence erupted in Delhi. They were then spirited away for a hastily arranged visit to Sri Lanka until things had improved. They returned for the First Test Match in Bombay, but the dramas were not over. Shortly before the match began, they were invited to a party of welcome by the High Commissioner, Percy Norris, a much loved figure. A good time was had by all but the next morning, on the way to his office, the High Commissioner was shot and killed. The tour management decided the First Test should go ahead. Fortunately, it proved to be the end of the trouble. England went on to win the series by two matches to one, never an easy feat on the subcontinent and England had been without the services of Ian Botham who had chosen to stay at home with his family.

The following summer in England the Australians, who had been weakened because a number of players had signed for a rebel tour of South Africa, were firmly put in their place. Gower, Gooch, Gatting and Tim Robinson all made big hundreds against an attack which was at best fitful. By the end of the series, England's main striking weapon was the out-swing of the tousle-haired Richard Ellison who took ten wickets in the Fifth Test at Edgbaston, one of the two for which I was allowed in the commentary box. The other was Lord's where Australia always won and this was no exception, but the overall result was 3–1 and the Ashes were back in English hands.

England tours to the West Indies had always been healthy breeding grounds for sensation and the side which David Gower took there after Christmas in 1985 was no exception. This aspect of the tour got off to an impressive start when a tabloid came up with the story that one of the players was having an affair with the wife of another who had only just got married. Mercifully, it was never printed and I don't for a moment believe it was true. Then, in front of many too many people most of whom goggled with jealousy or disapproval, our illustrious captain had what I can only describe as a highly insensitive swim in the pool at the Hilton in Port of Spain with an air hostess who worked for British Airways. She wasted no time in revealing all to another tabloid.

These were nothing more than mere starters. The pace hotted up when news came that the police in Devon and Cornwall were looking into allegations concerning the misuse of drugs on the walk Botham had done that autumn from John o' Groats to Land's End when he had raised almost a million pounds for leukaemia research, although Botham was never charged. The information had come to the police from the same paper Botham was suing for accusing him of smoking pot in New Zealand two years before. It was all being kept in the family. The smoke from this had hardly cleared when his celebrated agent, Tim Hudson, was reported as saying to a journalist at a party in Malibu, 'Of course Botham smokes pot. Everone does and so what?' One English paper devoted its entire front page to Hudson's remark and Botham now had a very public telephone conversation with his agent from the press box at the Queen's Park Oval in Port of Spain. Hudson was already in Miami on his way to Trinidad to watch some cricket. He altered his plans when he had put the telephone down and flew straight back to Gatwick where, with undue modesty, he immediately told the press that Botham needed him badly.

It was now time for the *News of the World* to get in on the act and it did so with a bang. The first five pages were devoted entirely to an exclusive exposure of an alleged drugs and sex scandal with Botham playing a starring role. Linda Field, who had sold the story, had once been selected as Miss Barbados, although since the comely photographs which had been taken of her at that sylph-like stage of her life, she had obviously acquired the habit of tucking into three square meals a day. She said that they had gone at it hammer and tongs to such an extent that Botham's sturdy bed had been badly broken. The lady went on to give extremely high ratings to Botham's performance which I am sure will have cheered him up. By then, Miss Field was holed up in a West End hotel in London with a spanking great cheque to help ease any belated pangs of conscience. Over the next few days it was almost impossible not to bump into a writ or an injunction for they were thick on the ground.

While it had all been most entertaining and highly diverting, it may not have done much to help England's cause on the cricket field and, alas, the world's greatest all-rounder made a somewhat less than overwhelming contribution. It was the tour, too, where

GOWER TO GATTING

David Gower made quite an impact with what he described as 'optional practice'. After the first two Tests had been lost, the players retired to Barbados for the Third which they lost by an innings in only just over three days. With the island overflowing with critical English visitors, Gower did not win a diploma for public relations. My own personal adventures in the West Indies did not, alas, stand comparison with any of this, although only the most solemn could fail to enjoy being sentenced to the Caribbean for the best part of four months.

The sequel to some of this came soon after the start of the 1986 season in England when the *Mail on Sunday* printed an admission by Botham that, in spite of all his previous denials, he had on a couple of occasions smoked pot at a party just to see what it was like. The cynics may have thought that Botham who was suing the *Mail on Sunday* for their story about him taking drugs on the 1983/84 tour of New Zealand, had been faced with some pretty solid evidence and this 'admission' had been part of a deal. Whatever caused it, he was suspended from Test and county cricket for nine weeks.

Peter May who was still chairman of the selectors, had announced his original appointment by summarily sacking Keith Fletcher as captain, but now, after Gower's highly questionable captaincy in the West Indies, he appointed him for only the First Test against India in 1986. He had already captained his country in twenty-three Test Matches and surely the selectors knew everything about his captaincy without having to insult him by putting him back in L-plates. They should either have sacked him before the series against India began or appointed him for all three of the Tests and then thought again before the series against New Zealand began in July. The First Test against India was lost and at the end of it Gower was ushered into the press conference in the writing room of the Lord's Pavilion by Peter Lush, the PR guru. Lush said that the captain had a statement to make and with great dignity Gower announced his own sacking. I thought it was disgraceful he should have been asked to do it himself and it said much for the shattering insensitivity of the people who ran the England set-up.

Mike Gatting took over from Gower but was unable to stop India winning their second series in England and New Zealand their first. Botham, having served his suspension, was reinstated for the last Test of the summer at the Oval, and it was marvellous to see his delight when he had Bruce Edgar, one of the openers, caught in the slips by Graham Gooch with his first ball. Botham later hit 24 off one over, from Derek Stirling, which equalled the record for runs scored from a six-ball over and so he was back with a vengeance and loving every minute of it. There was always something wonderfully compelling about Botham. Whenever he picked up a bat or a ball I always felt something was about to happen. He made me inch forward in my seat and had the same effect on millions of others. He had a happy knack of rising to the occasion and it was almost as if there was something pre-ordained about that wicket with his first ball. As well as being an extraordinary player, I felt that Botham was a lucky cricketer. He took wickets with bad balls and with the bat he got away with things that others would not have done. A cricketer with Botham's ability, and with luck on his side as well, is a formidable opponent. It was in this match he broke Lillee's record of 355 Test wickets.

That summer had been a particularly sad one for me. My father had hated being put on the sidelines at Hoveton and, although he and my mother still lived at Hoveton House, the running of the farm and the estate had been taken out of his hands. It not only made him feel unwanted but I know it also made him feel, right at the end, that his life had been rather a waste. I well remember having a number of extremely sad conversations with him about it all. He shut himself away more and more in the library at Hoveton and tried hard not to notice what was happening. In a sense, he had brought it on himself by being too nice and refusing to face up to the realities of the modern farming world. He had refused to get rid of people who had worked for a long time on the farm and were his friends. At the final count, it made no economic sense which he must have known, but he hoped that it would not all have to change until after he had died. He will have known, deep down, that he went on too long but perhaps that was the fault of John and myself. With sons whose main interests were the law and cricket, there had been no one to take over from him. I know that he suddenly felt redundant and unloved which was extremely sad. It drove him to the library in solitude, whereas my mother, who had a harder shell, wanted to fight back but was enough of a realist to know that changes had to be made, even if she disapproved of the way in which some had been carried out.

I had been asked by PBL Marketing to fly out to Australia for three or four days immediately after the Lord's Test Match late in June to take part in a television commercial for their forthcoming cricket season. I can't think how my old friend Lynton Taylor let this invitation slip through. Just before the start of the Lord's Test, my father had had a slight fall but by the time I caught my aeroplane on the evening of the last day of the Test match, he appeared to be recovering. I fear that by then all the fight had gone out of him and when, on that last evening at the Sheraton Wentworth before I flew home, I heard that he had died, I was not altogether surprised. He was eighty-three and in the last quarter of his life had become a splendid Norfolk figure who clearly belonged to an earlier age that was more gentle and relaxed. His and my mother's great passion had been the art world and in the middle of their lives they had collected some lovely things. I have to admit that it all rather passed me by because when they were at the height of their antique fever in the fifties and sixties, I am afraid I took a dim view of anything that got in the way of my cricket. They were well-known figures in the galleries and the antique shops of both London and Amsterdam. It was extremely sad though, that my father should have felt, as he did, that he had been diminished at the end, however inevitable it may have been.

I went to Australia in October 1986 for the England tour, by way of Houston, and while I was there I had one of the great sporting experiences of my life. I was taken by a friend to the vast Astrodome with its astonishing roof, to watch the Astros play the New York Mets in the second match of the best-of-seven finals of the National League Championship series. I had never watched an important baseball match before and I longed to see if it really was a more exciting, faster game than cricket which is another growth off the same old root. There was a crowd of about 45,000 which did not nearly fill this huge stadium and they were soon lapping up all the attendant showbiz razzmatazz of cheerleaders and dancing girls. There were unending supplies of popcorn, monkey nuts and beer and by the time the players got down to it, the entertainment had already been going on for some time. It was not a particularly exciting game. The Mets won 5–1 to make up for their unexpected defeat the night before. It was work-a-day baseball, without any home runs, which disappointed me. The most astonishing part of it was that it all had a roof over its head.

If I had had a stopwatch and had been able to tot up the seconds of genuine action and then have done the same with a Test Match, I am sure that cricket would have come out as the faster game. The hold-ups in baseball were endless but something was always coming over the tannoy and the cheerleaders were doing their stuff. There was never a shortage of things to look at. The character who interested me the most was the umpire, a large fierce-looking man dressed in black. He stood about three or four feet behind the striker – the cricketing equivalent would be a ridiculously close first slip. I called him Oddjob and if the need had arisen, I have not the slightest doubt he would have been a dab hand at throwing a steel rimmed bowler hat with deadly effect. From time to time the managers of both sides would run on to the pitch to argue with him but I could have told them they were wasting their time. At one point the Mets pitcher was accused of doctoring the ball with an illegal substance and this was by no means the only comparison with cricket. The standard of the catching and the throwing was phenomenal and put cricket to shame. I came away hugely exhilarated by what I had seen and wondering how the audience would take to a jazzed up cricket match of perhaps twenty-five overs a side. It might cause a flicker of excitement but I suppose in the end they would have wanted to go back to what they knew best and which was not, in any case, a million miles from cricket. My most obtuse memory of Houston was of being in the first car up to a level crossing as the gates shut and then having to watch a goods train loaded with corn take forty-five minutes to go through. While I had long enough to enjoy the benefits of each wagon, it didn't exactly dawdle and was pulled by no less than four huge diesel engines. I had never before realised that forty-five minutes lasted for so long.

Soon it was time for Australia and my tour got off to an exciting start after England, playing abject cricket, had lost their first serious match to Queensland with almost a day to spare. It was South Australia next and, after beating a weakened state side on the fourth afternoon, a party of us left by the Australian Pacific Express for the old mining town of Kalgoorlie where a Western Australia Country Eleven was waiting to do battle. There were six of us intrepid travellers, led by Peter West who was covering the tour for the *Daily Telegraph*. The others were David Gower, Phil Edmonds, Scyld Berry, writing for an august Sunday newspaper, and Adrian Murrell, one of the game's leading photographers. The other chap who became an honorary member of our party was our steward who was called Squizzy Taylor. He was short and fat; he never stopped smiling and laughing and was a genius at carrying four plates of soup at once while the train lurched this way and that without ever spilling a drop. A special carriage had been put on for the six of us and the only complaint I had concerned the overall stock of wine on board which suggested they had thought they were catering for the annual outing of Alcoholics Anonymous. It was poor thinking not to have brought our own for we had drunk the train dry when we were still eight hours short of Kalgoorlie.

The journey from Adelaide to Kalgoorlie took twenty-eight hours and the day we had climbed on board in Adelaide, the Melbourne Cup was run at Flemington. We had a sweepstake on the train, although the staff a trifle piously refused to join in saying that if they drew the winners everyone would say it was a put up job. Mercifully, Trevor, our admirable barman who by that stage we had virtually drunk out of a job, decided he would overcome whatever scruples he had been having a problem with, and organise it. While all this was going on, the train put into Cook which must be one of the driest, dustiest and remotest habitations on the planet. It is on the border of South Australia and Western Australia. Fewer than a hundred people live there and they are employed by either the Australian Railways or by Telecom. They didn't have much to boast about except an impressive amount of dust, a hot sun and a big modern swimming pool which they insisted we had a look at. In all honesty though, one swimming pool is very much like another. Close to the station there were two small cabins which looked as if they might have been either prehistoric telephone boxes or portable loos. They turned out to be Cook's two jails where, in the old days, passengers who had done themselves too well on the trains, were taken off and locked in until they had sobered up and the next train had come along to take them back home. They were now tourist attractions and I don't think they had serious thoughts about dusting them down for any of us.

I shall never forget waking up that day at six in the morning and opening the curtains of my compartment. The scene outside was incredible. Scorched red earth and scrub stretched away to the horizon and already the blazing sun was doing its worst. This was the Nullarbor Plain. Lying there in my air-conditioned hutch, I could almost feel the intense heat sweeping over me and the red dust climbing into my nostrils. I have never seen anything so arid and bleak and desolate and it went on for mile after mile, for hour after hour. Perhaps it was the first time I had truly sensed the size of Australia. In its way, it was as awe-inspiring as the Houston Astrodome.

I don't know what the train journey did for David Gower who, as England's recently sacked captain, had seemed out of sorts. He made nought in each innings against Western Australia. Rain on the last day saved England from defeat. The party went back to Brisbane for the First Test, fearful of the worst, but they were up against a poor Australian side. Micky Stewart, on his first tour as the England coach, and the captain, Mike Gatting, somehow managed to reinvigorate the England dressing room and they won this First Test by seven wickets. Ian Botham produced the most responsible innings I ever saw him play for England, batting just over four hours for 138. This victory gave England a big psychological advantage which was not checked until after they had regained the Ashes. Then, in the Fifth Test at Sydney, on a turning pitch, Australia played Peter Taylor, an off spinner who had played in only six first-class matches, and he and leg spinner Peter Sleep spun Australia to victory by 55 runs.

While Stewart had his most successful series as England's team manager, his opposite number, Bobby Simpson, was still trying to come to grips with the mess in which Australian cricket had been left after the Packer revolution. The members of Ian Chappell's formidable side in the mid-seventies had now retired and the next generation had been slow to take over. Australia had not been helped by the turmoil which had led to Kim Hughes's resignation as captain, as well as the unsettled aftermath. Australia's new captain, Allan Border, seemed at this stage of his career to be a stodgy thinker and he and Simpson probably did not see eye to eye all the time. Their cricket reached an all-time low when, in the Fourth Test in Melbourne, they lost by an innings in three days. I wrote a piece the next day in *The Australian* comparing the two coaches and saying how much better it was turning out for Stewart than Simpson, who was always mortally offended by criticism of any sort. The day the article appeared we had flown to Perth and in the evening Simpson came up to me in the large entrance hall at the Perth Sheraton and showed how absurdly sensitive he could be. Australia's performance in Melbourne had been too ghastly for words and was impossible to defend. It always surprised me that someone like Simpson, who was vastly experienced, should have bothered to go through the newspapers as he did. It showed an extraordinary and rather futile insecurity for which there was no need, as he was soon to show when he built up one of the best Australian sides they have ever had. Sadly, I don't think our relationship has ever been quite the same since I wrote that piece and our friendship had gone back to the mid-sixties when, after he had retired the first time, he came to England each summer to write for the *Evening Standard*, as it then was. There was a time when we both had flats in Chelsea Cloisters, Sloane Avenue. Simpson was one of the few Australian cricketers who was never as popular as he might have been with his colleagues from his playing days. His first venture into county cricket, with Leicestershire, was not a success and I shall be interested to see if, even now, he can make it work with Lancashire.

CHAPTER

19

ONE CRISIS TO THE NEXT

THE EIGHTIES embraced controversy almost until the end. After watching England hold on to the Ashes in Australia in 1986/87, I could not resist the temptation to nip over the Tasman Sea and have a look at the West Indies playing three Tests against New Zealand. It was their first visit since that extraordinary tour at the start of 1980 when they had let themselves down so badly by the way in which they made a fuss about umpire Goodall. I arrived in Wellington which is about as windy as its reputation suggests and landing at that small airport on a gusty day is an adventure. Built on a series of hills, Wellington is a most delightful and attractive city and its cricket ground, the Basin Reserve, is probably the largest traffic island in the world. Sadly, on its invariably docile pitch, I have had to endure some draws that have been as boring as any I have seen and, if the wind is in the wrong quarter, it can be chillingly cold. The West Indies fast bowlers seemed to have won the First Test before Martin Crowe and John Wright both made hundreds and saved the match for New Zealand. Goodness knows why, but Viv Richards allowed his bowlers to use the same ball for 177 overs, by which time it must have felt like a battered ball of wool.

The series now moved on to Auckland where Fred Goodall had been chosen as one of the umpires and, with the memory of that series in 1979/80 still abundantly clear in everyone's minds, it was bound to be a notable confrontation and was the reason I had come to New Zealand. I was not disappointed, even though I had to wait until the third day for the flashpoint which came when Malcolm Marshall bowled to Jeff Crowe. He played back, was beaten for pace and hit on the pad. The appeal was deafening and Goodall stared impassively, but challengingly, down the pitch for an appreciable time before turning it down. The West Indies seethed and jostled with discontent. A few minutes later it happened all over again. While the replay of the first incident revealed that a fertile imagination might just have perceived an area of doubt, it showed that on the second occasion there was none. Once again Goodall, who was loving every half second of it, peered down the pitch with his chin stuck out and his hands clasped behind his back. With every eye upon him, he straightened up quickly like a guardsman and with ill-disguised relish, flicked one of the coins he used to count the balls, from one hand to the other with a certain *brio*. While he was still leaning forward looking down the pitch, it began to occur to the West Indians that he was not going to give Crowe out.

When he eventually said, 'Not out,' the attention turned to Richards at first slip. Slowly, with that familiar mixture of confidence and arrogance, he walked the full length of the pitch to Goodall's end. I wish I could have lip-read what was being said. It was sharp and to the point and for a few seconds the future of the tour, relations between New Zealand and the West Indies, and the general health of the game of cricket were in the balance. Then Richards shrugged his shoulders and sauntered back down the pitch. It had been a close run thing and I wouldn't have missed it for the world. While this was happening, I saw Steve Camacho, the West Indies manager who was sitting just below the press box, make a bid for a place in the *Guinness Book of Records* for the fastest cigarette ever smoked. The West Indies won that Test by ten wickets. The Third was played in Christchurch where the New Zealand seam bowlers, led by Richard Hadlee, returned the compliment, although New Zealand lost five wickets in scoring the 33 they needed to win.

I enjoyed Pakistan's victory in the five-match series in England in 1987 because it came about when they won by an innings at Headingley and Imran Khan, bowling perhaps better than he had ever done, took ten wickets in the match. Whether bowling or batting, there was something faintly noble and old fashioned about Imran. He was a giant on the field and the only captain of Pakistan I ever saw who was able to control his troops and cope with the petty infighting within the team which so often prevented a talented side from producing its best. Alas, the cricket in this series came to be of almost secondary importance to the inept manner in which the Test and County Cricket Board handled Pakistan's complaints about the selection of David Constant to umpire in two of the Tests. The Pakistanis had fallen out with him during the 1982 series.

When they had arrived in England the Pakistanis had let it be known they would not be happy if he stood in the Test series and their manager, Haseeb Ahsan, complained each time he was chosen. Lord's treated the Pakistan manager in an unforgivably high-handed manner and sent him packing apparently oblivious to the fact that England were to tour Pakistan the following winter. It was almost a certainty that they would feel the need to complain about at least one umpire during that series. They had now made sure they would receive a dusty answer when they did. Haseeb Ahsan was nobody's fool and was cunning to boot. I met Peter Lush, the marketing manager for the TCCB, who was to manage the side in Pakistan that winter, in the passage outside his office in the Lord's Pavilion and I asked him if he thought the decision to stick with Constant might not backfire. His memorable answer was that he did not think the Pakistanis would be so silly, but before England settled down to tour Pakistan the following winter the World Cup was to be played in India and Pakistan.

The England season had been over for just three weeks when I flew off to India for the first World Cup to be played away from England. On 9 October I found myself in Madras for the opening match between India and Australia. The previous summer we had been visited in the commentary box by our old friend the Maharajah of Baroda who had been with us for the Indian series in 1974. In the meantime he had been putting together a number of coffee-table books about India and when I got him in front of the microphone, I asked him about his latest literary adventures. He told me he was writing a book about Indian ports. I asked him which vintages he recommended and, after a good chuckle, he told me it was forts, not ports. Before he left the box, Trevor Bailey and I told him we would be covering the matches played in India during the World Cup and when he kindly offered to look after our travel arrangements and hotels, we gave him out itineraries. I was rather pleased to think that my travel agent was a Maharajah, but when I got to India I discovered that he had in the meantime been struck down by a lingering bug and had been unable to fulfil his promises.

Arriving in India without any hotel bookings is a bit of a risk. Before I had left England I had discovered that Trevor was staying at the Connemara Hotel in Madras and when I arrived I went straight there and, most obligingly, they found me a room. I then ran into an old friend, M.L. Jaisimha, who was one of the Indian selectors, and he promised, with the help of their team manager, to arrange rooms for me for all the other matches. It was a great piece of luck and got me out of a nasty hole, although having the Indian manager as a travel agent was not quite the same as a Maharajah.

Those few weeks left behind many good memories, not least of which was Australia's victory over India by one run in that first match in Madras. A stupendous 141 by David Houghton took Zimbabwe to within four runs of victory over New Zealand in Hyderabad. There was a splendid visit in Chandigarh in the northeast from where on a good day it is possible to see the Himalayas and which is the home of Inderjit Singh Bindra, the organiser of the World Cup in India. Australia were playing New Zealand and one evening a most unlikely supply of claret turned up at a party for the two teams. It had, I think, been donated by Cornhill who were the inestimable sponsors of the England side at home. That evening I met Sir Edmund Hillary who was the High Commissioner for New Zealand in Delhi. I am glad to say he enjoyed the claret as much as anyone, besides speaking movingly about Sherpa Tensing with whom he had conquered Everest in 1953.

There was an extraordinary match in Nagpur which is almost in the centre spot of India. The hosts were playing New Zealand and, in order to qualify for the semi-finals, they had to score the 222 they needed to win in less than forty-three overs so that their run rate was higher than Australia's. This would mean they would have a semi-final against England in Bombay rather than against Pakistan in Lahore. It also meant that if things went according to plan, India would play Pakistan in the final.

In spite of a fever and a high temperature, Sunil Gavaskar opened the innings for India and launched an astonishing assault on New Zealand's bowlers. In Ewen Chatfield's third over, he swung him to mid-wicket for six, drove the next ball straight into the Governor's enclosure in the main stand above the sightscreen where there was a peacock-like fluttering of sarees and the bobbing of the odd turban. The third ball was driven over mid off for four and the fourth, a full toss, tucked away to the square leg boundary. In two overs Chatfield went for thirty runs. Gavaskar who had never made a hundred in a one-day international, reached three figures in eighty-five balls with three sixes and ten fours. It was one of the most incredible innings I have seen in any type of cricket and India scored the runs they needed from only 32.1 overs.

I have two other reasons for remembering that visit to Nagpur. Trevor and I had flown down from Delhi the day before the match and, as usual, our bags were weighed at the airport. The man who did so looked most suspiciously at mine which I had carried round India blamelessly and without incident for the last month. Having studied the scales, he looked up and told me with the friendliest of smiles that I would have to pay him 200 dollars for overweight. I expostulated and told him it was ridiculous and that I had no intention of doing so. I told him I had not been asked for this at any other Indian airport and when he was adamant, I demanded to see his superior. I had already broken the golden rule which is never to overreact when confronted by the imponderable face of subcontinental bureaucracy. I was taken to a room where three Indians dressed in khaki were waiting for me. I explained and I protested and I was furious and I should have known better than to say many of the things which came frothing up. In short, I was shamefully rude. It became increasingly clear that if I did not pay what I had been asked for, I would have no chance of reaching Nagpur that night. What I did not know was that Trevor had followed on behind and had been standing in the door when I was at my most eloquent. As I shuffled off back to the counter to pay the overweight, Trevor, with rather a stern look, did a certain amount of well-justified tut-tutting. I had undoubtedly made a fool of myself.

The morning after India beat New Zealand in Nagpur, we departed for the airport to fly down to Bombay for the semi-final. Before leaving England Trevor had acquired an American Express Gold Card of which he was proud and he had already waved it around a time or two. I settled my hotel bill first and then told him I would make sure the luggage was put safely in the taxi and wait for him outside. I did as I said and was waiting by the side of the taxi when I heard angry voices inside the hotel. I raised my ears and heard Trevor's not just among them but leading the way. I walked quickly back to the door for I sensed that this was something not to be missed. What had happened was that Trevor had presented his Gold Card to pay his bill and the chap at reception told him he had never seen one before and wouldn't accept it. At this point Trevor must have been grateful that he had heard me at Delhi airport, for it had given him a few tips on the way he should continue the conversation. I can only say that he not only remembered my lines pretty well, but he added one or two extremely telling ones of his own. He didn't speak in a whisper either. In the end he was forced to pay by some other method before stumping out of the hotel red-faced and bothered and still muttering. We settled into the taxi and when we had begun to move, he asked me if I heard the conversation and I said that indeed I had. He thought for an awkward moment before saying, 'I wasn't very good was I?' I laughed and told him that I thought it was at least thirty-fifteen to me. Straws can break camels' backs. There is no excuse but it does happen, although from then on there were no two more polite and charming Englishmen in India than Trevor and I.

The semi-final against England in Bombay was a mixed blessing for India who were well beaten. Graham Gooch made a splendid hundred, punctuated as always with those satisfyingly crisp cuts and drives and India were left to score 255 but never came to terms with the target. I shall never forget Kapil Dev's hopeful swing when Eddie Hemmings threw one up in the air and Gatting's joy when he hugged the skied catch to his chest at mid-wicket. That was the wicket which effectively ended India's chances. With Australia defying the odds and beating Pakistan, the final was between England and Australia which was not exactly what the organisers had been hoping for.

When I arrived in Calcutta, it was not until one o'clock in the morning that I was eventually allotted a room in the Oberoi Grand on Chowringhee, the street which runs alongside the Maidan. It was only because I had become a friend of Inderjit Singh Bindra that I had the luck to get in at all. I remember him sitting in an alcove near the bar with sheets of paper in front of him and masses of people trying to talk to him all at the same time, while furiously scratching his head through a voluminous turban. The West Indies had complicated things by arriving in Calcutta to watch the final when they had already been kicked out of the competition. By the end of that long hot evening I am not sure they hadn't been kicked out of the hotel as well. The festivities took in endless visits to the club at Tollygunge, presided over with great charm and no little whisky by Bob Wright, a David Niven lookalike. There was polo on the Maidan where prizes were presented by the Rajmata of Jaipur, with whom Johnny Woodcock and I had played golf in Jaipur after our drive to Bombay. Pierson Surita, the cricket commentator who lived in Chowringhee in a large flat of Dickensian gloom and turned up in the unlikeliest places resplendent in an MCC tie, did the on-course commentary at the polo. His voice made Jim Swanton's sound strangely middle of the road. He also had a box at the races at Alipur where I found it as easy to lose money as it is at any other racecourse in the world, and while we were there the Indian Open was being played at the Royal Calcutta Golf Club. The old city really pushed out the boat and for those few days it was almost impossible to get to bed before the sun was up.

On the day of the final, transport was at a standstill with taxis impossible to find and I walked across the Maidan to Eden Gardens, normally a fifteen-minute journey, but it took much longer because of the teeming crowds. We were commentating back to England on *Test Match Special* from a particularly cramped spot in the upper reaches of the pavilion. I shall never forget poor old CM-J's arrival. He was looking like a more than passable imitation of a ghost, with a combination of Delhi belly and Calcutta cramps and was in a bad way, but he stuck nobly to his task almost until the end. From England's point of view, an excellent match was ruined by Gatting's attempt to play a reverse sweep to Allan Border. Although Australia won by only 7 runs, it was never quite as exciting as that made it sound. When it was all over, I walked back across the Maidan to the Grand Hotel, while a magnificent display of fireworks let off at Eden Gardens, lit up the sky. There were thousands upon thousands of Indians on the Maidan that night and most were standing still, spellbound, staring up to the heavens watching something they had, most of them, never seen before as the rockets screeched skywards and the wonderful colours burst time and again in great umbrellas under the night sky. Only a mile or two away, hundreds of thousands were eeking out their existences in conditions of unbelievable squalor and filth. Calcutta showed us all that night, in case we needed reminding, that it is a city of astonishing contrasts.

The next day I flew off to Australia where my first port of call was Brisbane in order to watch Ian Botham play his first match for Queensland. During the England tour of Australia the year before he had announced his intention of playing for Queensland and he had promised he would go on playing for them until they managed to win the Sheffield Shield for the first time, which was not how it turned out. He had said at the same time that he would not be going on tour again with England which explained his absence from the World Cup. He now announced himself with a tail-end wicket in Victoria's first innings and a whirlwind 58 with four sixes and seven fours in Queensland's first innings. It was a story which was to have a sad ending, even though

Queensland reached the final of the Sheffield Shield in which they had to play Western Australia in Perth.

On the flight to Perth for that match, Botham was one of those playing a tape with the volume turned up to its maximum and he then had a violent argument with Allan Border which contained much flowery language. A passenger in the row in front asked him to quieten down and Botham's reaction was to pull the passenger's hair from behind and to give him a good shaking. When another passenger had the temerity to tell him to stop it, Botham retaliated by telling him he would be the next if he didn't shut up. The police met Botham at Perth airport and he was charged on two counts. He was kept in the cells until Dennis Lillee arrived to bail him out. Botham was in court the day after Queensland lost the final, and was fined A$800. In emerging from court, his first reaction was to launch a scathing attack on the press. After all this, Queensland astonished only Botham when they decided not to renew his contract.

Meanwhile, things had been coming to the boil in Pakistan. In the First Test, which was played throughout in a most unfriendly atmosphere, Chris Broad had refused to leave the crease when he had been given out which is always a pointless procedure, however unfairly treated a batsman may have been. Gooch had to go down the pitch to shoo him away. The England players were beginning already to feel the backlash from the treatment Haseeb Ahsan had received from the authorities at Lord's. The umpiring now was officious and abrasive and extremely bad. The Second Test in Faisalabad produced some of the worst scenes ever to be enacted on an international cricket field. Towards the end of the second day, Mike Gatting, at backward short leg, moved a leg-side fielder as Eddie Hemmings was coming in to bowl. Gatting had told the batsman what he was doing but umpire Shakoor Rana ticked off the England captain in no uncertain terms for unfair play because he had moved a fielder behind the batsman's back. Gatting and Rana had a shouting match in the middle of the pitch. The umpire refused to continue until he had received an apology from Gatting and the third day's play was lost as a result. The tour was almost cancelled and the British Foreign Office even became involved.

In the end Gatting wrote a terse note of apology which Rana accepted, but the Pakistan Board would not reinstate the third day. I would hate to think that was because Pakistan were losing the match.

Of course, it was an appalling piece of umpiring and almost certainly a put-up job. None of that can, however, excuse Gatting for his behaviour. The game is in the hands of the umpires and no matter how incompetent they are, their word has to be accepted. Gatting had been put under extreme pressure by the umpiring in both the first two Tests but what he did was unacceptable. Unfortunately, the matter did not rest there. The manager, Peter Lush, in my opinion pompous and humourless, and the cricket manager, Micky Stewart, took the side of Gatting and were seen therefore to condone something which struck a mortal blow at the intrinsic values of the game. But that was not all. The chairman of the TCCB, Raman Subba Row, immediately flew out to Pakistan and each England player was given a bonus of a £1,000 for enduring hardship. There is no nicer man involved in the administration of the game than Subba Row and he has been a friend of mine ever since we met on the station at Norwich Thorpe in 1959 soon after I had been sent down from Cambridge. For all that, I still find his decision to distribute bonuses after bad behaviour extremely baffling, coming from someone who could not normally be more anxious to uphold the traditions of the game. As an international match referee, it is still his job to do so. I have no doubt that by publicly engaging in a slanging match with Shakoor Rana, Gatting forfeited his right to captain England, although the pusillanimous cricket authorities at the time allowed him to get away with it. The older Gatting became, the more of a barrack-room lawyer he turned into, as those who have tried to run Middlesex cricket will confirm.

When the series in Pakistan had ended, with Pakistan the winners, England came to Australia to play the Bicentenary Test Match at the Sydney Cricket Ground. I had by then watched an entertaining series of three Test Matches between Australia and New Zealand. Australia had won the first easily but almost lost the third when their last pair had to survive for twenty-nine balls at Melbourne. Richard Hadlee took ten wickets in this match and five wickets in an innings on three occasions. Hadlee had begun his career as a tearaway fast bowler, but it was not until he cut down his run and became arguably the best fast medium seamer of all that he turned into such a relentless wicket taker. I enjoyed nothing more in county cricket than watching Hadlee and Clive Rice take Nottinghamshire to the County Championship when they cut swathes through all the other batting line-ups in England. It has to be said though, that the Trent Bridge pitch gave them all the help they wanted, but they could not have used it better. They made the journey to Trent Bridge, which has always been my favourite ground in England after Lord's, even more worthwhile.

The Bicentenary Test Match was held at the end of January 1988 to celebrate Australia's two hundredth birthday. The great day was 26 January, when the famous Sydney Harbour was filled from soon after daybreak with boats of every size and description. I walked down to Pier One at eight o'clock to join a boat called, appropriately enough, *Matilda I*. The first glass of champagne was in my hand soon after I had walked across the gangplank. The plan was to steer a course out between the heads and join the fleet of boats which was going to re-enact the arrival of the first fleet two hundreds years before. The boats taking part in this re-enactment were copies of the original fleet and they had themselves been brought out from England by volunteers on a journey which had lasted for several months. The night before they had tucked themselves away in Botany Bay to prepare for the great day. Tuckers, the company who, among other things, imported wine and had laid on *Matilda I*, had sponsored one of these boats. When we reached the heads after what must have been a nightmare journey for our navigator with so many small boats all over the place, we could see in the distance the tall sails of the replica fleet. We found the boat Tuckers had sponsored, the SS *Svanen*, and came slowly back into the harbour with her. It was hour after hour of non-stop celebration and, as the day went on, there was a most impressive fly-past of aeroplanes which revealed just about their full history. It began with some which looked as if they too must have been about two hundred years old and then it took us through most of the subsequent stages of development until we came to the early jets and eventually to representatives of the contemporary Australian Air Force. My day ended with a party on the roof of the International Hotel to watch a firework display which even outshone that at Eden Gardens three months before. The final *tour de force* came when the Harbour Bridge was lit up and that made everyone catch their breath.

The Test Match which began two days later was not quite able to live up to this high level of entertainment. England had the satisfaction of making Australia follow on before David Boon batted out the rest of the match. By then, Chris Broad had scored another hundred to add to the three he had made in Australia the year before, but it was a great pity that he again let himself down when he was out. He had made 139 when he tried to get out of the way of a lifter from Steve Waugh which hit him on the body and bounced on to the stumps. Broad was so angry that he spun round with his bat and knocked his leg stump out of the ground. I have seldom seen such a disgusting display of petulance on a cricket ground. On his return to the pavilion Broad was lucky to find that the England manager fined him only A$500. But I suppose after what had happened in Pakistan, he may have been hoping for a pat on the back and, who knows, a bonus from the TCCB. The England side had gone back to England for two weeks over Christmas and maybe Lush and Stewart had had their thinking altered by the time they arrived in Australia. Even after all this time, I still find it almost impossible to believe that Broad could have behaved as boorishly as he did in Sydney so soon after all that had happened in Pakistan.

I enjoyed the Australian season enormously because Brian White had moved from Radio 3AW in Melbourne to become the general manager of Radio 2UE in Sydney. One of his innovations was to widen the cricket commentary on UE so that we covered all the Test Matches and the one-day internationals. Our output was heard in Sydney and any of the stations affiliated to UE in the other states. It was the greatest of fun and we tried to give listeners a less intense and more light-hearted commentary than they would get on the ABC. Our output was much more like *Test*

Match Special and we had a splendid team. Dennis Cometti, who came from Perth, and I were the two main ball-by-ball commentators and we had a fine array of experts for the between-over comments. Ray Jordon, a legend as an Australian Rules Football coach who toured India and South Africa as the reserve wicket-keeper with Bill Lawry's side in 1969/70 but never played a Test Match, was always with us. He was one of the funniest and most delightful men I have ever shared a microphone with. He had a real Ocker Australian voice and you never quite knew what was going to come out next because he could get very near the knuckle, especially when he spotted a pretty girl in the crowd which was not an uncommon occurrence.

Ian Meckiff, 'the Count', who was drummed out of cricket for throwing by umpire Colin Egar in the First Test in Brisbane against South Africa in 1963/64, was usually with us when he wasn't engaged in his abortive efforts to try and come to terms with the local fish population. Bill Jacobs, who managed a number of Australian sides in the sixties and seventies and whom I once photographed riding a donkey in Grenada, was with us in Melbourne. Kerry O'Keeffe, the leg spinner, who dressed as if he was a late convert to flower-power, joined us in Sydney. We were also helped by several of the Channel Nine commentators and Tony Greig did ball-by-ball for us, while Richie Benaud, Max Walker, Bill Lawry and Ian Chappell sat in the summariser's chair. We flew around Australia for most of the summer under the guidance of Andrew Moore who joined as our scorer soon after he left school. He was soon allowed to lug the equipment round the country too, and by the time it all came to an end in the early nineties, he had become a more than competent broadcaster. I've no doubt he'll make a name for himself somewhere. He soon acquired a taste for the good things of life and didn't make much of a job of trying to keep us on the straight and narrow which was another of his duties. That was rather like employing King Alfred in a bakery.

When UE was bought by Kerry Packer, who was not always in agreement with the way Brian White ran the station, we all had to be a bit more careful because Tony Greig was a great confidant of Packer's. It was in my contract that I should travel first-class while some of the others had to sit in the back. One evening Greig found himself in the front of the aeroplane with me and White had a telephone call from Packer the next day. There were times when I was talking to Greig when I found myself wondering if it was he or Packer who owned Channel Nine. There was also the sad occasion when Rod Marsh was with us on UE at a match in Sydney and said how much he preferred Test cricket to one-day cricket. This was not the preferred option of Channel Nine and PBL Marketing and the next day Marsh was sacked from our broadcast by Packer himself. There was no malice in what he had said, it was just what he believed. It was Marsh who had called Randall back to the wicket that time during the Centenary Test Match and it was also Marsh who registered such horror when Trevor Chappell had bowled the infamous underarm ball.

Immediately after the Bicentenary Test, we all moved on to Melbourne where England played a one-day game against Australia and the crowd of 54,000 will have helped pay for a few more of the overall expenses. From there, we returned to Perth for Sri Lanka's first Test Match on Australian soil which lasted a fraction over three days with Australia winning by an innings. The crowds were so small they will have been hard pressed even to pay the gate-keeper's wages. By the time I arrived in New Zealand, England had already drawn the First Test in Christchurch. I joined the Television New Zealand commentary team for the last two Tests which were also drawn, and for the four one-day internationals after that. John Morrison and Glenn Turner, both former New Zealand opening batsmen, were with us and we were also joined by Bob Cunis who played twenty Tests as a medium fast seam bowler. It was Cunis of whom it was once memorably written by Alan Ross in the *Observer* that, 'His bowling, like his name, is neither quite one thing nor the other.' There have been a number of writers who have laid claim to those few words but Ross was the man who came up with them for the first time.

During the Third Test in Wellington, Iain Gallaway, New Zealand's best known and most experienced radio commentator and now president of New Zealand Cricket, asked me if I would

ONE CRISIS TO THE NEXT

like to visit the Valley of Peace Cricket Club when we were in Christchurch for the second of the one-day matches. It was no more than half an hour from the middle of Christchurch. The last mile of the journey was down a narrow winding country road and as we came round a bend I could see white flannelled figures through the green foliage of the trees a couple of meadows away in the small valley on the right. It was the most idyllic spot, even if the ground was not much bigger than a pocket handkerchief. We turned right over a small bridge and parked behind the pavilion. I was greeted warmly by John Waters who runs the club now and is the son of the founder. A glass of beer was soon in my hand and Ken Rutherford, who was to captain New Zealand, was batting. For me, it was exactly as if I was watching a village match on a lovely country ground in some remote part of England. The ground itself cannot then have been more than about an acre and three-quarters in size, although it has since been slightly enlarged, but boundaries still only count two and four. There was no doubting the seriousness of the cricket either.

The Valley of Peace, Christchurch Cinematograph Cricket Club, was founded by Harry Waters in 1928. He owned the Christchurch Cinematograph Company and wanted to find a ground where his employees would be able to play cricket on Sundays. In those puritanical times this was generally frowned upon but it was the only free day for those operating the cinemas. A Miss White, who lived in Huon Hay Valley in the house on the hill just above the ground, came to his aid. She agreed to rent them a paddock, provided they were prepared to clear it, and the fee was a shilling a week from each of those who played. Miss White was in the habit of giving a lot of money to the Roman Catholic Church and one day when she peered through her curtains at the cricket she was horrified to see lots of women watching. She told Harry Waters in the most vehement terms that if his chaps wanted to continue to play there, 'painted hussies' would not be allowed. To this day, the fairer sex is forbidden and on that first occasion, Jeremy Coney had the temerity to turn up with a girlfriend and there was much pointed whispering before she was forced to beat a retreat. The local feminists have mercifully not yet turned their attention to the Valley of Peace and, if they do, I am sure the members will man the ramparts. I hope John Waters and the members of this remarkable club will forgive me for saying that it is an extraordinary acre or two of England just about as far away from England as it is possible to be. I go back to the Valley of Peace without fail every time I go to Christchurch. It is the most perfect setting for cricket I have ever seen and the hospitality is second to none. It is, too, a wonderful reminder of the origins of the game. I have a lovely print of the ground hanging in our breakfast room at North Farm and it helps to give each day a better start.

When I returned to England, the new order at Hoveton had sorted itself out. My mother was now living in the house I had moved out of for John, while he and Judy and the family had moved into Hoveton House which they gradually turned into a less formal and more practical establishment for modern living. I am not sure my mother approved but she said very little. In her old age my mother became a priceless relic of a bygone age. To some, she was a frightening figure and she could never resist the temptation to tell people exactly what she thought of them. Verbally, she did not take prisoners. She now proceeded to build a life for herself and one of the joys of going down to Hoveton was to go and see her wrestling with her television set and complaining bitterly about something she had heard on the news or read in the papers. She always had a good bit of gossip to pass on and the best time to go and see her was six o'clock when she liked to be given a decent glass of her own special whisky. Having lived at Hoveton House for more than thirty years, it was quite a step down for her but she took it in her stride and had brought some of her favourite things from the big house with her. Mentally, she was as alert as ever and nothing got past her right up until the day she died. She hated what was going on all around her but she was sensible enough to realise that change was inevitable. Whenever she listed the latest catalogue of events of which she disapproved, she would usually say, 'It's just as well your father's dead. I can't tell you what he would have said about it.' Well into her eighties, she would come to lunch or supper with me in her

...ten with one of Bubbles's eleven puppies born ...e night before England's Test Match against Sri ...nka at the Oval in 1998.

The two of us at Haugh's End with Hudson's Bay in the background.

...rth Farm towards the end of summer when the Virginia creeper and the wisteria make their annual ...eover bid.

Talking to Bob Willis in Karachi in 1983/84 after England had lost the First Test. I feel sure the military was there to protect him from my question.

A couple of sailors on shore leave! Geoff Boycott and H.C.B., television comrades in the West Indies in 1992/93.

...osie McWhirter (widow of Ross), Jack Lee (brother of Laurie), tennis commentator Richard Evans, ...C.B., Rex Neame, Tony Facciolo (concierge supreme), Chris Martin-Jenkins and John MacKinnon at ...iana Fisher's daily picnic, at the Sydney Cricket Ground.

...ary Sobers, Glenn Turner, a TV executive, H.C.B., Mark Mascarenhas (owner of World Tel), Tiger ...taudi, Ravi Shastri and Kris Srikkanth – television comes to Eden Gardens, Calcutta.

Champagne and boules in Reims with Nasser Hussain and Mike Atherton and masses of Veuve Cliquot

Adelaide Oval – the most beautiful Test Match ground of all presided over by the cathedral.

rfu town square – a charming but unlikely venue where I once put on 50 with Bill Edrich.

rd's – the incomparable with its astonishing media centre and the stylish new grandstand.

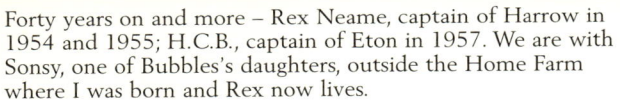

Forty years on and more – Rex Neame, captain of Harrow in 1954 and 1955; H.C.B., captain of Eton in 1957. We are with Sonsy, one of Bubbles's daughters, outside the Home Farm where I was born and Rex now lives.

My mother and father on the terrace at Hoveton House on my father's eightieth birthday.

Thorunn and David Gower and H.C.B. outside the Taj Mahal on a day off from commentating in 1992/9

The noses tell the story. My daughter Suki and I enjoy something cold in my London garden.

C.B. with stepson Rumple (Alexei) on his knee, sharing a laugh in London.

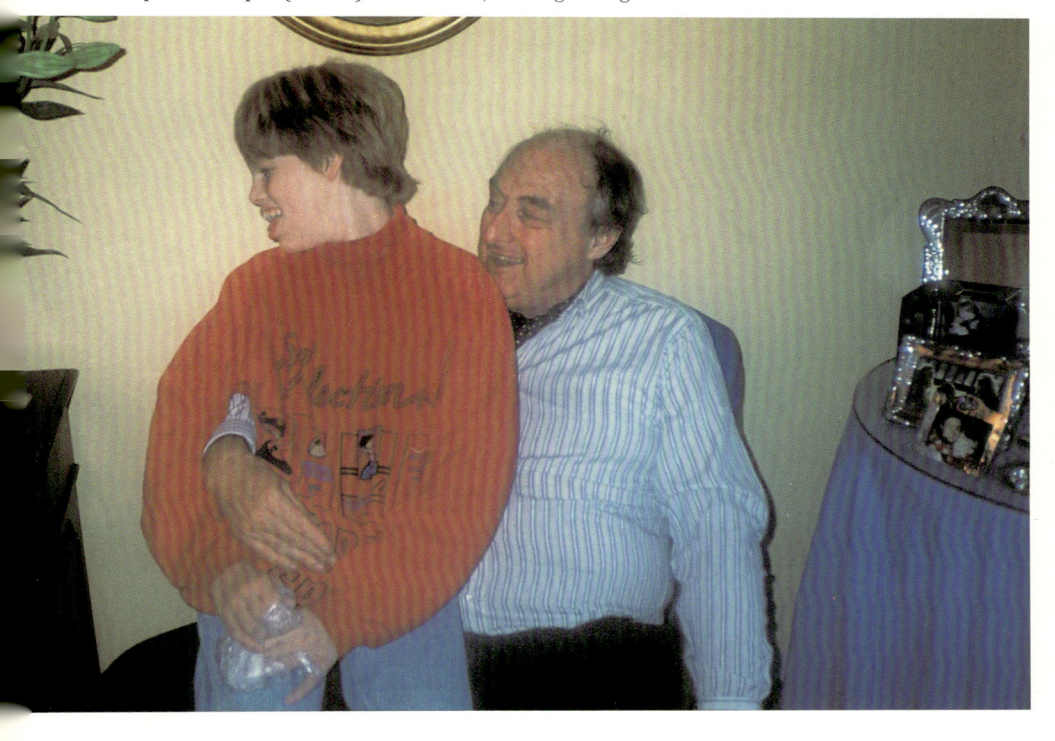

Saffron, one of the two puppies we kept, in the garden at North Farm.

ONE CRISIS TO THE NEXT

tiny red Fiat which she drove steadfastly after a certain amount of imperious revving in the early stages.

England lost four of the five Test Matches to the West Indies in 1988 and the only surprise was that they managed to hold on to the first, at Trent Bridge. Mike Gatting had somehow survived Shakoor Rana, although he had only been appointed for the first two Tests. Ever since he first played for England in Pakistan in 1977/78, I had felt that there was something reassuringly chunky and determined about Gatting, as a batsman and then as a captain. His chunkiness had got the better of him in Pakistan and he must surely have realised how lucky he was still to be in the job and he should have known the penance he had to pay was to walk with caution for quite a while. After England collapsed on the first day at Trent Bridge, it came to light that Gatting was in trouble with the TCCB over a book in which he had written his version of the Shakoor Rana incident. So bad must it have been that Alan Smith, the chief executive of the TCCB was prepared to break the habit of a lifetime and actually go on the record during the Test Match as saying that if it appeared in its present form it would not help Gatting's chances of retaining the captaincy. Alan Smith had an inborn reluctance to saying anything that was for public consumption unless he was wearing both a belt and braces. Then, during this First Test, Gatting allowed himself to be floored by what seemed to be a prearranged plot. While staying at a hostelry not far from Leicester, he made the acquaintance of a comely barmaid who was working at a rival establishment. She found an enthusiasm for Gatting which he was unable to deny. After disengaging herself from his arms, she threw herself greedily into those of a tabloid newspaper who had no doubt offered an appreciable financial inducement.

Their combined adventures made big news and the authorities were in more of a turmoil than ever. Having got away with it in Faisalabad, Gatting must have felt that the rules no longer applied to him. I suppose the offer of a big advance to write the authentic story from Pakistan may have made up his mind for him. It was absurd for the same people who had allowed him to continue in the job after Faisalabad to have conscientious objections about the England captain bonking a barmaid somewhere along the A6 between Nottingham and Leicester. Only Lord's could have had such a distorted sense of values. Which episode brought the game into greater disrepute? What must have happened was that they realised they had got it badly wrong in the first place when they had sided with Gatting in Pakistan and then distributed gold for the offence. They saw this as the chance to put things right and to embrace the rotten philosophy that two wrongs make a right which is the prerogative only of weak men. By all means, have a chat with Gatting, give him a bollocking and call him into line, but to pretend to become sanctimonious as they did about a copulatory detail was sickening. They were interesting times.

It was always likely to be a bad summer for England's cricketers on the field, but those who thought they were running it made everything a great deal worse. Their lack of man management cost English cricket dear. There was no obvious replacement for Gatting, and John Emburey did the job for two Test Matches but without making any impact whatever. For the Fourth Test, at Headingley, Peter May, who was still chairman of the selectors, gave the captaincy to his godson, Chris Cowdrey, who would probably never have got into the side on merit as a player, but he had captained Kent well and with a sure instinct. England still lost massively, but on the rest day David Gower told me that it was a long time since he had enjoyed playing cricket for England as much as he had over the last three days.

I am afraid that the cricket manager, Micky Stewart, will not have applauded Cowdrey's appointment or Gower's attitude. He will not have wanted someone who did not have all the necessary qualifications dropped in on top of him in the dressing room. Stewart may have been technically efficient but seemed to have no feel for flair and hitched his wagon irrevocably to method, discipline and logic, as he saw it. Stewart did not have a successful run as cricket manager and if only he could have been more flexible and imaginative and had been prepared to look at the players and his job with more of an open mind and even a sense of fun, I believe he would have got more out of his players. When

ONE CRISIS TO THE NEXT

Cowdrey was hit on the toe playing for Kent against Derbyshire and was unable to play in the Fifth Test, Stewart will have been determined to push Graham Gooch's claims to take over the job. They thought along the same lines with a stereotyped and unimaginative approach to everything. I sometimes wonder how Stewart would have coped with Mike Brearley. I suspect it would have been Brearley who would have had to do the coping. As it was, Stewart was now given Gooch who, the year before, had handed the Essex captaincy back to Keith Fletcher because he had not made much of a job at it. Cowdrey had been one of the selectors to chose the England side for that Fifth Test, but said later that the management had not made him particularly welcome in the England dressing room during the match.

Chris Cowdrey was not brought back for the one Test against Sri Lanka at the end of the season and I couldn't help smiling when Stewart, normally such a voluble talker, refused to discuss the question when asked about the unfair treatment which had been handed out to Cowdrey. But it was not such a big laugh as when our selectors chose Gooch to captain the side in India that winter and, because of his involvement with rebel tours to South Africa, the Indians said at once that Gooch was unacceptable and the tour was cancelled. You did not have to be a crystal ball gazer of great repute to have foreseen that would happen. Stewart will have fought hard for Gooch, particularly while Cowdrey was the only alternative. What an intolerable mess it all was and one could only watch helplessly as England's cricket was allowed to lurch from one crisis to the next without any discernible direction whatever. Those in charge at the time have a lot to answer for and should be ashamed of themselves. I have no doubt these were the origins of the even deeper mess it all got into during the nineties.

CHAPTER

20

BSKYB

TWO THINGS HAPPENED in 1989 which were to have a big impact on my life, one for the good while the other turned out in the end to be rather less than exciting. I was also fifty that autumn which filled me with unspeakable gloom and was the only birthday which ever gave me that dreadful feeling of hopelessness. Thirty was a logical progression and a pretty good one, too; forty had made me aware that the arithmetical equation was beginning to work against me, although it was still a long way off, but for some reason fifty made me feel that I should ring up the undertakers and make a booking. Funnily enough, sixty was nothing like so bad, perhaps because I had just been desperately lucky to survive a heart operation which had come uncomfortably close to forcing somebody else to ring up the undertakers on my behalf. It was lovely to be alive and, after that, it had all become a most exciting bonus.

In 1989 the satellite television invasion of Great Britain started. The redoubtable Rupert Murdoch put Sky Television in place, while a consortium of businesses financed the founding of BSB Television. With their own sports channel, Sky focused sharply on cricket. David Hill, who had been in charge of Kerry Packer's Channel Nine sports department in Sydney at the time of World Series Cricket, was now a Murdoch man and was in charge of Sky's sport at Isleworth, down London's Great West Road. Like most radio commentators, I wanted to do more television and I think, if I am honest, the lure was probably for all the wrong reasons. Television paid quite a lot more money than radio. At that time *Test Match Special* paid those of us who commentated not much more than £100 a day. Television could afford to be more generous. Another rather wet reason was that television sounded much more glamorous than radio, especially when the participants were seen on camera. Looking back on it now though, I am not sure that was right because many of the commentators who have been the best known over the years plied their trade mainly on the radio. Undoubtedly, there was more of a mystique attached to television than there was to radio and most of us were drawn in that direction at one time or another. I did not do a great deal on the box, but I very much enjoyed all that I did, although I was never very good at it.

Radio had always been my natural home and, like many others, I found television difficult and I don't think I was ever fully at ease in the television commentary box. On radio the commentator is the listener's eyes and must obviously go on talking and, because the listener can see nothing, his scope is limitless. Television is very different. The viewers can only see the picture and it is therefore bad television to talk about something which they cannot see offscreen. Also, while it is almost impossible to talk too much on radio, on television silence can be golden. The viewer can see the bowler coming in to bowl and does not need to be told. The television commentator should only speak when he can add to the picture. Television commentators are nowadays almost invariably former players. Who is better qualified to explain a picture than someone who has played Test cricket and knows what it is like to be out there in the heat of battle? In radio, professional broadcasters are important in the commentating role which is not quite the doddle many people seem to think and requires an expertise which does not automatically come from having played Test cricket. Perhaps those who have been brought up in the medium they are using are also better able to draw the best out of the experts who come in at the end of the over and whenever else the commentator wants to bring them in. The only man to cope with television and radio equally well is Tony Cozier and I envy the ease with which he moves directly from one box to the other and is able so effortlessly to adjust his style.

I allowed myself to get too carried away on television. If I saw something hysterically funny off camera that viewers were unable to see, I could not resist the temptation to have a laugh at it. I well remember commentating on a number of series on the subcontinent and in Sri Lanka for both TWI and WorldTel and upsetting the deeply humourless Australians who ran Murdoch's Star Television out of Hong Kong. We have a good deal of spontaneous laughter on the radio, but it is frowned upon on television which takes itself much too seriously. I sometimes think that listening to television is like tuning into a religious broadcast with Geoffrey Boycott playing the part of Moses, whom I have no doubt he could have taught a thing or two.

On *Test Match Special* we have masses of letters from listeners who tell us they love to watch the picture on television with the sound turned down so that they can listen to us on the radio. This makes me wonder if television has got its commentary as right as those in charge think it has. Laughter is an essential ingredient to life and I am not sure that any of us laughs enough. I wish sports broadcasters on television in general were allowed to see the funny side of things. It would lighten the load so much.

In 1989 England were massacred by Australia who won the six-match series 4–0, and Bobby Simpson was now able, with some justification, to shove my words of criticism at the end of 1986 back down my throat. He had produced a fine Australian side which was scarely checked for the next decade. While Australia had gone up under Simpson, England had moved in the other direction under Stewart who now had to deal with another, perhaps less familiar, chairman of selectors. Ted Dexter had succeeded Peter May and become the overlord of English cricket, a job, he told us, for which his whole life had been preparing him. His first act was to appoint David Gower as captain against Australia in place of Graham Gooch, a move which is unlikely to have had Stewart's blessing. Gower did not survive that drubbing by Australia and it was Gooch who took the side to the West Indies in the New Year. They were accompanied by Sky Television who were going to show the entire Test series and the one-day games on their sports channel. This was a terrific innovation for English viewers who for the first time were to have the chance of watching England play overseas.

The pictures were produced by Transworld International from London and that job was presided over by Gary Franses who, through the nineties, was to make a considerable name for himself as the best cricket producer around. He now masterminds Channel Four's coverage of England's cricket at home and is a spectacularly nice man, being the only man of influence in television I have ever met who has no problem whatever with his own ego. They all had a great piece of luck when England, thanks to fine seam bowling by Gladstone Small, Angus Fraser and Devon Malcolm, and a brilliant hundred from Allan Lamb, won the First Test in Kingston and, after the Second had been washed out in Guyana, would have won the Third in Port of Spain but for some blatant time-wasting by the West Indies captain Desmond Haynes, standing in for Viv Richards who was ill. England went on to lose the series 2–1, but it gave England's cricket a big lift and the series also helped Sky Television win credibility.

In 1989 I had one of my better years with *TMS* and was allotted four of the six Test Matches. My first of the year was at Lord's and for two nights during the match Rex Neame, who ran a smart hotel at Kinlochbervie, just about the most north-westerly point of Scotland, came to stay with me in my new flat in Rossetti Garden Mansions at the bottom of Flood Street in Chelsea. We had been asked by David Lewis to his annual Lord's Test Match party. David had bowled leg breaks intermittently for Glamorgan when they had won the County Championship in 1969 and was now a sort of entrepreneurial wheeler-dealer. He lived for much of the time near Cardiff but also had this enormous apartment just over the Vauxhall Bridge in the same block as Jeffrey Archer. I don't know whether David's parties rivalled those upstairs, but they were always the greatest of fun.

It must have been about half past eight by the time Rex and I made it to Alembic House. As we pushed our way into the big room on about the eighth floor with its amazing views of London and the bend of the river, there were a lot of people there. We hadn't gone far when I saw across the room a blonde lady who was amazing. I turned to Rex and said, 'That's the girl I'm going to marry.' It took me sixteen months, as I had to prise her apart from one or two others, but on 23 October 1990 Bitten Pernert-Hansen and I were married at the Chelsea Registry Office in the King's Road. I was potty about her and this was the only forecast I have ever got right in my life. Bitten's family lived in Malmo in the south of Sweden and she had spent more than twenty years in London. She had been christened Karin Britt-Marie and Bitten had come about as her attempt as a child to say her own name. Many people put an R in it, like the bird, and Johnny Kimberley, the Earl, who has been a legend in Norfolk and Montego Bay and almost everywhere in between, still refers to her as 'the boomer'.

Bitten had a son, Alexei, from her first marriage, who was nine when we met. He had, poor chap, drawn the short straw in a big way for he had been born without the fifteenth chromosome and was unable to speak and, when he grew older, it became almost impossible for him to walk without help. When I first knew him, he lived at home with Bitten in London and went to a day school for handicapped children in Fulham. He has always been the most gregarious of people with a winning smile and much more intelligence than people often give him credit for at first sight. Although he cannot answer a question, he can most certainly show his preferences. Television is the saving grace of his life and, for whatever reason, he adores watching sport. Tennis and snooker are his two favourites with golf not far behind. He finds cricket too slow and does not much care for football and is inclined to crawl over to the set and turn it off. His real passion on television is Terry Wogan and when Wogan used to have a programme each evening at half past six, Alexei would take Bitten or me by the hand at about twenty-seven minutes past and make sure we turned it on. Those were the days before he was able to push the switches for himself.

I had never known a handicapped person before I met Alexei whom I was quick to nickname Rumple, short for Rumpelstiltskin from Hans Christian Andersen. I can't remember how or why it first occurred to me but it seems to have stuck for all time and he responds to it almost as well as he does to Alexei. He and I have always got on well and I am sure that if there is a secret, it is to treat him as a normal person, as I would like to think I always have. There are some who are unable to cope with handicapped people which is sad for them because they can be marvellously rewarding. If it had not been for the immense love and care which Bitten has given to him, I think it is extremely unlikely he would have survived. In return, Rumple is capable of great love and trust. Of course, like everyone else, he can have his moments. When he does not want to do something he can be as obstinate as they come and there is nothing he enjoys more than pushing something over and hearing the resulting crash when he chuckles hopelessly and perhaps a trifle maliciously. Well, why shouldn't he. Small tables in the drawing room are his speciality.

One of his great favourites was Bob Willis when we commentated together for Sky and Bob often used to come round to our house in London. Rex Neame is another for whom he has an undying love, but his greatest hero of all is Bitten's father, Sven-Eric Pernert, who, whenever he comes to Hoveton, is submerged by Rumple. The trouble is that Sven-Eric is now in his eighties and has to walk with a stick and a galumphing twenty-one-year-old, who only uses maximum strength sometimes, makes it hard for his grandfather to hold his own. Rumple also loves our four dogs and it is extraordinary how the animals know and understand, because they allow him to bully and even to hurt them in a way that I would never be allowed to. When we first moved into North Farm in 1992, Bubbles, our black Labrador bitch who is the best friend I ever had, was extremely protective of him. When someone was staying at North Farm, Bubbles would invariably sleep on the carpet outside Rumple's bedroom door. Rumple now lives permanently at North Farm where all the dogs are wonderful with him and never more so than when he is eating because some of the food usually drops on to the floor. For just over a year he went into residential care near Aylesbury which in the end came close to killing him when the carers seemed to give up on him.

His only method of protest was not to eat and to have epileptic fits which he appeared to be able to bring on almost at will. We had no option but to take him away when, at the age of sixteen, they had allowed his weight to fall to just four stone. Of course, finding the right people to look after him has often been a nightmare although at the moment we have the best team in the world at North Farm, led by Christine Webster. It all works so well there where Rumple knows every step by heart and the stairs are wide and gentle.

During the eighties I had become more serious about collecting the first editions of P.G. Wodehouse. For years I had been giving the books he wrote towards the end of his life to my father as Christmas and birthday presents. When he died, John nobly gave them all back to me in their shining dustwrappers which are so important if you are a serious collector. Wodehouse's first books which came out around the turn of the twentieth century were beginning to be extremely valuable and it was not a cheap hobby. Each winter I returned from Australia and New Zealand with a few additions and I always had enormous fun visiting the network of secondhand bookshops in both countries. My greatest coup in Australia was coming across a first edition of the second book he ever wrote, *A Prefect's Uncle*. It had bright red covers and the boy drawn on the front cover wearing an Eton bum freezer had the most gloriously supercilious look I have ever seen on any face in my life. The copy I came across at this bookshop in Melbourne's Glenferrie Road was as bright as if it had been published the week before. I paid rather a lot of money for it but it was well worth it.

In Australia and New Zealand I would often come across copies with first edition pages and covers but which had *The Colonial Edition*, stamped at the top of the title page. Extreme purists had problems with this but they were good enough for me. My luckiest break of all came in Wellington. I rang an old bookseller who dealt from his home not far from the cricket ground, the Basin Reserve. He told me he had one or two things I might be amused by and I went round to see him. Just as I was about to go with the few books I had bought, he told me that he had a waterlogged copy of the first edition of *The Prince and Betty*, which was published in 1912, and that it had a faded dustwrapper. He fetched it and let me have it for next to nothing, 10 or 20 New Zealand dollars. The book, as he had suggested, was a write-off but the eighty-year-old dustwrapper was in fine condition and when I checked it out in the Wodehouse bible, a catalogue of all his work produced by an American, I found it was for the first issue of the first edition. In time, I found another first edition of the book and put on the dustwrapper. When I came to sell my entire collection, this was the star of the sale and it collected more than £4,000. It's that sort of luck which makes collecting such fun.

The best piece of Wodehouse I ever managed to get hold of came from Tony Aldridge in Bristol who dealt in high-quality secondhand books. It was not all that long after we had met that he showed me a copy of a lesser known book by Kenneth Grahame called *Pagan Papers*. On the inside front cover, it was signed, in black ink 'P.G. Wodehouse'. It was a young but educated hand and as *Pagan Papers* had been first published in 1898, Tony suggested that it had belonged to PGW during his last year at Dulwich. I bought it at once for a speculative £200 and, on taking it home, I made further fascinating discoveries. On page fifty-nine, vertical pencil lines had been drawn down the side of a sentence which read, 'Of all forms of lettered effusiveness that which exploits the original work of others and professes to supply us with right opinions thereanent is the least wanted.' Alongside the vertical line on the right-hand margin is written in pencil, 'Text for essay on "Notes" PGW.' The fourteenth chapter of the third book he wrote, *The Tales of St Austin's* (1903), is called *Notes* and this same sentence appears at the top of the chapter. On page 147, there is another vertical pencil line and beside it, the legend, 'Text for Essay on "Relations". PGW' and on page 169 there is a vertical line but no marginal addition. When I sold my collection at Christies in South Kensington, I put these two books together with, I am glad to say, too high a reserve and I still have them both. I hope these stories convey something of the fun I had putting together my collection.

The book that all PGW collectors would die for is the first

edition of the *By the Way Book* which was a paperback edition of the compilations of his columns in the *Globe*, a London evening paper. I never had the luck to come by one and even if I had I very much doubt I would have been able to afford it. I remember one piece of bad luck I had in Australia when I thought I had come across a first edition of Ian Fleming's *Casino Royale*, the first James Bond book, in a small bookshop at King's Cross in Sydney. The dustwrapper was maroon and there were a number of red hearts on it. The owner of the shop also thought it was the first edition and priced it accordingly. It was only when I came to sell it that I discovered that it was the second impression of the first edition which is not remotely as valuable. I suppose I should have known because there was a brief extract from a review on the inside flap of the dustwrapper which the first impression would never have had. It was an expensive mistake.

The Wodehouse collection was my pride and joy, but unhappily financial activities have never been my greatest strength and towards the end of 1993 I found a number of rather large bills were distinctly pressing. After wringing my hands a good deal, I took a deep breath and decided that if I sold the Wodehouse collection I would be able to breathe more easily elsewhere. At the end of January 1994 they came under the hammer and the proceeds were gratefully received. It broke my heart at the time, but these sort of things have to be used as the last line of defence if need be.

When everyone returned to England in mid-April, I had a telephone call from Tony Greig who had been one of the Sky commentators in the West Indies and was now going to remain with their team for the coverage in England in 1990. He and David Hill arranged to meet me in Joe's Café, a trendy little restaurant and bar at the top of Draycott Avenue in Chelsea.

I met them at about six o'clock in the evening. Although I was regarded as an enemy to the cause at the time of the Packer revolution, David was reasonably friendly and in the years after 1977 we occasionally shared the odd glass and once met for dinner at Lucio's in Paddington in Sydney. With that resonant voice and curly hair which by now was going grey, he was always full of good cheer and he greeted me warmly. On the other hand, Tony Greig and I had had our moments, not least when I scooped him on his epilepsy when I wrote *The Packer Affair*. I don't think he could help talking down to me in every sense. Apart from being enormously tall, Greigy likes to think he knows the answers to almost everything and I was always given the irritating impression that he was doing me a favour. I don't think he meant to do it but, having spent so much time with Kerry Packer and his chums, a good deal of it had washed off. Leaning forward on the stool in Joe's Café, Greigy was in his most avuncular 'Now, Blowers, listen to me' mood.

Of course, I hoped that they wanted me to work for Sky Television and indeed they did. Sky's coverage of domestic cricket consisted only of the Sunday League which was a forty-over slog-about on Sunday afternoons. I think they offered me £250 a day and I couldn't wait to begin.

I must have done about ten matches that year and it was always a good party. We drove to a posh hotel as near to the ground as possible on the Saturday evening, unless we were covering a match in London, and did ourselves extremely well. Greigy's second wife, Viv, was director of those operations and I remember some excellent dinners. We stayed at the Cavendish Hotel near Chatsworth for a match at Chesterfield and there was a particularly good evening at the Flitwick Manor Hotel from which we covered a match at Northampton. Clive Lloyd, Bob Willis, David Lloyd and Simon Reed, the younger brother of Oliver Reed who, disappointingly perhaps, did not possess quite the same extravagant thirst or tastes, were the other commentators and it was all terrific fun. I don't think we were that special on air, at least I'm pretty sure I wasn't. In those days Sky had not sold that many dishes and the audience must have been tiny. No one said anything much about how it was going. We were all caught up in Greigy's enveloping wave of enthusiasm which led us to believe, for no very good reason, that we were winning.

During the summer of 1990, England beat both New Zealand and India in series which were not particularly memorable, except for the First Test against India when Graham Gooch scored a small matter of 333 in England's first innings, the highest score ever made at Lord's. Needing 454 to save the follow on, India reached this figure with one wicket in hand. In an astonishing onslaught, Kapil Dev drove Eddie Hemmings more or less straight for four successive sixes which is the only time that has been done in a Test Match. England won and I remember the match particularly well because I was on the air when Gooch made his 300th run and in describing the moment I unfortunately managed to spoonerise 'Never before at Lord's has a *crowd clapped* like this one' for which I received only a mild rebuke from the Controller of Radio Three who told me that when he heard it he did not believe it.

The Australian seam attack, consisting of Terry Alderman, Bruce Reid, Craig McDermott and Merv Hughes, were too strong for England's batsmen the following winter in Australia. Mark Waugh made a superb hundred in his first Test at the Adelaide Oval and, once again, Allan Border's side was out on its own and they won 3–0. Besides my usual rounds of commentary with 2UE and the others, I did some work for the BBC and also for Sky. They took the Channel Nine coverage but after the close of play a number of us under Greig's command had a look back at the day that had just ended. While we were in Australia news came through that the two satellite channels in England had merged with Sky very much the senior partner. It was exciting that the new channel, BSkyB as it was to be known, had taken over all of BSB's old cricket commitments which included the Benson & Hedges Knock-Out Cup, edited highlights of each day's Test cricket, the one-day internationals, and the NatWest competition, in addition to the existing Sunday League commitments. It was going to be an exciting summer.

There were more meetings with David Hill when I returned to London. We met for lunch in an intriguing little restaurant on the corner of Kew Green. He told me of the large amount of cricket Sky would now be covering which amounted to just over ninety days and asked me to leave *Test Match Special* and to work all the summer for Sky. I was keen to do it but I wanted a contract for more than one year. My solicitor went into bat for me. While he was unable to persuade Sky to give me any assurances beyond that summer of 1991, he did manage to persuade them to double the daily match fee they had already offered which made me think that they must want me and, if they were prepared to pay that much, perhaps they had taken a long-term view of me after all. I fear they may have done and it was not the one I wanted. A fee of £1,000 a day, as opposed to just over £100 a day from *TMS*, was not to be sniffed at and, of course, I badly wanted to commentate on television. I several times rang up Brian Johnston for advice and in the end I think he felt that I had no alternative but to accept, in view of the amount of money involved. So, with something of a fanfare, I very sadly severed my links with *TMS* and joined Sky. I did not know it at the time but it meant that I had done my last broadcast with Brian himself.

It was a hectic summer and a huge amount of fun. The presenter was Charles Colvile whom Sky had inherited from BSB. He had worked for some years for the BBC where for a long time one of his jobs was to present the sports slot for the *Today* programme before breakfast. One of our jobs with *TMS* was for one of the commentary team to get up early and be in the box soon after eight o'clock, ready to be interviewed about the prospects for the day in the sports section in the second edition of *Today*. Colvile was usually our interrogator and I seem to remember that the questions often used to go on for longer than the answer. Now he attacked the television microphone with the same animated enthusiasm and did a difficult job well. Willis and I teamed up together and spent the summer negotiating the motorways of England and just occasionally Wales, for we covered a Sunday League game at Ebbw Vale and something else at Cardiff. It was the first summer of the M40 and we spent many happy hours upon it heading for the Brockencote Hall in Chaddesley Corbett which was one of my most favourite watering holes and which did duty for Birmingham and Worcester and was a good halfway house on the journey from London to Manchester.

The authorities at the Test Match grounds were stumped when they had to find accommodation for a second television broadcaster. It wasn't too bad at Old Trafford, Headingley and

Edgbaston. At Lord's we were given pews in a very recently converted ladies' loo on the first floor of the Warner Stand. There was still the pungent reek of the disinfectant cleaner, although maybe a little had been sprinkled on the floor as a deliberate hint for us not to let our commentary become too lurid. We were perched on high stools to be able to look through the small windows which made me feel I was sitting in an eye-level grill. The only real problem was that those stalwart ladies who had been popping in to use the loo for years merely thought the sign on the door must have fallen down during the winter, and came bursting in just the same. Luckily I don't think any of them had started to loosen their belts before they realised that the geography had changed. It was quite a surprise for them and highly entertaining for us. The Oval and Trent Bridge found cabins of a sort for us at deep third man which at least kept us dry when it rained. It was a wonderful series against the West Indies which was drawn 2–2 and the innings I shall never forget was Graham Gooch's 154 not out when he carried his bat through England's second innings in the First Test at Headingley. England won the first and last of the five Test Matches.

After all that, the summer had a pretty devastating end for us. On the Saturday of the NatWest final at Lord's, David Hill gave a party to celebrate his marriage in the gardens of his apartment block in Kensington. That morning the TCCB had announced the results of their deliberations about the distribution of the television contracts for the next three years. Sky had lost just about everything. The Benson & Hedges competition, which had belonged to the old BSB, had reverted to the BBC, the recorded highlights had been taken away and we were left with the measly old Sunday League as a sop for the future. The party had therefore been somewhat stopped in its tracks before it even began and needed alcohol in large dollops. What was forthcoming was lukewarm tequila, which even circumstances as dire as these did not quite warrant, and a certain amount of beer. I am not sure that warm tequila would make even a good party go with too much of a bang.

The following winter saw the World Cup taken to Australia

and New Zealand. It was being televised in England by Sky who were taking the local output and I had been hoping they would use me in an additional role as they had in Australia the year before. I was working in New Zealand for TVNZ who were the host broadcaster there and so Sky will have had to take bits and pieces of my commentary but they gave me nothing extra. When I returned to England, it was to discover that I was still in their commentary team for the Sunday League matches which was something. I was then requested to accept a fifty per cent cut in pay which I was not so keen about and this may, in the end, have counted against me. In any event, I never again worked for Sky after the summer of 1992, although I worked for other broadcasters whose output was shown on Sky. It was an extremely depressing period in my life because, although I was writing for the *Independent*, it was a seriously underfunded newspaper and the retainer they paid me had started at a pittance and had never risen, though they were great people to work for. Sky covered the Sunday League again in 1993, but my telephone never rang. I made endless telephone calls to Mr Hill but I never got further than his resolute Scottish secretary and he failed to return a single one of them, nor had he even bothered to write me a letter. One evening in June, I plucked up courage and rang him at home. He answered the telephone in his usual hearty way and then became rather shifty and evasive, not that I had even got on to the subject of my future with Sky. Then the conversation took a strange turn.

'Hang on,' he yelled, 'the most wonderful apparition in red has just come through the door. You must have a word with her.'

I heard some feverish whispering and then this girl came on the line. We had not the first idea who we were and couldn't have cared less. We had one of those absurd conversations which complete strangers have on the telephone. Then she said she must be going and I said goodbye and I held on waiting for Mr Hill to come back to the phone. But she had put the handset back on the holder and all I heard was the exchange line ringing in my ear. I put the telephone down and waited for him to call me back. I am still waiting. Soon after that, Rupert Murdoch took him away to Fox in Los Angeles where I gather he has become a mega-hero. I was told some time later that he hated more than anything having to pass on bad news. Thanks a million, Mr Hill.

The World Cup in 1991/92 caused a mild furore before the teams even began to think about packing their bags for Australia or New Zealand. In 1991 the President of South Africa, F. W. de Klerk, had dismantled the odious policy of apartheid and in July of that year South Africa was readmitted to the International Cricket Council. The paradox was that at the same meeting it was announced that, on the recommendation of the chairman, Colin Cowdrey, South Africa would not be allowed to take part in the 1991/92 World Cup. The logic was crazy. South Africa had been re-elected to the top table of the club and then told that they must not use it. It was interesting that no one was more put out by this than the African National Congress, but what was good enough for Nelson Mandela was not good enough for the men of goodwill who ran cricket. Of course, feelings ran high and in the end sanity prevailed.

An emergency meeting was held in the desert at Sharjah during one of the tournaments there. I was in Sharjah working for Pakistan Television who were covering the competition. The ICC meeting was held at the plush Marbella Club next door to the Holiday Inn and I well remember waiting outside on a hot desert evening for the delegates to come out and the press conference to begin. We were told that all the member nations had agreed that South Africa should take part in the competition. In July, they had been refused entry. It's almost impossible to believe that this whole episode took place, for it was so absurdly stupid and unnecessary. It is yet another example of the endemic barminess which singles out the delegates of the ICC on almost every occasion when they have something serious to discuss. We will come to other instances before this book ends. Perhaps Sharjah and the ICC deserved each other because that tournament which began with such high hopes has degenerated into yet another one-day shenanigans which is ruled by money and appears to be played only for the benefit of television and the glorification of those who run the cricket there.

Because of the World Cup and my potential involvement with Sky, I was unable to join the commentary team for 2UE in Sydney. By then Brian White, the station manager, had died from a heart attack and those who were now running the station had never been that keen about the cricket and after one more season they gave it up. This was sad, for it had brought a good alternative commentary to quite a large section of people and had perhaps made cricket appear a rather more entertaining game.

The World Cup began in February and I stayed in New Zealand working as a commentator for TVNZ and doing bits and pieces for my various newspapers. All went well until one Sunday evening in Auckland in early March 1992 when the telephone went in my room at the Centra Hotel where I was staying. It was Bitten ringing me from Norfolk to tell me that my mother had died. She had dinner with Bitten at Haugh's End on the Saturday evening and Bitten had collected her from the Green where she lived just about a quarter of a mile down the drive. John and Judy, my brother and sister-in-law, came to have a drink before dinner and although my mother, who was a week short of her eighty-ninth birthday, had not been particularly well, she was in reasonable form during the evening. I am glad to say she enjoyed a decent glass of champagne and some claret later. She had asked Bitten to take her home at about a quarter past nine. Bitten saw her into her house, said goodnight and left. John rang her at about nine o'clock the next morning and Joan Ives who helped her with breakfast, found her, still in her clothes, slumped on the floor by her dressing table. She had been sitting on the stool just beginning to take the pins out of her hair. She was formidable to the end. It was not that long before her death that I asked her what she thought of one of Suki's friends who had come down to Hoveton. 'He seemed very nice, darling. I just do wish his vowels had been a *trifle crisper*.' It came back as sharp as mustard.

She was buried later that week, on what would have been her birthday, in the same grave as my father at the east end of the Hoveton St John church. Since my father died, whenever I said goodbye to my mother before going off on a cricket tour, she had invariably said to me, 'Darling, if I die, you must promise me not to come home. There is no point and I shall be very cross.' I took her at her word which in many ways I still regret. I don't think her death really hit home to me until I returned to Hoveton and then I found the gap she had left was enormous. Hoveton had become an infinitely less humorous place without her. I still think, eight years later, whenever I drive past the Green what fun it would be to be able to pop in and see her. A few pithy comments always did me good. In New Zealand I was not certain I could really believe she was no more. There was something that was so timeless and indestructible about her.

England played three Test Matches in New Zealand before the start of the World Cup and won 2–0 against a New Zealand side which was now looking much more vulnerable than it had done in the eighties. They still had some good cricketers but there was no longer the cohesion, the spirit or the captaincy which had taken them through the eighties without losing a single series at home. The World Cup was unusual in that Pakistan were as good as out of the competition before they won their first match and then they never looked back. As they played their matches in Australia, I did not catch up with them until they took on New Zealand in the semi-final in Auckland. New Zealand, captained by Martin Crowe, were the surprise of the competition and there was some original thinking behind their success. They decided to open the bowling with the off breaks of Dipak Patel who had learned his cricket by the banks of the Severn in Worcester before emigrating to New Zealand. Opening batsmen were not at all sure how to cope with an off spinner at the start and he not only picked up valuable wickets, but he also bowled his ten overs extremely cheaply. They were almost bound to have cost many more runs if he had come on later in the innings.

New Zealand made 262/7, batting first, and Pakistan only won because of Inzamam-ul-Haq's ferocious hitting in the closing stages which brought him 60 runs from thirty-seven balls. He had become one of the most exciting players in the competition and had already helped Pakistan out of a few holes in Australia. He was a big man who came from Multan and could barely speak English. He had been discovered by Imran Khan. In the other semi-final, South Africa put England in to bat and kept them to 252/6 which proved a big enough score after rain had interfered. When play was finally resumed, one ball remained to be bowled and the system in use for calculating the target after stoppage for rain had changed it from 22 being needed from thirteen balls to 21 being required from the final ball which was something only a cynic or the ICC could have dreamed up. It was a system which lasted until Messrs Duckworth and Lewis dreamed up the present system which, if anything, is even more incomprehensible although fairer. Pakistan batted first in a final which never got off the ground. England were left to score 250 to win and failed to come to terms with their target losing by 22.

While I was in Melbourne for the final I received a cable from Gary Franses, who ran the cricket for TWI, asking me to call him in London. When I did, he asked me if I would be able to come to the West Indies to commentate on the mini-series which South Africa were playing in the Caribbean. They were going to play a one-day match in Kingston, two more in Port of Spain and then a Test Match in Barbados. I was delighted because I was certain that Sky would be taking the coverage and also I was pleased to be working with TWI who had suddenly become a big player in cricket. My fellow commentators were Tony Cozier, Michael Holding and Bob Willis.

It was a most exciting adventure and they were going to give me the chance to present as well as commentate. My first job was to do brief interviews with almost all the players on both sides so that when one of them did something remarkable, there would be a soundbite with him talking about his cricket which could be slotted in. The first game in Kingston went off well enough with the West Indies winning a one-day match, but there was a little bit of local trouble because Richie Richardson from Antigua had been appointed to succeed Viv Richards as captain. The Jamaicans all felt that their own Courtney Walsh should have been the man and Richardson was roundly booed by the good crowd when he came out to bat. It didn't sound very friendly but it was probably inevitable. My most enjoyable task was to interview the former Jamaican Prime Minister, Michael Manley, one morning. We talked about post-apartheid South Africa and his feelings about welcoming a South African cricket team to Jamaica. He was pleased because it signified the re-acceptance of South Africa by the world and this meant that the coloured man was once again free in that country. He had great admiration for Nelson Mandela and was immensely relieved that change had come about peacefully but was concerned that further progress should not be too precipitate if it was not to end up by being counter-productive. It must be a constant and continuing process and he felt that all the signs were right, even though the South African side was still all-white.

We left Jamaica the day after that match and flew on a direct flight to Port of Spain. It had been laid on especially because of the cricket. Normally that flight takes most of the day as the aeroplane hops from island to island around the Caribbean. There were good crowds for the two games in Port of Spain, although they stopped well short of being full houses, at the ever lovely Queen's Park Oval. We then moved on to Barbados where TWI had installed us all in some comfort in Tamarind Cove, a lovely hotel on the St James's Coast presided over by a good friend of many of us, Theo Williams. The Test Match turned out to be a wonderful game of cricket which the South Africans should have won, for they started the last day at 122/2 needing 79 more to win. Not for the first nor the last time, Curtly Ambrose and Courtney Walsh rolled up their sleeves and saved a seemingly desperate situation for the West Indies. On that last morning Ambrose took 4/16 in 10.4 overs and Walsh 4/8 in eleven overs. It was magnificent bowling against inexperienced batting. The great disappointment about the match was that the people of Barbados had got it into their heads that Anderson Cummins, a distinctly ordinary fast medium seam bowler, should have been in the West Indies side. He was not, and they decided to boycott one of the best Test Matches ever. On that exciting last morning there were only 300 spectators in the ground. This protest had been building up for some time and probably it would have been sensible for the West Indies selectors to have picked a squad of thirteen players which included Cummings who would then have been left out on the first morning. Cricketing brains trusts seldom twig things like this. Cummings went on to play three Test Matches.

The flight from Kingston to Port of Spain had been of some personal significance for me. I sat next to our executive producer, Bill Sinrich, and he asked me if I knew anyone in Pakistan who might be able to raise a million US dollars in commercial revenue to make it possible for TWI to televise the series the following year between the West Indies and Pakistan. TWI had a contract with the West Indies Cricket Board to televise all the international cricket played in the Caribbean and had opened up for the Board a considerable and completely new source of income. If England, Australia or South Africa were the opposition, there was no problem because enough networks round the world would be prepared to pay good money to transmit the product. Pakistan was a problem because broadcasters like Sky in England would not be willing to pay a significant amount of money for the pictures. It was crucial, therefore, that Pakistan's own internal network, PTV, should be prepared to show it and to pay a realistic sum for the privilege. The only way for that to be possible was to put together a consortium of businesses who would be prepared to pay to advertise while the cricket was being shown and therefore to finance the telecast. The only man I knew who might conceivably fit the bill was Arshed Gilani, a retired commander in the Pakistan Navy. I had met him at various of the tournaments in Sharjah and he looked after the interests of a number of major western companies inside Pakistan. When we returned to England, I called Karachi and, planting a germ in his mind, I arranged for the three of us to have lunch when he was next in London in about three weeks' time.

Over lunch on a sunny pavement on the edge of Chiswick, the Commander became even more interested in Bill Sinrich's proposition. By the time he had fought his way through a plate of langoustines, a trifle messily but they are the hardest things in the world to eat if the shells have been left on, he was going to have a go. To his enormous credit he succeeded and TWI were able to televise Pakistan's series in the Caribbean and Arshed had started a relationship with TWI which lasts to this day.

CHAPTER

21

PASSAGE TO INDIA

As soon as the English season had finished in 1992, I was asked by Bill Sinrich to go with Andrew Wildblood, his senior lieutenant, to India to try and make sure that TWI secured the rights to televise the forthcoming series against England. My purpose was simply to be a genial man-about-town who knew most of the Indian Board (BCCI) anyway and I suppose Bill thought that my presence might give TWI's bid a certain increased credibility. The BCCI were holding their annual meeting at Poona under the presidency of the former Maharajah of Gwalior, Madhavrao Scindia, as he was now known. The meeting was taking place at the Blue Diamond Hotel where Tony Greig's England side had stayed for a match at the start of their tour in 1976/77. To my great joy I found I was able to buy six P.G. Wodehouse paperbacks from the newspaper shop in the hotel which kept me going for much of the tour.

Andrew and I flew to Bombay where we stayed the night before boarding a train to Poona at five o'clock in the morning, along with most of the Board of control. Inderjit Singh Bindra and Jagmohan Dalmiya, two of the most powerful men in Indian cricketing affairs, were on the station, but there is something rather daunting about meeting anyone, however well you may know them, at such an ungodly hour. Andrew was much better at pre-dawn chit-chat than I was. Indian stations are always an adventure. Every one I have ever been to on the subcontinent is invariably teeming with millions of people at all hours. There are those who are trying to catch trains or who have just got off one that has arrived; then there are those who, in their thousands, appear to be loitering in the hope that something may turn up, in addition to the considerable number who live and sleep rough in the purlieus of the station. There is also a veritable army of porters who prowl around like the Hosts of Midian and descend on you the moment you set foot out of your taxi. The chaos is not helped by a number of extremely energetic policemen doing nothing very much. The queues are interminable, the chaps who look at your tickets before you get on board are both disbelieving and slow and the likelihood of finding your pre-booked seat unoccupied is remote. There was also an excellent chance that we would lose contact with our porter who was humping our bags. By the time we arrived at our carriage we both felt that we had been in a fight. By the time we had found ourselves somewhere to sit, our state was one of total exhaustion. We had teamed up with several members of the Board and, had it not been for their help, I should think we would both still be on the platform.

When we got to the Blue Diamond, I could only feel that skulduggery was afoot. Hurried whispered meetings between Board members were soon taking place in the corridors, in the coffee shop, outside the lifts, round the pool and goodness knows where else besides. Bindra, who was to succeed Scindia as the president, and Dalmiya, the secretary of the Board with his glistening hair, were at the centre of most things. If they had sold Brylcreem in India, Dalmiya would have made the perfect advertisement. Andrew and I busied ourselves about the place, meeting as many of the Board as we could while doing our best to plead our cause. Although I tried to enter fully into the spirit of it, I have to admit that I found it all slightly embarrassing. Andrew was brilliant as he convinced them one after the other that TWI's bid was undoubtedly the best when all the factors were taken into account. We would make the best pictures, cause the least trouble, be much more highly organised, pay the most money and, of course, be as good as our word.

Naturally, the delegates we spoke to gave nothing away beyond vague promises that they would do what they could for us. We

PASSAGE TO INDIA

were not the only ones lobbying for the business. There was Seamus O'Brien who had come to Poona from Hong Kong in search of the rights. He once worked for CSI, a company mainly based in Surrey, and then joined a rival, and I cannot remember for whom he was working that day, but I was always confident that Andrew's know-how would win the day. That afternoon we went off to the stately Poona Club, set in magnificent grounds, originally no doubt by the British Raj, to watch a game of cricket between the club itself and the Board of Control who in general made a rather measured progress in the field. I remember the great skill my old friend Raj Singh showed at extra cover when he positioned himself in such a way that he was able to bend down and pick up a stationary ball with something approaching aplomb. I was co-opted for a time to commentate over the Tannoy and, as much as I wanted to pull the legs of the Board members as catches went down and the ball for ever disappeared between their legs, I kept being reminded by Andrew of how badly we wanted their votes when it came to the crunch. As a result, I was positively fulsome in my praise of some of the worst fielding it has ever been my lot to see. I was reminded of the lovely story told to me by Jack Mercer who for years between the wars had bowled his heart out for Glamorgan. In those days the amateurs fielded in the slips and when Jack Hobbs had once come out to bat at Swansea, Jack Mercer produced the perfect out-swinger. The Great Man played forward and the ball flew off the edge and hit first slip on the tummy button. As the offending amateur bent down to pick it up off the ground, Jack found himself saying, 'Well stopped, sir.'

The next day the meeting began in earnest and Andrew and I spent the time in the hotel hovering and hoping. It was not until late that night, when the official meeting had broken up into lots of smaller ones, that the issue was decided. We were summoned to Dalmiya's room and told in the presence of Bindra and a couple of others that we had won the day, provided a couple of points could be cleared up. Andrew spoke on the telephone to Bill Sinrich in London and eventually everything was sorted out to Dalmiya's liking. We shook hands on it and had a drink. We felt pleased with ourselves until, just before going to bed, Dalmiya said that everything was fine unless CSI came up with a higher bid in the morning. I was not altogether sure that he was only joking and Andrew told me later that he also had had an uneasy night. The next morning before departing for Bombay, we were taken round with the rest of the Board by bus to Scindia's house and stud farm – Poona is a horse-racing centre. It was a memorable journey because, after the bus had been making steady progress for an hour, it was discovered that we were going in entirely the wrong direction. When at last we arrived, the princely president, an old boy of Winchester, was extremely friendly and by the time we set off in the same rickety old bus, which had never heard of air-conditioning, back to Bombay, our agreement had been signed and sealed.

I was back in India soon afterwards on a reconnaissance mission with Gary Franses who was producing the television coverage, Neil Harvey, the chief engineer and his main asistant, and Jonathan Riley who looked after the day-to-day logistics of the operation from hotels to taxis, to meals at the ground, to transport for the huge amount of equipment, the flights from place to place and so on. Bill Sinrich sent me again on the basis that some of the locals in each place will have known me, which I suppose may have helped smooth the path of our initial introductions. I found it all the most fascinating experience and I was staggered at what was involved to make it all happen. This was only a recce and in every place we met all those who would be involved in supplying everything we wanted from generators as a back-up for the power supply, to the installation of telephone lines, the position for the satellite dish, a control room which was adequate for the purpose and goodness knows what else besides.

The Indians were wonderfully enthusiastic and fell over themselves to help. They nodded their heads like mad and smiled charmingly while writing down instructions and promising everything and more with that lovely sideways movement of the head. We left each venue confident that everything would be in place by the dates we had set for them. Sadly, the promises were one thing and the fulfilment quite another and in the end only the genius of Gary, Neil and Jonathan made sure that it all worked when the time came. They were brilliant at dealing with people who were not used to the demands being made of them or indeed of sticking to a tight time schedule. They were all three completely unflappable which was why the many telecasts they supervised together in the subcontinent went as smoothly as they did. In 1995/96 it was thanks to Gary that the World Cup television, produced by Alan Pascoe and Associates on behalf of WorldTel, was such an outstanding success.

England's tour of India at the start of 1993 was a conspicuous failure. They were outplayed in all three Test Matches before going on to Sri Lanka and losing the only Test Match there. Gooch was the captain in India, although Alec Stewart took over the job for the Second Test in Madras when Gooch fell foul of a plate of not notably fresh prawns at dinner the night before, and was also in charge in Sri Lanka. It was while we were in Madras that Bindra and Dalmiya succeeded in winning the 1995/96 World Cup for India and Pakistan in the face of strong western competition. By promising them a much bigger percentage of the final hand-out than they had ever received before, they made sure of the votes of the associate member countries and they had also secured the support of Zimbabwe who had only just been elected as a full member of the ICC. There is a huge amount of money in India which has become probably the most profitable venue of all for international cricket. Bindra and Dalmiya, friends then but the bitterest of enemies now, were both in impressively high spirits that night in Madras. Whether the methods they adopted to secure their second World Cup would have passed a steward's enquiry, I cannot be too sure. My best memory of that tour came towards the end when we played a one-day game in Gwalior. There was a dinner party at the Maharajah's palace one night in a huge hall and the decanters of wine were brought round on a small silver train which chugged up and down the tables, the guests helping themselves when it passed. I am not certain whether the membership of the Junior Gannymede in Curzon Street, P.G. Wodehouse's club for manservants and gentlemen's gentlemen, would have approved. I can see Jeeves writing a prompt letter to the secretary and entering a sharp *nolle prosequi*.

After a month in London and weekends at North Farm where we were getting ourselves organised, I was on my travels again. The Commander had not only found enough money in Pakistan to make it possible for TWI to go ahead with the television coverage of their tour of the Caribbean, he had also decided to accompany the tour in what I can only describe as the grand manner. The Commander never did anything by halves and was one of the most amusing and charming men with whom cricket ever brought me into contact. The tour began with five one-day matches which, as usual in the West Indies, means careering all over the Caribbean at breakneck speed and always seems to involve that boring journey from Jamaica to Trinidad. The best venue was the Windward Island of St Vincent where we stayed in a most delightful hotel overlooking the cricket ground and the airport which were side by side. It was run by a chap called Tony Sardine who was lethal behind the bar and not to be sniffed at in front of it either. The day after the one-day match in St Vincent the Commander acquired the services of a most impressive looking yacht and we started uncomfortably soon after breakfast and went by way of Bequia where we put in for drinks, on to Mustique, the island made famous by Princess Margaret. Imran Khan, who was also working in the commentary box, came with us that day bringing his German girlfriend who did not for a moment make us think he had lost his cutting edge. We had the most delicious lunch in a restaurant by the water near to our anchorage in Mustique where we ate fish and drank white burgundy in impressive quantities.

After the one-day matches, there was almost two weeks pause before the Test series began. I flew back to England where I was soon to read that the Pakistanis were in trouble in the lovely island of Grenada with the captain, Wasim Akram, and one or two of the others being arrested for 'constructive possession' of marijuana. There was a distinct chance that the tour would be cancelled but in the end compromises came to the rescue, the Test series went ahead and I flew back out. The Pakistanis were well beaten. Our commentary team included Michael Holding and Tony Cozier from the West Indies, Imran and Asif Iqbal from Pakistan. The Commander was with us all the time and, because he had to see that his sponsors received the publicity they had paid for, he was never far away from the box as he checked up that we gave the somewhat extravagant commercials a good going over. I was particularly involved in this, singing the praises of Singer and Samsung and all the others. One or two of the broadcasters who were taking the product did not care for these rather obtrusive advertisements. Sky was one to protest and I fear it was held against me even though I was, for once, only doing what I was told.

CHAPTER 22

GRASPING THE ENGLISH NETTLE

IN LATE NOVEMBER 1993, Brian Johnston was going down by train to Bristol one morning where he was to make a speech at a lunch. His usual taxi driver turned up for him at his house near Lord's and on the journey to Paddington station he heard some coughing in the back. When he looked through his rear-view mirror, he saw Brian slumped on the seat. He drove him straight to hospital where he remained for a while before returning home, but his mind was all over the place. I rang up one day not knowing that he was back at home and was amazed and delighted to hear him answer the telephone before Pauline, his wife, quickly took over. Soon after Christmas his condition got worse and he had to go back into hospital where he died a few days later and one of the great characters of broadcasting had finally been extinguished. His funeral was for family only but there was the most wonderful memorial service I have ever been to. Westminster Abbey could have been filled three times over.

During the spring, I realised that if I was ever going to get back on *Test Match Special* it would have to be soon. The first three Test Matches were against New Zealand and I didn't get a touch, but Peter Baxter gave me a ring quite early in the summer saying that he was pushing my cause and, if my chance came, it would be later in the summer. He rang again getting on towards the end of June and with a deadpan voice asked me if I would be available to commentate for *TMS* in the First Test against South Africa. I have never been more pleased or excited, even when I heard I was going to do my first Test twenty years before. But I did have one salutary thought which was that I knew full well that the chance would never have come if poor Brian had still been alive.

I arrived at the box earlier than usual on the first morning and I was extremely nervous which I had not been for years. I knew lots of people would be listening most critically. I realised it was very important that I did not try and be too clever and for my first two twenty-minute sessions I played it right down the middle. I enjoyed it so much and I was well aware after about thirty seconds that I was more relaxed at the microphone than I had been at any stage of my abortive television career. It was marvellous to be back. I can only remember one thing about the commentary from that match. This was the first Test Match Jonty Rhodes had played in England and the full joy of his fielding had not yet been appreciated by the English public. He's worth the gate money all on his own and in one over from Fanie de Villiers, after stating that the bowler had bowled and the batsman had played a stroke, my commentary concentrated entirely on Rhodes at cover point. I don't think I had ever watched Rhodes so closely before and it was extraordinary to see what he got up to. He was never still for a single moment. I think my return must have received at least grudging approval from within the BBC, for soon after this Test, which England lost with embarrassing ease, Peter Baxter was again on the telephone asking me if I was available for the Third at the Oval. I was. That was the match when Devon Malcolm for once got it so right that he took nine wickets in South Africa's second innings and England levelled the series.

Although England drew 2–2 with the West Indies in 1995, the inability of the England side to make much of an impact against the best countries had become a matter of considerable concern. The structure of the domestic game in England was being carefully examined to see if it was still the breeding ground needed to produce Test cricketers good enough to win matches. For a great many years, England had been the only country to play professional cricket, but since the Packer intrusion, cricket had turned into a professional game in all the other Test-playing countries and England had been left behind. The England season had become more and more of a treadmill and what made it so was the amount of limited-over cricket which was played. A one-day game is more wearing for players than a four-day County Championship match. Providing the weather holds, an enormous amount has to be crammed into the one-day affairs and the game is played at full pressure from first ball to last. A one-day match takes far more out of players than a day's Championship cricket when a good number of players may spend most of the time in the pavilion.

When players from a bygone age protest at the complaints made by modern cricketers at the amount they play, they point out that they themselves often played as many as thirty-two three-day Championship matches in one season. But they should remember that they had every Sunday off and did not have to make the big journeys around the country for the one-day games which is the lot of contemporary cricketers. Not only that, but one-day cricket, by its very nature, teaches bad habits when it comes to the longer drawn out game and is one of the reasons our cricket is in such a poor way. Facing a top-class fast bowler when he has one slip and one gully and is not allowed to bowl bouncers is a much more attractive proposition than when he has three slips and two gullies and can bang the ball in short. One-day cricket has dramatically changed the emphasis of the game because it is essentially a defensive game. If, in fifty overs, your side manages to restrict the batting side to a score of 100 for no wicket, it has done better than bowling them out for 120. From this, one can see that the fundamental values of the traditional game of cricket have been hopelessly distorted. The best way to win a two-innings match is to bowl the opposition out twice.

The Test and County Cricket Board's inspired answer to these problems was to set up working committees and to commission reports. They achieved almost nothing except to underline the inevitable clash between those who ran the individual counties and those in charge of England's cricket. Cricket has always been a poor game and the county chairmen and their committees naturally strive desperately to keep their counties afloat. They were unable or unprepared to see the wider picture which is that without a successful England side, interest in the game will decrease and it will become less profitable with sponsors nothing like so willing to stump up. This will come to mean that in time the central handout from the Board to the counties, which is their financial lifeline, will get smaller. In 1999, the ECB were unable to find as many main sponsors for the World Cup as they had hoped. A year later Cornhill pulled out of sponsoring Test cricket in England and a replacement was hard to find.

There was one attempt in the late eighties to try and make the county game a more satisfactory breeding ground for Test cricketers by introducing four-day cricket instead of three. This idea, which on its own was never likely to have been of more than marginal benefit, was scuppered by the appalling standard of the pitches being produced. They ensured that far too many matches still ended in three days or even less. On the few good pitches there were, Parkinson's Law came into operation and work expanded to fill the time allotted. The plan had been that four-day matches would give batsmen the time to play the big innings which are so important in the context of Test cricket. Then, in 1996, in a move of which I have always been a great supporter, Sir Ian MacLaurin, soon to become Lord MacLaurin, was chosen as chairman of the Board. On 1 January 1997, the TCCB became the England and Wales Cricket Board (ECB). MacLaurin was soon to retire as chairman of the supermarket giant, Tesco, which he had taken from well down the ladder and turned into England's most successful supermarket chain. He had also been a good cricketer and, after leaving Malvern College, had played a certain amount of second eleven cricket for Kent. A businessman's approach was felt to be what was needed and Brian Downing from Surrey, who was an important member of the old Board's marketing committee, had secured MacLaurin's appointment.

The opposition were outflanked and most unhappy, partly because people such as Doug Insole, still an immensely powerful figure in English cricket, and Alan Smith, the chief executive of the old TCCB whose original appointment Insole will have helped secure, were intransigent and inflexible. I wonder if Insole has ever changed his mind about a single thing in his entire life, while Smith's sitting on the fence was a joke which became legendary. I have never forgotten his initial appointment as secretary of the TCCB. He had been secretary of Warwickshire and was now introduced to the press in his new role by Raman Subba Row, the chairman, at a press conference in the pavilion at Worcester. When asked if this new job meant that he would be moving from the Midlands to London, he characteristically sucked in an enormous amount of breath between his teeth before saying, 'You could say yes to that question, but then you could say no.' He never became any more decisive. He had played for England himself and was in the best possible position to give his committees positive advice and to sweep aside the dead hand of mindless tradition which so stifled the game in England and prevented realistic progress. MacLaurin's brief now was in effect to bring the game shaking and screaming into, at any rate, the second half of the twentieth century.

He soon found that running a supermarket chain was a great deal easier than trying to reorganise English cricket. At Tesco, what he said as chairman went. At the ECB, every decision he wanted to make and any change he planned had to be ratified by the First-Class Forum, composed almost entirely of the representatives of the counties. MacLaurin soon realised that to preserve the county system as it was, with eighteen sides, was spreading the mixture far too thin and was condemning English cricket to eternal mediocrity as far as the international scene was concerned. There were too many indifferent players and too many cheap runs and wickets on offer and players spent too much of the time going through the motions. His first attempt to shake everything up came when he spent the latter part of 1996 and the first half of 1997 preparing the blueprint 'Raising the Standard' with the intention of changing the format of the English game to make it more internationally competitive.

He wanted to see the counties divided into two tiers for the County Championship. When he found support was not forthcoming from the counties or his advisers, he decided not to dig in his heels and launch a PR offensive to try and persuade the doubters, some of whom would, with certain guarantees, have been willing to change their minds, but ran for cover. 'Raising the Standard' then tried to foist on the counties a system whereby the eighteen counties were divided into three conferences and the final positions would be decided by a series of play-offs at the end of the season. It was almost impossible to understand and, mercifully, the counties threw out what was in any event only a compromise. Having rejected the conference idea, the counties voted on a two-tier plan which had always been MacLaurin's own favoured option and this was beaten by eleven votes to seven. This latter made far more sense and I am sure that, in retrospect, the chairman will have felt that he was wrong not to have devoted all his energies to persuading the counties to understand the benefits he felt it would bring to the English game.

It was in 1999 that the two-tier system was agreed upon which became a fact in 2000. To win this battle MacLaurin deployed his troops more cleverly and at the various meetings of the First-Class Forum the opponents, if not wholly convinced, were made to realise that English cricket had come to such a pass that action was desperately needed. The existing system was never going to work again as it had done in the good old days, and this was the most acceptable alternative. A year had been lost and, while some who should know better are only too eager to blame MacLaurin for this, I can well understand how, in his first year in the job, he wanted to try and get to his goal by consensus rather than by gunboat diplomacy. He obviously learned the lessons from the failure of 'Raising the Standard' to bring about changes to county cricket, did his homework better the second time round and also prepared the ground more thoroughly.

The two-tier system is not, on its own, going to make England competitive at the top level overnight but in my view it is a start in the right direction. I have no doubt that it is absurd to expect the old system with which we have all grown up to produce winning England sides at the top level of today's game. England's cricket has been overtaken and needs to reinvent itself. The old farts need to be patted sympathetically on the head and given a whisky and soda and, if that isn't enough, there is always the padded cell. 'The trouble about MacLaurin is that he doesn't know anything about cricket,' is the bleat I have often heard from the old farts, which is as absurd as it is untrue. He has a good background in the game, has been a brilliant businessman, has a great mind and a good deal of steely determination. I regard him as an excellent man for the job and I only hope he serves a third term as chairman of the ECB. If he does, he will with any luck have kicked the old farts firmly into touch by the end of it.

To persuade the counties to accept the two-tier system, MacLaurin had to agree that the bottom county in the second division would receive as much money from the annual central hand-out as the top county in the first division. This would prevent a financial crisis which might lead to bankruptcy and extinction for some sides. Fair enough. But from now on, it is crucial that things must be arranged so that the best sides and top players are better rewarded than those lower down. When that happens, human nature will come into play and produce the biggest incentive of all which is man's urge to better his lot. It will make sides in the second division determined to gain promotion and it will make good players in the lower reaches want desperately to lift themselves up the ladder. To do this, there must be a proper transfer system. The only way the two-tier system will lift English cricket is if excellence is concentrated in the first division and the best players and the best sides are continually playing against each other. Ideally, there are three too many sides in the first division. It may be that one or two counties will go to the wall, which would be one way of bringing down the numbers; or it may be that after a couple of years with two tiers in operation, other ways of achieving the same thing may appear. Australia, who at the moment have set the benchmark, have six first-class sides, in South Africa there are nine, while there are six in the West Indies. The domestic first-class competitions all over the world run at a huge loss but they are a prior charge on Test cricket. In all the other countries they prepare players for the step up to the Test scene because there is this concentration of excellence which is able to recreate the pressures of Test cricket.

It is no good being squeamish about what must happen. The best advertisement for cricket in any country is to have a winning national side. English cricket has suffered for far too long from having an absurdly ineffectual Test side. Something has to happen and Lord MacLaurin has grasped the nettle and deserves support for attempting to bring some sense to the structure of the modern game in England.

There is, of course, only one thing which needs to be done to have an immediate impact on the standards of English cricket and that is to go back to playing on uncovered pitches. This always used to give England's cricket a built-in advantage and I see nothing wrong with that and it wouldn't half smarten up both batting and bowling techniques. The best possible solution for English cricket would be to play three-day County Championship matches on uncovered pitches and hey-presto. There will be a lot of toffee noses stuck up in the air at this suggestion and most of them will belong to the marketing fraternity. They may help provide the life blood of the game but perhaps they are the ones who 'don't know anything about cricket', not Ian MacLaurin. After their unavailing attempts to sell the World Cup in 1999 and their present search for sponsors, surely to goodness they must realise how much simpler their job would be if England were in the habit of going to Australia and winning. It seems to me to be another indication of the terrifying lack of common sense among those who preside over the game.

England's cricket meandered on through the nineties supervised by the intense self-justification of Micky Stewart who found criticism unusually hard to take and was quick to justify all his actions, although he was hardly blessed with success. He passed the baton on to an apologetic, perplexed and unlucky Keith Fletcher who was not helped by the comments of Raymond Illingworth. Illingworth had never been shy of pointing out where his predecessors had gone wrong and he now stepped far from shrinkingly into Fletcher's shoes. There was a time when perhaps Illingworth might have done the job well, but I am afraid that by the time he ascended to the throne – he was the overall supremo, not just the coach – the game he had known had become a thing of the past. In 1995/96 on the tour of South Africa, he publicly executed Mark Ramprakash, Devon Malcolm and Robin Smith, and after a bad World Cup later the same winter, he beat a somewhat undignified retreat to his house in Spain, an emperor who had indeed lost most of his clothes, humbled into a state of belligerent nakedness. Nonetheless he still finds the time to come forward with a deafening 'I told you so' whenever the opportunity is there, which tells either of a Yorkshire cussedness or an insufferable bloody-mindedness.

His replacement, Lancashire's David Lloyd, an extremely funny man with whom I had worked a good deal both on radio and television, now entered the dressing room. His arms were full of tapes of Winston Churchill's most inspiring wartime speeches and recordings of 'Land of Hope and Glory' and probably 'Rule Britannia' as well. He hung up big signs on the walls, proclaiming things like 'Win' and 'Commitment'. India were beaten by a single victory, while Pakistan won two of their three Test Matches. The dressing room was frightfully gung-ho and Lloyd so upbeat that a rank long hop if bowled by an England player acquired the deadly subtlety of a cobra. As far as Lloyd's public pronouncements were concerned, the occupants of the England dressing room were a band of angels who would have kept even our old friend Gabriel on his toes. The trouble was that like Gabriel they were not very good at cricket either. There was never any doubting Lloyd's admirable spirit and determination to try and make something of the England side. He was soon telling everyone that it was the best job in the world, although his teeth became progressively more clenched. There's more to winning a Test Match than playing 'We shall fight them on the beaches' and 'We shall never surrender' on the tape recorder in the dressing room. It helps to be able to bowl in the right place to the Waugh brothers and to know how to cope with a short one from Curtly Ambrose.

I went to Zimbabwe with the England side for the first leg of their winter tour in 1996/97 which was to take them on to New Zealand. I have never been on a more chaotic tour or with a team so full of complaints, about the hotels, the country, the people, the food and anything else they could find to have a go at. It is

GRASPING THE ENGLISH NETTLE

not too much to say that they let England down with a colossal bang. The first Test Match was the first in the game's history to be drawn with the scores level. With five wickets in hand, England needed three from the last ball and could only manage two of them. Lloyd's immediate riposte was to shout to all and sundry that 'We *flippin'* murdered 'em,' which was not true. This should find a place in any book of contemporary quotations for it caused quite a stir. Ian MacLaurin, who was about to be installed as the chairman of the ECB, came to Zimbabwe to review his troops rather as Hannibal would have done when about to be sent another consignment of elephants, and he did not like what he saw. Tim Lamb, the chief executive of the ECB, gave purpose to his boss's thoughts when he said, 'Lord MacLaurin and I were horrified by what we saw in Zimbabwe. We were not happy with the way the England team presented themselves. Their demeanour was fairly negative and not particularly attractive.' Coming from Tim Lamb, the mildest of men, those words represented a considerable megaton explosion. England drew both Test Matches and lost all three of the one-day matches. Even Lloyd could hardly have agreed with his tape recorder when it blurted out that this was his finest hour. Contrary to the coach's public thoughts, I found Zimbabwe a most delightful country with charming people, wonderful things to see, delicious food and a good supply of extremely adequate South African wine. I spent Christmas day on a farm about forty miles from Harare and I do so wonder now what has happened to my charming hosts, to their farm and to their lovely home.

My outstanding memory of the tour was not, sadly, the Victoria Falls which I did not have the chance to see, but of interviewing that good-for-nothing stinker, Robert Mugabe. During the Second Test, which was played at the Harare Sports Club, Mugabe, who lives in a considerable fortress behind the trees just across the road, decided to come to the cricket. We watched his movements with interest because, like most of his ilk, when he moved around it was at speed with a convoy of soldiers and police positively hotching with weaponry and a procession of huge cars which made President Clinton's movements round the world look like a Sunday afternoon family outing. Sirens would blare their heads off and everyone using the road scattered in fear of their lives. When Mugabe emerged from his homestead, his route almost invariably took him down the road at the opposite end of the ground from the pavilion. He had agreed before coming to watch the Test Match that he would be prepared to allow the press to interview him. He was to meet them in the room at the top of the pavilion. On those occasions the plan is that the first few questions are asked by the representative of the BBC, although, of course, everyone else is listening. It makes it sound as if the BBC have obtained an exclusive interview.

I had come to Zimbabwe to commentate for *Test Match Special* and Peter Baxter, our producer, had decided that I was to be the man to ask those first questions. I had not done this before and was a little bit nervous as we climbed the stairs in the pavilion to await the great man's arrival. There were a lot of us hovering around in the upper room. Mugabe was submerged rather than surrounded by bodyguards and a pretty ghastly lot of blackguards they were, too. A job lot of fifty identical black suits had been bought and the bodyguards had been issued with one each, no matter their shape or size. The only unmistakable feature about them, apart from their general scruffiness, was the sinister bulge by the left shoulder. The security chaps had come on ahead and, just as we heard that the President was in the next room, one came up to me and suggested in the unfriendliest of manners that I shouldn't be there at all and started to push me back. I waved my microphone furiously and told him I was about to interview his President, which I doubt would have impressed him overmuch, when the situation was saved by Mugabe himself.

At that very moment he stepped, bespectacled and smiling, into the room and everyone stopped talking. The chap who had latched on to my arm stopped pulling and a couple of moments later Mugabe and I were facing each other. It was an entirely trivial interview. I remember asking him if he had ever played cricket and he said he had, in South Africa. I suggested that he should take it up even now and play in Zimbabwe on the basis that no bowler would dare get him out or umpire give him out. He would undoubtedly finish high in the averages. The idea amused him and he told me that he sometimes played tennis with his predecessor, ex-President Canaan Banana, whom he usually beat. I suggested he should hire the centre court at Wimbledon for the next contest between the two of them. You can see from this, the dramatic intellectual heights we touched. When I had finished, the chap who had been persecuting me had made a swift withdrawal – to see his tailor, perhaps. It's interesting to meet someone like Mugabe and talk to him, even like this for a few moments. I must say, he looked and sounded intensely unlovable and his breath smelt particularly unpleasant. None of us had the slightest clue about what lay ahead, of course. Maybe his goons in ill-fitting black suits are better at security than they looked for otherwise surely someone would have bumped him off by now. I doubt he will be granting me another interview. This was two and a half years before he finally lost his senses and allowed himself to become a pawn in the hands of his bully boys.

England surprised even themselves when they beat Australia by nine wickets in the First Test Match, at Edgbaston in 1997, even though Australia's captain, Mark Taylor, who was on the point of resigning because of his bad form, made a splendid hundred in their second innings. After the match David Lloyd rubbed his hands and said 'I told you so' and several other things which also came to be hostages to fortune well before the summer was out. The Australians, who had been underprepared, were so stung by this defeat that England never sniffed them again until the sides came to the Oval for the Sixth Test of the summer, by which time Australia had already won the series. In the fourth innings under the famous gas holders Australia had to make 124 to win and were bowled out by Caddick and Tufnell for only 104. I expect by now that the match-fixing sleuths will have been casting their eyes over that result, too. Being beaten 3–2 by Australia doesn't look too bad in the record books, but in reality England were comprehensively outplayed when in mattered.

In October I went to Pakistan when they played three Tests against South Africa. Karachi airport in the middle of the night was surprisingly jolly and my old friend Commander Arshed Gilani had laid on the sort of reception usually reserved for visiting royalty or bank robbers who have been extradited from South America. I was met at the aeroplane door, or as the dreadful modern word has it, 'planeside'. (The poor old English language is daily desecrated beyond belief.) From planeside to the Commander's car, having collected my bags on the way, took all of twenty minutes and that involved much passport stamping besides. The Commander's chauffeur, Amir Baig, is a gem who has elbowed his way out of the pages of Rudyard Kipling. Like all the Commander's staff, he comes from the tribal areas by the North-West Frontier. Amir Baig is tiny with a lovely, cheerful round face and a warm smile which poked its way through a well-regulated moustache as he greeted me. He led our procession through teeming millions to the car before making a serious assault on the land speed record between the airport and the Commander's house. He regarded red traffic lights as a decoration, pedestrians as justifiable targets and policemen as objects of ridicule.

I reached my bedroom in time to have the briefest of lie-downs before breakfast. In no time at all the Commander burst in full of good cheer and fired off a series of instructions as if he was a talking timetable. We had to fly that morning to Rawalpindi where the First Test Match began the next day and everything from then on was done at the double. Travelling with the Commander was like it must have been trying to keep tags on Christopher Columbus when he had a following wind. Doors were continually being opened and sanctuaries were for ever being offered, red carpets were all over the place and there was always a glass of this or that in the most improbable places. There were three Test Matches and two of them, at Rawalpindi and Faisalabad, were entertaining. At Rawalpindi, two Pakistanis, Ali Naqvi and Azhar Mahmood, made hundreds in their first Test Match and Azhar and Mushtaq Ahmed put on 151 for the last wicket which equalled the world record, although the match was drawn. The Second Test in Sheikupura, an hour's taxi drive from Lahore, was ruined by rain. Our daily journeys marked the start of an ongoing crusade by

Geoffrey Boycott to sort out the traffic problems in Pakistan and rewrite their Highway Code.

This came to a head on the drive from Lahore to Faisalabad for the Third Test, a journey that can take anything from three to five hours, depending on the traffic. This was the outstanding game of the series and it was won by South Africa. Boycott always assumes the front seat of a taxi, as of right, without ever considering the needs of the elderly and infirm who may crouch in the back. The traffic that day was beyond belief and the issue was complicated by a considerable political rally which meant that hordes of people dressed predominantly in green were bearing down on Faisalabad. Lorries, buses and cars were packed to the gunwales and for the last fifty miles second gear was the height of any driver's ambition. Boycott who had relegated the former Pakistan captain, Rameez Raja, to the back seat, became increasingly indignant about the inability of Pakistan's drivers to obey the Highway Code as he saw it. In the outskirts of Faisalabad he had apparently jumped out of the taxi which was inextricably entwined in an interminable traffic jam and began to act the role of traffic policeman. He waved his arms frantically and shouted vehemently and no one paid the slightest attention. King Canute would have said I told you so. In the end, to avoid injury he had to leap somewhat inelegantly back into the taxi where he continued to expostulate. It was a little bit like his running between the wickets.

Our relationship which, as far as he was concerned, had always been very much *de haut en bas* – I was always the *en bas* part of it – broke down completely after Christmas in the West Indies. He had by then been convicted *in absentia* by a court in the South of France for beating up a girlfriend with whom he had been staying in a fashionable hotel at Cap d'Antibes. He was given a three-month prison sentence which was suspended and was fined £5,000. He was adamant that the verdict had been unjust and his whole life became geared to trying to make sure it was reversed at the retrial. During the last Test Match of the series, in Antigua, the Great Man approached me one morning just outside the gents loo in the media area and asked me if I would write him a letter saying that as far as I was concerned he was not and never had been a violent person. I refused and told him that after the way he had behaved with the waiters and taxi drivers in Pakistan, it was but a short step to physical violence. This did not suit him at all and we have been off the air from that moment. Most people he asked dutifully wrote a letter saying that he was not a violent person and he sent the correspondence to his lawyers and a fat lot of good it seems to have done him. When he returned to the South of France for a retrial, the lady judge found him guilty as before and, as he had lost his temper in court, she remarked that he did not behave like the perfect English gentleman he had been at pains to point out that he was. He had found it almost too much to bear that proceedings in a French court of justice should be conducted in French, of which he had spectacularly little. A *Daily Telegraph* reader wrote a letter to the paper suggesting that the French lady judge, who was more than usually attractive, should become the first lady member of the Marylebone Cricket Club (MCC).

That wasn't the end of it for he was to appeal and early in 2000 that effort was thrown out as well, by which time it was estimated that his legal bills were more than half a million pounds. It wouldn't have surprised me if he had managed to get someone to sponsor his court appearances and, if so, maybe we still haven't heard the last of it. When he gave evidence in that famous libel action in Court Thirteen in the High Court in the Strand, brought by Ian Botham and Allan Lamb against Imran Khan in 1996, Boycott turned up from the commentary box at Lord's wearing a shirt emblazoned with Air India's name. He told the judge he had not had time to put on his jacket. Admirable, nuts, vainglorious, the manifestation of a truly sensational inferiority complex, sheer perverse bloody-mindedness or a combination of any or all of them? You pays your money and takes your choice.

In the Caribbean in that winter of 1997/98, the First Test was played at Kingston where the scene was set for one of the most bizarre happenings I shall ever be likely to see at a Test Match. We all arrived at Sabina Park early on the first day only to find that the pitch was undergoing a more than usually extensive examination. A walk to the middle told the story. This pitch had recently been relaid and looked like corrugated iron gone mad. I could sense that the distinguished grey locks of the Australian match referee, Barry Jarman, were going greyer by the second as he bent anxiously over it. I doubt Sherlock Holmes would have wasted time with his magnifying glass. No matter whether I looked at it from sideways on or straight down from the pavilion end, that terrifying corrugation was there. The heavy roller had been used much too soon after the relaying of the surface, when it was still too wet. Even though various eminent West Indian cricketers, including fast bowler Wes Hall and Jackie Hendriks, their former wicket-keeper, who had been in charge of the relaying operations, said that it was a beauty, I thought it would have been clear to the meanest of intellects that the ball was going to fly all over the place, at your nose one moment and at your ankles the next. Even the groundsman had his doubts, for otherwise he would not have tried to roll in some extra mud to even the surface out, although that only made matters worse. I took my place in the *Test Match Special* box with Jonathan Agnew and CM-J and our gallant army of comments men and waited for the action. England won the toss and, I suppose on the reasonable premise that the one thing it was not going to do was get any better, Mike Atherton decided to bat.

After fifty-six minutes' play when ten overs and one ball had been bowled and England were 17/3, the England physiotherapist came out for the sixth time that morning as yet another batsman took a sickening blow amidships or on the fingers. Alec Stewart, who was still not out, took the chance to wave on his captain, Michael Atherton, who shuffled out in that unassuming way of his and had a word with Brian Lara, his opposite number. The captains were joined by the umpires, Srini Venkataraghavan from India and Steve Bucknor from Jamaica, and Barry Jarman also came out from the pavilion. It was soon clear they were all in agreement. They came off the ground shaking their heads and the first Test Match in the history of cricket had been abandoned because the pitch was unfit for play and too dangerous.

It was a brave decision by the umpires. Venkat is an admirable chap and would have had no doubt that this was not a fit surface for a Test Match, but it would have been much harder for Bucknor. He is a Jamaican himself and knows how important it is for the West Indies to beat England. He knew that the Jamaican crowd sensed a hatful of wickets for their own Courtney Walsh. He will have been only too well aware that this was the only Test Match of the year in Kingston and that he would not be a popular man if he was to have a hand in the abandonment of a game which had seen the West Indies get off to such a brilliant start. Yet he too, with great bravery, held up his hand alongside Venkat's. They were both given full and sterling support by Jarman who did not have the slightest doubt about the correctness of the decision.

The action now moved to the George Headley Stand which encompassed the pavilion. We walked across the ground, stopping once more to take in the extraordinary topsy-turvy surface of the pitch as we went. A press conference had been hastily arranged by Stephen Camacho, the infinitely harrassed chief executive of the West Indies Board who still miraculously maintained an equable and cool exterior. The room provided was not big and packed with hacks, so the lack of air-conditioning was soon keenly felt. We waited for a long time, until eventually, trooping in like new occupants of the condemned cell, came Camacho, Pat Rousseau, the Jamaican president of the West Indies Board and a lawyer, and Jackie Hendriks.

Rousseau told us that it was impossible to arrange another Test Match in Jamaica but that an extra game would be fitted in during the tour so that we still had the full quota of five. This had not helped the president's temper and while he spoke it was easy to see that he was seething below the surface. He clearly wanted to have a go at someone but was unable to make up his mind who should be the target of his anger. His moustache quivered and he seemed still unable quite to comprehend what had happened. Hendriks was more straight forward. He said that he honestly thought that, in spite of its appearance, the pitch would play well enough and he apologised. Camacho told us that two Test Matches would be played back-to-back in Trinidad which was in any event our next destination. He had had a busy time on the telephone and those in charge at Queen's Park Oval in Port of Spain had come to his rescue. The rest of the day was hectically involved in telling the story to the rest of the world. That evening gave me the chance to dine at the Blue Mountain Inn high above Kingston, which was not quite the occasion it had been when I first went there thirty years before. The view up in the Blue Mountains was now more staggering than the banana flambé, while before I felt the banana flambé had won on a tight rein.

If anyone had bowled even half as well as Angus Fraser in the First Test at Port of Spain, the West Indies would have got nowhere near the 282 they needed to win. Fraser took eleven wickets in that match and nine wickets in the next, where he found more support, and England won by three wickets in the tensest of finishes. They then found themselves on the wrong end of the toss and a poor pitch in Georgetown and lost in four days. My visit to Guyana was enlivened by the arrival of that great cricket enthusiast Mick Jagger for a brief visit to the *TMS* box. England arrived in Bridgetown 2–1 down in the series. Mark Ramprakash played a wonderful innings of 154 there and showed form he has never yet been able to reproduce. If it had not rained for most of the last day, England would have had an excellent chance of winning. Then it was on to Antigua for the last Test and, on the Recreation Ground, England were comprehensively demolished and lost a series which they should at worst have drawn, by three matches to one.

At the end of this last Test Mike Atherton resigned the captaincy, after leading England for fifty-two Test Matches. Although he had become England's longest serving captain, it was a job which had never appeared to rest easily on his shoulders. He was not the most imaginative of captains, although, to be fair to him, the raw materials at his disposal were often pretty sketchy. I once accused him on *TMS* of being a consensus captain which did not please him. He did not exude either confidence or great authority when he was in charge, although that may in part have come from his slightly hang-dog manner. Spin bowlers as a breed may have found him sullen and unresponsive, but he is the most delightful of men, with an excellent sense of humour and is liked and respected by his colleagues. But he was not Mike Brearley.

Tours to the West Indies always leave behind a string of splendid memories. There was a visit one evening to the *Sea Goddess*, the last word in cruise ships, in the harbour at Bridgetown where the ninety-one-year-old Jim Swanton helped draw the raffle. On this visit to Barbados, his invariable habitat in the new year, Jim had a number of golf lessons from the pro at Sandy Lane, which spoke volumes for both his enthusiasm and his optimism. With his strong silvery grey hair, his booming voice and his still stately manner, Jim cut a hugely impressive figure. Another evening, in St Vincent, was spent having drinks with their highly entertaining Prime Minister, Sir James Mitchell. I was driven to this party by a splendid sixty-year-old Vincentian taxi driver who answered to the name of Fuzzy and sauntered carelessly in to join us at the Prime Minister's drinks party. It was all delightfully democratic. Tony Cozier gave his usual beach party at his house on the Atlantic side of the island. Getting there was a problem. My navigator was Geoffrey Nicholson who watches his cricket at Hove and on one splendid occasion at the Oval many years ago was twelfth man for Sussex. I only hope he was better able to distinguish between third man and long leg than he was at navigating in the West Indies. Then there was the Cobblestone Inn in Kingstown, the capital of St Vincent. They provided me with a room over the top of a karaoki club which seldom seemed to weigh anchor until three o'clock in the morning, by which time all 328 people present had made a valiant and increasingly tuneless attempt to sing 'My Way' at least twice each. But they served excellent omelettes for breakfast. My final memory of St Vincent, which is the loveliest of islands, was of the Royal St Vincent police going around with the letters RSVP in silver on their shoulders.

Towards the end of the one-day series in the West Indies my right knee became increasingly sore and the journey home did nothing to improve it. When I arrived back at North Farm, climbing the stairs was quite an adventure. Next on the agenda came Bitten's birthday, an occasion when I fear she thinks I rally round in rather a half-hearted manner. I suppose birthdays are a matter of upbringing. Without actually dismissing birthdays, my family tended to underplay them. Bitten's birthday was on 14 April and while she was working in London, my knee kept me in Norfolk and I have no doubt that I lost brownie points. Two days later I woke up to find that it was badly sceptic and I was hastily admitted to the Norfolk and Norwich Hospital where a Mr A.D. Patel had a look at it and decided that it needed operating on that same day. I had a problem because the following evening I was taking a dinner at the Petersfield Hotel in Horning on behalf of the Hoveton St John church roof. I had let them down once before when I had had suddenly to go to Pakistan and I told Mr Patel that come hell or high water he had to let me out on a stick or even a crutch. He agreed and Rex Neame, who always lends a hand on those occasions, picked me up, having first lent me a pair of fiercely blue shorts because my leg was in a splint and wouldn't go into a pair of trousers. My top half was covered by shirt, collar, tie and jacket but the nether regions did not bear inspection. Anyway, I turned up and did my stuff and then about a quarter to twelve Bitten drove me back to the hospital where I gave the night staff in the Alpington Ward the shock of a lifetime. It was, I suppose, a gentle net for what was to come a year later.

I was back in action by the time the series against South Africa began. Cricket all that summer was played to the background of the debate about what should happen to county cricket. The backwoodsmen were still determined to change nothing but one heard that some of the counties, now that the problems had been better explained to them, were more likely to accept change. The preferred option seemed to be to split the County Championship into two tiers, although there were some who favoured the idea of playing regional cricket to bring the best players together, and to leave the Championship as it was. I was a strong advocate of the two-tier system because, once that was in place, I was confident that other necessary adjustments would follow on behind and it would give England's cricket its best long-term chance.

Predictably, the England captaincy was given to Alec Stewart with Nasser Hussain the only other serious contender for the job. Stewart's appointment was a bad mistake because he had shown what an unimaginative and ordinary captain he had been with Surrey. They had the best side in the country at the Oval and yet during his years in charge won only a single trophy, the Sunday League, perhaps the least significant of all the titles, in his last season in 1997. The job should have been given to Hussain if the selectors had not been thoroughly wet and pusillanimous. But Hussain had acquired a reputation for being something of an awkward chap. I felt that Stewart's appointment wasted what turned out to be just over a year before Hussain was eventually given the job. No one could admire Stewart as a player more than I do, but there is, understandably perhaps, a certain bureaucratic son-of-the-father aspect to his captaincy, and his man management skills were suspect. For example, during Stewart's tenure of office Andy Caddick never played once under him and yet was to become England's most successful strike bowler under the more flexible regime of Hussain and the Zimbabwean coach, Duncan Fletcher. Caddick had upset a number of people with his indifferent bowling during the tour of the West Indies in 1997–98.

The Test series against South Africa in 1998 began with a draw at Edgbaston where England scored their runs too slowly in the first innings and rain on the last day then ruined their slender chances of victory. At Lord's, England indulged in one of those spectacular batting collapses which had recently become the unenviable hallmark of their cricket. Six wickets fell for 11 runs on the Sunday afternoon after Hansie Cronje and Jonty Rhodes had organised a spirited South African batting recovery on the first two days. Then in front of almost empty stands at Old Trafford, came a remarkable draw. Only the ECB still believed the game to be as popular as ever and during the match journalists who had had the temerity to think otherwise were subjected to a patronising lecture from one of their minions. He was clad, exceedingly irreverently in my view, in an England blazer which, like the cap and tie, should be reserved only for those who have played for their country, but many more are these days allowed to wear the sacred garments. He talked irrelevant nonsense about the number of children who played Kwik cricket. It was rather like suggesting that the increasing number of British children using water pistols spoke volumes for the back up strength of the armed forces. Anyway, in their different ways, Atherton and Stewart and then Croft and Gough held the South African bowlers at bay. But in the end, with the scores level, it was England's number eleven, Angus Fraser, who managed with great courage to survive Allan Donald's last over before Robert Croft played out a maiden from Paul Adams. It was brilliant theatre.

The action now moved on to Trent Bridge where England won an extraordinary Test Match by a margin of eight wickets which sounds far more convincing than it was. After South Africa had gained a first innings lead of 38, they were bowled out in their second for 208, with Fraser taking five wickets in both innings. England needed 247 to win. Allan Donald began at a blistering pace but somehow Atherton and Butcher survived the new ball. Shaun Pollock accounted for Butcher when they had put on 40 and, with Hussain taking his place, every run had to be mined out of solid rock. Nothing was given away. The umpiring during the match by Mervyn Kitchen from Somerset and Steve Dunne from New Zealand had not been the best and this had not helped the tension between the two sides. The game now almost caught fire. England had reached 82 and Atherton was 27 when he appeared to have been caught behind off his glove as he fended another torrid bouncer from Donald. The South Africans went into paroxysms of delight but Dunne remained motionless at the bowler's end and suddenly it occurred to the South Africans that Atherton was not going to be given out. Donald could hardly control himself and when his very next ball flew off the inside edge of Atherton's bat to the boundary, Donald snarled at him. This was the start of one of the most dramatically exciting pieces of cricket it has ever been my luck to see. Donald was beside himself with fury and he can never have bowled faster, while Atherton remained calm and composed, as unworried by bouncers as he was by sledging. His very calmness will only have annoyed the South Africans even more and Atherton stayed until the end, when he was 98 not out. Stewart applied the finishing touches with a remarkable exhibition of strokeplay which brought him 45 runs and nine fours from thirty-three balls.

Headingley came next and this match only seemed to compound the tensions and dramas of Old Trafford and Trent Bridge. For some years one neutral umpire had been standing in each Test Match which had stopped the increasing number of accusations of home-town bias. But the effectiveness of this arrangement was brought sharply into question with the appointment of the Pakistani Javed Akhtar for this crucial Fifth Test Match. The players of both sides were still seething at perceived injustices they had suffered in the Fourth at Trent Bridge. The ICC make these appointments and, when queried about the wisdom of selecting an umpire who did not have perhaps the best of credentials for such an important game, they answered with terrifying ineptness that these decisions had to be made with plenty of time to spare so that the people involved could make the necessary arrangements. Now, although the ICC could hardly be said to be one of the great advocates of the art of flexibility, surely in circumstances such as these, late adjustments could and should have been made. It can only make sense to try and ensure that two of the best umpires are in control of such a needle match.

Javed Akhtar's appointment hung over this match before the start like the approaching monsoon and while he may not have had the best of games, there were those ready to complain about every decision he made which hardly gave him a chance. This time South Africa gained a first innings lead of 22 and when Donald and Pollock bowled out England for 240 in their second innings, South Africa were left to score 219 to win. After fifteen overs they were 27/5, Gough having taken three much to the delight of the Yorkshire crowd, and Fraser the other two. Jonty Rhodes and Brian McMillan took the score to 144 and were playing with ever-increasing confidence when McMillan top edged a hook against Dominic Cork. Gough disposed of Rhodes soon afterwards and when the fourth day ended South Africa were 185/8 needing 34 more. Nine more had been scored the next morning when Donald felt for Fraser and was caught behind and finally Javed Akhtar gave Makhaya Ntini lbw to Gough who had taken 6/42. There were those who thought this last ball would have slipped down the leg side but there was someone who doubted every decision. The indisputable fact was that, however fortunately, England had beaten a major cricketing power for the first time since 1986/87 when Mike Gatting's side had won in Australia. I lived every ball of this match from inside the brilliant new press box at Headingley which is behind the arm and gives the best view in the ground. The last word on the umpiring and the result of the series was indirectly spoken by Ali Bacher, the managing director of the United Cricket Board of South Africa. He decided to pay the South African players the same bonus they would have received if they had won the series.

It was almost two years later when Dr Bacher, giving evidence to the King Commission in Cape Town, accused Javed Akhtar of being in the pay of bookmakers. Akhtar has vigorously denied the charge and it remains to be seen whether there is any truth in the accusation. It was almost as if Dr Bacher had forgotten that South Africa was the focus of the King Commission's inquiry. Perhaps he was simply throwing up a smokescreen to deflect attention from what was going on in South Africa. Cronje himself was always said to be obsessive in his pursuit of victory for South Africa. Yet I well remember the detached calm he showed when facing the press almost immediately after the match was over. He did not give the impression of being a man who felt his side had just been cheated out of a Test Match.

There remained a single Test Match to be played against Sri Lanka at the Oval and it brought a cock-a-hoop England alarmingly back to earth. The one-day World Champions had adapted their game successfully to the demands of Test cricket. They had outstanding cricketers in their freakish off spinner Muttiah Muralitharan, whose action caused constant controversy, in Sanath Jayasuriya whose dramatic strokeplay was as effective at the start of a Test Match as it was at the start of a one-day game, and in Aravinda de Silva, one of the outstanding batsmen of his generation. They were captained by the rotund Arjuna Ranatunga who was a shrewd leader and an important batsman coming in at the fall of the fourth wicket. But England were delirious after their victory over South Africa and David Lloyd could hardly stop himself from making non-stop verbal cartwheels of delight.

It was an extraordinary Test Match. Arjuna Ranatunga won the toss, put England in and watched contentedly while they made 445 with Graeme Hick and John Crawley making hundreds. With a superb and delightful piece of bowling, Muralitharan took 7/155 in 59.3 overs, figures which had an old-fashioned ring to them. Jayasuriya, who had had a bad time of it since taking a small matter of 340 off the Indian attack, now produced a familiar whirlwind of strokes as he reached 213 in five and three-quarter hours, while Aravinda de Silva brought his more classical influence to bear with an innings of 152 and Sri Lanka reached 591. It was now that Muralitharan produced a magical piece of bowling which left England bowled out for 181 and brought him figures of 9/65, the seventh best return ever in Test cricket. He had taken 16/220 in the match which had only been bettered on four occasions. Sri Lanka scored the 36 they needed to win without losing a wicket. Ranatunga now said that he put England in so that Muralitharan could have a decent rest between innings which he would not have done if they had been made to follow on. What a nerve!

The figures alone tell only a small part of the story of those five days which centred around the right arm and elbow of Muralitharan. His action was considered to be suspect. The ICC had studied films of him bowling and had come to the conclusion that there was nothing unfair about his action and had cleared him of being a chucker. Nonetheless, two Australian umpires, Darrell Hair and Ross Emerson, had both called him for throwing when Sri Lanka toured Australia in 1994/95. Muralitharan's action is far from normal, but he is a freak of nature rather than an exponent of sly cunning. His deformed right arm is fifteen degrees out of straight and he also has a double-jointed right wrist. Of course his action looks strange, but whether it is 'diabolical', as umpire Hair was to describe it in a book he wrote the following year, is a moot point. In 1998/99, while England were in Australia, I spent a few days on the Murray River in South Australia staying on Barry Jarman's houseboat. Another member of the crew was John Reid, the former New Zealand captain, who was the match referee for that Ashes series. One day we watched films of Muralitharan's action. Jarman was certain he threw, but after studying these films most carefully for a long time, Reid was not convinced and I have to say that I agreed with him. I could not see any evidence of Muralitharan straightening at the point of delivery an arm which appeared to be bent but only as a result of his deformity. He is well past two hundred Test wickets and I hope that he will now be allowed to bowl in peace. He is wonderful entertainment to watch and with that double-jointed right wrist, he is probably the only off spinner ever to use his wrist to turn the ball.

On the fourth evening of that Oval Test, David Lloyd who had watched his umpire-inspired triumph over South Africa disappear down the Kennington drains, could contain himself no longer. At a press conference that evening when talking about the off spinner's action, he said meaningfully, 'I have my opinion and I have made it known to the authorities,' which was tantamount to saying that he thought Muralitharan was throwing. The Sri Lankan Board complained to the English Board and Lloyd was severely censured and rightly so. His was the reaction of a spoiled boy looking for an excuse to try and protect his England side which had been outplayed in the most comprehensive manner. He should have kept his thoughts to himself and used the proper discreet channels through which protests of this sort should be made. Of course it suited him to think that Muralitharan threw. The next day, Geoffrey Boycott said on BBC television that England needed a coach who talked less and got on with his job. Lloyd heard this in the England dressing room and stormed upstairs into the media centre to shout at Boycott who held his ground and said little. The media area was not the most discreet place in which Lloyd could have blown his top and his bosses at the ECB will again have made note.

The Greatest Living Yorkshireman will have enjoyed the whole episode because, being Boycott, he had the conviction that he would coach England better than anyone else, which was surely the mootest of points. England's cricket may be alarmingly ineffectual but it is seldom boring.

The summer was given its final pertinent postscript by Ian

Chappell, who had been at the Oval. He said afterwards that he had seen nothing about England's cricket to cause Australia the slightest concern in the Ashes series starting in October.

CHAPTER

23

STORM CLOUDS AND INDIAN BOOKIES

WE HAVE BEEN LIVING in North Farm for eight years and it is the most heavenly house. It looks bigger than it is because it is stretched at one end by a couple of garages and at the other by old bullock sheds. The body of the house was built in 1595. A date stone has been moved up from its original place in the cellar and installed over the fireplace in the hall. The house has been added to over the ages and in the 1920s was extended at the east end. Unfortunately the supply of the old two-inch bricks ran out after the new south front had been built and the gable end and the north wall are built of an austere dark red brick which the north-east winds have been able to do little to soften. The house is haunted, although no one knows by whom. The main staircase which goes up two floors has been the place where most people come across it, although Bitten is adamant that she has twice felt a presence and seen a dark shadow at night move across our bedroom. I am not sure that I make good ghostly encounter material for I have never seen or felt anything.

We have three Labradors and a Cocker Spaniel and in haunted houses dogs can sometimes behave strangely. There has been the occasional instance of Bubbles, who sleeps much of the time in a basket in our bedroom, refusing point blank to walk across the room and, normally the most biddable of dogs, she once refused to come in at all and insisted on sleeping downstairs. I know this is slender evidence. My mother who never lived at North Farm – I was the first of the family to do so – was always certain that it was a benevolent ghost and there have been tenants of the house this century who have sworn to their dying day they have seen it in mid-season form. There was one occasion when we thought that it had taken on reasonably violent if not quite poltergeist qualities, but this was an attempt by one of those who looked after Rumple, my stepson, to try and persuade us that we should pay him danger money in addition to everything else.

No one loves the house more than Rumple. The old staircase is wide and gentle with banisters he can easily clutch. He knows all the steps, although he should never walk on his own because if he does trip, he goes straight down, all twelve stone of him, like a bag of coal. If you take your eye off him for a moment, however, he moves like the Scarlet Pimpernel, with great speed and in total silence. The extraordinary thing is that the dogs, whom he loves, never get in his way and trip him up. Rumple lives at the top of the stairs on the first landing and the ghost has never yet upset him and I have always heard that handicapped people are very quick to sense and react to a ghost. It is a romantic mystery that will almost certainly remain unsolved, but I would love to know who, if anyone, was foully murdered in the house and if he or she still climbs the stairs at night. Bitten is sure the ghost looks after us all.

I find the wrench of leaving England for long periods becomes greater each time. Whenever I go away for two or three months, some part of my life seems to have gone when I return or something has changed for the worse. I delayed my departure for Australia as late as I possibly could for the England tour in 1998/99. I managed a couple of days' pheasant shooting at Hoveton before I went. It is sadly no longer the shoot it was in my father's day but the estate is too small for John to be able to justify a full-time gamekeeper. Roger Hearn, who is a frontline tractor driver, does his best in his spare time and produces some extremely enjoyable days but, like the England batsmen, we don't reach three figures very often. The duck shooting is still the most exciting but one has to be lucky to hit on a night that is rough and cloudy which is much the best for an evening flight. As the water level in the Broads rises, it becomes more and more difficult to get out to those places the duck love to come in to feed in the evening without going in over the top of your waders. Just occasionally the water recedes and the weather obliges and then it is an evening to remember.

I don't mind if I don't let off my gun because standing out in the marshes in thigh waders with the water up to your knees with all the sounds around you is worth anything. There are the duck – mallard, gadwall, wigeon and others. The teal are the most fun. When it gets almost dark you hear them swoop in and there is a gentle splosh on the water as they land. It is difficult to see them then and they are the hardest of all to shoot. There are thousands of honking geese, Canada and greylag, and the big flights of seagulls, the squawking of waterhens and occasionally the silent fluttering of an owl or the beautiful flight of a woodcock. Sometimes you will hear that intriguing and unforgettable call of a snipe jinking high over your head. There are the few dark trees among the oaks in Poker's Loke by the entrance to the marsh. The scraggy alders have been left in the Pulk in the middle of the marshes, which was a pheasant drive when I was young and the marshes had been reclaimed for cattle grazing. Now they have gone back to nature and the height of the water will eventually finish off the remaining ones. And then on the edge of the upland, between the Pulk and Poker's Loke, stand the handsome firs in the Firground wood. During the flight, pheasants will say goodnight to the world as they go up to roost with an audible fluttering of wings.

When I am thousands of miles away from Hoveton watching cricket in midsummer in Australia, say, this is the scene I remember and see in my mind more than any other. Not so much because of the actual shooting but because of the sheer unspoilt beauty of the marshes. They are stark and wonderful in the winter; in the spring when those eighty or more acres are full of nesting birds with their beautiful plumage at its best, it is more unbelievable than ever. The more quietly I manage to quant the boat round every bend in the dykes, the closer and better the surprises which await you. The marshes, like the Broads, are never the same two days running and it would be impossible ever to tire of them. There is an old mill on the edge of the Bure where the marshes come up to the river bank, Dydler's Mill, and Rex Neame is putting it back into shape. From the small glass conservatory at the top, the view of these marshes and their feathered inhabitants is remarkable.

The flight to Brisbane even though I had conned my way into the first-class cabin, was a let down after all this. England had already made their usual poor start to the tour. Michael Atherton's back was playing up and Graham Thorpe's was an unknown quantity. Graeme Hick who was not in the original party, even after that hundred at the Oval, was going out as a reinforcement and was on the same aeroplane now. The Sheraton Hotel in Brisbane was as comfortable as ever, but the dear old Woolloongabba, once a ground of great character, had been turned by the builders into a stadium which was well on its way to resembling the featureless Polo mint it has now become. The ground would soon be encompassed by one identical stand. Talk about the dead hand of conformity. The grassy banks of the hill, where a handful of people sat and cheered that faraway evening in December 1960 when little Jo Solomon from square leg threw out Ian Meckiff as he and Lindsay Kline scampered for the winning run in the First Test between Australia and the West Indies, are but a distant memory. That was the first tie in the history of Test cricket.

By the time I arrived in Australia, the West Indian players had turned their hands to gunboat diplomacy. They had successfully held their own Board of Control to ransom for better financial terms for their tour to South Africa. After losing to South Africa in Bangladesh in the final of yet another spurious one-day competition for all the Test-playing countries, Brian Lara and Carl Hooper, the captain and vice-captain, flew to London instead of going on to South Africa. There they met up with Courtney Walsh, Curtly Ambrose, Jimmy Adams and the four others who had been selected for South Africa but had not been required in Bangladesh. Holed up in a hotel at Heathrow, they demanded better terms and conditions from the West Indies Board. The immediate reaction of Pat Rousseau, their irascible president, was to sack Lara and Hooper as captain and vice-captain and to fine the others who were waiting on events at Heathrow before deciding whether to go to South Africa. This was old-fashioned Colonel Blimpish colonialism at its best. Great expectations for the tour had been building up for a long time in South Africa and Ali Bacher was so worried by the threat of cancellation or of the West Indies sending a second eleven, that he flew to Heathrow to help with the negotiations. Once that had happened the players knew they couldn't lose. Rousseau had to eat humble pie, a dish he always finds particularly indigestible, even though he has had a certain amount of experience at it, and reinstate Lara and Hooper and cancel the fines. He also had to fly to Heathrow where he was outplayed in the negotiations and the tour went ahead. He won't have enjoyed himself. It could hardly have been a more disastrous tour for the West Indies who lost all five Test Matches. The South Africans scarcely had to break into a sweat. Maybe Rousseau should have tried to organise a deal with his players which had something to do with their results. The ironical postscript was that when Rousseau visited South Africa to watch a Test Match or two, he was taken to see the new ground in the township of Soweto and while there he and his companions were held up by gunmen and robbed of all their valuables. There was a moral there somewhere.

England played the First Test in Brisbane after the usual thoroughly unsatisfactory start to the tour in the first few matches. In the final equation, England needed 348 to win with all the last day as well as seven overs at the end of the fourth at their disposal. At lunch on the last day they were 108/3 and, with Stuart MacGill weaving complicated spells with his leg breaks, defeat was a distinct possibility. England's main hopes rested on a storm of gargantuan proportions which was beginning to build up in the distance behind that stout fortress, the Boggo Road Jail, which is such a celebrated landmark near to the Gabba. There was no doubt that it was coming; the only problem was the time of its arrival. From our position high in the stand we had a perfect view of the gathering clouds and no impending storm can ever have been discussed in such intimate detail. These tropical storms in Brisbane can be fearful prima donnas though, and take an awfully long time to come to the point. After lunch three more wickets fell and the light became gloomier and gloomier. Someone, an Australian of course, told me that these storms have a habit of slipping round the back. The umpires, Darrell Hair and 'KT' Francis, were now meeting after every over but with sickening perversity for English eyes would not come off. What was even more frustrating for us English was that this impenetrable bank of black clouds, which was now making it look as if the world was about to come to an end, obstinately refused to produce any rain. The game struggled on in an *Alice in Wonderland* atmosphere of unreality. The black skies at the southern end were continually being lit up by great jags of forked lightning and the constant cracking and rumbling of the thunder made me think I was watching a movie of one of those dreadful Great War battles. Then the umpires met again after another anxious over of leg spin had been survived and this time they called a halt.

We handed briefly back to the studio in London and a minute or two later Peter Baxter asked me if I would mind giving the listeners an update. I did my best, although it had by now become the sort of scene that could only be found in the MGM studios in Los Angeles. It was as dark as it is in England at four o'clock on a December afternoon, the lightning was a firework display which might have been orchestrated by Dante for one of the juicier parts of his *Inferno*, but still it would not rain. I could not escape from the dreadful thought that it might slip round the back after all and England still might have to continue their innings. 'Oh, ye of little faith . . .' After one final belching thunderclap, the heavens opened and, my goodness, did it rain. In seconds the ground was under water and then it turned to hailstones which bounced off the Gabba like ping-pong balls. It was now so dark that it was impossible to see beyond the vague outline of the stand at the Stanley Street end of the ground opposite to us, and it was not easy even to see that far. Then the ground became submerged in cloud and even the glow from the street lights disappeared. It was half past three in the afternoon of a

Test Match and it might have been midnight in the middle of a power cut. I found it utterly thrilling and just a little frightening. I had the luck to be able to try and describe what was happening to listeners at home. Of course, it didn't go on for ever but it went on for long enough to ensure that England had escaped with a draw. I wondered if there had ever been such a storm, but my old friend Peter Burge, who made so many runs for Australia in the sixties, said as he gave me a lift back to my hotel, 'We get 'em like that, you know, Blowers.' I was disappointed, but at least it had been a considerable first for me and it was not by any means the first tropical storm I had sat through at the Gabba.

At the WACA ground in Perth the pitch was fast and uneven and it took Australia less than three days to put England in their place. They were without Graham Thorpe whose back had gone again and he was soon to return to London. Even so, if England's batsmen had shown greater resolution and the fielders had been able to hold on to even half the eight catches they dropped, Australia might have had to make 150 instead of 64 to win. Who knows what might have happened then, for the Australians did not much enjoy batting on that pitch either and they lost three quick wickets in this final innings. As it was, the pattern for the series had been inextricably set and I left Perth for Adelaide knowing that the Ashes were as far away from England's grasp as Methuselah was from a cot death.

While we had been in the West Indies the previous year, Barry Jarman, the match referee, had invited me to spend a few days on his houseboat on the Murray River in South Australia during the present series. I had run into Barry again during the First Test in Brisbane when he came up for a dinner for all those to have captained Australia. (He had been in charge at Leeds for the Fourth Test in 1968 while Tom Graveney had captained England in the same match. The two regular captains, Bill Lawry and Colin Cowdrey had been injured.) Barry told me in Brisbane that the dates for my visit had been set and a week before the Third Test he picked me up outside the Adelaide Club early one morning and, with John Reid and his wife Norleigh, we drove for three hours up to Lyrup where his boat was berthed. We drove along dead straight roads through parched dusty country and it is on journeys like these that you get some idea of the colossal size of Australia. When the road took us close to the Murray River the land was extremely fertile and we drove through thousands of acres of green vines. As we passed the old Tailem Bend racecourse Barry told me a wonderful story of how he and his three co-owners of a horse called Sleepwalker had engineered a killing. Richie Benaud, Norman O'Neill, Ray Steele, who managed several Australian tours, and Barry had owned a leg each. They had entered Sleepwalker for a five-furlong sprint and the locals knew nothing about the horse which began at a good price. Barry had used a suitcase to bring up enough money from Adelaide and they had distributed it among the bookies. Then they had had a supremely anxious few minutes before the judges decided that Sleepwalker had won by a short half head. Barry's father had come with them and put a pound on Sleepwalker with each of the twenty-seven bookies at the meeting. When Barry asked him what on earth he was doing, he replied that it had always been his ambition to take money off every bookie on the course.

Barry's boat was called *Gooda's Gold* and had been named after Tony Gooda, one half of the Gooda-Walker syndicate which had lost many people a lot of money when Lloyd's of London caught a bad cold. Barry had met Gooda several times in England and had gone to stay at his house in Sussex which Gooda had eventually renamed as Jarmans. Barry, happily for him, did not allow himself to be lured into Lloyd's. We spent three nights on the Murray River which stretches from Port Adelaide to the northern reaches of New South Wales. There were seven of us on board and we had a delightful three days chugging up and down and eating splendid food cooked most capably by Captain Jarman. Needless to say, we also worked our way through a great many of South Australia's finest red wines. The country was starkly beautiful and the river almost completely empty of other boats, apart from a few waterskiing yuppies up for the weekend from Adelaide. It was now that we had the chance to watch the videos of Muralitharan's action which produced plenty of intense but inconclusive argument.

STORM CLOUDS AND INDIAN BOOKIES

The annual Test Match at the Adelaide Oval is one of the most glorious occasions in the cricketing year and I have been lucky enough to have watched more than a dozen of them. It is a lovely ground with the twin spires of the Cathedral looking down from one corner from behind the green Moreton Bay fig trees. In the far distance behind the Victor Richardson Gates are the rolling hills of the Mount Lofty Ranges, while the new Bradman Stand at the City End of the ground is a most tasteful addition. It could hardly be in greater contrast to what the commercial architects have done with the Gabba. It is as though the stand has always been there and yet it was built in late eighties. The old members' stand, which incorporates the pavilion, goes the full length of the ground opposite the Richardson Gates. It is wonderfully peaceful and it still makes me feel that cricket is not all ruthless modernity, at least while they play in white clothes and with a red ball. On the spacious lawns behind the pavilion, some of the winemakers from the Barossa Valley put up tents and display their wares and the picnic lunches are formidable. The ladies of Adelaide dress up for the occasion. It is all very tempting. There is something of P.G. Wodehouse's Blandings Castle about the Adelaide Oval and one wonders why God had to invent sin and go and spoil it all.

I suppose it is yet another manifestation of Sod's Law that over the years the Adelaide Oval has attracted more than its fair share of controversy. It was here in the Bodyline tour that Harold Larwood hit both Bill Woodfull and Bertie Oldfield sickening blows which almost caused the end of the tour and a major diplomatic incident. When we arrived in Adelaide now, venality had taken over. Mark Waugh and Shane Warne had been exposed by some brilliant and persistent investigative journalism by Malcolm Conn of *The Australian* for accepting money from the illegal Indian bookmaking fraternity when they were in Colombo in 1994. They had been paid US $6,000 and $5,000 respectively for giving information about the weather and the pitch. The Australian Cricket Board had come to know about it soon afterwards and had fined the players but had kept it all secret. As luck would have it, Sir Clyde Walcott and David Richards of the ICC were passing through Sydney at the time and were also informed but they too promised to keep it secret. In the light of subsequent events, when Mark Waugh, Warne and Tim May accused Salim Malik of trying to bribe them to play badly on their visit to Pakistan after the Sri Lankan leg of the tour, the continued silence by the president and chief executive of the ICC was shameful. In the pavilion two days before the start of the match, both Australians read apologetic statements to the press which had been prepared with the help of the Board and which claimed that they had revealed nothing of any significance.

The chairman of the Australian Board, Dennis Rogers, took a press conference during the Third Test and he was hard pressed to find an adequate defence for the manner in which his predecessors had covered up what had happened. It was clear to me that he had no idea whether any other Australians had been involved. He was keeping his fingers crossed and almost certainly still is. It was just before the Ashes series, while Australia were touring Pakistan, that Waugh and Mark Taylor in the absence of the injured Warne had given evidence to the Qayyum Commission in Lahore which had been set up to look into accusations of match-fixing and bribery. Malcolm Speed, the chief executive of the Australian Board, had flown to Lahore to be with the players in court, knowing full well of Waugh's and Warne's involvement with the bookies but without letting on. It defied belief. Of course, the Pakistanis saw it as an immediate let out for them and their Board had every right to feel highly indignant at the high-handed way in which they had been treated by the Australians.

I was not selected for the commentary team for the Adelaide Test and watched it throughout from the balcony on the top deck of the Bradman Stand which was primarily for the use of the television cameras. I sat with Eddie Bevan who accompanies us on most tours for BBC Wales, especially if there is a Welsh interest which there was now in the person of Robert Croft, the off spinner who, sadly, became rather a depreciating asset in Australia. Eddie had to supply his listeners in both English and Welsh and it was always a joy to have him on a tour for he has a lovely sense of humour and prevents us all from taking ourselves too seriously. Australia made 391 with Justin Langer contributing an excellent 179 not out and then England did their favourite party trick. They were going along in pretty good order at 187/3 but fourteen overs later they were all out for 227. In the end, Australia left England to score 443 to win and they got no further than 237 with the last five wickets falling for only 16 runs.

I was given a good chuckle when I arrived in Melbourne immediately after the match by the pronouncements of none other than Mr Raymond Illingworth from his pad in Spain. He had said that England were bloody awful and indulged in some joyous I-told-you-somanship. At least he welcomed the decision which had been made just before the start of the Adelaide Test Match, to divide the County Championship up into two divisions. He put the icing on the cake when he said, no doubt portentously, 'I proposed two divisions in 1976.' There is something warmly comforting about the path of predictability. It was reassuring, too, to read that Tim Lamb, the chief executive of the England Board, had said at about the same time, 'Great strides are being made at the junior level.' It always does one good to hear about the invincibility of the under-nines when you are two down in an Ashes series. All this gave me a great laugh one morning in bed at the Melbourne Club. I had forgotten what a jolly old world it is out there.

When I arrived in Melbourne I stayed for two days with Jeremy and Jen Oliver at their charming house in Hawthorn. He is one of Australia's leading wine experts with a cellar to match and I had the most exceptional two days drinking. We had met many years before when he was at University and, trying to earn a bob or two over Christmas, was working in Dan Murphy's wine store in the suburb of Prahran when I had turned up to buy my Christmas booze. He offered to drive it all round to the Windsor Hotel that evening and I had agreed as long as he was prepared to help me see off the first two bottles. He had no problem with that and we've been firm friends ever since, although my liver is probably glad I don't see him too often. We soon found now that our thirsts had not grown less, merely more discriminatory, since we had last seen each other in 1992.

Early service at Melbourne Cathedral passed off without incident on Christmas morning, which is more than can be said some years before when I was late. I had burst in through a small door at the east end to find the service under way and that I was standing close to the altar in the midst of the bishop and the assistant clergy which had all been very embarrassing. All I could see was Johnny Woodcock chuckling away to himself in a pew in the middle distance. Christmas lunch with the daughter and son-in-law of Judy Casey, who was also there and at the very peak of her form, was considerably assisted by a superb bottle of Grange Hermitage of a very good year, but I still arrived at the vast Melbourne Cricket Ground (MCG) the next morning fearful of what lay ahead. I need not have been so apprehensive for the two sides served up one of the best Test Matches I have ever watched and the excitement was dramatic throughout.

The first day was washed out after the captains had tossed and Mark Taylor had put England in to bat. This meant that the teams had been selected and could not therefore be changed whatever the weather. Boxing Day at the Test Match at the MCG has been a popular ritual for the inhabitants of Melbourne for a long time and, although it did not require any great intellect to know that play was doubtful, no less than 61,580 of them turned up and most of them waited until the umpires had decided late in the day that no play would be possible. England had already had to face the disturbing news that Alex Tudor who seemed certain to play, had suffered what was described as a light injury to one of his hips playing football on Christmas Day and was unable to play.

Because of the lost day the rules now allowed for a start to be made half an hour earlier and for play to continue half an hour later each day. This would mean that four of the six hours lost on the first day would be made up. It made excellent sense, although it is a rule which still needs fine tuning as we saw on the fourth day of the match when the final session of play went on for more than four hours, which is too long for anyone. Australia, who were batting last, had claimed the extra half hour on top of everything else, as they were fully entitled to do, as they felt it would give them their best chance of winning

England's start was as agonising as ever. Atherton and Butcher were quickly out and the score stood at 4/2. The noble collection of insomniacs back at home who had switched on *TMS* must have reached gratefully for their sleeping pills. While it always gives me a tremendous kick to be the bearer of good news, I tend to feel partly responsible if the tidings are less than joyful. The messenger usually gets it in the neck anyway. The good news was that Alec Stewart had begun to bat like a man possessed and his 50 arrived in only sixty-six minutes with eight spanking fours. What a terrible pity it was that he had ever been asked to bother with the wicket-keeping gloves. Later in the day a square cut for an all-run four brought him to his first hundred in a Test Match against Australia. Four runs later he was bowled round his legs sweeping and England were all out for 270, which did not seem enough. Australia were 59/2 at the close and the next day only Steve Waugh held up the England bowlers. Australia's eighth wicket fell at 252 and it looked then as if England might even have the luxury of a small first innings lead.

Waugh's batting had been relentlessly solid as he refused all risks and scored his runs only when they were sensibly on offer. During the tea interval he changed his thinking and afterwards he went for his strokes and found just the partner he needed in Stuart MacGill. While Waugh reached his hundred, MacGill threw his bat around with telling effect and they put on 88 in just over an hour and a half. In the end Australia had a lead of 70 which, in the context of a fairly low-scoring match on a pitch with an uneven bounce, I was sure had given them a decisive advantage. Atherton completed his pair of spectacles in the second over of England's second innings when Damien Fleming bowled him one of those which pitched on the leg stump and hit the top of the off. The enigmatic Atherton shuffled off with his crash helmet under his arm looking much the same as he did when he had made a 150. When England were four wickets down their lead was only 8. Nasser Hussain went on to reach a good 50 but then got out driving hard and low to cover, which has become something of a pastime for him. Hick also played well for a time but at 221/9 England were only 151 ahead and all that was left was Alan Mullally whose batting in this series so far had been horribly comic. In six attempts he had only once got past nought. He now faced Glenn McGrath and we all watched in humorous expectation as if it was Corporal Jones about to come up with the answer for Captain Mainwaring yet again. McGrath pranced in full of menace and Mullally went through a windmill swing of the bat and, lo and behold, the ball screamed back over McGrath's head for four. McGrath stood there looking as if he had seen a ghost. He raced in again and this time Mullally unwound another wild swing and the ball whistled over long on for four. While Mullally lent amiably on his bat, McGrath was hard pressed to see the funny side of it and gave Mullally what he no doubt would have considered to be some excellent advice. Mullally's next swing sent the ball high in the air to mid-wicket where Michael Slater waited for the catch until he was trampled on by McGrath, who held on nonetheless. By then, Fraser and Mullally had put on 23 runs which had assumed enormous importance by the end of the day.

Australia needed 175 to win and, after an early tea, perhaps the longest session ever to have been played in a Test Match got under way. The score was 31 when Slater was lbw to one from Dean Headley which kept low and 10 runs later Taylor hooked Mullally to fine leg. But Hick dropped Langer low to his right at second slip and at 100/2 it began to look as if it was all over. Three runs later Mullally bowled a short one to Langer who hooked it square out of the middle of the bat and Ramprakash at square leg threw himself far to his right and held a staggering one-handed catch two feet from the ground. This was the piece of luck England needed and the game underwent a dramatic change. When the Waugh brothers had put on an uneasy 27, Mark tried to play Headley to leg and was quickly caught by Hick at second slip. After one straight drive for four, Darren Lehmann drove again and was caught behind and then Ian Healy pushed forward, also to Headley, and was caught at second slip. When Fleming stumbled half forward and was lbw Australia were 140/7, 35 runs away from victory. But Steve Waugh was still there and Matthew Nicholson now made him a stalwart partner.

STORM CLOUDS AND INDIAN BOOKIES

They had taken the score past 160 when Nicholson groped forward to Headley and was caught behind. With 14 needed Waugh played the first ball of the next over from Gough to fine leg for a single without any thought of trying to protect MacGill, his partner, for whom Gough now produced the perfect yorker which made a terrible mess of his stumps. McGrath took his place and peered at the first ball which he was unable to locate. He did not pick up the next one either which hit him on the pad and umpire Daryl Harper was quick to agree with the Englishmen that it would also have hit the stumps and England had won by 12 runs. Waugh, who had made 152 runs in the match without being out, seemed wrapped in thought as he made his way back to the pavilion. It was a game which had electrified Australia and if the reports we heard on *TMS* from London were anything to go by, the same had happened at home.

I flew to Sydney the next day after one last deliciously punishing evening trying to come to terms with Jeremy Oliver's cellar. The next day I went to see an old friend, Peter McFarline, who wrote cricket for many years for *The Age* in Melbourne before he contracted the most appalling illness which has just about shut down his whole central nervous system. He cannot move and sits in a wheelchair in hospital unable to speak audibly because, while having treatment for a respiratory arrest, his vocal cords were damaged. He is on a respirator and has not been able to breath on his own or swallow anything down his own throat since 1995. His bravery and determination in the face of such desperate odds as these have been staggering. He still has the guts to come occasionally in a wheelchair to watch the cricket at the MCG and he manages to write occasional pieces for *The Age*. Del, his wife, who is as big an inspiration as Peter is himself, can lipread the words as he mouths them, and writes them down. Although he cannot even turn the page of a book, he can read what Del has written and correct what he wants. While I was there he was full of enthusiasm and was as well if not better informed than I was about all the match-fixing dramas. He told me triumphantly that, while all his food is poured through a tube into his stomach, they also pour some whisky in when he wants it and it has a wonderful effect. I wonder if there is a braver human being. What an object lesson he is to all of us and especially to those who spend their lives whingeing about anything and everything. I came away feeling extremely humbled.

Then it was on to Sydney where Mark Taylor won his fifth successive toss and England got the worst of a turning pitch. Australia brought back Shane Warne, whose shoulder was at last better, but it was MacGill who did the damage, taking 12/107 in the match. Even so, England had one piece of bad luck. In Australia's second innings, Slater played an extraordinary innings scoring 123 or 66.84 per cent of their total of 184, a proportion which has only been exceeded once and that in the very first Test Match of all in 1877 at Melbourne by Charles Bannerman who made 165 out of Australia's total of 245, or 67.34 per cent of the runs. When Slater was 35 he appeared to be run out by a direct hit from Headley, but the replays were not conclusive because Such, the bowler, obscured the view. It is absurd that there are not two cameras square with the wicket, one on each side, to help the third umpire. If Slater had been out then, England's final target might have been within reach.

Bitten had arrived in Sydney for the New Year which we celebrated in some style at the Sheraton on the Park in the middle of town. By the time the Fifth Test Match started we had been joined from Pakistan by the Commander and his wife Shano who had not visited Australia before. As always, they added greatly to the gaiety of nations. The day after the match was over, the four of us flew from Sydney to Cairns in North Queensland and from there by small aeroplane to Dunk Island where we boarded a motor cruiser for the final half hour of the journey to Bedarra Island. One of the Family Islands, it was discovered, needless to say, by Captain Cook who appears to have missed nothing in this neck of the woods. It is tropical bliss and our tiny resort had fifteen small villas with a maximum of three people in each, so it was hardly overcrowded. We had paid for our four days in advance and once we were there no money changed hands. There were four high-class chefs living on the island and all the meals were superb. At the bar guests helped themselves to whatever they wanted and the wine list was impressive. We found an unlimited supply of Bollinger which we drank at almost every opportunity. It was the perfect way to unwind after a hard tour. Because I paid a long time in advance I kept feeling that I was getting it all for free. My only problem was to make the Commander understand that inactivity sometimes has its merits, for he is someone who likes always to be up and doing. By the time we arrived for breakfast on the first morning, he had already walked round most of the island. He had also arranged for a huge catamaran to take us to the Great Barrier Reef the following day and for a supersonic cruiser to take us on a private visit to another part of the reef the day after that. Our only companion that day, apart from the crew, was a sensational picnic provided by the staff at Bedarra Island with unlimited Bolly. They were a heavenly four days in which we were all spoilt to bits and the Commander's nautical roll became daily more pronounced.

Then it was back to Sydney, a final dinner at Peter Doyle's splendid fish restaurant in Watson's Bay and the flight home the next day. I managed to avoid the one-day series which was not noteworthy except for two particularly nasty pieces of unpleasantness which both happened in Adelaide which, as I have shown, has a habit of attracting this sort of thing. First, umpire Ross Emerson, a former police officer from Perth, came to Adelaide to umpire England's game against Sri Lanka. He had called Muralitharan for throwing five years before. Muralitharan came on to bowl the sixteenth over of the match and, in his second over, Emerson called the fourth ball a no-ball from his position at square leg. This on its own was a shoddy enough performance for there is a discreet and accepted way for umpires to deal with bowlers whose actions they suspect. Emerson was now making a public fool of Muralitharan. This was bad enough, but Arjuna Ranatunga's reaction to it as captain of Sri Lanka was nothing short of scandalous. After wagging his finger at the umpire, he led his troops to the boundary's edge where they were joined by the manager and, on a mobile telephone, rang their own Board of Control in Colombo. Play eventually continued and Ranatunga was now insistant that Emerson should stand close to the stumps when Muralitharan bowled from his end. Emerson demurred and Ranatunga went up to him and said, 'I'm in charge of this game. You'll stand where I want you to. If you don't stand there, there won't be a game.' So much for the ICC's celebrated Code of Conduct. The referee, South Africa's Peter van der Merwe, wanted to throw the book at Ranatunga but, after repeated telephone calls to Lord's, was prevented from doing so because the ICC appeared to be doubtful that their own Code of Conduct would stand up in a court of law. You would be forgiven for thinking that they might have thought of this before.

I have been through this tour of Australia at some length because it provides a good example of the way the game has changed, at the same time as making it clear that there is still an awful lot of fun to be had from the constant hurly-burly of a modern tour. It was not quite the end of my winter's adventures either.

CHAPTER

24

RETIRED HURT

January was not yet over which meant a long and chilly wait until the start of the English cricket season. *Cakes and Bails*, my book about my progress through the year 1997/98, had come out the previous autumn and had not bombed completely, so the same publishers were brave enough to ask me to try again. *It's Just Not Cricket* was the result. However I felt I needed another adventure which might stretch to a chapter or two and so I decided to go to New Zealand for three weeks in March to watch them play a couple of Test Matches against South Africa. I have always enjoyed the country enormously and, having not been back there since 1993/94, there were a great many friends I wanted to catch up with and a considerable number of new vintages that urgently needed to be tasted.

I flew through Los Angeles to Auckland and arrived at the ParkRoyal Hotel in Christchurch the day before the Second Test Match began. After a successful sortie to Christchurch's two secondhand bookshops on the day I clocked in, I watched a laboriously dull Test Match which Hansie Cronje did not seem in the least interested in winning. There was a fair amount of rain but, even so, more imaginative thinking would have allowed South Africa an excellent chance of victory. As it was, Herschelle Gibbs was allowed to bat for ever and a day for more than 200. In the light of the involvement of both these players with the bookmakers, I suppose one has now to wonder if either or both were helping themselves to a bob or two even then. What happened made such poor cricketing sense.

A THIRST FOR LIFE

The match was played at what has always been called Lancaster Park and is the home of both cricket and rugger in Canterbury. To my horror, I found that it was now masquerading under the strange name of the Jade Stadium. The administrators of the ground had been persuaded that it was financially sound to hawk the name of the ground around to potential sponsors. They had first attracted the Auckland Savings Bank, but at the last minute realised that it might not be the wisest course of action if the famous Lancaster Park was now to carry the name of a North Island city. The ASB were sent packing and a local computer software billionaire took his chance and his company, Jade, paid around NZ$400,000 (£130,000) a year for the privilege, which was peanuts. Back home, financial necessity had, of course, driven those in charge of the Oval to do a similar deal with Fosters, but the Fosters Oval sounds only mildly offensive in comparison. While I was in New Zealand, Walter Hadlee, the *eminence grise* of New Zealand cricket and a Canterburian who had first played rugger at Lancaster Park in 1927, was scratching his head rather vigorously about this piece of *lese-majesty*.

I was grateful to leave cricket for a few days after watching this match. Before I left Christchurch I found time to pay yet another pilgrimage to the Valley of Peace where, only the week before, one of the club's regulars, Eric Jackson, who was admittedly seventy-four, had collapsed and died at the non-striker's end when he was 4 not out. At a touching little ceremony, we all gathered round the spot with various members of his family, and a short eulogy was delivered. I can't think of a much better way of putting your cue in the rack although I suppose, for choice, I would rather have been facing the bowling with a few more than 4 against my name. My visit to Christchurch also enabled me to catch up with one of my favourite cricket writers, Dick Brittenden, who wrote for many years for the *Christchurch Star*. Although he has long since retired, he sat with us in the press box throughout the match. Dick has written many fine books about New Zealand's cricket, becoming their unofficial historian, and his distinctive chuckle has blessed press boxes all round the cricketing world.

On the last day of the Test Match, I flew to Blenheim at the top of the South Island where I became the first house guest at Clayvin, a thirty-five acre vineyard, a half share of which had just been bought by Richard and Johnny Wheeler on behalf of their family firm of wine merchants, Lay and Wheeler, who over the years have had the same sort of impact on teetotalism in the home counties as Aphrodite had on celibacy on a rather larger scale. Leisurely mountains sweep their way across the skyline to the north with the vines stretching away almost to the foothills. I spent three nights there, absorbing far too much delicious pinot noir and a certain amount of chardonnay, and providing the name for the splendid black cat which behaved as if it owned the place and by the time I left was beginning to answer to 'Blowers'. I met an old friend, Graham Thorne, the former All Black, who needed some catching on the wing. He was about to open his own winery restaurant, the Gumdigger's Dog, for which he later inveigled me into making a radio commercial. At lunch I also met Kevin Judd, the redoubtable winemaker at Cloudy Bay whose original Sauvignon Blanc had given not only Cloudy Bay but also the whole New Zealand wine industry a significant push in the right direction. We visited Cloudy Bay's tasting room after lunch where we did rather more than just taste his 1997 pinot noir which was exceptional. We then went back to christen the Gumdigger's Dog which was opening for the first time the following morning and it was there that my memory ran out on me that afternoon.

The short flight across the Cook Strait to Wellington for the Third Test Match delivered me up into the safe hands of Laurie Bryant – and his hands were considered to be so reliable that for three years he had been a courtier at Buckingham Palace where he had been assigned to the heir to the throne. He lives in both Wellington and Masterton and cuts a considerable figure in political and gourmandising circles, for he is nothing if not a *bon viveur*. Over the next few days South Africa's batsmen managed to leave their bowlers time to win the Third Test at the Basin Reserve. Then after a quick visit to Auckland to make a speech at a luncheon club, I returned to Wellington to pick up the pinot noir trail again under Laurie's direction. I was now in the Wairarapa where winemaking is at least as big an obsession as it is in Marlborough and we must have visited about six wineries, one of which was the home of Ata Rangi, run by Clive Paton, who paid me the compliment of naming one of his four huge steel wine tanks 'Blowers'. A black cat and a wine tank in the same week was not bad going. Laurie and I bought sundry bottles, six of which I managed successfully to transport all the way back to England in my large briefcase.

Some luncheon club talking and much serious imbibing later, I was back in Auckland and, on the eve of departure, was interviewed on a television show where I met for the last time that great New Zealand left-handed batsman, Martin Donnelly. He had made a double century in the Lord's Test Match in 1949, one day of which I watched with my parents. He lived in Australia and had been over to New Zealand to watch the Wellington Test Match and was the next to be interviewed. I was extremely lucky to run into him for he died only a few weeks later.

I had had a hectic three weeks and returned to London by way of Sydney and Frankfurt. I had felt as well as ever while in New Zealand and I spent the next two weeks in England getting on with *It's Just Not Cricket*. I spent both weekends in Norfolk and on the second one I set about giving the lawn in front of North Farm its first mow of the year. It usually took me about three hours with the cylinder mower but, after doing just over half of it, I felt absolutely whacked and retired hurt for the day. I had also felt some rather strange pains in the underside of my wrists which I put down to carrying a heavy mower down ten steps to cut another small piece of lawn. We returned as usual to London on the Sunday evening and on the Monday I had to make some radio commercials for Vodafone. I caught a bus to Piccadilly and walked to the studio just behind Carnaby Street.

On that walk my wrists again ached and throbbed, but I didn't give it much thought, made the commercials and walked back to Piccadilly to catch another bus home without ill effect. The following evening I had arranged to meet Bitten at six o'clock at the World's End Nurseries in the King's Road in Chelsea to try and sort out what to do with our little garden in London. James Lotery runs the establishment and is always ready to dispense liquid hospitality while giving advice. Our house is about ten minutes away. I walked through Westfield Park and was well into the King's Road when my chest suddenly began to tighten, not painfully but to the extent that I could hardly breathe and I was extremely lucky there was a seat on which I could plonk myself. I wondered what the hell had happened but after about three minutes all was back to normal and I set off again. I had just got over the traffic lights by Somerfields when my chest tightened once more. This time there was no seat and so I lent as best I could against a lamp post and after a minute or two the tightness went away. James's inner sanctum, with its disguised entrance at the end of a potting shed-cum-greenhouse full of plants, smells of a cocktail of greenhouses and geraniums and freshly watered peat with the odd dash of fertiliser and a good splash of brandy thrown in. I daresay it would have made Lady Chatterley and Mellors feel thoroughly at home. I told James what had happened and he put me in a chair and offered me some of the aforementioned brandy. I don't quite know why, but I refused it. I found it difficult to keep my mind on things when James discoursed on the advantages of trees rather than shrubs for the far end of our garden by the wooden fence.

Bitten arrived soon after six and reckoned, I suspect, that I was making a fuss about not very much and turned her attention to the horticultural problems. I waited and then she drove us home where we found Suki, who was having an early dinner with us, busily ringing the bell. When I told her what had happened she insisted I should ring up my doctor, Trevor Hudson. As we were only going to potter round the corner to the Chelsea Ram for dinner, I said that if it happened again on the way, I would go back at once and ring him. It did happen, about fifty yards before we got to the pub, and I went home and rang Trevor. He said immediately that it was angina and that I was a prime candidate for it. He told me to go straight to bed and not to get up until he rang me in the morning, unless I wanted to go to the loo. He then told Bitten to go at once to a chemist and buy some pills which I was to suck if I had the slightest suspicion that my chest was again tightening.

Bitten came back with the pills, I sucked a couple for good measure, had a plate of pasta before settling down for the night and slept extemely well. I visited the bathroom without ill effect too. My main worry was that the following day was Bitten's birthday and the year before I had been on my way to the Norfolk and Norwich Hospital with my knee. I had remembered to buy her birthday card but I was intending to buy her present the next morning and we had tickets for the new Abba musical that evening. Bitten had left for her office at about half past eight and at getting on for nine, I could bear it no longer and rang Trevor Hudson. All the arrangements had been made. I was booked into the Harley Street Clinic – thank heavens for medical insurance – under a cardiologist called John Muir. He would decide who would operate on me when he had found out what needed to be done. I rang Bitten who promised to come back and drive me to Weymouth Street, and flung a few clothes into a grip bag, but no pyjamas because I didn't have any, which later proved to be no more than a mild embarrassment. More to the point, I did manage to throw in half a dozen bottles of claret which were lurking in the kitchen, and a corkscrew.

I don't think the possible enormity of it all had hit me until the journey to the Harley Street Clinic. Bitten was being determinedly optimistic and kept telling me she was sure I would be out in no time and we would be able to enjoy Abba that evening. I was not so sure. Formalities took a long time at the clinic and it must have been close to lunchtime before I was taken upstairs in a wheelchair and climbed into bed in a rather poky little room. I was immediately given an ECG which did not prompt anyone to issue a May Day call. Endless heads poked round the door as the afternoon wore on and the first of them belonged to John Muir, my cardiologist. He told me that my ECG was not too bad and asked me to tell him exactly what had happened in the King's Road the evening before. He then told me that I was undoubtedly suffering from angina and he would be back the next morning to do an angiogram which would tell the full story. Then they would decide what was to come after that. I was told I could watch it all happening on a television monitor. I didn't like the sound of that at all. It seemed to be voyeurism gone mad.

During the evening they began to take ECGs thick and fast and before I turned in I was connected to a sort of permanent ECG machine so that the nurses could keep a close eye on me through the night by watching a monitor in their own room. I heard afterwards that my ECGs were deteriorating and I was getting closer to a heart attack. John Muir told me later that he didn't think it would have killed me, which I suppose was some consolation. I was not allowed breakfast the next morning as the nurses busied themselves about the place taking more ECGs and, before long, John Muir appeared and was clearly preparing to bowl the first over. I was skilfully shipped from my bed on to a trolley and we set off down the corridors which had as many right-angled bends as the Monaco Grand Prix circuit. I really can't remember what went through my mind at that time, although I know I was pretty nervous while doing my best not to show it. Our destination was just like a television studio with cameras and monitors everywhere. I was lifted off the trolley onto a sort of bed. All I could see was masses of machinery to my left, and in front of me a kind of opaque sheet of perspex from the other side of which rose John Muir, looking faintly ridiculous in a turquoise two-piece outfit with a white V neck which made him look like a high-ranking officer in a surrealist army.

He gave me a brief run through of what was going to happen, telling me that it would kick off with a slight prick to the groin which might be followed by a stinging sensation. I felt the prick but there was no stinging and nothing happened for a bit while the local anaesthetic was given time to work. Then it all got very exciting and I thought I could see from John's movements that he was feeding something into me. It was an uncanny sensation. Here they were feeding this pipe up from my groin to my heart and I could feel nothing. I kept thinking that I ought to be cringing with pain. I glanced upwards to my left and saw this animated black snake making excellent progress on its way to my heart. Then the cameras started to move backwards and forwards across the ceiling and when I looked back at the monitor I saw what looked like puffs of black smoke gushing from the mouth of the tapeworm which had been pushed up into my heart. Suddenly, I found it compelling viewing and couldn't take my eyes off it. There were some more puffs of smoke and then it was all over. The cameras stopped, John Muir reeled me in and I was wheeled back to my room while my cardiologist told me he was going off to have a look at the evidence. By the time I got back to bed I had decided that I wouldn't have missed any of it for the world. I had by now persuaded myself that I was going to have to have an angioplasty which is when they stick another tube up into your heart and blow up a small balloon at the end of it which is then pushed through the blockage and removes all the gunge. For all that, I was apprehensive about the next visit I would receive from John Muir.

It was not long before he was back in another immaculate Savile Row suit, clutching a wad of papers which was the photographic evidence and looking a trifle pensive, I thought. He showed me the pictures and tried to explain them to me. The main arteries to my heart were at the top of their form which was something. The problems lay elsewhere. There was one artery hardly any smaller than the big ones which was jammed solid and there were two smaller ones which were between sixty and seventy per cent blocked. He told me there were three possible options. The first was to do nothing and hope that the angina would not recur for a long time. My lifestyle effectively stood that one on its head. Only a soldier in the trenches at the battle of the Somme, who had been ordered to go over the top, would have grasped at those odds. It was not Muir's favoured option either. The second was an angioplasty, but he told me that I would have to have another within nine months at the latest which seemed to me a bit like being moved from the condemned cell into the hospital block because of toothache. The third was bypass surgery which, if successful, would guarantee me at least fifteen years before it would have to be done again. As far as I was concerned there was only one answer and I cheerfully submitted myself to it. John Muir left saying he would be back before long with Christopher Lincoln who would be sharpening his knives for an eight o'clock start in the morning.

RETIRED HURT

My surgeon and I had been up at Cambridge together, although we had not met. He was a couple of inches over six foot, ramrod straight and a trifle austere, with greying hair. He came in with a sister and I rather took to him, especially when he stopped in mid-sentence and said to the sister, pointing at the small table on which my six bottles of claret were resting, 'You see those bottles, Sister?' She said that she did and I thought, Oh dear, you win some and you lose some.

'Mr Blofeld can have those at any time he wants,' was his splendid response. Then, turning to me, he said, 'The full benefits of red wine with heart illness are not beginning to be understood.'

It had been a long time since I had had a much better conversation than that one and I had a couple of glasses before I swallowed my sleeping pills later that evening. I am sure they complemented one another. I had one slightly worrying moment when Christopher Lincoln unscrewed his fountain pen while telling me that there was a failure rate of one to two per cent, who presumably snuffed it, and that I would have to sign the usual disclaimer just in case anything went wrong. I started to read it but very soon I realised that it would extremely bad for my morale, so I signed with as much of a flourish as I could muster, grateful that I was going to be allowed a glass or two of claret.

That evening we had one of those bedside conferences which I think are probably best avoided. Bitten and Suki were both there, and my sister Anthea, who is a retired doctor, had come along to see me, as had our splendid GP, Trevor Hudson, who had masterminded everything so far. I think more or less everyone had glasses in their hands and there was a deafening reverberation of false bonhommie. Everyone agreed that it was such a simple operation and that, apart from a little discomfort, I would be up and about in no time at all and back at home the day after that.

I have to say that I did once find myself wondering if I would ever see any of them again, but the feeling didn't last for long. Bitten was the last to go and left with a cheerful, 'See you tomorrow.' That was the worst moment of all. Bitten told me much later that as she left me she had a horrid premonition that something was going to go badly wrong. I was now alone and there was nothing between me and it. I had P.G. Wodehouse's *Luck of the Bodkins* with me and I was immensely grateful for the few chuckles it gave me that evening – only PGW could have done that at such a moment – and by the time I put out my light I felt fine. They probably popped a tranquilliser or two into the impressive selection of pills I was given by way of a nightcap. Then suddenly it was six o'clock in the morning and a nurse appeared with two and a half white pills and a tiny amount of water with which to swallow them. She was back again an hour later with an injection and after that I can remember nothing, although my anaesthetist later told me we had quite a conversation before she finally slipped me the lead piping.

By then, it must have been getting on for eight o'clock on the Friday morning. I did not come to again until some time after lunch on the Sunday and I can only tell the story of what happened in the interim from what has been told to me. I'm still not quite sure I can piece it all together in the proper sequence and I have a nasty feeling that my rather vague and disjointed recollections of what I was told don't make any sort of medical sense. The operation was a success and I only needed a double bypass. While it was happening, I was taken off my own heart and put on to a heart/lung machine in the normal way. The problem was that I refused to come round from the anaesthetic and my own heart was reluctant to take over again. Bitten had arrived at lunchtime, when it had been generally felt I would be taking a renewed interest in life. Everyone at the hospital assured her that it was not unusual that I had not come round. When I had been operated on, apparently the top half of my body was frozen and Bitten told me that during the afternoon it began to convulse horribly, which can't have been much fun for her. As the day wore on I obstinately refused to return to this world and Bitten sensed they were all becoming more worried than they were prepared to admit. Just before she went home that evening, Trevor Hudson told her they would not now try to bring me round until the morning and everyone again did their best to assure her that there was nothing unusual about any of this. She naturally smelt a rat. When the telephone rang at half past three in the morning and it was a nurse at the Harley Street Clinic telling her to come round as quickly as she could because things were not going according to plan, it was even less fun. Bitten told me that she cannot remember getting dressed or even driving round to Weymouth Street.

When she arrived, the porter on the door told her she had to go and see Christopher Lincoln before she saw me. She was certain that was because he wanted to tell her that I had died. Can you imagine? The dark of the night, the drive, the gloom of the clinic and that disconcerting message; it must have been too dreadful for words. Lincoln wanted to see her first because they had had, in the emergency of the situation, to operate on me where I was in my bed in the intensive care unit. They did not want to risk the journey to the operating theatre. But they had not cleaned me up, there was still blood everywhere and they wanted to warn her of the mess. Bitten is not easily deterred and went straight to intensive care to see me and the bloody remains. Bitten first galvanised the nurses and then turned her attention to the doctors and surgeons who seemed to be resigned to the inevitable. She told them to get back and save me and, shamefacedly, I hope, they did just that.

John Muir told me later that the medics went into a huddle and that he felt I was short of liquid, so they decided to inject me with something. Once this had been done, my kidneys, which had been showing every sign of giving it up as a bad job, suddenly perked up no end and I began to pee which apparently was a triumph. My lungs were not at their sprightliest either, but they also began to feel that things were looking up. My blood pressure hereabouts had been lingering at 59 over 43 which in cricketing terms is a bit like finding yourself and your partner in the crease at the bowler's end and cover point's throw on the way to the wicket-keeper. As they watched now, it suddenly stole a quick single and rose to 60 over 43 which had everyone leaning forward in their seats. It was not long before another single was scored and soon it rose to the dizzy heights of 62. There is no doubt that I had been poised to hand in my dinner pail when the Almighty chose to lend me a helping hand.

Bitten had rung Suki during the night to warn her of the gloomy news. It must have been desperate for her as only the summer before she had watched her poor mother disintegrate with cancer of just about everything. Suki arrived at the clinic at breakfast time, just after Anthea and Anthony, my brother-in-law, had turned up. Anthony, a retired parson came equipped with a bottle of holy oil and proceeded to give me the last rites. These moments, however grim, have their humour and Anthony was a trifle loose with the oil as if I was a salad in dire need of dressing and Bitten told me that quite a lot of mopping up had to go on afterwards. While Anthony may have ensured that the Almighty was on the case, I have no doubt that it was Bitten, with her love and determination, who had made the difference when everything was at its most critical and that it was to her that I owed the most. I gathered over the following few days that what had happened was that while the sewing was going on, and I had been put on the heart/lung machine, although temporarily out of use, my heart had elected to go into heart-attack mode. By the time it was reconnected to my body and the sewing was complete, there was no method of reverse signalling. This was what I gleaned from those around me and is probably at best a wild over-simplification. I don't think anyone who knew really wanted to give me a blow-by-blow account of what had happened in those two days.

Surgeons I have met since have told me that the person I owe most to for my survival was my anaesthetist, Barbara Callum. She was the most delightful woman who always managed to introduce the human touch into an atmosphere of impersonal clinical efficiency and know-how. She was kindness itself. On that Saturday I was stable enough for Bitten and Suki and the others to feel that they could go out for a reasonable lunch without the likelihood of me giving the bucket the most imperial kick somewhere between the entree and the main course. On the other hand, those with whom I had taken out life insurance policies will still have been biting their nails. At dinner, I daresay muted sounds of revelry were permitted and when Bitten arrived at the clinic on Sunday, she met Barbara Callum on the stairs who told her that I was beginning to show signs of regaining consciousness.

It was not until after lunch on Sunday that I returned properly to life, although I had begun to take a mild interest in things during the morning. My own first awareness of anything came in a horrible way. I can remember a dark grey window appearing in my world of blackness. I had obviously just come round briefly, but I was unable to speak and I could not open my eyes. I discovered later that I was on a ventilator and there was a large tube going down my throat which had effectively neutralised my larynx. The greyness came from whatever light was able to penetrate my closed eyelids. I could hear Bitten's voice asking me how I was and then she told me that Rex was there. Rex Neame had driven up from Norfolk which was way beyond the call of duty. Bitten then asked me if I was in pain and the best I could do was to nod vigorously because my chest hurt like hell. Then I was asked by someone else, probably a nurse, where it hurt and I moved my hands up towards my chest. I was then injected with a further supply of morphine and I remember the delicious feeling as a blanket of warmth and comfort swept over me, knocking the pain on the head and leaving me feeling that I was sinking blissfully into a mass of velvet.

This happened two or three more times as the Sunday morning wore on. On one occasion Bitten told me that her sister, Wiveca, who is a doctor, had arrived from Sweden. Still I could not speak or open my eyes and these windows always ended the same way, with me being asked if I was in pain. Each time I nodded and pointed to my chest and the morphine followed. Once I indicated that I wanted to write something down and a pen was put in my hand but I was unable to control it. In these brief and frustrating sessions of consciousness I heard all too clearly how frantic Bitten sounded. I desperately wanted to tell her that all was well and she was not to worry and I just needed time. In my befuddled state I tried to do this by pushing her away because in my mind, such as it was, I thought I was telling her not to fuss and that I was all right. Instead, it sent out exactly the opposite message and she thought I was telling her to go away. It was not until later that I realised what I had done. I woke up properly that afternoon and I remember John Muir telling me what a desperate time Bitten had had but, of course, I did not then realise what a close run thing it had been.

When I was taken out of intensive care and returned to a normal room, I had lots of time over the next four weeks to reflect. I found myself thinking back to the bicycle accident at Eton almost forty-two years before. My urge to get back into life then came, I suppose, from the natural exuberance of youth when everything lies ahead and it is one's instinct not to start looking backwards or inwards. Now I was just as keen to get on. I knew I would be out of action for the World Cup which was taking place in May and June, but I was determined to be back in front of the microphone for the Test series against New Zealand which began on 1 July. When I told people of my hopes, they thought I was mad, but that was always my goal and I am sure that my determination to make that date helped the speed of my recovery. There was no point whatever in feeling sorry for myself – there seldom is. I grew irritated at having to remain so long in hospital and angry when it was clear that the scar on my chest had gone sceptic and that I would have to have another operation. Bitten, too, was beside herself at the prospect, but although it meant another five or six hours under anaesthetic, it went off without a hitch and my wound was cleaned up and the screws in my sternum were tightened. Six days later I was allowed out of hospital, although I had to stay in London until my stitches had been removed and John Muir had given me another ECG – which he still does every six months.

In the Harley Street Clinic I soon became extremely bored. My chest hurt like hell, it was a hot early summer, I had to spend the Bank Holiday weekend in captivity, the food was pretty ghastly and monotonously the same. The poor physiotherapist, who harrassed me to take exercise each day which involved the excitement of walking the corridors and up and down one flight of stairs, got it in the neck. I suppose it may have been a sign that I was getting better, but I am ashamed to say I began to show zero tolerance. What I longed for more than anything else in the world was to be back at North Farm and to be allowed to take the dogs for a walk up the North Farm Loke to the Belt and back again; not far, I admit, for it is a round trip of less than a third of a mile, but the idea was heaven. I longed to hear Holly bark which, like most

Cocker Spaniels, she does unceasingly. She is a dear dog but with nothing much between the ears. Bubbles who was then six and a half and beginning to go grey, was already very much the matriarch. She had had' no less than eleven puppies five days before her sixth birthday, all of whom had survived with something of a flourish. Bubbles expected favoured treatment and she got it. Then there were the babies, Saffron and Alice, the two of the litter we had kept. Alice, with her white patch on her chest, was a nervous child but was steadying down as womanhood approached, and Saffron, the bigger of the two, was rangy and had an impressive degree of obstinacy which simply meant that, while she was not wholly averse to doing what she was told, she very much preferred to do it in her own time. I missed them all irretrievably while I was in hospital; and there was Rumple, too, who for all his handicaps is the dearest of chaps and the greatest of friends.

The great day came and Bitten drove me back to North Farm where I began to mend fairly rapidly. The North Farm Loke was every bit as therapeutic as I knew it would be with the dogs in close attendance. Then, on 1 July, less than two and a half months after that first highly eventful operation, I was in my position in the commentary box at Edgbaston for the First Test against New Zealand. England won that one when Alex Tudor made an extraordinary 99 not out in the fourth innings. After that the series was lost and England never once scored as many as 200 in the first innings which was, more than anything, the reason for the defeat. I like to think my commentary in that First Test at Edgbaston did not sound too bad and I can't tell you how wonderful it was to be back – for that match and for the rest of the series too.

I have no doubt that this whole experience has changed my thinking about a number of things. I am sure that I am much more aware of life than I was and I am certain that I enjoy it more. We none of us have a clue when its going to end but an experience like this has made me sharply conscious of the fact that it is going to do so and that therefore the maximum must be extracted from every day. All my life I have been terrified of the thought of dying and the thought that I, like everyone else, have in the fullness of time to go through it, has never been that far away. How will it happen and what then are the unanswerable questions. But after all of this, I find I am no longer afraid of the prospect of dying. I don't know if I can remember anything from the time I was deeply unconscious or maybe my mind is playing tricks on me. I am nonetheless convinced that when the time comes it will be both a relief and a release, more of a welcoming home than a full stop. Having crawled out of the end of my own particular tunnel, my mind tells me that I was not approaching the end of anything. Of course, there is no evidence and there never has been. The cynics have said to me that that is what morphine does to you. When I returned to the commentary box, Michael Holding, who has also been though a life-threatening experience, strongly advanced the case of the morphine syndrome. But when the time comes, either God will be at the end of the tunnel or he won't. From all I went through, my belief that he will be there was strengthened. I don't believe my survival was just a piece of good luck.

While all of this was going on, there were two indirect assaults on my life. While I was recovering in the Harley Street Clinic, the news broke that TalkRadio, the brainchild of the redoubtable Kelvin Mackenzie who, in cricket matters, has the sterling advice of none other than Geoffrey Boycott to aid and comfort him, had bought the radio commentary rights for England's series in South Africa the following winter. *Test Match Special* had a serious competitor. Peter Baxter and Jonathan Agnew came to visit me and told me some of the gory details. I had already gathered that Mackenzie appeared to have done a deal with Ali Bacher behind the back of the BBC who were not allowed the chance to make a bid. Mackenzie had paid £150,000 which would have disappeared the moment any competitors were alerted. They later bought the rights for England's tour of Pakistan in 2000/01 and, although not everything went the way of Mackenzie and Boycott, it was worrying for us at the time. The other setback came when I had returned to North Farm to convalesce. The unstoppable Ivo Tennant of *The Times* rang me up to tell me that he was writing my obituary and wanted to talk to one of my family about me. I felt the great obituarist's timing was, to say the least, mildly awry. I'm still wondering what he wrote.

As far as the future is concerned I now know more than ever that the joker is going to come up in the other bloke's hand one day. But meanwhile I have been given a bonus and intend to enjoy it all to the maximum. I have no intention of forgetting that red wine is good for the heart and, within reason, I intend to carry on as before. If I gave this up and cut that out and had only a little of this, I would be an even bigger bore than I am already. There is surely no future in being mealy mouthed about it all. Much better look it straight in the eyes. I just keep my fingers crossed that when the time comes, it is swift and decisive and not lingering and beastly. But I am sure that when we get there in the end, whatever the means, there will be a big welcome waiting for us all.

CHAPTER 25

DRAWING STUMPS

I DROVE FROM NORTH FARM to Brockencote Hall where the *Test Match Special* team stay for the Test Matches at Edgbaston and I don't think I have ever enjoyed a journey more. I was going to see my friends again and I was about to return to *TMS* which I have enjoyed far more than anything else I have done in my life. I knew only too well how desperately lucky I had been to survive those ghastly operations and their unhappy aftermath. I had suffered the agonies of listening to the World Cup which was played in England in 1999 while I was marooned in Norfolk, unfit to participate. When I was in hospital, Jonathan Agnew had asked me if I would like to do a piece on the telephone for his weekly cricket programme on Radio Five Live and I turned him down as I didn't feel I was ready for it. As the World Cup drew towards its finish Peter Baxter asked me if I would be prepared to talk to him on the telephone during the break between innings at a match being played at Trent Bridge. I couldn't resist it and we had a spirited chat for about five minutes and it gave me the taste for it all over again.

As I drove the two hundred miles that afternoon my mind galloped all over the place. I remembered that drive to Gravesend all those years ago to cover my first game for *The Times*. I spent a short time in Ady's Rolls throwing the boxes of matches to the children by the side of the road in Afghanistan. Then there were the lies I had told Alan Richards at the Courtleigh Manor in Jamaica which had got me started as a commentator. There were the days I had kept wicket for Norfolk with Bill Edrich at first slip when the conversation flowed effortlessly from first ball to last. I remember very clearly when I scored some hectic runs at the start of our second innings against Suffolk the year we won the championship. When I was out, Bill met me at the front of the pavilion at Lakenham and gave me my county cap. My mind now was everywhere but on the road, although I arrived at Brockencote Hall in one piece. After I had unpacked, I went down and drank a glass of wine in the lovely evening sunshine on the terrace which looks over a broad pasture to a tall hedge. This hides the Chaddesley Corbett Cricket Club and muffled appeals told of a game in progress.

I had been there for about ten minutes when the glass door behind me to my right was pushed open and standing there was 'Foxy' Fowler who was one of our three comments men for the Test Match. I greeted him but for a few seconds he just stood there and then without saying anything, walked slowly down the steps and over to me. He enveloped me in a colossal bear hug. Still he said nothing and he told me later that he was too choked to speak. I can't think of any other moment after I had left hospital which affected me as much as this. Foxy has always been a great man to work with and a true friend, but I don't think it was until that moment that I realised quite what friendship meant.

The whole summer was the most wonderful voyage of discovery. I now realised that there was so much in life which I had taken for granted for such a long time. I had got to the point where I had not seen things which had been in front of my eyes. Now I found myself taking everything in and I was anxious not to miss anything. Everywhere I went, people were pleased to see me and it was tremendously touching to see how concerned they were about me. I also received a great number of letters welcoming me back to the air waves. When I woke up on the first morning of the match, there were butterflies all over the place in my tummy. If, after all the hoo-ha, I made the most fearful mess of it all, it would be too awful. But once I set off at the start of my first spell, it was as if I had never been away. It all came flooding back to me and dear old Vic Marks had remembered to wear one of those lovely check shirts of his which had not been ironed since Queen Victoria was on the throne. It really made me feel at home. In the end I did all four of the Tests for *TMS*, as Brian Waddle, the New Zealand commentator, had been called home after the World Cup and Radio New Zealand had then decided not to send him back for the Test Matches. As New Zealand won the series with some ease, it was perhaps not the best decision ever made but I had no complaints.

Edgbaston always brings back ghosts from the past for it was there that I had made my second appearance for *TMS*. In 1972 England played the first series of one-day matches in England, against Australia, and I had been asked by Michael Tuke-Hastings, Peter Baxter's predecessor as the cricket producer at the BBC, to commentate on the matches at Lord's and Edgbaston. The old commentary box is bigger than it is today, although the path to reach it, over wooden planks on the pavilion roof, was more precarious than the flight of stairs we now have to climb. This match was the only occasion I shared a commentary box with Alan Gibson, a brilliant commentator and a most amusing and entertaining man. I came to know him well later on when he wrote his delightful and highly idiosyncratic accounts of county matches for *The Times*. On that first occasion he kept his distance and was probably justifiably suspicious of new young commentators. It was Alan and Jack Fingleton, who on his day could be decidedly crotchety and was always smilingly cynical, who became involved in that discussion about what made a cricket ball swing. It ended up with me being ticked off by Jim Swanton for daring to mention my own cricket in the company of Test cricketers. I can still hear his opening words, 'Now, young Henry'. Jim coming into the commentary box to do his summary at the end of the day was like an old galleon in full sail. He needed plenty of room to manoeuvre. John Arlott was extremely kind to me in both games and concerned that I should not feel nervous or left out. I shall never know how I came through it for I was certain I must have sounded dreadful in comparison to the others. It was frightening to have to try and compete. Whenever I visit Edgbaston, this far-off day always comes back to haunt me.

I don't remember ever enjoying anything as much as the next two and a half months. I had made the firm decision not to write and broadcast on the same day so that I did not immediately put myself back under too much pressure. I felt fine but sudden twinges of pain in my chest were constant reminders that I had just spent getting on for sixty hours under anaesthetic and a fair amount of chopping and cutting and sawing had gone on, to say nothing of the sewing. I was pursued too, by rattling pill boxes for I had to take two pills every morning and two more before I went to bed. At first I had to go and see John Muir every three months after having a blood test to discover how my cholesterol was coming along. He always gave me an ECG and soon told me that the operation and recovery could not have gone better. The job now was to stop it happening all over again. I was told to take off some weight and to take more exercise.

In the Second Test Match, New Zealand beat England for the first time at Lord's and, although we did not know it then, this was the last Test Match for which Fred Trueman was with us as a summariser. He had been a regular since 1974 and I had always enjoyed commentating with him as long as he did not spend too much time on some of his pet hobby horses such as Geoffrey Boycott and the administration of Yorkshire's cricket. For those like Fred and Trevor Bailey who used to play for England in the days when they won a great many Test Matches, the present standards were unacceptable. Fred was nothing if not forthright in his comments. I always thought he was at his best when you steered him back down memory lane and he would start talking about Test Matches and tours in the fifties when it was a very different game. But Bob Shennan, the head of sport at the BBC, decided that the time had come for both Fred and Trevor, who began in 1967 and whom I also miss, to be put out to grass. I am sure the challenge of TalkRadio had something to do with this, as well as the need to appeal to younger listeners who will not have been born when Fred and Trevor retired from the game. It was a pity there was not a dinner to mark the ending of this particular era. The *TMS* box will never be quite the same again without Fred's pipe and Trevor's succinct, penetrating and dismissive comments on new players of, 'Can't bowl', or 'Can't bat'. This Lord's Test Match was the first time I had commentated from the amazing new media centre at the Nursery End which looks more than anything like a space ship. It was much better than I had feared but I would still far rather have been back in the left-hand turret of the Pavilion where we had been for so long that we had become part of the fabric of the place. But having said that, it made sense to have all the media under one roof, rather than for them to be scattered around as they had been.

For me, there is no more evocative cricket ground in the world than Lord's. As I looked out now from the Nursery End facing the Pavilion, I found myself taking everything in as I not done for years. Of course my mind went back to my first Eton and Harrow match at the age of fifteen when we had driven though the Grace Gates in General Burrows's Rolls-Royce with ink still on our fingers, I should think. There was that dreadful moment when I was unknowingly the third victim of Rex Neame's hat-trick in the same match. It is my eternal penance that he should now live in the Home Farm where I was born. We both have photographs of that ball which I had elected to try and play from two yards down the pitch. They are prominently displayed in both our houses. I tell him I have mine to show that I am not proud. Then there were the two hundreds I made at Lord's on pitches on the Grandstand side of the ground. The thrill of walking off and daring to raise my bat in appreciation of the applause will give heaven something to live up to. Fielding while Denis Compton made 71 against Cambridge in the match when I scored my only first-class hundred, was just as memorable.

Another innings which always returns when I look back reflectively at Lord's is the amazing, almost contemptuous, strokeplay of Ted Dexter when he made 70 in eighty-one minutes against the West Indies, Wes Hall, Charlie Griffith, Gary Sobers and all, in 1963. If James Bond had played cricket he would have batted as Ted did that day. Three years before, in 1960, I had settled down in the Grandstand with Joanna, Suki's mother, to watch the third day's play in the Test against South Africa. We were engaged and I was trying to break her in to cricket. Brian Statham who took eleven wickets in the match, destroyed the South Africans in their first innings. When he had got rid of Jackie McGlew at the start, Joanna glanced at her engagement ring and saw that one of the stones was missing. We had, there and then, to go to South Molton Street, off Oxford Street where the jewellers lived and when we got back to Lord's the innings was almost all over, on a day that Statham took 6/53. This was the match when Geoff Griffin, one of South Africa's opening bowlers, was no-balled out of the game for throwing, having just become the first bowler ever to take a hat-trick in a Test Match at Lord's. The next time I came across Griffin was at Kingsmead in Durban when South Africa were playing Australia in 1969/70 and he was running a bar called the Bent Arm Inn. Years later at Lord's there was Gooch's 333 against India and I was on the air when he reached 300 and I came out with that unfortunate spoonerism. Then, of course, there was that one-day international back in 1972 which was the only time I used the old commentary box in the Warner Stand. I was terrified throughout and cannot remember much about the day. At the end of the match I do remember receiving the ultimate accolade from Jack Fingleton. He put his hand on my shoulder and said, 'You'll do for me, Blofeld, whatever Swanton may say.'

The drive to Manchester for the Third Test was almost as exciting as the one to Edgbaston for the first. I remembered all too clearly my first drive up to the Swan at Bucklow Hill, where the *TMS* team used to stay, the day before my first Test Match commentary in England. I can remember how nervous I was on that drive and the agonies of the next five days and all that laughter with Brian Johnston. The old commentary box has long since gone. It was there that I had that difference of opinion with Alan McGilvray in 1981. I was reminded now of the story which was told to me by that great South African fast bowler, Neil Adcock, many years later when he was living in Australia. In the Test Match in 1955 Denis Compton had made 158 and 71 with a borrowed bat. In the second innings, Neil told me, he had bowled three identical balls in succession to Denis. They had all pitched just outside the off stump on a length. The first hit the boundary just behind square on the off side. The second disappeared first bounce into the crowd at deep mid-wicket and the third went to the rails over extra cover's head. It was all done with the twelfth man, Fred Titmus's bat. Denis who turned absent-mindedness into an art form, had forgotten to bring his own with him. A year later, of course, Jim Laker took a small matter of nineteen wickets for 90 against Australia, in a match which is still deeply implanted in the Australian psyche.

Rain saved England at Old Trafford in 1999 and we came to the Oval at one-all. England's batting was as dreadful as ever and New Zealand won in under three and a half days. The Oval is a friendly ground with less outward formality than Lord's and more of a homespun atmosphere. After coming though the Hobbs Gates, where for years the gatemen regarded potential entrants more as intruders than spectators, and well before I had seen a blade of grass, I was always stopped by Eric Budd. He ran the bookshop at the Oval until the end of the 1999 season and he is the most delightful of men. We always had a good old gossip. After that, it's up to the new media centre by the slowest lift in the world. When I first went to the Oval in 1962 it was nothing like it is today. The cold, draughty and uncomfortable press box was at third man and it was from there that I was lucky enough to see the last of Peter May's strokeplay and to withstand the occasional invective from Lyn Wellings whose every utterance from the front row was pithy. May retired, much too young, in the early sixties, leaving us all with the memory of a cover drive which was an exceptional work of art. The Oval was the home of Lock, Laker and Loader and it was here that the County Championship found a home for seven years from 1952–58. Zaheer Abbas for Pakistan in 1974, Viv Richards two years later for the West Indies, David Gower and Graham Gooch against Australia in 1985 have provided some of the exhibitions of strokeplay that went through my mind during this Test against New Zealand. The pitch, under the learned supervision of Harry Brind, had been the best in the country for some years, and now his son, Paul, carries on the good work. It was in the Oval commentary box in

1976 that Brian Johnston had informed the world that, 'The bowler's Holding, the batsman's Willey.' Fifteen years later in a newer commentary box, he and Jonathan Agnew were summing up the day's play when Aggers, in describing Ian Botham's dismissal when he trod on his wicket, said, 'And then Botham failed to get his leg over.' At which point Brian began to subside into a fit of the giggles which went on and on and on. It must have been the most hysterical moment *TMS* has ever known and as funny as anything that could ever have been broadcast.

Soon after the end of the 1999 cricket season, on 23 September, I was sixty. It is fair to say that I was the only surprise guest at my own birthday party. I asked sixty friends and almost all the stages of my life were represented: family, nursery and lessons at the Home Farm, Sunningdale, Eton and Cambridge and then my journalistic and broadcasting careers and of course Trevor Hudson who had helped pull me back from the brink that April. We had dinner and danced in Bitten's splendid offices in Dover Street which had not long before been given a serious facelift – for the greater good of her firm, not my birthday party. This was another evening of memories about all those who were present and about others who were unable to make it for the simple reason they were dead. One of my oldest friends, Jane Seymour, who now lives in the lovely gabled house in east Norfolk which had been the home of that well-known landscape painter, Ted Seago, had bravely made the journey to London. She and I had virtually shared the same pram and had done lessons together under the eagle eye of Mrs Hales. We were talking about my mother and father when she told me a splendid story about my mother I had not heard before and which had been handed down to Jane by her own mother.

At a dinner party at Hoveton, one of the guests was a neighbouring God botherer called Bill Batt who today would probably have been called a born-again Christian. In the drawing room after dinner he was banging on about the Bible when he noticed that my mother, who had almost had enough of it, was allowing her concentration to wander. He lent forward in his chair and said in the sort of voice used to call meetings to order, 'Surely Grizel, you believe in Our Lord Jesus Christ?'

'Not in the drawing room after dinner,' came the withering reply in a voice which had a good deal of emphasis.

You can see why I loved her so much and she would have enjoyed that evening in Dover Street. So would my father, although he would have come up to London under protest. Once he had arrived, he would have beguiled all and sundry with his charm as he fiddled with his eye glass. In his later years he cut a faintly piratical figure with a black patch over his right eye because of a detached retina which had refused to be put back into place. I would have loved Brian Johnston to have been there, too, and volleys of raucous laughter would have followed him round the room. As far as I was concerned, Johnners never changed. The only time I ever saw him when he was less than ebullient was occasionally in restaurants, for he was nothing if not a fastidious eater. Three of his pet hates were garlic, nouvelle cuisine and what he called fancy sauces. He liked simple, traditional fare. Peter Baxter and I were talking about him during the party and he told me that Johnners had once said to him that his idea of a perfect evening at home was to eat steak and kidney pie on a tray in front of the television while watching *Dad's Army*. I well remember the awful time he had on his first-ever visit to India when he was on the verge of eighty. The idea of eating curry was too awful for words and, like Dickie Bird when he was umpiring on the subcontinent, he ate a huge number of boiled eggs. He did not much care for foreign food and even trod a very suspicious path when confronted by the delights of a French menu. He was abstemious, too, although he could be tempted by white wine from the Loire and eventually by white burgundy.

It always takes a great deal of arm-twisting to persuade Johnny Woodcock, who Alan Gibson always described in *The Times* as the Sage of Longparish, to appear on these occasions. It was only when I promised him that he would not have to dance that he decided to venture north. He, of course, was the chap who started the whole business when we met at that party in the Hyde Park Hotel for the Arabs back in 1962. It was right that he should be there now for he had an awful lot to answer for. I have had more fun with Johnny than anyone else I have known in all my years with cricket. We've flown around the world together on any number of occasions, as well as making our way from London to Bombay by car. What an adventure that was. In a quiet way, Johnny has a wonderful sense of humour, although there were occasions, too, when the iron could enter into his soul. We were in Georgetown, Guyana for the Fifth Test Match in 1967/68 and when Gary Sobers came in to bat on the first day, it was not long before he played back to a ball from John Snow which hit him just above the ankle when he was standing in front of middle stump. Umpire Cecil Kippins, a Guyanese, gave him not out and he went on to make 150. Johnny wrote in *The Times* that 'whatever infinitesimal amount of doubt there was in umpire Kippins's mind, he gave unerringly to the batsman.' The airmail edition of *The Times* arrived two days later. When the England manager, Les Ames, visited the press box later the same day, Jim Swanton who was sitting in front of Woodcock, turned round and took Johnny's copy and handed it to Les Ames saying, 'In your day, Les, responsible journalists did not make imputations of this sort.'

While Les was reading, Johnny suddenly realised what had happened. He lent forward and snatched the paper out of Les's hands, saying in a loud voice as he did so, 'There are many people in this life who think you are a shit, Swanton, and as from now you can count me amongst them.'

There were no two greater friends in the press box than Swanton and Woodcock and it was not long before they were laughing about what had happened. A fund of good stories were told about Jim who was a huge man, and it was once remarked of him, by whom, I am not sure, 'What an uncomfortable life he must lead, sitting on the fence with his ear close to the ground.' I rather suspect that Jim was happy with Oscar Wilde's dictum that the only thing in life worse than being talked about, is not being talked about.

The autumn swept into winter by which time I was the proud possessor of my first Senior Railcard. When I found out how much money it saved me, it helped me to forget about my age. The autumn at Hoveton was lovely and as I looked out at those glorious russets and yellows in King's Wood, just a field away, I realised again how lucky I was that I was still around to see it all. Autumn may not give off the same feelings of hope which appear at the start of the year from the time of the first snowdrop and continue at an ever-increasing speed until sometime in May when summer takes over from spring. But it has a wonderful rounded mellowness all of its own which becomes more overwhelming each year, no matter how often you have seen it before. Then come the winds and the final shaking of the branches and winter has arrived, as those leaves, no longer so beautiful on the ground, linger to block up drains and blow about the garden. Perhaps it is all a touch too symbolic.

The leaves had almost gone by the time I boarded a huge aeroplane for Johannesburg to watch the first two Tests between South Africa and England. South Africa cannot be a happy country. Of course, the hideous days of apartheid are over but the yawning gap between expectation and fulfilment remains and with Mugabe getting up to his tricks in Zimbabwe, there can only be a distinct unease in South Africa. The First Test was in Johannesburg where murder is nowadays so commonplace that we all stay twenty miles away in the sanitised comfort of the Sandton Sun where, with all the shopping complexes and restaurants, it is more than possible to live for days without ever seeing the sky. The pitch was much too wet on the first day. England lost the toss, were put in and were beaten by a distance, the urge to fight not always being apparent. Bitten joined me the day after the match ended and we drove seven hundred kilometres from Johannesburg almost to Tzaneen in Northern Transvaal where we spent three days at the Coach House, a coaching inn made famous by John Buchan who had stayed on the same property a hundred years before. It was this part of the world in which he set the third of his Richard Hannay books, *Prester John*. The veldt was wonderful and vast, empty and irresistible.

After three nights at the Coach House we drove down to the Mala Mala game reserve on the edge of the Kruger Park. We started off at Harry's Camp and then moved up the road to the Main Camp, spending seven nights there in all. It was the best holiday we had ever had together. It was incredible to be able to see so much wildlife at such close quarters. We started off in the Land Rovers at six o'clock in the morning, coming back to camp after four hours for a late breakfast. Then we were off again at four o'clock in the afternoon for another four hours. We saw lions, cheetahs, leopards, elephants, rhinos, hippos, crocodiles and a great many other wonderful animals besides perhaps no more than ten yards from our vehicle and not in the least perturbed. They have grown used to the Land Rovers and have come to realise that they are not a threat to them. We had one experience which promised to be more interesting than it actually turned out to be when an irascible female elephant felt we were encroaching too much. With her ears waving and much roaring she came after us at quite a pace but Ralph, our splendid ranger, was quick on the accelerator and we were away. The vehicles were extraordinary and able to drive through swamps, up steep banks and through almost anything. The camps were superbly appointed and it was almost uncanny to be living deep in the bush in such remarkable luxury.

After that wonderful week, Bitten returned to London and I went down to Port Elizabeth where the players and press were billeted in a supremely uncomfortable hotel. The rooms were basic, there was no dining room, and breakfast was the only meal they served. England survived this Test Match and then I flew home to prepare for Christmas and the New Year. The England side moved on to Durban where they might have won the Third Test Match, but they were hopelessly beaten at Cape Town. Then followed the final match at Centurion Park near Pretoria when the two captains, Nasser Hussain and Hansie Cronje, agreed to forfeit an innings. England were left to chase 249 in 76 overs on the last day and won by two wickets with five balls left. At the time, the move seemed as refreshing and enterprising as it was unexpected. Cronje was the last person in the world I would have expected to give England a ghost of a chance of pulling back a match so that they only lost the series by two matches to one.

Alas, we all now know that Cronje accepted money to ensure that this match had a definite result. We know, on his own evidence to the King Commission in Cape Town, that he had been receiving money from the bookmaking fraternity for at least five years. His statement of guilt has implicated other players in other countries and enquiries look like going on for quite a while. The Pakistanis have long been under suspicion for match-fixing, but the Qayyum Commission, set up in Lahore to find out the truth, seems in the end to have pulled its punches. The illegal bookmakers of Bombay appear to have been the driving force in all this and it would be surprising if none of the Indian players were involved. We know that while they were in Sri Lanka, Mark Waugh and Shane Warne took money from Indian bookies for supplying information about the team, the pitch and the weather. This has thrown the cricket world into complete turmoil for no one can be sure how far it all goes. There is a strong belief that some administrators may be involved and that the deals fixed with those who buy the television rights may not bear close examination. Goodness knows where it is all going to end and what the eventual damage to cricket may be.

Conclusive proof of match-fixing is hard to come by, but circumstantial evidence would seem to be pretty strong. It may be, though, that the self-interest of some countries will prevent the truth from ever coming out. There are a lot of people out there who know much more than they have been prepared to tell. When the Indian police, looking for drug dealers, stumbled on Cronje's telephone conversations with the forces of evil, they will have had no idea of the ramifications of their discovery. I have never come directly into contact with match-fixing and bribery and at the moment I cannot begin to tell how it has affected the cricket I have watched in recent years. The thought that I may have been watching close and exciting finishes which had already been arranged by the unscrupulous is too awful. I have shown how England's stirring victory over South Africa at Leeds in 1998 is under suspicion. If cricket cannot again become a sport which is above suspicion, there is no point in playing it. It would be better then if it was adapted for the green baize of the casino for that is where it would belong.

In blissful ignorance of most of this, I had to clear the decks at North Farm in the new year and start writing this book with the animated assistance of Rumple, Bubbles, Holly, Saffron and Alice and, of course, Bitten at the weekends when she was freed from taking Erco Lighting to new frontiers. It was still not a year since my prolonged visit to the Harley Street Clinic but already life was tasting better than ever and long may it continue, even if my weight obstinately refused to budge. By then we had heard that TalkRadio had paid the Australian Cricket Board half a million pounds for the radio rights for England's next tour of Australia in 2002/03. Kelvin Mackenzie, backed by Rupert Murdoch's money, was becoming a serious player and *TMS* was going to be under increasing pressure.

I had to wait three months for the best New Year's present of all. Two weeks before it arrived, the BBC had been asked by the England Cricket Board to pitch for the radio rights for all international and county cricket in England. At nine o'clock on 1 March, I foregathered with a good many others in the Council Chamber at Broadcasting House. Led by Greg Dyke, the new Director General who was most impressive, the BBC put on a really good show. TalkRadio, which had been translated into TalkSport, were mounting fierce opposition and they also made their pitch. Kelvin Mackenzie had let it be known that they were prepared to bid half as much again as anything the BBC offered. Negotiations must have continued apace during the intervening two weeks and I believe the BBC had to raise their initial bid. I had come up to London for a couple of days by kind permission of my Senior Railcard and had caught a number eleven bus from Liverpool Street Station to the outer reaches of Chelsea. I was on the top deck which is so much more fun than it is downstairs, and we were in a traffic jam by the Grosvenor Hotel at Victoria Station when my mobile telephone rang. It was Shilpa Patel, *TMS*'s assistant producer.

'Blowers,' she shouted in my ear, 'we've won. *TMS* have got the rights for all home cricket for another five years.' There could not be a better way than that to end this particular story.

INDEX

Abid Ali 106
Abrihim (in Teheran) 142–3
Adams, Jimmy 356
Adcock, Neil 393
Adelaide
 ground (Oval) 179–80, 361–2
 rest days in 116–17
 Tests 308
'Ady' see Liddell, Adrian
Afghanistan 144–8
Agnew, Jonathan ('Aggers') 341, 386, 388, 395
Ainsworth, Mike 37, 38
Air India (HB's sponsor) 131
Alan Pascoe and Associates 323
Alderman, Terry 233, 235, 308
'Alderman, The' see Mosey, Don
Aldridge, Tony 305
Alexander, Bob 167–8
Ali Naqui 338
Allan, David 81
Allen, Gubby 19, 155
Alley, Bill 62, 124
Altham, Harry 30
Ambrose, Curtly 316, 356
Ames, Les 83, 196, 217, 397
Amiss, Dennis 111, 114, 116, 117, 153, 159
Ankara 136–7
Antigua 86, 224, 226
apartheid 88, 94, 118, 312, 316
Arabs 55, 60, 79, 80–2
Argentina 197–8
Arlott, John
 and B. Johnston 219, 220
 Bill Edrich plays prank on 157
 and HB 101, 104, 105, 109–10, 191, 218–20

last commentary 218–19
mastery of language 106–7, 119
poem on E.W. Swanton 102
reluctance to believe Packer story 162–3
and TMS team 120
Armstrong, Warwick 40
Arshed Gilani ('The Commander') 317–18, 324, 325, 338, 368–9
Ashes see England v Australia (except 1976/77, 1979/80, 1980, 1987/88)
Ashraf the Elder 253, 254, 255
Ashraf the Younger 255, 256–7
Asif Iqbal 325
Atherton, Mike 341, 343–4, 347, 356, 365
Austin, Richard 182, 183
Australia
 v England
  (1932/33) Bodyline tour 125, 361
  (1948) 19–21
  (1956) 394
  (1968) 87–8
  (1972) 110
  (1974/75) 110–18
  (1975) 119
  (1976/77) Centenary Test (Melbourne) 125, 156–60
  (1977) 166–7, 230
  (1978/79) 190, 192–5
  (1979/80) 200, 201, 202–3
  (1980) Centenary Test (Lord's) 218–19, 220
  (1981) 231–5
  (1982/83) 241–3

403

Australia – *cont.*
  v England – *cont.*
    (1985) 269
    (1986/87) 276–7
    (1987/88) Bicentennial
      Test 289, 290
    (1989) 300
    (1990/91) 308
    (1997) 337
    (1998/99) 357–70
  v India
    (1977/78) 169, 173, 179–80
    (1980/81) 221
  v NZ
    (1980/81) 221
    (1987/88) 288–9
  v Pakistan, (1983/84) 249–50
  v South Africa, (1969/70) 93–4
  v Sri Lanka, (1987/88) 292
  v WI
    (1960) (first ever Test) 356
    (1968/69) 89–91
    (1975/76) 121–3
    (1977/78) 181–3, 185
    (1979/80) 200, 203
    (1984/85) 265–6
  World Cup
    (1975) runners-up 118–19
    (1983) 247
    (1987/88) winners 282, 285,
      286
  limited-over matches
    (1980/81) 221
    (1982/83) 243
    (1987/88) 292
  Super Test sides 173, 178, 179
  other matches 163, 172
The Australian 191–2, 235, 277, 361
Australian Cricket Board 268
  and I. Chappell's suspension 202
  and Lillee's aluminium bat 202
  and match-fixing cover-up 361–2
  and Packer 161, 190, 199–203
  post-Packer confusion 235–6,
    243
  sells rights to TalkRadio 401
Australian radio 190, 235, 266,
  290–2, 313
Australia's Bicentennial
  celebrations 289–90

auto-rickshaw drivers 257–9
Azhar Mahmood 338

Babolsar (Iran) 141, 143, 144
Bacher, Ali 94, 349, 386
Baig, Amir 338
Bailey, Peter 95
Bailey, Trevor 104, 105, 282–4,
  391–2
Bakht, Sikander 174
Bannerman, Charles 368
Barbados
  HB as player in 79, 80–2
  refuses work permit to HB 96
  E.W. Swanton's home on 86–7
  tour crisis (1980/81) 223–4
Barber, Bruce (*pseud.* of B.
  Chapman) 86
Barber, David 35–6
Baring (boy at Sunningdale) 17, 23
Barlow, Eddie 93
Barnes (Australian Test cricketer
  1948) 19, 20
Baroda, Maharajah of
  ('Jackie' or 'Prince') 104, 105,
    150, 281–2
Barrington, Ken 85, 119, 153, 155,
  179, 225–6
Barrow, Errol 224
baseball game 273–5
Batt, Bill 395
Baxter, Peter 93, 104, 239, 241,
  252–3, 336, 386, 388
BBC 91–3
  HB commentates for 99 *onwards*
  wins 5-year rights to home
    cricket 401
  see also TMS
BCCI (Indian Board of
  Control) 319–23
  Golden Jubilee 204
Bedarra Island 368–9
Bedi, Bishen 154
Bedser, Alec 20, 114, 232, 239
Beitzel, Harry 266
Benaud, Richie 170–1, 291, 360
Bennett, Fred 183, 268
Bennett, Michael 128, 129
  characteristics 128, 129
  overland to India with HB 28–50

INDEX

coincidental meeting 145
death 150
Bennett, Murray 265
Benson and Hedges Cup 229, 308, 310
Benson and Hedges World Series Cup 203, 267
Bequia 324
Berbice (Guyana) 223
Berry, Scyld 275–6
Bevan, Eddie 362–3
Bhutto family 174–6
Bindra, Inderjit Singh 282, 285, 319–22, 323
Bird, Dickie 205, 396
Bird, Lester 224
Bird, Vere 224
Birkbeck, Christo 211
Birley, Robert 41
Bland, Colin 119
Blenheim (New Zealand) 373
Blofeld, J.C. (HB's grandfather) 10
Blofeld, I.C. (HB's grandmother) 10–12
Blofeld, Anthea (HB's sister) 2, 379, 382
Blofeld, Bitten (HB's 2nd wife) 209, 344–5, 368, 395, 401
  marries HB 302
  and ghost 353, 354
  and HB's heart surgery 374–85
  and 'Rumple' 302, 303
  trip to SA 398–9
Blofeld, Grizel (HB's mother)
  character and habits 1–2, 3, 8–9, 210–13, 273, 314, 395–6
  and North Farm ghost 354
  passes on share tips 53–4
  premonition of HB's accident 43
  old age 272, 273, 294–5
  death 313–14
  other references 12, 14, 15, 24
Blofeld, Henry
  early life 1–25
    prep school (Sunningdale) 14–25; early cricketing experiences 16, 18–25
  Eton 25–45
    Eton–Harrow matches at Lord's 30–4, 37; century for Public Schools side 38, 392; accident and aftermath 42–4, 209–10
  games for Norfolk 37, 39–41, 45, 49–50, 55;
  Cambridge 44, 45–9
    awarded Blue 48; century against MCC 49, 392
  marriage and family matters
    marries (first) Joanna 56–8, 208, 392–3; birth of daughter 73; moves house 124; robbed in Trinidad 222–3
    moves to Haugh's End 263–5; father's death 211–12, 272–3, 294; 50th birthday 298; marries (second) Bitten 301–2; mother's death 313–14; heart bypass surgery 374–85; 60th birthday 395
  career highlights
    uncongenial City job 50–5, 56, 59, 64–5; first writing assignments 59–64, 67–73; first trip to India 74; tries TV commentating 77–9; and mistakes woman for man 79; to Barbados as player with Arabs 79, 80–2; first trip to Australia 89–91; trial radio commentaries 91–3; first Test broadcasts (for WI radio) 94–8; first commentaries for BBC 99–104; joins TMS 104–8; at Melbourne Centenary Test 156–60; joins Australian commercial radio 190; enjoys Sydney fans' leg-pulling 193–5; South American tour with young players 196–8; at Australia's Bicentennial 289–90; leaves TMS for Sky TV 306–11; interviews Michael Manley 316; as commentator and negotiator for TWI 319–23; rejoins TMS 326–7; interviews Robert Mugabe 335–7

405

Blofeld, Henry – *cont.*
　pleasures and pursuits
　　book-collecting 236–7, 304–6
　　(*see also* Wodehouse, P.G.);
　　getting around by train to
　　Kalgoorlie 89; driving overland
　　to India 125–50; driving in
　　UK 246; loves flying 240–1
　　horse-racing and gambling 59,
　　285; love of India 152–3; and
　　of Lord's 187–8;
　　shooting 4–5, 261–2, 354–6;
　　smoking 51–2; taste for wine
　　and good living 74, 123–4,
　　237, 239, 268, 360, 363, 364,
　　368–9
　　(even in hospital 376, 379)
　leisure days and friends' hospitality
　　at home *see* Haugh's End, North
　　Farm; in Australia 89, 117,
　　268, 289–90, 359–60, 363–4,
　　368–9; (clubs 115); in
　　India 149, 150, 282
　　problems 281–5; in NZ 117,
　　373–4; in Pakistan 337–8; in
　　SA (holiday with
　　Bitten) 398–9; watching
　　baseball in Houston 273–5; in
　　West Indies 86, 87, 224, 324,
　　344; (honeymoon 57–8)
　reflections
　　on match-fixing 400; mid-life
　　self-analysis 206–10,
　　214–15; post-
　　operative 385–6, 387, 389;
　　on radio v TV
　　commentating 298–300; on
　　restucturing of domestic
　　game 327–33; on women
　　commentators 250–1
Blofeld, Joanna (HB's first wife)
　engagement and marriage 56–8,
　208, 392–3
　accompanies HB 61, 62–3, 79,
　86, 240
　gives birth to Suki 73
　accident 91
Blofeld, John (HB's brother)
　childhood 2–3, 7, 8–9, 21
　at school 15–16, 25

　21st birthday 10
　and HB's accident 43
　takes over Hoveton 213, 263–4,
　272–3, 294
Blofeld, Suki (HB's daughter) 73,
　208, 375, 379, 382
Blofeld, T. (HB's father) 2, 4–5, 7,
　12, 18, 21, 34, 39
　character and habits 8, 14,
　210–14
　friends 210–12
　old age 263–4, 272–3, 396
　death 211–12, 244, 273
Bogota 196
Bojnourd (Iran) 144
Bombay
　eclipse 204–5
　Golden Jubilee Test 204
　HB drives overland to 125–50
　HB's favourite city 152–3
Bond, Jack 49, 71
Boon, David 290
Booth, Brian 71
Border, Allan 241–2, 265, 266, 277,
　287, 308
Botham, Ian 189–90, 229–35, 239,
　241, 242, 272, 276–7, 395
　behaviour off the field 174,
　226–8, 230–1, 260, 287
　drugs allegations 254, 269–70,
　271
　sex scandal 270
　Best Man to Viv Richards 226
　Bombay Golden Jubilee Test 204
　as captain 216, 221–2, 224,
　231–2
　charity walk 270
　debut for Queensland 286–7
　libel action against Imran
　　Khan 340
　runs out Boycott 180–1
bouncers 118, 124–5, 191, 328, 347
Bowen, Rowland 101
Boycott, Geoffrey 36, 85, 86, 106,
　125, 167, 174, 351, 386
　as captain 174, 180
　convicted of assault 339–40
　libel action against Imran
　　Khan 340
　and Packer 161–2, 177

INDEX

and Pakistan traffic problems 261, 339
  rebel tour to SA 237-8
  run out by Botham 180-1
Bradman, Sir Donald 20-1, 42, 170, 201, 202
Brasher, Chris 69
Brazil 198
Brearley, Mike 159, 174, 177, 231
  as captain 166, 202, 216, 232, 233
  and Packer 166
bribes *see* match-fixing
Bright, Ray 232, 234
Brind, Harry 394
Brind, Paul 394
Brisbane
  ground ('The Gabba') 110-11, 356
  stormy weather 357-8
Brittenden, Dick 372
Broad, Chris 287, 290
Brown, Bill 90
Brown, Freddie 89
Bryant, Laurie 373
BSkyB TV
  loses main England contracts 310
  see also Sky TV
Bucknor, Steve 341-2
Budd, Eric 394
Budd, Lloyd 125
Buenos Aires 197-8
Burge, Peter 359
Burgess, Mark 97
Burnham, Forbes 223
Burrows, Mr (Sunningdale tutor) 18
Burrows, Richard 31, 37
Butcher, Basil 85
Butcher, Mark 347, 365
buzkashi (Afghan game) 146

Caddick, Andy 337, 346
Cairns, Lance 248
Cakes and Bails (H. Blofeld) 371
Calcutta
  city 285-6
  World Cup Final (1987/88) 285, 286
Caldwell, Tim 201
Callum, Barbara 382

Calthorpe, Henry (*pseud.* of HB) 83
Camacho, Steve 280, 342
Cambridge University 44, 45-9, 188
Cardus, Neville 49
Carrington, Desmond 78
Carter (Hoveton gamekeeper) 5
Cartwright, Buns 41-2
Cartwright, Tom 88
Casey, Judy 127-50, 364
Cecil, James and Sarah 60
Champness (Harrow cricketer) 34
Chandigarh 282
Chandrasekhar, B.S. 154, 155
Chapman, Brian 86
Chappell, Greg 121, 159-60, 221, 249, 251, 265
Chappell, Ian 90, 93, 113, 121-2, 251, 291, 352
  as captain 115, 170
  suspension 202
Chappell, Trevor 221, 234
Chatfield, Ewen 118, 180-1, 248, 283
Chevalier, Grahame 93
Chile 197
Christchurch
  Lancaster Park Ground/Jade Stadium 372
  Valley of Peace CC 292-4, 372
Clapp, Bob 230
Clayton, Geoff 49
Clegg, Richard 253
Clooney, Rosemary 33
Close, Brian 84, 124, 125
Collinge, Dick 180
Colombia 196
Colvile, Charles 309
Combined Services side (1956) 37-9
Compton, Denis 19, 35, 36, 48-9, 84, 230, 393-4
Compton, Leslie 35
Coney, Jeremy 293
Congdon, Bevan 97
Conn, Malcolm 361
Constant, David 281
Constantine, Learie, Lord 78
Cook (Australian town) 275-6
Coomb, Arthur 39, 50
Coote, Cyril 46-7, 188

407

Cope, Geoff 175
Cork, Bob 22
Cork, Dominic 348
Cornell, John 163
Cornhill Insurance 190, 282
Cottenham, Earl of 82
county cricket
   County Championship 301, 394
   restructuring and two-tier
      system 327–33, 345, 363
   Robins tours for young
      players 195–6, 216–17
Cowans, Norman 241, 242
Coward, Noel 58
Cowdrey, Chris 296, 297
Cowdrey, Colin 38, 75, 78, 114–15, 116
   as captain 84, 85, 88, 359
   as selector 297
Cozier, Gary 160
Cozier, Tony 120, 299–300, 315, 325, 344
Crabtree, Harry 35
Crafter, Tony 237
Craven, John 149
Crawley, John 350
Cricket Dialogue (Macindoe and Taylor) 29
Cricket Ground Trust (Australia) 193
Croft, Colin 182, 218
Croft, Robert 347, 362
Crombie, B.L. 96
Cronje, Hansie 346, 349, 371
   and match-fixing 399–400
Croser, Brian 237
Crouch, Maurice 49–50
Crowe, Jeff 280
Crowe, Martin 279
Crusaders 55
Cubitt, Reggie 210–12
Cummins, Anderson 316–17
Cunis, Bob 292
Cunningham, Ken 250

Daily Express 190, 253
Daily Mail 161
Daily Sketch 72–3
Daily Telegraph 82–6, 121, 163, 275
Dalmiya, Jagmohan 319–22, 323
Daniel, Wayne 106, 124

Davies, Barry 78
Davies, Dai 49, 188
Davis, Charlie 97
Davis, Ian 159
day/night matches 200, 236
de Silva, Aravinda 349, 350
de Villiers, Fanie 327
deKlerk, F.W. 312
Delhi 149, 150
Denness, Mike 104, 111, 118, 119, 217
Denning, Lord 168
d'Erlanger, Minnie 46
Dexter, Ted 46, 113, 300, 392
Dilley, Graham 232, 233
Doggart, Hubert 30
D'Oliveira, Basil 87–8
Donald, Allan 347, 348
Donnelly, Martin 374
Douglas-Pennant, Simon 29, 33, 34
Dowling, Graham 97
Downing, Brian 329
Doyle, Peter 117, 369
Duckworth, Frank 315
Duckworth, George 78
Dudley, Doust 227
Dunedin
   rest days 117
Dunne, Steve 347
Dyke, Greg 401

Eagar, Patrick 222–3
East Africa 118
Easter, Miss ('See-Saw', HB's father's secretary) 6
ECB (England and Wales Cricket Board) 329–33, 346, 401
Edgbaston 390
Edmonds, Phil 275–6
Edrich, John 85, 88, 112, 114, 124, 125
Edrich, W.J. ('Bill') 18, 19, 20–1, 40, 49–50, 157, 389
Edwards, Richard 81
Edwards, Ross 115
Egar, Colin 291
Elkins, Gloria 58
Ellis, Timmy (of RBL) 54
Ellison, Richard 269
Emburey, John 235, 238, 296

INDEX

Emerson, Ross 350, 369–70
Endean, Russell 94
England
  v Australia
    (1932/33) Bodyline tour 125, 361
    (1956) 394
    (1968) 87–8
    (1974/75) 110–18
    (1977) 166–7, 230
    (1978/79) 190, 192–5
    (1979/80) 200, 201, 202–3
    (1980) Centenary Match at Lord's 218–19, 220
    (1981) 231–5
    (1982/83) 241–3
    (1986/87) 276–7
    (1987/88, Bicentennial Test) 289, 290
    (1989) 300
    (1990/91) 308
    (1997) 337
    (1998/99) 357–70
  v India
    (1963/64) 74–7
    (1974) 104, 106–8
    (1976/77) 153–5
    (1979) 199
    (1979/80, Golden Jubilee Test) 204
    (1981/82) 237, 238
    (1982) 239
    (1984/85) 268–9
    (1986) 271–2
    (1988/89) tour cancelled 297
    (1990) 307–8
    (1992/93) 323
    (1996) 334
  v NZ
    (1974/75) 118
    (1977/78) 178, 180–1
    (1983) 248
    (1986) 272
    (1987/88) 292
    (1990) 307
    (1991/92) 314
    (1999) 385, 388, 390, 393, 394
  v Pakistan
    (1977/78) 174–8
    (1978) 188–90
    (1981/82) 252–3, 260
    (1982) 239
    (1987) 280–1
    (1987/88), umpiring problems 287–8
    (1996) 334
  v SA
    (1955) 393–4
    (1960) 392–3
    (1994) 327
    (1995/96) 333–4
    (1998) 346–9
    (1999/2000) 398, 399
  v Sri Lanka
    (1981/82) 238–9
    (1988) 297
    (1992/93) 323
    (1998) 349–52
  v WI
    (1967/68) 397
    (1973/74) 113
    (1976) 124–5
    (1980) 221
    (1980/81) 221–2, 223–6
    (1984) 264
    (1985/86) 269, 270–1
    (1988) 295–7
    (1989/90) 300–1
    (1991) 310
    (1995) 327
    (1997/98) 340–3, 346
  v Zimbabwe, (1996/97) 334–5
  World Cup (1979) finalists 198–9
    (1987/88) runners-up 285, 286
    (1991/92) runners-up 314–15
    limited-over matches
      (1981/82) 243, 246
      (1987/88) 292
  other matches 156, 191, 223, 275
  drugs story 253–4
  problems of the 1990s 327–33
Erzerum 138
Essex (1963) 71
Esso (HB's sponsor) 131
Eton College Chronicle 41
Eton Ramblers 30, 41–2, 56
Evans, Godfrey 20, 233
Evening Standard 171

Facciolo, Tony ('Facci')   243, 244–5
Faisalabad   260–1, 339
   day's play lost (1987/88)   287
Falcon, Mike   18, 40
Fasken, David   55
Fenner's   188
Field, Jimmy   40
Field, Linda   270
Fiji v USA (ICC Trophy match, 1974)   118
Fingleton, Jack ('Fingo')   90, 101, 103, 194, 390, 393
First-Class Forum   330
First-class sides, numbers of   332
Fisher, Diana   117
Fitzpatrick, Kate   250–1
Fleming, Damien   365, 366
Fleming, Ian   58
Fletcher, Duncan   346
Fletcher, Keith   118, 237, 238, 239, 333
'Foe' *see* Fox, Mr
Ford, Christopher   69
Forest, Martin   26
Forty Club   35–6
four-day cricket   329
Fowler, 'Foxy'   389
Fox, Mr ('Foe')   15
Fox, Mrs   15, 23
Francis, 'KT'   358
Frankfurt   132
Franses, Gary   301, 315, 322–3
Fraser, Angus   301, 343, 347, 348, 366
Fredericks, Roy   122–3
Free Foresters   56
Frindall, Bill   100
'Fuzzy' (St Vincent taxi driver)   344

Gallaway, Iain   292
Gandhi, Indira   268
Gaskin, Berkeley   91, 183
Gatting, Mike   234, 269, 272, 276, 287–8, 295–6
Gavaskar, Sunil   107, 199, 283
Georgetown (Guyana)
   debate on WI Packer players   182–5
   politics cause Test cancellation   223–6

rest days   87, 117
ghost at North Farm   353–4
Gibbons (chauffeur to E.W. Swanton)   82
Gibbs, Herschelle   371
Gibbs, Lance   86, 89
Gibson, Alan   103, 390
Gibson, Clem (Jr)   30, 31, 32
Gibson, Clem (Sr)   40
Glamorgan   163, 301, 321
Gleeson, J.W.   88
Gloucestershire   163
Goddard, Trevor   93
Gomes, Larry   237
Gomez, Gerry   96
Gooch, Graham   225–6, 269, 310, 394
   as captain   297, 300–1, 323
   consequence of rebel tours to SA   297
   record 333 at Lord's   307–8
Good, Tony   360
Goodall, Fred   217–18, 279–80
Gore-Booth, Sir Paul   76–7
Gosein (umpire)   185
Gough, Darren   347, 348, 367
Governor of Sind's Eleven   174
Gower, David   226, 269, 275, 276, 296, 394
   as captain   261, 268, 269, 271, 300
   Test debut   188–9, 190
Grace, W.G.   26
Grapes, Sidney   11
Graveney, Tom   85, 359
Gray, David   71
Great Barrier Reef   369
Greece   134–5
Green, David   35, 48
Green Jackets   30
Greenidge, Gordon   179, 182
Greig, Tony   107, 112–14, 116, 154, 159, 160
   as captain   114, 119, 153, 155, 158
   and HB   307
   and Packer   114, 158, 162, 163–4, 165–6, 184, 291–2
   and Sky TV   307
Grenada   324

INDEX

Griffin, Geoff 393
Griffith, Charlie 84, 85, 90, 113, 181
The Guardian 83
   and HB 69–71, 77, 86, 93,
      109–10, 162–3, 191, 205, 235
   and J. Arlott 109–10, 162–3, 191,
      219
Guyana *see* Georgetown
Gwalior, Maharajah of *see* Scindia,
   Madhavrao
Gwalior (place) 323–4
Gwen (hairdresser) 53

Habeeb Ahsan 287
Hadlee, Richard 123, 180, 181, 218,
   248, 280, 289
Hadlee, Walter 181, 248, 372
Hair, Darrell 350, 358
Hales, Mrs (HB's tutor) 7–8, 10, 395
Hall, Wes 84, 85, 113, 341
Hamilton Island 268
Hampshire 63–4, 229–30
Hancock, Colonel
   Fitzhardinge ('Hardy') 24
Hansen, Alexei ('Rumple', HB's
   stepson) 302–4, 354, 385,
   401
Harare 335–7
Harper, Daryl 367
Hart, Len 39
Harvey, Charles 70–1
Harvey, Neil 322–3
Haseeb Ahsan 281
Hassett, Lindsay 20
Hastings, Brian 97
Haugh's End 263, 264–5
Haynes, Desmond 182, 183, 301
Hayter, Reg 231
Headingley 349
Headley, Dean 366, 367, 368
Healy, Ian 366
Hebeler, Joanna *see* Blofeld, Joanna
Hector, Tim 224
Hemmings, Eddie 287, 308
Hendrick, Mike 107
Hendriks, Jackie 95, 341, 342
Hennessey, John 60
Herbert, Percy, Bishop 57
'HH' (Cambridge don) 188
Hick, Graeme 350, 356, 365, 366

Higgs, Ken 46, 112
Hill, David
   at Channel Nine 173, 250–1
   and BSkyB 298, 306–7, 308–9,
      310
   and HB 306–7, 311–12
Hill, Eric 229
Hill Smith, Rob 116
Hill Smith, Wyndy 116
Hillary, Sir Edmund 282
Hilton, Colin 49
Hilton, Malcolm 49
Hislop, John 117
Hobbs, Jack 230, 321
Hogg, Rodney 191, 192–3, 195
Holding, Michael 106, 121, 124,
   181–2, 265, 315, 325, 386
Holland, Bob 265
Hookes, David 159
Hooper, Carl 356–7
Hope Wallace, Philip 71–2
Houghton, David 282
Houston 273–5
Hoveton
   cricket at 9–10, 21–3, 56
   House and estate 1–13, 124,
      210–14, 263–4, 272–3, 294,
      354–6, 397–8
   see also Haugh's End, North Farm
Howarth, Geoff 118, 218
Howland, Chris 45, 48
Hudson, Robert 93
Hudson, Tim 231, 270
Hudson, Trevor 375, 376, 379, 380,
   395
Hughes, Kim 234, 265
Hughes, Merv 308
Hunn, Freddie 9
Hunn, Hilda 9
Hussain, Nasser 345–6, 347, 365,
   399

ICC
   Code of Conduct 370
   impossible target calculation 315
   and SA's readmission 312
ICC Trophy
   (1974) 118
   (1982) 247
Illingworth, Ray 333–4, 363

Imran Khan 281, 315, 324, 340
  as captain 249–50, 251
  and Packer 176–8
The Independent 311
India 281–5
  v Australia
    (1977/78) 169, 173, 179–80
    (1979/80) tour postponed 200
    (1980/81) 221
  v England
    (1963/64) 74–7
    (1974) 104, 106–8
    (1976) 113–14
    (1976/77) 153–5
    (1979) 199
    (1979/80) Golden Jubilee
      Test 204
    (1981/82) 237, 238
    (1982) 239
    (1984/85) 268–9
    (1986) 271–2
    (1988/89) tour cancelled 297
    (1990) 307–8
    (1992/93) 323
    (1996) 334
  v NZ (1975/76) 123
  World Championship of Cricket,
    (1984/85) winners 267
  World Cup
    (1983) 248
    (1987/88) 282, 283, 285
  limited-over matches 323
  other matches 321
  and TWI 319–23
  Vaseline controversy 154
India (country)
  accommodation and other
    problems 281–5
  assassination of Mrs Gandhi and of
    Percy Norris 268–9
  eclipse 204–5
  HB's love for 152–3
  stations 319–20
Indian Board of Control *see* BCCI
Ingate (Hoveton bailiff) 1–2
Ingleby-Mackenzie, Colin 48, 80, 81
Ingram-Johnson, Colonel ('Inky') 22
Inniss, Eric 80
Insole, Doug 329–30

Inverarity, John 88
Inzamam-ul-Haq 314–15
Iqbal Qasim 189
Iran 139–45
Irvine, Lee 93
Isaacs, Wilfred 94
Istanbul 135–6
It's Just Not Cricket (H. Blofeld) 371, 374
Ives, Joan 313

Jackman, Robin 223–6
Jackson, Eric 372
Jacobs, Bill 291
Jagger, Mick 343
Jaipur 150
Jaipur, Rajmata of 285
Jaisimha, M.L. 282
Jamaica
  tour crisis (1980/81) 223–4
  see also Kingston
  Jamaica Colts 86
Jardine, Douglas 154, 158
Jarman, Barry 88, 341–2, 351, 359–60
Jarvis, Terry 97
Javed Akhtar 348–9
Javed Miandad 237
Javed Zamaan 262
Jayasuriya, Sanath 349, 350
Johnson (Hoveton head marshman) 6
Johnston, Brian ('Johnners') 92, 101, 104, 107–8, 120, 123, 309
  character 105, 396
  and John Arlott 219, 220
  jokes, puns and 'clangers' 107, 119, 174, 395
  and Packer 171
Jones, Clem, mayor of
  Brisbane 110–11
Jones, Jeff 86
Jordan, Cortez 81
Jordon, Ray 291
Judd, Kevin 373
Julien, Bernard 122

Kabul 146–7
Kabul Gorge 147
Kalgoorlie 275
Kallicharran, Alvin 97, 182, 185

INDEX

Kandahar 145
Kanhai, Rohan 85, 86
Kapil Dev 248, 308
Kardar, Abdul Hafeez 177
Keating, Frank 77
Kent 40, 46
    HB's first assignment (1962) 61–3
Kerrigan, Pat and Edith 57
Khyber 148
Kimberley, Earl of (Johnny) 302
Kingston (Jamaica)
    pitch problems (1997/98) 340–3
    radio stations 95
    spectators riot (1967/68) 85
Kingstown (St Vincent) 344
Kippins, Cecil 397
Kirby, David 47
Kitchen, Mervyn 347
Kline, Lindsay 356
Knott, Alan 86, 158, 167, 204
Knowles, Raffie 96
Kureishi, Omar 177
Kwik cricket 346

Lahore
    HB's adventures in 253–60
    riots at Test 174
Laker, Jim 167, 394
Lamb, Allan 260, 301, 340
Lamb, Tim 335, 363
Lancashire 46, 49
Lane Fox, Edward 23, 29–30, 33, 44
Langer, Justin 363, 366
Langley, Mr (of RBL) 53
Lara, Brian 341, 356–7
Larwood, Harold 157, 158, 361
Lashley, Peter 81
Lawry, Bill 87, 90, 291, 359
Lawson, Geoff 233
Leary, Stuart 37
Leewards Islands 86
Legge-Bourke, Bill 44
LeGrice, Hylton 123–4
Lehmann, Darren 366
Lever, John 153–4
Lever, Peter 118
Lewis, David 301
Lewis, Ivor 205–6
Lewis, Mr (of RBL) 52

Lewis, Tony 315
Lewis, Tony (A.R.) 241, 261
Liaquat Ali 188
Liddell, Adrian ('Ady')
    drives Rolls to India with HB 127–49
    attitude to Judy 128, 130, 132, 139
    dislikes 'hot' food 148
    driving skill 129, 132, 134, 135, 136, 143
    language skills (lack of) 131–2, 150
    life after the trip 150
Lillee, Dennis 106, 110–18, 121, 122, 173, 234, 241, 287
    and aluminium bat 202
    bets on England (1981) 233
    in Melbourne Centenary Test 158
    and Miandad incident 237
    and Packer 161, 164
    retires 251
Lima 197
limited-over cricket 161, 203
    30-yard rule 172, 200
    early games 200, 236
    pressure on players 267–8, 328
Lincoln, Christopher 378–9, 381
Listowel, Judith, Countess of 56–7
Lloyd, Clive 85, 123, 125, 179, 218, 307
    last Test 265–6
    and WI Packer debate 182–4
Lloyd, David 115, 350
    complains of Muralitheran's action 350
    as manager 334, 335, 337
    and Sky TV 307
Loader, Peter 89
Lock, Tony 86
Long John Scotch whisky (HB's sponsor) 131, 132, 133, 134
Lord's
    broadcasters' accommodation 100, 310, 392
    Centenary match (1980) 218–19, 220
    HB's affection for 19–21, 187–8, 392

Lotery, James 374–5
Luckhoo, Sir Lionel 183, 223–4
Luckhurst, Brian 111, 115
Lush, Peter 271, 281, 288
Lynam, Desmond 100

McDermott, Craig 266, 308
McDonald, Colin 115–16
McFarline, Peter 162, 367–8
MacGill, Stuart 357, 365, 367, 368
McGilvray, Alan 120, 183, 193, 234, 235
McGlew, Jackie 393
McGrath, Glenn 366, 367
McGregor, Sue 199
Macindoe, David 29, 42
McKechnie, Brian 221
McKenzie, Graham 88, 90
Mackenzie, Kelvin 386, 401
Mackenzie, Ron 191
McLachlan, Ian 46
MacLaren, Archie 40
MacLaurin, Sir Ian (later Lord) 329–33, 335
McMillan, Brian 348
Madan Lal 248
Maddocks, Len 166–7
Madras 154
The Mail on Sunday 253, 260, 271
Mailey, Arthur 25
Majid Khan 177
Majzub, Fuad 140, 141–2
Makins, Clifford 64, 71
Malcolm, Devon 301, 327, 334
Maley, John 169, 179
Mallett, Ashley 88
Manchester Grammar School 35
Mankad, Vinoo 90
Manley, Michael 316
Marks, Vic 389–90
Marlar, Robin 224, 226
Marner, Peter 49
Marsh, Rodney 159–60, 233, 249, 292
 retires 251
Marshall, Malcolm 280
Martin-Jenkins, Christopher ('CM-J') 104, 105, 106, 120, 190, 241, 286, 341
Massie, Bob 110

match-fixing 337, 361–2, 399–400
Maud (Hoveton parlourmaid) 6
Maxwell, Lois 58–9
May, Peter 38, 239, 271, 296, 300, 394
May, Tim 362
MCC 19, 48–9, 220
 see also England
Meares, Peter 192
Meckiff, Ian ('The Count') 291, 356
Melbourne
 MCG 156–7
 Centenary Test 125, 156–60
 first ever Test match (1877) 368
 and HB's blue jeans 266–7
 VFL Park 169–70, 171
Melford, Michael ('Mellers') 75, 121, 123, 224
Mercer, Jack 321
Merriman, Bob 265
Milburn, Colin 87
Miller, Geoff 242
Miller, Keith 48, 90, 157, 194
Mitchell, Mr (of RBL) 52–3
Mitchell, Sir James 344
Mohammed Husain, Chaudri 177
Moore, Andrew 291
Moore, Nigel 39
Morgan, Jane 222–3
Morris, Arthur 19–20, 35, 193–4
Morrison, John 292
Moseley, Hallam 230
Mosey, Don ('The Alderman') 120, 174–6, 199, 239, 247
Mudassar Nazar 174–5
Mugabe, Robert 335–7
Muir, John 376–84, 391
Muldoon, Robert 221
Mullally, Alan 366
Muralitharan, Muttiah 349–51, 360, 369
Murray, Deryck 182–3, 218
Murrell, Adrian 275–6
Mushtaq Ahmed 338
Mushtaq Mohammad 177–8
Mustique 324

Nagpur 283–4
'Nanny' (Hoveton) 6, 13

INDEX

Neame, Rex
  friendship with HB 301, 345, 356, 383
  plays for Harrow against HB 31, 32, 33, 34
  and 'Rumple' 303
New Zealand
  v Australia
    (1980/81) 221
    (1987/88) 288–9
  v England
    (1974/75) 118
    (1977/78) 180–1
    (1983) 248
    (1986) 272
    (1990) 307
    (1991/92) 314
    (1999) 385, 388, 390, 393, 394
  v India (1975/76) 123
  v Pakistan (1976/77) 149
  v SA, (1998/99) 371, 373
  v WI
    (1971/72) 94–8
    (1979/80) 217–18
    (1986/87) 279–80
  World Cup
    (1987/88) 282, 283
    (1991/92) 314–15
  limited-over matches
    (1980/81) 221
    (1982/83) 243, 246
  other matches 188, 195
  and Packer 181
  rest days 117
News of the World 270
Nicholson, Geoffrey 344
Nicholson, Matthew 366–7
Nickerson, Mark 25
Nickson, Geoffrey ('GWN') 26–7
Nimmo, Derek 250
Nixon, Bob 247–8
Norfolk 18
  HB plays for 37, 39–41, 45, 49–50, 55
Norris, Percy 269
North Farm 12, 303–4, 353–4, 384–5, 401
Nottinghamshire 40, 48, 289
Ntini, Makhaya 348

Nullarbor Plain 276
Nur Khan, Air Marshal 249
Nurse, Seymour 81, 85

O'Brien, Seamus 321
The Observer 68, 71, 93, 292
O'Connell, Max 202
O'Grady, Desmond 139–43
O'Keeffe, Kerry 160, 291
Old, Chris 177, 232, 233
Old Trafford 105–6
Oldfield, Bertie 361
Oldroyd, Eleanor 251
Oliver, Jeremy and Jen 363, 367
one-day matches *see* limited-over cricket
O'Neill, Norman 360
O'Reilly, Bill ('Tiger') 90, 158
Oval, Adelaide *see* Adelaide
Oval, The 372, 394
Oxford University (1959) 48, 49, 392

The Packer Affair (H. Blofeld) 178–9
Packer, Kerry 117, 125, 158, 160–8
  and ACB 190, 195, 199–203, 243
  and Brian Johnston 171
  HB's book 178–9
  innovations 193, 200
  interviews with 171–2, 184–5
  and NZ players 181
  and Pakistan players 176–8
  and UE radio 291–2
  and WI players 182–6
  see also PBL Marketing, World Series Cricket
Paine, Mr (of RBL) 54, 64, 65
Pakistan
  v Australia, (1983/84) 249–50
  v England
    (1977/78) 174–8
    (1978) 188–90
    (1981/82) 252–3, 260
    (1982) 239
    (1987) 280–1
    (1987/88), umpiring problems 287–8
    (1996) 334
  v NZ (1976/77) 149
  v SA (1997/98) 337, 338–9

Pakistan – *cont.*
  v WI
    (1981/82) 237
    (1992/93) 324–5
  World Championship of Cricket
    (1984/85)
    finalists 267
  World Cup, (1991/92)
    winners 314–15
    limited-over matches, (1983/
      84) 249
    other matches 174
    drugs scandal (1992/93) 324–5
    and Packer players 176–8
    and TWI 317–18, 324
Pakistan (country)
  HB drives through 148–9
  traffic 257–60, 261
Pakistan TV 312
Parfitt, Peter 39, 75, 196
Paris 132
Parish, Bob 199–201
Parker, Jack 35
Parks, Harry 40
Parks, J.M. 119
Parry, D.R. 182
Parry, Ray 29
Pataudi, Nawab of ('Tiger') 36–7
Patel, A.D. (surgeon) 345
Patel, Dipak 314
Patel, Shilpa 401
Paterson, Miss (Sunningdale
  tutor) 16, 18
Paton, Clive 374
PBL Marketing 199–200, 201–3,
  243, 267, 273
  see also Packer
Peebles, Ian 29, 35
The People 227
Pernert, Sven Erik 303
Pernert-Hansen, Bitten *see* Blofeld,
  Bitten
Perth (Australia)
  first Test there
    (1970/91) 191
  WACA ground 156
Peru 197
Peshawar 148–9
Piachaud, Danny 81–2
Pollock, Graeme 93–4

Pollock, Peter 93
Pollock, Shaun 347, 348
Poona 319–22
Porcher, Mrs (Hoveton cook) 5–6
Port of Spain
  HB robbed in 222–3
  rest days 117
Powell, Peter 39, 40
Prasanna, E.A.S. 154
Pretlove, John 40
Prideaux, Roger 87
Prior, Tom 267
Procter, Mike 93
Public Schools side (1956) 37–9
Pugh, Tom 31, 33, 34

Qayyum Commission 362, 400
Queensland
  Botham's debut 286–7
  v England 275

Radley, Clive 177, 191
'Raising the Standard'
  (MacLaurin's blueprint for
    change) 330–1
Ramprakash, Mark 334, 343, 366
Ranatunga, Arjuna 349–50, 369–70
Randall, Derek 159–60, 177, 181,
  192–3
Raven, John 47
Rawalpindi 149
Rea, Chris 138
rebel tours to SA 237–8, 269, 297
Reddy, Santosh 66–7
Redpath, Ian 90, 121, 181
Reed, Barry 30
Reed, Simon 307
Reid, Bruce 308
Reid, John 351, 359
rest days 116–17
  total eclipse in Bombay 204–5
Rest of the World sides 161, 164,
  179
Rhodes, Jonty 119, 327, 346, 348
Rice, Clive 289
Richards, Alan 95, 120
Richards, Barry 93–4, 179, 229
Richards, David 361–2
Richards, Viv 119, 121, 173, 179,
  181, 182, 248, 394

INDEX

as captain 125, 279, 280, 315
wedding 226
Richardson, Peter 252–3
Richardson, Richie 315
Riddell, Henry 92–3, 234
Ridgard, Winston 95
Rigby, Paul 89
Riley, Jonathan 322–3
Roberts, Andy 106, 121, 123, 124, 229, 230
Robertson, Austin 163
Robins, Derrick: tours for young players 195–8, 216–17
Robins, Walter 35
Robinson, Lionel 39
Robinson, Tim 269
Rodriguez, Willie 217
Rogers, Dennis 362
Ross, Alan 292
Rousseau, Pat 342, 357
Rowe, Lawrence 97
Roy, Fred 22
'Rumple' *see* Hansen, Alexei
Ruscoe, Sybil 251
Rutherford, Ken 293

St Lucia 87
St Vincent 324, 344
Salim Malik 362
Salmon, Anthony [HB's brother-in-law] 382
Samuel, John 69, 162
Santiago 197
Sao Paolo 198
Sardine, Tony 324
Sarfraz, Nawaz 249–50, 260
  HB stays with 253–9
Sayer, David 49
Scargill, Arthur 247
Scindia, Madhavrao 319–22
Scott, Archie 25
Scott, Edward 35, 37, 44
Scott, Ruth 25
'See-Saw' (Miss Easter) 6
Seymour, Jane 395
Seymour, Kelly 196
Shakoor Rana 287–8, 295
Sheffield Shield 286–7
Sheikapura 338
Shennan, Bob 391

Sheppard, Revd David 48
Shiell, Alan 162, 166, 184
Short, Peter 80, 183, 184
Simpson, Bobby 170–1, 277–8, 300
  as captain 173, 179–80, 183, 195
Simpson, Reg 48
Sinclair, Ian 33, 34, 37
Sinrich, Bill 317–18, 319, 321, 322
Sinstadt, Gerald 91
Sky TV 298, 301, 306–11
  see also BSkyB
Slade, Mr Justice 167
Slater, Michael 366, 368
sledging 122, 347
Sleep, Peter 277
Small, Gladstone 301
Smith, Alan 49, 225, 254, 329–30
Smith, Mike 76
Smith, Robin 334
Snow, John 158, 162, 397
Sobers, Gary 85, 89, 91, 97, 113, 114, 397
  as captain 84, 85–6
Solkar, Eknath 106
Solomon, Jo 356
Somerset 61–2, 229–30
South Africa
  v Australia, (1969/70) 93–4
  v England
    (1955) 393–4
    (1960) 392–3
    (1965) 119
    (1994) 327
    (1995/96) 333–4
    (1998) 346–9
    (1999/2000) 398, 399
  v NZ, (1998/99) 371, 373
  v Pakistan, (1997/98) 337, 338–9
  v WI
    (1991/92) 315–17
    (1998/99) 356–7
  World Cup, (1991/92)
    semifinalists 315
  apartheid problems 88, 94, 118, 312, 316
  rebel tours to 237–8, 269, 297
South Africa (country) 94
South America: 1979 tour by Derrick Robins side 195–8

417

South Australia   191, 202, 275
Southern Schools v the Rest
    (1956)   37
Soweto   357
Speed, Malcolm   362
Spencer, Tom   119
Spring Out programmes
    (Rediffusion)   77–8
Sri Lanka   118
    v Australia, (1987/88)   292
    v England
        (1981/82) inaugural Test
            Match   238–9
        (1988)   297
        (1992/93)   323
        (1998)   349–52
Sri Lanka (country)   238
Statham, Brian   46, 112, 157, 392–3
Steele, Ray   360
Stepney, Howard   16
Stevenson, Graham   198, 226
Stewart, Alec   323, 341, 345–6, 347, 365
Stewart, Micky   76, 276, 277, 288, 296–7, 300, 333
Stoddart, David   31
Stollmeyer, Jeff   117, 182, 183, 184
Stollmeyer, Zara   117
streaker   119
Subba Row, Raman   38, 238, 288, 330
Such P.M.   368
The Sun   267
Sunday Express   83, 84, 93, 191, 222, 235
Sunday League games   307, 309, 310, 311, 346
Sunday Telegraph   83, 241
Super Tests   161, 173, 178, 179, 190, 195
Surita, Pierson   285
Surrey   188
    Stewart's captaincy   345–6
Sussex   48, 162, 163
Sutherland, Mr (of RBL)   52–3
Swanton, E.W. ('Jim')   30, 78, 85, 101–4, 121, 344
    and Arabs club   55, 79, 80
    and HB   82–4, 86–7, 103, 390
    and J. Arlott   219

and J. Woodcock   397
Sydney
    Bicentennial Test and
        celebrations   289–90
    rest days   117
    SCG ground   156–7, 193
Sydney Morning Herald   251
Symmonds, Donna   251

TalkRadio   386, 391, 401
Tariq Saeed   255, 266
Tasmania
    v South Australia   202
    young players tour   216–17
Tattersall, Roy   46, 49
Tavare, Chris   242
Taylor, Bob   204
Taylor, Bruce   97–8
Taylor, Claude ('CHT')   28–9
Taylor, Clive   160
Taylor, Lynton   201, 202, 236, 267–8, 273
Taylor, Mark   337, 362, 364, 366, 368
Taylor, Peter   277
Taylor, Squizzy   275
TCCB
    and BSkyB contract   310
    and reorganisation of cricket in the 1990s   328–9
    replaced by ECB from 1997   329
    and umpiring rows with
        Pakistan   281, 288, 295
Teheran   139–43
Teheran Cricket Club   143
Tennant, Ivo   387
tent pegging exhibition   149
Test match Special *see* TMS
Thessalonica   134–5
Thicknesse, John   85, 171–2
30-yard circles   172, 200
Thomas, Bernard   118, 154, 225, 226–7
Thomas, Bill   39
Thompson, Wilfred   18
Thomson, Jeff
    against England
        (1974/75)   106, 110–11, 112–13, 114–15, 116, 117
        (1982/83)   241, 242

INDEX

against WI 121, 181–2
and Packer 164, 180
Thomson, Peter 243–4
Thorne, David 56
Thorne, Graham 373
Thorpe, Graham 356, 359
The Times 60–4, 68, 172, 387, 390, 397
Tink, Arthur 22
Tink, Mona 22
Titmus, Fred 76, 85, 394
TMS (Test Match Special)
  annual dinner 119–20
  Arlott's last commentary 218–19
  book by Don Mosey 176
  fees 299, 309
  HB leaves 308–9
  letters 300
  loses rights for England v SA (1999/2000) 386
  and Mugabe interview 336
  and Today programme 309
  women commentators 251
  see also under Blofeld, Henry
Tokanpur 149
Tolchard, Roger 154, 155
Traicos, John 93
Transworld International *see* TWI
Trent Bridge 289 *see also* Nottinghamshire
Trevor (barman on Pacific Express) 275
Trinidad
  HB robbed in Port of Spain 222–3
  Radio Trinidad and Raffie Knowles 96
  rest days 117
Trueman, Fred 69, 391–2
Tudor, Alex 364, 385
Tufnell, Phil 337
Tuke-Hastings, Michael 93, 99, 100
Turkey 135–9
Turner, Glenn 95, 97, 292
Turner, Graham 77
Turner, Mark (HB's uncle) 50, 64
TVNZ (New Zealand television) 311
TWI (Transworld International) 301
  bid for India TV rights 319–23

and HB 315–18, 319–23
and Pakistan rights 317–18, 324
and WI rights 317
two-tier system 330–3, 345

Udaipur 150
'Uncle Malik' 253, 254, 255
uncovered pitches 333
Underwood, Derek 88, 158, 238
USA v Fiji (ICC Trophy match, 1974) 118

Valley of Peace CC (NZ) 292–4, 372
van der Merwe, Peter 370
Vanter, Leslie 84, 254
Ventakaraghavan, Srini 341–2
Victoria v Queensland 286–7
Vizianagram, Maharajkumar of 76–7

Wadsworth, Ken 97–8
Waite, John 94
Walcott, Sir Clyde 96, 183, 361–2
Walker, Max 158, 291
Walmsley, Peter 39
Walsh, Courtney 315, 316, 342, 356
Walters, Doug 90, 115, 159
Walters, Keith 82
Wanderers (Barbados) 81
Wareham, George 84
Warne, Shane 361–2, 368, 400
Warwickshire v Middlesex (1962) 64
Wasim Akram 324
Waters, Harry 293
Waters, John 293, 294
Waugh, Mark 308, 361–2, 366, 400
Waugh, Steve 290, 365, 366–7
Wayman, Laurie 61, 62, 63, 64
Webster, Christine 304
Weekes, Everton 80, 81–2
Wellings, E.M. ('Lyn') 72–3, 76, 84, 394
Wellington
  city 279
Wessels, Kepler 112
West Indies
  v Australia
    (1960) (first ever Test) 356
    (1968/9) 89–91

419

West Indies – *cont.*
  v Australia – *cont.*
    (1975/76) 121–3
    (1977/78) 181–3, 185
    (1979/80) 200, 203
    (1984/85) 265–6
  v England
    (1967/68) 83–7, 397
    (1974) 113
    (1976) 124–5
    (1980) 221
    (1980/81) 221–2, 223–6
    (1984) 264
    (1985/86) 269, 270–1
    (1988) 295–7
    (1989/90) 300–1
    (1991) 310
    (1995) 327
    (1997/98) 340–3, 346
  v NZ
    (1979/80) 217–18
    (1986/87) 279–80
  v Pakistan
    (1981/82) 237
    (1992/93) 324–5
  v SA
    (1991/92) 315–17
    (1998/99) 356–7
  World Cup
    (1975) winners 118–19
    (1979) winners 198–9
    (1983) 247, 248
  World Series Cup winners
    (1984) 267
  limited-over matches, (1980/81) 223
  other matches 172, 173
  bad behaviour in NZ (1979/80) 217–28
  bouncers 124–5
  debate over tour (1980/81) 223–4
  and Packer 164, 182–6
  pitch problems 340–3
  players' demands (1998/99) 356–7
West Indies Board of Control 317, 342–3, 356–7
West, Peter 275
Western Australia
  win Sheffield Shield (1987/88) 287

Country Eleven v England 275, 276
Wheeler, Richard and Johnny 373
White, Brian 266, 290–2
White, Crawford 79, 190
White, Miss (owner of Valley of Peace ground) 293
White, Tony 196
Williams, Theo 316
Willis, Bob 177, 189, 222, 233–4
  as captain 239, 241–2, 261
  as commentator 307, 309, 315
  friendship with HB 239, 309
  and 'Rumple' 303
Winchester School 30, 36–7
Witherden, Ted 39
Wodehouse, P.G. 8, 206, 213, 236–7, 304–6, 319, 324, 380
Wolfe-Murray, Angus ('Gus') 31, 33
women commentators 250–1
Woodcock, Johnny
  auto-rickshaw scheme 257
  and HB 56, 60, 151, 224, 261, 364, 396–7
  overland to India 123, 125–50
  and Packer 172
  writing skill 151
  minor references 75, 114–15, 121, 253, 285
Woodward, Steve 218
Wooldridge, Ian 161
Woolmer, Bob 159
World Championship of Cricket 267–8
World Cup
  (1975) inaugural 118–19
  (1979) 198–9
  (1983) 246–8
  (1987/88) 281–3, 285, 286
  (1991/92) 310–11, 312, 314–15
  (1995/96) 323, 334
  (1999) HB misses 388
World Series Cricket (WSC) 114, 158, 169–73, 190, 192, 267
  television coverage and audiences 179, 192
  World Series Cup 203, 267
  see also Super Tests
WorldTel 323
Worrell, Frank 84

INDEX

Wright (Australian Test cricketer 1948) 20
Wright, Bob 285
Wright, John 279
Wright, Kingsley 83, 121
Wyatt, Bob 222

Yallop, Graham 179, 195, 234
Yallop, Neville 22–3
Yardley, Norman 20, 101
Yorkshire 162
Young, Jack 35

Young, Jimmy 199
Yugoslavia 133–4

Zaheer Abbas 177–8, 249–50, 260, 394
Zia-ul-Haq (President of Pakistan) 177–8
Zimbabwe
  v England, (1996/97) 334–5
  World Cup
    (1983) 247
    (1987/88) 282